Environmental Justice and the Rights of Indigenous Peoples

Environmental Justice and the Rights of Indigenous Peoples

International and Domestic Legal Perspectives

Laura Westra

London • Sterling, VA

First published by Earthscan in the UK and USA in 2008

ISBN: 978-1-84407-485-3

Typeset by JS Typesetting Ltd, Porthcawl, Mid Glamorgan
Printed and bound in the UK by TJ International, Padstow
Cover design by Andrew Corbett

For a full list of publications please contact:

Earthscan
8–12 Camden High Street
London, NW1 0JH, UK
Tel: +44 (0)20 7387 8558
Fax: +44 (0)20 7387 8998
Email: earthinfo@earthscan.co.uk
Web: **www.earthscan.co.uk**

22883 Quicksilver Drive, Sterling, VA 20166-2012, USA

Earthscan publishes in association with the International Institute for
Environment and Development

A catalogue record for this book is available from the British Library

Library of Congress Cataloging-in-Publication Data

Westra, Laura.
  Environmental justice and the rights of indigenous peoples : international and domestic legal
perspectives / Laura Westra.
      p. cm.
  ISBN-13: 978-1-84407-485-3 (hardback)
  ISBN-10: 1-84407-485-4 (hardback)
  1. Indigenous peoples–Civil rights. 2. Indigenous peoples–Legal status, laws, etc. 3. Offenses
against the environment. 4. Conservation of natural resources–Law and legislation. I. Title.
  K3247.W47 2007
  342.08'72–dc22
                              2007021165

The paper used for this book is FSC-certified and
totally chlorine-free. FSC (the Forest Stewardship
Council) is an international network to promote
responsible management of the world's forests.

Contents

We live today in a world filled with fundamental challenges to our health, personal security, economic and spiritual well-being, and even our very survival. Our identities as citizens of increasingly less significant states; as members of religious, ethnic or cultural groups who are often in conflict with other groups; as workers in a global economy in which unseen forces can suddenly cause our financial houses to crumble; as parts of families increasingly under threat; all of these factors can give rise to feelings of fear, anger and simply being overwhelmed. More recently, we have moved from a situation of many localized environmental disasters to one in which the future of the entire globe is threatened by climate change. Those who have achieved this realization the earliest, about whom Laura Westra draws upon the analogy of the 'canaries in the coal mine', are those indigenous peoples around the world who have managed – despite colossal intrusions upon their societies and the ravages of generations of colonization – to sustain a symbiotic relationship with their traditional territories. They and their lands are also frequently the most directly threatened by the environmental depredations that have occurred, and are continuing to occur at an ever accelerating rate.

Laura Westra has sought to build upon the foundations laid in her two most recent books involving the intersection between environmental health and a broadly interpreted concept of human rights. In *Ecoviolence and the Law: Supranational Normative Foundations of Ecocrime* she argued passionately and cogently that pollution was not merely a civil wrong justifying access to financial compensation for its victims but should be viewed as a form of violence that warranted criminal sanctions. In *Environmental Justice and the Rights of Unborn and Future Generations*, she sought to apply principles of ecojustice to the special case of children's right to health, including a healthy environment, and then to extend this approach to protect future generations. Now, in the present work, she moves from children as the particular category of the most vulnerable *individuals* into exploring the situation of *peoples* that also are highly vulnerable yet have the capacity to pursue collective action. This natural progression leads Dr Westra to examine in detail the threats confronting indigenous peoples throughout the world and the challenges they face in seeking to protect their identity, their traditional lands, and the interdependence that exists between the two. In this regard, she raises the specific situations of indigenous peoples in a number of countries and the significant environmental risks that threaten their collective survival.

The author assesses the two most common models for advancing the collective aspirations of indigenous peoples – the cultural identity and self-determination models – and finds them lacking. She asserts persuasively that both models pay inadequate attention to addressing the immediacy of the threat to the air, lands and waters on which indigenous peoples rely, as well as to the growing scientific evidence of major risks to their physical health. Thus, Laura Westra seeks to emphasize the importance of supplementing these two prevailing frameworks for human rights analysis and political action by adding a third: the 'biological/ecological integrity' model. In doing so, she is passionate and provocative in building a truly multidisciplinary approach in which she draws upon legal principles, population health information, environmental and social science research, and the impact on domestic economies of the actions of transnational corporate and financial entities upon the most essential concerns of indigenous peoples. She is almost as energetic as a force of nature herself as she seeks to prod readers to consider new ways of thinking to solve longstanding problems. Throughout this important book she continues to keep the spotlight on ethical questions as being at the core of public debate while aggressively attacking governments and the World Bank for permitting multinational corporate polluters to profit from ecoviolence with virtually no sanctions and little recourse to international environmental and human rights law principles. Her efforts involve the exploration of existing international covenants confirming environmental and human rights standards, the continuing relevance of customary international law and the potential importance of new emerging indigenous rights instruments under discussion within the United Nations and the Organization of American States.

Domestic law in key settler states that have yet to decolonize in any way is also a central feature of this volume. Dr Westra devotes particular attention to the prevailing legal regimes in Canada, the United States, Australia and New Zealand as they impact upon the original owners of these lands. Exploring the utilization of domestic law to consider breaches of 'the law of nations' by foreigners before the American judicial system through invoking the Alien Torts Claims Act of the USA is an especially valid and novel aspect.

The over 370 million indigenous peoples spread across the globe possess extra-ordinarily vibrant cultures, political systems, values and immense traditional knowledge about their homelands and the environmental changes that have been rapidly escalating in recent decades. They have much to teach the rest of the planet's population in this regard. They have faced the devastating consequences of colonization and marginalization yet they are also survivors who generally continue to be willing to share their expertise and their generosity while seeking an accommodation with adjacent or dominant societies. As citizens of the world, we must all confront the human injustices that exist within our borders while simultaneously addressing fundamental environmental threats from within and without. Laura Westra provides us with very timely reminders of these pressing issues while offering new ideas on how we should respond. I urge you to read this book with care. More importantly, I encourage you to take action. It is a distinct pleasure to add these few words in support of her clarion call for change.

Bradford W. Morse
Professor of Law
University of Ottawa, Canada

Both economic and biological indicators require a baseline against which future conditions are assessed. For IBI (Index of Biotic Integrity), that baseline biological integrity is the condition of a site with a biota that is the product of evolutionary and biogeographic processes in the relative absence of the effects of modern human activity.
(Karr, 2006)

This book stems from two concurrent strands of thought I have been pursuing: the centrality of biological/ecological integrity to human rights, and, therefore, the criminality of depriving humans of that natural, ecosystemic condition. In 2000, I returned to graduate school to study for a second PhD in Jurisprudence in order to better argue for the issue of criminality, rather than easily demonstrated immorality. Basing my argument on the research of the World Health Organization (WHO) and of epidemiology and public health in recent works, I termed any and all activities that result in harms to humans, following upon that deprivation, as 'eco-crimes' or forms of 'eco-violence', that is, violence practised in and through the environment (Westra, 2004a).

If that argument is accepted, it follows that the most vulnerable among those gravely at risk are children – both born and preborn, according to WHO research (2002) – and future generations. Both are unable to move to avoid the harm or to defend themselves from those attacks on their lives, health and normal function, and environmental justice requires that their rights, that is, the rights of the future, be respected (Westra, 2006).

In a somewhat natural progression, the next question that arises is whether there are any groups and communities that are particularly affected today. The answer is clear once aboriginal peoples are considered. Children and future generations of these groups are often involved in litigations as the conflict between the economic interests of state and non-state actors is increasingly obvious with the spread of globalization.

No corner of the world is spared as land-based minorities find that their interaction with, and their lifestyle on, their territories is no longer possible: mining and extractive interests put their survival and culture under attack as climate change accelerates and exacerbates the damage, rendering their traditional, age-old knowledge obsolete.

Having been commissioned in January 2006 to work with the lawyers of the First Nation at Walpole Island (Chief Dean Jacobs), on the impact of climate change, I could not rest without further exploring this topic as the natural completion of a 'law trilogy' of sorts, starting first with the contention that environmental harms are and should be treated as crimes. The second argument, supported by a Health Canada grant and with the collaboration of the Geneva office of the WHO (Child and Adolescent Health), asserted that the most vulnerable individuals, the 'canaries', are the children and unborn generations. The present work now adds to these the crimes against aboriginal communities: these appear to go beyond even simple crimes, being comparable with the highest criminal activities proscribed by international law, that is, crimes against humanity and genocide.

That is the basic argument of this work as I review instruments (both domestic and international) and the case law from all continents in the quest for environmental justice. Even if I do not succeed in proving the presence of genocide under present definitions and regimes, or the presence of crimes against humanity, the reader will judge whether or not at least some valid doubts should be raised about the way environmental harms are handled in the courts, when these embattled and endangered groups attempt to receive justice.

The book is divided in four parts. The first part reviews the main present models of protection of aboriginal peoples in international and domestic law, as it considers the historical background of 'self-determination' and 'cultural integrity' models. A third model is proposed in the first chapter of this part: the 'biological/ecological integrity' model, as foundational to the other two and hence necessary for their survival. The meaning of ecological integrity is also analysed, as is the original natural law approach to indigenous groups in North and South America, and the need for a universal, cosmopolitan approach today.

The second part reviews some selected case law from all continents in order to show the recurring themes brought to the courts in those complaints. The 'facts' repeatedly show the centrality of biological and ecological integrity, and the need to radically re-evaluate the present treatment of all environmental cases, if justice is to be achieved.

The third part is at the heart of the book's argument, as it discusses the meaning of 'genocide', and examines views on how far that concept can reach, and how far it would be desirable to extend that reach, beyond the examples in present jurisprudence.

A special situation, that of the Nunavut people of Canada, emphasizes the criminality of the corporate actors, whose practices have had a near-fatal and ongoing effect on their life as individuals and as a people. A review of the conditions of Nunavut clearly supports the proposition that, if not deliberate genocide, then at least 'wilful murder' or criminal negligence is present against those Arctic peoples. This is the crux of this work, and I leave it to the reader to judge whether this argument is convincing.

Finally, part four discusses the responsibility for these harms (and crimes) and the question of accountability of both state and non-state actors for the irreversible results of their hazardous activities. The final chapter proposes some possible and desirable ways of ensuring that global governance acknowledges and entrenches in all legal instruments, as, for example, the Earth Charter already does, the biological integrity, health and normal function of individuals and the ecological integrity of the land base upon which aboriginal peoples depend for their survival.

Acknowledgements

The research that inspired this work started with a paper I was asked to write by lawyer Kate Kempton for the First Nation at Walpole Island (Ontario, Canada) and then Chief Dean Jacobs, in early 2006. That research and my conversations with Kate opened my mind to the importance of the relation of indigenous peoples to their lands, and to the immense vulnerability of their communities to the harms, the 'ecocrimes' I had been studying since I returned to law school in 2000.

As I noted in my 2006 work, the most vulnerable individuals in society are indeed the children, the unborn and future generations (Westra, 2006). But the most vulnerable groups and communities are, without a doubt, the indigenous peoples of the world. In order to confirm my insights, I returned to school to audit some courses, and my research reinforced and helped to focus my beliefs on this issue. I was eventually admitted as a post-doctoral student to the University of Ottawa, under Professor Bradford Morse. I learned a lot in his class on Comparative Aboriginal Law, thus my greatest debt is to him. My deepest thanks are due to him for his time, despite a full teaching and research schedule before my arrival, and for his illuminating conversations.

I am also extremely grateful to Dr Colin Soskolne (University of Alberta) for his invaluable help with the medical and epidemiological research required by my argument. Also, the final months of William Rees's Social Sciences and Humanities Research Council of Canada (SSHRC) grant ('Controlling Eco-Violence: Linking Consumption and the Loss of Ecological Integrity to Population Health, EcoJustice and International Law'; three year award from April 1, 2004, File #410-2004-0786; PI: W. E. Rees, UBC; Co-Applicant, C. L. Soskolne; Collaborator, L. Westra) helped support this work, as both attacks on eco-justice and human rights breaches are clearly in evidence when the ecological footprint of Western nations extends to the impoverished but resource-rich indigenous communities.

My desk research was confirmed after I became co-chair (with Melinda Janki) of the IUCN Commission on Environment and Law, Specialist Indigenous Peoples Group, as Melinda and other group members were invited to attend the Ecological Integrity and a Sustainable Society Conference of the Global Ecological Integrity Group (GEIG), as they presented their research at Dalhousie University, in Halifax, Nova Scotia (June 24–27, 2007).

Once again, special thanks to Osgoode Hall Librarian Diane Rooke and to Luc Quenneville of the University of Windsor, without whose technical support this book could not have been done.

PART ONE

Basic Issues, Principles
and Historical Background

The Rights of Indigenous Peoples: Eco-footprint Crime and the 'Biological/Ecological Integrity Model' to Achieve Environmental Justice

INDIGENOUS PEOPLES AND INTERNATIONAL LAW

Indigenous people and their communities and other local communities have a vital role in environmental management and development because of knowledge and traditional practices. States should recognize and duly support their identity, culture and interest, and enable their effective participation in the achievement of sustainable development.[1]

This declaration provides an excellent starting point from which to evaluate other regimes pertaining to the rights of indigenous peoples. One of the major instruments that supports those rights is the Declaration of Human Rights,[2] which has been viewed as an 'expression of general principles of law' (Castaneda, 1969). The International Court of Justice (ICJ) has also 'taken judicial notice of the Declaration' (Cancado Trindade, 1985) and, in general, various UN organs have used the declaration as an 'authoritative interpretation of human rights provisions of the United Nations Charter' (Cancado Trindade, 1985; see also Humphrey, 1979). In fact, although some argue that the UN General Assembly resolutions on human rights are not 'law making', as they can only be declaratory in character (Guradze, 1971), it is beyond doubt that they have influenced the standards of international behaviour and that they have helped in the formation of international law, as well as state practice, particularly on the highly relevant topics of 'decolonization, recognition of the right to self-determination of peoples, and permanent sovereignty of States over their natural resources' (Cancado Trindade, 1985).

All rights are interrelated (Cancado Trindade, 1985), and that holds true especially for the rights supported by the International Covenant on Civil and Political Rights (ICCPR) and the International Covenant on Economic, Social and Cultural Rights (ICESCR); 'without the latter, the former would have little meaning for most people' (Cancado Trindade, 1985). This approach has been characteristic of the 20th century. Parallel developments appear to be, first, the emerging importance of individual rights within this scenario, and second, the increasing awareness of the relationship between human rights and environment. For instance, the Stockholm Declaration states that:

... man has the fundamental right to freedom, equality, and adequate conditions of life, in an environment of a quality that permits a life of dignity and well-being.[3]

In addition, Principle 14 states that indigenous peoples have the right 'to control their lands and natural resources and to maintain their traditional way of life' (Shelton, 1994).The Convention on the Rights of the Child (CRC)[4] emphasizes the need to protect health and the obligation of state parties to fight both malnutrition and disease and to take into consideration environmental pollution. The 1989 Convention of the International Labour Organization Concerning Indigenous and Tribal Peoples in Independent Countries supports environmental protection,[5] and the Sub-Commission on the Prevention of Discrimination and the Protection of Minorities also states that human rights violation may lead to environmental degradation and that, in turn, can result in human rights violations. The 1994 Principles declared by that commission affirm 'the interdependence and indivisibility of human rights, an ecologically sound environment, sustainable development and peace' (Shelton, 1994).

Moving beyond international law regimes, the African and Inter-American regional rights systems guarantee the right to a 'safe and healthy environment',[6] and recognize the right of all peoples to 'a generally satisfactory environment favorable to their development'. The Additional Protocol to the American Convention on Human Rights in the Area of Economic Social and Cultural Rights, 22 November 1969, Additional Protocol Art. 11, OAS Treaty Series No. 36, at l, provides that everyone shall have the right to live in a healthy environment, and similar concerns are expressed in several constitutions and are supported by litigation.[7]

These instruments and cases should be considered against the background of the 'fundamental unity of the conception of human rights, as they all ultimately inhere in the human person' (Cancado Trindade, 1985). But if the 20th century is characterized not only by the emergence of treaties and declarations supporting human rights, hence the inherent interrelation and the expanding presence of human rights related to the environment, the 21st century may be the locus of developing 'third generation' rights, even 'ecological' rights, as Prudence Taylor argues (Taylor, 1998).

If the unity of civil and political, with economic, social and cultural rights, together with the emergent diminution of state control over individual rights, is the present trend, then the rights of peoples as well as individuals to environmental/ecological 'third generations' rights is indeed the portent of things to come. Individuals have to be recognized through a cosmopolitan approach to human rights before special groups may follow and expect to be considered separately and not only as part of a state party.

The main point is that all these rights are fundamental, as well as interrelated. Hence they should be viewed as non-derogable, *jus cogens* rights, and the obligations they impose singly and jointly should be viewed as *erga omnes*, that is, beyond the limited reach of state and domestic law, and even that of treaties limited to those who are prepared to ratify them. This reality increases the gravity of any possible breach, and, at the same time, it demonstrates the complexity that is present when collective responsibility is to be imposed and enforced, justified though it might be.

THE BACKGROUND OF INDIGENOUS PEOPLES' RIGHTS IN INTERNATIONAL LAW

International law is not only rules. It is a normative system harnessed to the achievement of common values, values that speak to all of us. (Higgins, 1994)

The first thing to note is that there is not one absolute definition of 'indigenous peoples' in international law, although they are increasingly emerging both as players and participants in UN instruments, as well as other documents (Metcalf, 2004). The main international law instrument that attempts to define indigenous peoples and their rights, is the International Labour Organization's (ILO) Convention on Indigenous and Tribal Peoples.[8] It treats as 'indigenous' the following groups:

- peoples whose social, cultural and economic conditions distinguish them from other sections of the national community;
- peoples whose status is regulated wholly or partially by their own customs and traditions;
- peoples who descend from populations that inhabited a country at the time of conquest or colonization; and
- self-identification of a group as indigenous or tribal is regarded as a fundamental criterion (Metcalf, 2004).[9]

There are other legal instruments that are relevant to both indigenous peoples and their environment, but only two of these are legally binding: The International Labour Organization (No. 169) Concerning Indigenous and Tribal Peoples in Independent Countries, and the Convention on Biological Diversity.[10] James Anaya (2004) traces the rights of indigenous peoples to the earliest times of international law, as they emerged as a topic of discussion after Christopher Columbus's 'discovery'.

From the writings of Roman Catholic missionaries such as Francisco de Vitoria, the maltreatment of the 'other Indians' is clearly documented, as was the natural law basis for the severe critiques of those ongoing practices (Anaya, 2004). Despite later criticisms of the natural law-based argument for human rights (see, for example, Baxi, 1998), the natural law approach can best provide the basis for an all-embracing system of human rights protection, a system that Grotius later attempted to separate somewhat from that doctrinal origin: 'Grotius moved toward a secular characterization of the law of nature, defining it as a "dictate of right reason" in conformity with the social nature of human beings' (Anaya, 2004; see also Grotius, 1925).

Nevertheless, it is only because natural law claims a supranational source for its moral perspective, so that it is not simply 'humanist' (Anaya, 2004), that natural law could and did claim to be able to judge positivist laws. For natural law, a law that violated the moral code was not truly law at all (Anaya, 2004; see also Westra, 2004c; King, 1990).[11]

But in the century after Grotius, Emmerich de Vattel wrote his *Law of Nations* (1758) where he argued that natural law should simply be applied to nation/state as to individuals (Anaya, 2004). Perhaps this approach was foundational not only to the correct positivist law preference, but it may also be viewed as the origin of the later application of individuals' rights and norms to corporate legal entities. Both moves proved to be highly damaging to the individual rights of natural persons. In modern times, the prevalence of eco-footprint harms renders these rights particularly vulnerable when the individuals at risk are part of an indigenous population (Westra, 2006).

In sum, the step from the natural law protection of all individual basic rights to the positivist move to subsuming individuals under the category of nation/states, papers over a vast area of differences that exist, for example, between minority groups and others, rich and poor, colonizers and colonized. The lack of recognition of these fundamental differences is highly damaging to indigenous peoples as they are slowly attempting to regain, singly and collectively, the rights they might have retained historically under a different conceptual understanding of the law.

In order to apply international law regimes regarding indigenous peoples to First Nations and other aboriginal groups, the initial steps are: first, to see whether they fit under existing accepted definitions of indigenous peoples; second, to discover what binding or suggestive legal instruments may exist that are relevant to the protection of their interests; and third, to evaluate what soft law instruments may be used to their advantage. In addition to the covenants mentioned above, the Earth Charter should also be included, with its strong component of support for all habitats and natural entities through ecological integrity, and with its explicit support for respect for indigenous peoples.[12]

PROTECTION OF INDIGENOUS PEOPLES THROUGH INTERNATIONAL MECHANISMS

After considering the various legal instruments that might be available to defend environmental and other indigenous peoples' rights, the next question that should be raised is whether there is any group or body to monitor the regulatory instruments that exist for the protection of indigenous peoples. It is acknowledged that such protection is not adequate by most legal scholars, thus there is a 'protection gap' between human rights legislation and the problems faced by indigenous peoples (Anaya, 2004).[13] Some of these problems include:

> ... *impacts of development projects on indigenous communities, the implementation of recently enacted domestic laws to protect indigenous rights, the relationship between formal state law and customary indigenous law, indigenous cultural rights, indigenous children, indigenous participation in policy- and decision-making processes, and various forms of discrimination against indigenous individuals.* (Anaya, 2004, pp223–4)

The Committee on the Elimination on Racial Discrimination[14] has the authority to monitor human rights implementation, and it has adopted procedures to address all circumstances that could be viewed as 'early warnings' of situations that might escalate. This approach was urged by Aboriginal groups in Australia. The Committee often invokes the principal of self-determination, even when dealing with Canada and considering Canada's report in 1992 and the dispute between the Mohawks and the government of Quebec where the question of self-determination was raised.[15]

The ILO Convention No. 169 investigated the situation of several Amazonian communities, and noted that 'the right to life and to physical security and integrity is necessarily related to and in some ways dependent upon one's physical environment'.[16] This particular point cannot be overemphasized. In fact, when Cherie Metcalf lists two major categories of indigenous rights as the 'cultural integrity model' and the 'self-determination model', both also present in Anaya's work (Anaya, 2004; Metcalf, 2004), I believe there is an even more basic model that has been omitted, 'the biological/ ecological integrity' model. I believe that it is a model that is foundational to all considerations involving First Nations, with special emphasis on the Seven Generations Rule, as well as the legally binding international covenants, including the Convention on the Rights of the Child.

THE 'THIRD MODEL' AND FIRST NATIONS ENVIRONMENTAL RIGHTS ISSUES

The 'indigenous' perspective or world view is one of embeddedness and holistic integration and sharing, in which the environment is embedded within the identity and the existence of humans. (Kempton, 2005)

The 'right to life and to physical security',[17] is clearly a description of the rights that Henry Shue termed 'basic': the right to security and subsistence (Shue, 1996). These rights precede both conceptually and in time, civil and political rights, and economic, social and cultural rights. The use of normal functions and the capacity for independent agency both depend on developing in environmental circumstances that permit and foster, rather than hinder, a human being's normal development (WHO, 2002; see also Gewirth, 1982b; Westra, 2006). The biological integrity of individuals is entirely dependent on the ecological integrity of their surrounding habitat.

In the case of indigenous peoples, including First Nationss, the requirement for a healthy environment is vital: large cities and industrial centres *may* be able to mitigate some of the disastrous environmental conditions that affect us, including the effects of climate change, but mitigating conditions may not be available to peoples who live closer to the land and are entirely dependent upon it for their survival. In addition, as we saw in the case of the city of New Orleans and hurricane Katrina, even in a wealthy country and in a fully developed area, a city cannot count on escaping disaster. Of course, other seaside populations in developing countries and island states are facing even more disastrous conditions.

Even for landlocked groups, the problem is that despite the work of several decades of conservation biologists, such as Michael Soule and especially Reed Noss (1992), ensuring conservation and respect for an area's integrity implies the presence of buffer (or corridor) areas, as well as the designated 'core' areas, in order to ensure the security and survival of the targeted flora and fauna intended for protection. Unfortunately this requirement, though absolutely necessary to the achievement of the protection goals, has largely been ignored. Any natural reserve and, of course, any First Nation needs a surrounding 'buffer' of sufficient size to ensure that the populations and species within the protected area are not affected by pollutants, toxins and any effluent that may affect the mandated conservation (Westra, 1994a; 1998).

Recent work by the European Environmental Agency (EEA) and the WHO (EEA, 2006), provides details of the risk of exposing *all* populations to pollution and climate change, and they indicate that the problem is particularly acute for indigenous peoples in several areas:

> *Arctic human populations are at risk due to the long-distance transport of bio-accumulative substances, with the Arctic as an important sink, and the dependence of indigenous populations on traditional diets exposes them unduly to chemicals accumulated in the food chain. Europe and other developed countries have a clear responsibility for the global body burden of chemicals. This raises issues of equity and global responsibility.* (EEA, 2006)

Both wildlife and children serve as 'canaries' or sentinels to give early warnings of the effects of chemicals, especially those that are bio-accumulative, persistent and toxic. Links between climate change and health are emerging from scientific research as well, and they 'particularly affect vulnerable groups, ... raising issues of equity'. (EEA, 2006)

An example of this lacuna in environmental and human rights law can be seen in the recent discovery regarding the Aamjiwaang First Nations in Canada's 'Chemical Valley', near Sarnia, Ontario (Mittelstaedt, 2005). Scott Munro, general manager of the Sarnia-Lambton Environmental Association (financed by Shell Canada, Imperial Oil and 13 other large Chemical Valley firms), wants further research to be sure of data, a familiar ploy when facts emerge that may threaten the status quo. But the facts are that in the First Nation community there are twice as many girls born as boys, a finding greeted with alarm by the First Nation's environmental groups. Pollutants such as hormones and endocrine disruptors in general, alter parents' hormonal make-up:

> *The sexual characteristics of the child are determined during early development and are under the control of estrogen in girls and testosterone in boys. Under normal circumstances, the sex ratio is higher than one, i.e. more boys than girls are born. Several studies have reported a small but significant decrease in the sex ratio of several European countries.* (EEA, 2006)[18]

It is worthy of note that in the 1976 disaster of Italy's Seveso dioxin spill, 48 girls were born and only 26 boys. In addition, thyroid hormones are essential for normal brain development, especially in the first weeks of pregnancy, and much more could be said about a number of neurodevelopmental disorders related to polychlorinated biphenyls (PCBs), insecticides, herbicides and phthalates (Rogan and Regan, 2003).

The question is what is the environmental heritage the parents are forced to give their children, given the multi-causal health effects that result from our current practices according to business as usual? The main point is that these effects cannot be ignored, even if our normal approaches to epidemiology and toxicology do not quite capture them: 'We probably have to abandon the classical toxicological dogma of cause/effect relationship at the individual level and extend it to the generational level' (EEA, 2006).

Consideration of future generations is one of the pillars of traditional First Nations knowledge and belief. In contrast, to ignore the evidence of the harm perpetrated on First Nations by current practices that the Ontario and Canadian governments ought to regulate, or rather alter or eliminate altogether, may not be intentional genocide, but could be termed 'wilful blindness' in criminal law, and a case of 'attacks on the human person' in international law.

Nor is this a very recent discovery. Theo Colborn discovered similar effects in the bird, mammal and marine life in the Great Lakes (Colborn et al, 1996). It was yet another 'canary in the mine' situation that was not heeded at the time. Nor was her study unrelated to human health:

> *One way of understanding how environmental exposures affect health is to study animals in the wild. Despite many differences, many fundamental physiological processes in animals and humans are identical or very similar. An effect in wild animals carries a strong implication that a similar effect may occur in humans in a similar exposure situation.* (EEA, 2006)

Thus, we can say with some confidence that these effects on First Nations deny them their biological integrity, hence their natural functions, and – like the elimination of species well-documented by Colborn and others especially in the Great Lakes area – it indicates the presence of conditions amounting almost to genocide. Ken Saro-Wiwa so described the chemical alterations produced by the operations of Royal Dutch Petroleum in Ogoniland, Nigeria. He termed them forms of 'genocide and omnicide' as the security and subsistence of his people was being systematically eliminated (Westra, 1998).[19]

In sum, the biological integrity of indigenous peoples, including First Nations, is dependent upon the ecological integrity of their living environment, and it is their access to environmental regimes that single out their specific habitat conditions. Both the 'cultural integrity' and the 'self-determination' models, to which Anaya and Metcalf appeal, are important, but they need the presence of basic conditions with which individuals and groups can thrive. For all three models, the presence of existing international legal instruments emphasizes the importance of environmental and human rights law.

THE APPLICATION OF THE OTHER TWO MODELS TO ABORIGINAL COMMUNITIES' ENVIRONMENTAL RIGHTS

The current treaty-based framework of international environmental law is poorly equipped to accommodate non-state players with equivalent to state rights within the area of environmental management. (Metcalf, 2004)

Like the additional third model I proposed, of the other two models, the 'cultural integrity' model[20] is supported by the Organization of American States (OAS) Declaration that explicitly addresses the right to cultural integrity. The same can be said about the 'self-determination' model; that is, they are both firmly based in human rights instruments. For that reason, both models pose problems for state sovereignty (Metcalf, 2004). In both cases the holistic approach to environmental rights, typical of the indigenous world view, is fundamental.

The difference between these two models and the model for which I argued in the previous section, however, is that the latter addresses the most basic human rights of all, that is the right to life, health and normal function, whereas the other two models *assume* the presence of those conditions and proceed to add further rights to protect other possible choices. The 'self-determination' model replicates the Economic, Social and Cultural Rights Covenant, whereas the 'cultural integrity' model appears to be in line with the Civil and Political Rights Covenant. In order to benefit from the protection of the activities under either covenant, normal intellectual abilities and physical capabilities are required.

The main point is that in all three cases, the presence of a safe and healthy environmental quality is absolutely required, both for the general habitat and for the land itself. Indigenous peoples' traditional lifestyles, living close to the land, render them particularly vulnerable.

The cultural integrity model

The cultural integrity model emphasizes the value of traditional cultures in themselves, as well as for the rest of society. According to the Rio Declaration, Principle 22, traditional cultures and the knowledge they possess must be protected:

> *Cultural protection for indigenous peoples involves providing environmental guarantees that allow them to maintain the harmonious relationship to the earth that is central to their cultural survival.* (Metcalf, 2004)

Hence, not only their biological integrity but also their cultural integrity are entirely dependent on the protection of the ecological integrity of the areas they occupy. Any consideration of the economic value of these areas and forests is thus equally dependent on that protection.

Both the Biodiversity Convention,[21] Article 8(j) and the United Nations Convention to Combat Desertification in those Countries Experiencing Serious Drought and/ or Desertification Especially in Africa[22] incorporate cultural integrity as one of the indigenous environmental rights that are protected, while the Arctic Council of 1996,[23] ensures that 'indigenous groups gained status as permanent participants in an international inter-governmental forum for addressing environmental concerns affecting them and their ancestral lands' (Metcalf, 2004).

The cultural integrity model has two aspects. The first emphasizes the environmental closeness between environment and the traditional lifestyle of indigenous peoples, that in fact defines and delimits their cultural presence as a people. The second aspect has their traditional knowledge as its focus, and especially the value of that knowledge to the global community. The first element is akin to the ecological model I proposed earlier, and complementary to it, but the second aspect may be problematic.

Indigenous groups, and hence First Nations, appear not to be valued for themselves in this aspect of the model, as much as for their instrumental value, as holders of specific, commercially valuable knowledge (Halewood, 1999). When traditional knowledge is viewed as 'intellectual property', then some may conclude with Dinah Shelton (1994), that the best way to protect the environmental rights of indigenous peoples is through intellectual property law. I believe that this emphasis is misplaced, as the traditional approach of indigenous peoples to the land, for instance, is one of deep kinship and respect. The land, all the creatures it supports and all its processes are not viewed as a commodity.

Several articles of the Convention on the Rights of the Child[24] are far more appropriate for the protection of cultural integrity, and the CRC is an instrument that has been ratified by almost all of the global community (with the exception of the US and Somalia). Article 30 states:

> *In those States in which ethnic, religious or linguistic minorities or persons of indigenous origin exist, a child belonging to such a minority or who is indigenous, shall not be denied the right, in community with other members of his or her group, to enjoy his or her own culture, to profess and practice his or her own religion, or to use his or her own language.*

Here the respect for cultural integrity of children is easy to adapt to indigenous teachings, especially the Seven Generations Rule. If indigenous peoples are to survive as peoples, rather than being simply assimilated into the larger society in which they are embedded, *both* their biological integrity and their cultural integrity must be treasured, the latter not as a commodity but as a living tradition of great value, necessary to guarantee their survival.

The self-determination model

> *self-determination is a powerful expression of the underlying tensions and contradictions of international legal theory: it perfectly reflects the cyclical oscillation between positivism and natural law, between an emphasis on consent, that is, voluntarism, and an emphasis on binding objective legal principles, between a 'statist' and a communitarian vision of world order* (Cassese, 1995).

The second model is that of self-determination and appears to be the most firmly entrenched in international law (Anaya, 2004). Self-determination is a pre-eminent topic in UN law scholarship, hence it is – no doubt – the easiest model to defend (Gros Espiell, 1980).

But even this model is not free of difficulties for several reasons. The very concept of 'peoples' in this context is hard to define: limiting it to post-colonial groups is insufficient; understanding the concept as including whole populations is unnecessarily over-inclusive and too state centred. The third variant, based exclusively on 'ethnonationalist theory' also ignores the existence of overlapping groups and communities, all of which benefit from a definition based on human rights (Anaya, 2004). Perhaps the best approach may be found in the 'Great Law of Peace', as defined by the Iroquois Confederacy (The Haudensosaunee):

> *The Great Law of Peace ... describes a great tree with roots extending in the four cardinal directions to all peoples of the earth; all are invited to follow the roots of the tree and join the peaceful co-existence and cooperation under its great long leaves. The Great Law of Peace promotes unity among individuals, families, clans, and nations while upholding the integrity of diverse identities and spheres of autonomy.* (Anaya, 2004, p102; see also Wallace, 1994)

Hence the right to self-determination does not necessarily mean that any and all groups may have rights to independent statehood, although decolonization itself is indeed based on self-determination. Essentially, self-determination requires governing institutions where peoples 'may live and develop freely on a continuous basis' (Anaya, 2004).

The early background of self-determination

Despite the importance of the concept of self-determination, its clear historical background and its consistent presence in international law, there appears to be no comprehensive legal account of the concept. Anaya reports the difficulty of the concept of self-determination when it seems to imply 'a right of secession':

> *This understanding has been reaffirmed in subsequent sessions of the Commission on Human Rights Working Group even while a consensus on the precise formulation of indigenous self-determination has remained elusive.* (Anaya, 2004, p112)

Nor is the concept's prominence of recent origin, which might explain this lacuna. Indeed, Lenin was one of the original proponents to the international community, proposing the importance of self-determination to support the freedom of peoples (Cassese, 1995; Lenin, 1969).

Internal self-determination, given its origin, was seen as necessarily based on socialism. It had three aspects: first, it maintained that the 'ethnic or national group' could freely decide their own destiny; second, internal self-determination was to be applied after military action, to decide on the appropriate allocation of territories; and third and most importantly, it was intended as the basis for anti-colonialism and for the liberation of colonized territories (Cassese, 1995). For Lenin that goal was to be accomplished by secession:

> *In the same way as mankind can arrive at the abolition of classes only through a transition period of the dictatorship of the oppressed classes, it can arrive at the inevitable integration of nations only through a transition period of the complete emancipation of all oppressed nations, i.e. their freedom to secede.* (Lenin, 1969)

In contrast, as Cassese points out, US President Woodrow Wilson viewed self-determination as free choice and, ultimately, self-government (Cassese, 1995). This goal was to be accomplished through 'orderly', progressive reforms, whereas Lenin called for the immediate halt to colonial rule, thus undermining present power structures if the right of minorities to separate from the state was admitted. Nevertheless, aside from political principles, 'State sovereignty and territorial integrity remained of paramount importance' (Cassese, 1995).

It is after the Second World War that these political principles emerged as international legal standards. At first the principles were used for Europe, hence the historical development of the concept of self-determination, though interesting, is not relevant to the topic of this work. At any rate, even in Europe, 'self-determination was deemed irrelevant where the people's will was certain to run counter to the victors' geopolitical, economic and strategic interests' (Cassese, 1995). This point is worth keeping in mind, as 'victors' may be understood today to include 'powerful states and corporations', and the same results will follow, as we shall see below.

In 1941, F. D. Roosevelt and Winston Churchill drafted the Atlantic Charter and proclaimed self-determination as a general standard governing territorial changes, as well as a principle concerning the free choice of rulers in every sovereign state (internal self-determination) (Cassese, 1995; see also Grenville, 1974). But, although self-determination (internal) is important, as it strengthens the ability of indigenous groups to stand up to those who would exploit them, and perhaps provide them with a stronger voice in the governance of the host country, it is necessary but not sufficient to support indigenous rights. Even the UN Charter does not define either 'external' or 'internal' self-determination, and despite the wording of Article 1(2) and Article 55, the document does not impose hard and fast obligations on member states. Its merit lies primarily in being the first multilateral treaty that actually includes 'self-determination' (Article 1(2)) and addresses the question of the purpose of the United Nations: 'develop friendly relations among nations, based on respect for the principle of equal rights and self-determination of peoples, and to take the appropriate measures to strengthen universal peace'. Article 55(c) states the goals of promoting, inter alia, 'universal respect for and observance of, human rights and fundamental freedoms for all without distinction as to race, sex, language or religion'.

After the Second World War, both Eastern Europeans and developing countries wanted to see Lenin's thesis developed principally as anti-colonialism, whereas Western countries were not immediately willing to accept that conception of self-determination (Cassese, 1995).

From developing countries' approach to self-determination to the impact of neo-colonialism

> For developing countries self-determination meant three things: (1) the fight against colonialism and racism; (2) the struggle against the domination of any alien oppressor illegally occupying a territory (an idea that was fostered largely due to the insistence of the Arab states after 1967 with the case of Palestine in mind); (3) the struggle against all manifestations of neocolonialism and in particular the exploitation by alien powers of the natural resources of developing countries. (Cassese, 1995)

The 1966 Covenants on Civil and Political Rights, and on Economic Social and Cultural Rights, are clear on the topic of both the political and economic aspects of self-determination, as the common Article 1 states:

> *All peoples have the right to self-determination; by virtue of that right they freely deter-
> mine their political status, and freely pursue their economic, social and cultural
> development.*
> *In no case may a people be deprived of its own means of subsistence.*[25]

These rights appear to be unequivocal, and they stand unless a 'public emergency
which threatens the life of the nation' and which is proclaimed officially (Article 4(1)),
permits a state to disregard the rights. Yet many cases brought before the courts by
indigenous peoples groups are deemed 'not to rise to the level of the law of nations'
(see Chapter 5). Cassese (1995) points out that 'The problem lies not in understanding
the nature of the right, but in ensuring State compliance'.

In contrast, it is clear that the collaboration between states and multinational
corporations (MNCs) violates Article 1(2) of the covenants, and the added presence of
'complicity' between these actors when the deprivation of necessary resources results
in genocide, demonstrates yet another criminal aspect of these cases in international
law (see Chapter 7). At the present time, however, at best it is possible for dispossessed
people to seek compensation, totally ignoring the fact that many of the harms perpetrated against them are simply incompensable (see Article 47 of the ICCPR and Article
25 of the ICESCR, both of which reiterate, 'the inherent right of all peoples to enjoy
and utilize fully and freely their natural wealth and resources').

Since 1945 and the proclamation of the UN Charter, self-determination, primarily
in its internal form as self-government, has been accepted in law, but it is primarily a
'goal', with no specific obligation imposed on states to accept it, even in this weakened
form (Cassese, 1995). Nevertheless in 1971, the International Court of Justice gave
an Advisory Opinion on Namibia. The UN set up Namibia in 1946 as a separate state
'under the direct responsibility of the United Nations', because South Africa refused to
acknowledge it as a separate territory with a separate, freely elected government (Res.
435/1978 of 29 September 1978; Namibia's independence was declared on 21 March
1990) (see also Schmidt-Jortzig, 1991).

But our main concern is with the disenfranchised victims of globalized 'development', where resources, lands, water and way of life are taken and destroyed. The states
wherein these groups live, in general, do not respect the law of self-determination, nor
the mandates of international law regarding indigenous rights to their own resources.
Nor is the principle of territorial integrity fully appreciated in its quantitative and
qualitative aspects (see Para. 6 of the UN Resolution 1514 (XV): 'Any attempt aimed at
partial or total disruption of the national unity and territorial integrity of a country is
incompatible with the purposes and principles of the Charter of the United Nations').

The problem becomes more complex when one tries to extend the argument for
interference with self-determination to encompass the standpoint of economic 'neo-
colonialism'. In 1977, the Geneva Protocol to the four 1949 Geneva Conventions on War
Victims, Article 1, 'supports the thesis that the right to self-determination is considered
to arise when a State dominates the people in a foreign territory using military means'
(Cassese, 1995). In that document the phrase 'alien occupation', the meaning of which
lends itself less easily to an interpretation linked to economic development, militates
against the interpretation I propose, but 'It should be added that in the United Nations
a minority of States – Mexico, Afghanistan, Iraq and Pakistan – considered economic
exploitation of a foreign State (chiefly in the form of neo-colonialism) a breach of self-
determination' (Cassese, 1995).

At best what is addressed here is the issue of economic interference in the affairs of a separate state, whereas our concern is the exploitation and domination of specific peoples. A further question remains the definition of indigenous peoples and land-based minorities in this regard, and the possible inclusion of 'local people' in that category, especially those based in the African continent.

Decolonization, self-determination, natural resources and indigenous peoples

> The term 'indigenous' refers to those who, while retaining totally or partially their traditional languages, institutions and lifestyles which distinguish them from the dominant society, occupied a particular area before other population groups arrived.
> (Tomei and Swepston, 1996)

There are two major problems that will have to be considered in relation to this work. First is the question: who are 'indigenous peoples'? This issue is be explored in the first two chapters of this work. Second is the grave problem of the evaluation of the well-documented gross violations of human rights, under the categories of 'neo-colonization' or 'second conquest', in a way that lays bare their insidious and racist aspects, that masquerade presently as 'development' or 'trade', both well protected under international law.

S. K. Date-Bah (1998) considers some of these questions from an 'African perspective'. It is clear that the local peoples in the African and Asian continents may lack the protections (weak as they are), that are available to indigenous peoples, despite their long history in certain areas. Present clear-cut definitions might exclude too many people affected by corporate 'development'. The major difficulty, however, remains the need to consider that vulnerable people suffer through economic domination, exploitation and deprivation of resources. These deprivations are promoted and protected as 'free trade' or simply 'economic development', imposed with or without outright force, and sometimes even through the force of the law itself.

The argument I want to propose and develop is that the eco-footprint of Western developed countries is the foundation of the 'second conquest', and a direct attack on both the right to survival and the right to self-determination of indigenous and local populations. But, if 'decolonization' is now a major principle of international law, and a *jus cogens* norm, then the elimination of the practices that impose the precarious conditions forced on local and indigenous peoples by corporate actors, with the cooperation of state governments and the support of international trade laws, should represent an obligation *erga omnes* on legal individuals as well as states.

Further critiques of the self-determination model

Self-determination may well include 'free' developments that run contrary to both moral development or just institutions, or even ecologically sound ones. Even the collective will of the people may be based on misinformation and falsehoods, and may lead to conditions that do not represent the best interests of all, although the decisions leading to these conditions may be the result of free self-determination.

Paul Gilbert (1994) discusses self-determination in the context of ethnicity and national identity: 'I suggest then, that the proper grounds for a group's claim to statehood, are that it is living or could live a decent communal life which would be protected or enhanced by statehood.' For Gilbert, therefore, it is not simply a voluntarist model of self-determination that is sufficient to establish a group as entirely separate, 'not [only] what people desire, but what is desirable for them, that generates that right', although Gilbert (1994) acknowledges that such a group will be in the best position to judge what is its most desirable choice. This is indeed what Anaya (2004) concludes, as he cites Ian Brownlie (2003) on that topic: for people the best option may simply be to live in a political order that enables them to live as a distinct group, with a different character, and 'to have their character reflected in the institutions of government under which it lives'.

A non-controversial definition proposed by Metcalf is closer to the environmental requirements of indigenous peoples in general, and First Nations in particular:

> ... *this model recognizes a limited form of self-determination in which indigenous peoples have internal sovereignty rights over their own cultural, social, and economic development, including the exclusive ability to control and manage indigenous lands and resources.* (Metcalf, 2004)

This definition does not attempt to redefine 'peoples', but its meaning is clear regarding the model and the sort of 'peoples' Metcalf intends to cover within this model. In addition, this definition is consonant with the UN Draft Declaration on the Rights of Indigenous Peoples, which includes one of the strongest statements of the rights of indigenous peoples in the context of international law.[26]

At first sight it may seem as though the emphasis on environmental land issues makes this model quite similar to the 'cultural integrity' model discussed above. But in this model, indigenous peoples' rights to their lands are based on their rights to control their own social life and development. A troubling corollary of this approach is that there is, at least in principle, no necessary connection between a group's free choices and any ecologically sound policy. However, Article 39 of the UN Draft Declaration states:

> *Indigenous peoples have the right to have access to and prompt decisions through mutually acceptable and fair procedures for the resolution of conflicts and disputes with States, as well as to effective remedies for all infringements of their individual and collective rights. Such a decision shall take into consideration the customs, traditions, rules, and legal system of the indigenous peoples concerned.*

Thus, at least this article recognizes the essential presence of 'tradition' and 'customs', although it stops short of making the presence of such traditional choices mandatory in order to legitimize an indigenous people's or First Nation's choices.

Perhaps this is the most disturbing aspect of this model. If self-determination is the ultimate value, aside from any other consideration, then in theory (although most likely not in practice), an aboriginal group could decide to rent their land to a Monsanto affiliate, or a chemical company or any other hazardous industry, as long as it was the general will of the people to do so.

Therefore, although all three models include positive aspects for First Nations, it seems that the third model, or the biological/ecological integrity model proposed in the previous section might be the best choice, on its own or in conjunction with either of the other two models, to provide and ensure a solid and sustainable ecological foundation.

INDIGENOUS PEOPLES AND ECO-FOOTPRINT CRIME

The previous sections emphasized the interdependence between the basic/survival rights of indigenous peoples, their biological integrity and the ecological integrity of their lands. But that integrity is constantly under attack through the economic activities of developed countries that view the use of aboriginal lands and peoples as their right, with little or no consideration for the gravity of the consequences that ensue.

I have described these consequences as 'eco-footprint harms' and even 'crimes'. Thus the first issue to consider is whether any industrial operation in the developing world, and in the vicinity of indigenous populations, is to be taken as routinely allowable. The problem is not only the 'accidents' that can be expected regularly, such as that at Bhopal, but also the day-to-day operation of these activities that under the present legal regimes is just as disastrous (consider for instance Ogoniland, Nigeria, in this regard). Note that I am referring to them as 'accidents' not because I have any indication, or belief that there was any criminal intent, or *mens rea* involved. But it seems clear that, even in technologically advanced countries, a certain amount of technical failures/human error *must* be expected. Bluntly, the operation of chemical industries and related corporate activities, even in the most advanced countries and under the optimal circumstances found in affluent Western countries, is *not* safe for all stakeholders, even when all possible precautions, legislated by the regulatory regimes of Western nations, are implemented.

Most of all, these operations are unsafe for the ecosystems that are affected by their products, even under 'ideal' conditions. But this is by no means their only effect. Any pesticide leaves residues not only in the fields, but also in all foods that are not organically grown. The increasing rates of diseases, such as cancers in both the developed and the developing world, attest to the accuracy of medical research (Epstein, 1978) and most of all that of the WHO. There the effects of routinely used chemicals on the most vulnerable of human beings, the children, are discussed. Hence it must be acknowledged that industries that have produced some comforts and advantages for mankind in general, and huge profits to many, have also been a dangerous and insidiously harmful presence in the lives of almost everyone.

Chemical companies' immense profits are the result of their worldwide marketing drives. But the 'side effects' of these operations affect the life and health of too many to be simply dismissed as 'externalities' or the cost of doing business. Royal Dutch Shell has been accused of complicity in acts of genocide, crimes against humanity, multiple rapes and assaults on behalf of the military government of Nigeria (see Appendix 2), and yet their alleged eco-crimes are not even factored in the Alien Torts Claims Act (ATCA) indictments. The destruction of the environment also destroyed the Ogoni people's way of life, and their present and future health.

In this regard, it might be instructive to consider the Statute of the International Criminal Court,[27] which, unlike the Nuremberg Charter, envisions the possibility of internal crimes against humanity, committed by individuals, not states (Article 7), although the environment as such is only spoken of in connection with situations of armed conflict. Article 7(h) refers, for instance, to 'the crime of apartheid', a crime that may be politically motivated but that is not exclusively or even primarily a 'war crime'.

I have argued that even negligent harms of the magnitude of these industrial disasters should be included as 'crimes against humanity' (Westra, 2004a). I am well aware, however, that we are considering *lex ferenda*, at best. Perhaps the best hope to see these crimes indicted and properly categorized may eventually be found in the definition of Article 5(d), in the crime of 'aggression' (under the provisions of Article 121, and 123), as its full extent is, as yet, undefined. Similarly, it is not too far-fetched, I believe, to acknowledge with the language of the 'Preamble' the presence of *erga omnes* obligations, based on *jus cogens* norms, as applicable to all peoples, as they are in the worst crimes:

> *Recognizing that such grave crimes threaten the peace, security and well-being of the world. Affirming that the most serious crimes of concern to the international community as a whole must not go unpunished and that their effective prosecution must be ensured by taking measures at the national level and by enhancing international cooperation.*

When one considers the seriousness and the pervasiveness of the harms produced by the combination of corporate 'freedom' to pursue its goals with few restraints, on one hand, and the primacy of trade 'efficiency' (Heath, 2001), on the other, we discover that all human rights are at stake. Even, as Jennifer Downs argues, 'first generation rights' (Downs, 1993), which are codified in the International Covenant on Civil and Political Rights,[28] while second generation rights refer to the International Covenant on Economic, Social and Cultural Rights[29] are under fire. Neither first nor *second* generation rights, ever mention health, either human or ecological, yet according to the 'Preamble' of the latter: 'The ideal of free human beings enjoying freedom from fear and want can only be achieved if conditions are created whereby everyone may enjoy his economic, social and cultural rights as well as his civil and political rights.'

Freedom from 'fear and want' should include conditions of life that start with the 'basic rights' to 'subsistence' and 'security', as Shue describes them (Shue, 1996), that must include health and normal function, as well as a safe habitat able to support both. Below I return to the possibility of establishing in law third generation rights or 'solidarity rights' (Downs, 1993). But the argument proposed here is clearly supported by the Ogoni case, the case in Bhopal and in some measure, several other cases.

The many faces of eco-footprint crime

Before leaving the topic of eco-footprint crime, we need to move beyond examples in order to better understand its meaning and the different aspects under which it manifests itself. These various 'faces' are really masks, often bland and even benign manifestations, representing jobs, economic possibilities and even progress.

To understand eco-footprint crime better, the first thing to note is that the harmful/ criminal aspects of eco-footprints can be both direct and indirect. For instance, in the example of Ogoniland, there are direct physical harms arising from the oil extraction operations and we noted the direct impact on the health and the life of the local communities. But there are also at least two kinds of indirect impacts, no less heinous: first, the impact on the community's habitat, the land and water upon which they have depended for generations for their subsistence and survival; and second, the impact of support for the extraction operated by the Sani Abbacha military dictatorship, with the subsequent accusations of suppression of protests, and the rapes, murders and other attacks upon the populations.

The direct effects of the Western eco-footprint, therefore, do not only result in direct physical harms, but also, by their presence, produce indirect harms beyond the easily observed material harms and damages to local environment and public health. Indirect harms may be far more subtle. They include supporting racism, engaging in illegal business practices, and supporting industrial activities through the silencing of protests and other human rights violations.

Such cases include both direct and indirect material harms. The activities of Royal Dutch Shell Oil were directly harmful to the health of the inhabitants, and they also eliminated the basis for the population's survival as they made it impossible for the Ogoni to continue in their traditional lifestyles. Eventually, the strongest representatives of the protests, Ken Saro-Wiwa and the rest of the Ogoni Nine were indicted and murdered precisely for speaking out against the operations of Shell (see Appendix 2).

A glance at the recent jurisprudence under ATCA[30] indicates that intimidation, attacks and even murders occur even when the corporate entity responsible and intent on promoting and protecting the efficient operations of its business is *not* intrinsically harmful in its products or processes, as in the *Sinaltral v. Coca Cola* case.[31] Most of these eco-footprint harms are inflicted by a Northern corporate organization on a vulnerable population in the South or on an indigenous people, where regulatory regimes protecting human rights are not well entrenched and where impoverished governments are greedy for the economic benefits these organizations will bring. Hence, it is systematic exploitation of those who cannot defend themselves that characterizes the criminality of the harms imposed.

In conclusion, the biological/ecological integrity model I proposed is the best possible antidote against eco-footprint crime. If the rights of indigenous peoples are based, first, on their rights to biological integrity and natural function; and second, these rights cannot be separated from the protection of the ecological integrity of their lands; then third, entrenching such rights would limit the freedom of Western industrial operations to commit crimes.

The special vulnerability of such peoples is not only based on their poverty and their remoteness from the centres of power, but also on the fact that most such groups are not able to move freely from their present locations, regardless of the harmful conditions to which they might be exposed. Hence, their situation is truly hazardous if the rights I recommend are not legislated. In general, their situation may be compared to that existing in the US for many African Americans, whose neighbourhoods are often established through historical links to Jim Crow laws (Westra and Lawson, 2001, pp113–140), or simply defined by industrial brownfields. (Brownfields are areas that have been used for dumps or unsafe business operations. They are deemed to be appropriate locations for more of the same practices than are wealthier and relatively cleaner neighbourhoods.)

Indigenous peoples and 'local peoples' as land-based minorities

There is a case for arguing that the local communities as a whole should be given the benefit of the rights granted with a view to compensating local residents for the disruptions, inconvenience or other adverse effects resulting from the exploitation of natural resources in their locality. (Date-Bah, 1998)

As we saw, the exposures to which local communities are condemned are far more than 'disruption' and 'inconvenience'. Hence the importance of ensuring that even those who are not 'indigenous' – in the accepted sense of a people who are descendants of the 'pre-invasion inhabitants of lands now dominated by others' (Date-Bah, 1998) – have their rights protected. But many groups have not been part of an imperial conquest: the Inuit of the Arctic, the Aborigines of Australia, the Maori of New Zealand and tribal peoples of Africa, such as the Ashanti, the Yoruba, the Masai and others. Such groups can and should be considered indigenous in relation to the law (Date-Bah, 1998; see also Asiema and Situma, 1994).

The unifying concept for all these disparate groups is their land/culture connection. All these peoples: first, view themselves as a distinct people; second, have inhabited the same territory from time immemorial; third, possess a common language, culture and religion; fourth, view themselves as 'custodians' of their environment; fifth, define themselves, at least in part, through the habitat that provides for them; sixth, have tribal and communal forms of social relations and resource management, often based on directions from their elders; seventh, have an identity based upon their lands; and eighth, view the ecosystems they inhabit and have inhabited traditionally as religiously significant (Asiema and Situma, 1994).

This last aspect of their common characteristics is particularly relevant: they 'view themselves as the world's most experienced environmentalists with a role to play in environmental protection and conservation, especially of the ecosystem they have traditionally inhabited' (Asiema and Situma, 1994). This vital environmental role, only performed by land-based, aboriginal groups, together with their location, poverty and powerlessness, makes it imperative that we extend the protection they need, without resorting to semantics to distinguish 'local' from other 'indigenous peoples'.

Perhaps the addition of 'land-based' to the expression 'local', may help to distinguish these vulnerable people from other minorities whose situation may well be completely or partially different. The international legal instruments intended to protect defined indigenous groups are neither strong nor enforceable. Nevertheless, their very existence at least helps to frame and to declare their rights openly. At any rate, it would seem appropriate to ensure that all those who share most of the characteristics listed should be protected by the same laws, limited though they are.

The major problems that threaten indigenous and land-based minorities are essentially two sides of the same coin: their poverty and powerlessness renders them highly vulnerable to the 'development' that brings them a high dose of the hazardous exposure that their very poverty and isolation had helped them avoid. Hence they are the most vulnerable to climate change (Brown, 2002; Lovelock, 2006; Revkin, 2005). In addition, when their isolation has been breached, the full thrust of unchecked exposures renders their conditions close to untenable (Lyon, 2002).

The full import of North/South interaction after decolonization, the nefarious role of the International Monetary Fund (IMF), the World Bank Group and the World Trade Organization (WTO) is reviewed below and discussed in more detail in Chapter 4 in the context of the impact of globalization and economic 'collateralism'. However, for now, the expression 'indigenous peoples' or 'indigenous groups', should be understood to include all local land-based minorities in the South.

NOTES

1　Principle 22, *Rio Declarations on Environment and Development.*
2　UNDHR, GA Res.217A (III), UNCA at A/810, 10 December 1948.
3　*Stockholm Declaration on the Human Environment,* adopted 16 June 1972, UN Doc. A/CONF.48/141 Rev.l at 3(1973) Principle 1, 11 ILM 1416(1972).
4　GA Res. 44/25, 44 UNGA Supp. (No. 49), UN Doc. A/44/49.
5　ILO, 27 June 1989, Art.l(2) 28 ILM 138 (1989).
6　The African [Banjul] Charter on Human and Peoples Rights adopted 27 June 1981, Art. 24,21 ILM 58(1982).
7　See for instance *Minors Oposa v. Secretary of the Dept. of Environmental and Natural Resources* (Philippines 1993), 33 ILM 173 (1994).
8　*ILO Convention on Indigenous and Tribal Peoples,* No. 169 of 1989, International Labour Conference, (entered into force 5 September 1991).
9　See also a UN document (*UN Sub-Commission on Prevention of Discrimination and Protection of Minorities*) that has the following definition: 'Indigenous communities, peoples and nations are those which, having a historical continuity with pre-invasion and pre-colonial societies that developed on their territories, consider themselves distinct from other sectors of the societies now prevailing in those territories, or parts of them. They form at present non-dominant sectors of society and are determined to preserve, develop and transmit to future generations their ancestral territories, and their ethnic identity as the basis of their continued existence as peoples, in accordance with their own cultural patterns, social institutions and legal systems'.
10　5 June 1992, 1760 UNTS 79, Can.T.S. 1993 No. 24, 31 ILM 818, henceforth *Biodiversity Convention.*
11　Thomas Aquinas termed any law that did not promote and protect the interests of *all* citizens a form of violence by a sovereign or law-maker; as such it was the citizen's obligation not only *not* to obey it, but also to actively oppose it.
12　See for instance Chapter 10 and the Earth Charter (www.globalecointegrity.net).
13　See also *Report of Special Rapporteur on the Situation of Human Rights and Fundamental Freedoms of Indigenous Peoples,* M Rodolfo Stavenhagen, submitted pursuant to Commission res.2001/57, UN Doc. E/CN.4/2002/97, paras. 102, 109, 103.
14　CERD Report (1993): UNGAOR, 47th Sess. Supp. No. 18 Doc. A/47/18.
15　CERD Report (1992) 45 CERD Report (1992) 45.
16　*Report on the Situation of Human Rights in Ecuador* OAS Doc. OEA/Ser.L/V/II.96, Doc. 10, rev. 1 (1997), Chapter VII, on 'The human rights situation of the inhabitants of the Ecuadorian interior affected by development activities'.
17　ILO No. 169.
18　See also WHO-IPCS (2002) 'Global assessment of the state-of-the-science of endocrine disruptors', (WHO/IPCS/EDC/02.0).

19   See also the ATCA case, *Wiwa v. Royal Shell Petroleum et al*, 226 F. 3d 88 (2d Cir. 2000).
20   Codified for instance in the *Proposed American Declaration on the Rights of Indigenous Peoples* (1997), OR OEA/Ser./L/V/II.95 Doc. 6 [OAS Draft Declaration].
21   *Convention on Biological Diversity*, 5 June 1992, 17 UNTS 79, Can.T.S. 1993 No. 24,31 ILM 818 [Biodiversity Convention].
22   14 October 1994, UNTS 3, Can. T.S. 1996, No. 51, 33 ILM 1332 [Desertification Convention].
23   *Declaration on the Establishment of the Arctic Council*, Canada, Denmark, Finland, Iceland, Norway, Russian Federation, Sweden and the United States, 19 September 1996, 35 ILM 1387 [Arctic Council Declaration].
24   CRC, GA Res. 44/25, annex 44, UN GAOR Supp. (No. 49), UN Doc. A/44/49 (1989).
25   ICESCR, UN Doc. A/6316 (1996) 993 UNTS 3; ICCPR, UN Doc. A/6316 (1996) 991 UNTS 171.
26   Resolution 1994/45, Annex 26, 1994, adopted without changes from the *Report of the Working Group on Indigenous Populations on its Eleventh Session*, UN ESCOR, Commission on Human Rights, Sub-Commission on Prevention of Discrimination and Protection of Minorities, 45th Sess., Agenda Item 14, UN Doc. E/CN.4/Sub/1993/29, Annex 1.
27   Rome Statute, in force 12 July 2002.
28   GA Res. 2200, UN GADR, 21st Sess., Supp. No. 16, UN Doc. A/6316(1966).
29   GA Res. 2200, UN GADR, 21st Sess., Supp. No. 16, UN Doc. A/6316 (1966).
30   *Alien Torts Claims Act*, 28 USC 1350 (2000).
31   United States District Court S.D. Florida, *Sinaltral the Estate of Isidro Sequndo Gil, Plaintiffs v. Coca Cola Company et. al*, *256* F. Supp. 2d 1345.

CHAPTER 2

Cultural Integrity and Ecological Integrity:
The Interface and International Law

INTRODUCTION

The argument of the previous chapter hinged on the specific role that land, waters and air play not only in the cultural identity, but also on the survival and basic rights of indigenous peoples everywhere. Castellino and Walsh's work (2005) emphasizes the relation between the 'right to land and to self-determination'. There are several points of tension embedded within this seemingly unexceptional paragraph. For instance, 'the right to land' in most cases does not entail the right to a specific territory but only a certain territorial area embedded within a state. This condition, renders many of indigenous peoples' rights conditional upon the wider national entity wherein they reside, plus the status of the latter within the international community. 'International society consisting of individuals and groups existing within sovereign states ostensibly gain legitimacy and *locus standi* in international law by virtue of being a part of a sovereign state' (Castellino and Walsh, 2005).

In addition, as noted earlier, there is also a conflict between the presence and enforcement of human rights and state sovereignty itself: it is *individuals* and *groups* that often require protection in and from the state. Speaking of the World Social Forum, De Sousa Santos (2005) points out the need for a 'subaltern cosmopolitan legality' that relies both on political strategy and legal components, especially relevant for many exploited and oppressed groups, including indigenous peoples: 'whenever law is resorted to, it is not necessarily the nation-state law; it may be the local unofficial law as well as international or transnational law'. In fact, for the realization of most indigenous peoples' rights, state is both an 'enemy' and a 'potential ally', hence indigenous peoples' rights are at one and the same time part of both a national and a global struggle (De Sousa Santos, 2005).

TERRITORIAL RIGHTS AND STATE SOVEREIGNTY: *TERRA NULLIUS* OR *UTI POSSIDETIS*

In many ways indigenous peoples' lands conform to the definition of a state, with its inherent rights to sovereignty.[1] 'The state as a person of international law should possess the following qualifications: (a) a permanent population; (b) a defined territory; (c) government; and (d) capacity to enter into relations with other states' (Castellino and Walsh, 2005).[2]

Aside from the problematic aspects of considering states as 'persons' (of which more in Chapter 3 and in Chapter 1), even the final clause fits to some extent because indigenous peoples can, minimally, enter into relations with the state wherein they are embedded, and conclude treaties with it, as tribes have done in the US and First Nations are doing in Canada. Nevertheless the presence of indigenous peoples has helped develop not only collective rights, beyond the rights of individuals, but also contributed significantly to what Anaya terms, 'the softening of State sovereignty' (2001).[3]

Historically, the right to land or territory was based on either of two major approaches in existence since their introduction in Roman law: *uti possidetis* or *terra nullius* (Anaya, 2001) The latter had been used by colonizers on their arrival at a new continent, although there were certainly inhabitants living from time immemorial in the 'discovered lands'. But these inhabitants failed 'to organize themselves into units "recognizable" to colonists' (Castellino and Walsh, 2005), hence the tribes who lived on those lands were considered 'uncivilized'. This judgement left indigenous peoples and tribes unprotected from the greed and aggression of the imperial powers of the time (Castellino and Walsh, 2005). The international legal position on what constitutes *terra nullius* can be found in the Western Sahara case (1975), where the indigenous Saharan tribes were replaced by King Hassan and Morocco after Spain's departure (Franck, 1978). In general, the applications of this doctrine simply represent cases of racism in each instance.

In contrast, the doctrine of *uti possidetis juris* appears to be a better choice for the protection of the present stakeholder occupying a specific area. The current use of this doctrine is part of a general movement in international law towards the acceptance of 'ethnic self-determination', and it leads to an effort to reassess what constitutes a 'people' and whether being a people may permit secession from a state. Examples include the events that followed the disintegration of Yugoslavia.[4] In the case of the former Yugoslavia, however, this approach led to a confirmation of the legal status of 'units' or the former republics that constituted Yugoslavia, rather than of any specific ethnic/indigenous group *within* the borders of the states thus protected under the doctrine of *uti possidetis juris*. The international community was thus intent on recognizing borders and self-determination for the 'whole people' of those states (Pentassuglia, 2002). This recent result shows that, although 'the concept of people has been implicitly described, for legal purposes, by referring to the territorial unit of self-determination' (Pentassuglia, 2002), it follows upon the understanding of 'colonial people' as 'the whole people in a non-self governing territory' (UN Charter, Article 73). In fact:

> ... the typical territorial connotation of people is to be viewed in connection with the doctrine of sovereignty and its fundamental corollaries protective of state boundaries and political unity **(against claims by individual groups defined by ethnicity or other element)**. (Pentassuglia, 2002, emphasis added)

It is worth noting that because of this emphasis on 'whole people', the right to secession is not even envisioned for distinct peoples, for example, as the Canadian Supreme Court decided for the people of Quebec.[5] Hence, although it is increasingly obvious that in any state 'the notion of "people" is no longer homogeneous' (Pellet, 1992), democratic self-determination remains internal to the state (or to the newly formed unit), without involving the ethnicity of disparate groups.

The full translation of the doctrine of *uti possidetis ita possidetis* (based on Roman civil law) means 'as you possess, so you possess'. Clearly the doctrine is of little use in territorial disputes because the territory is treated 'as the *de facto* as well as *de jure* legal possession of the current occupier' (Castellino and Walsh, 2005). It is a useful principle to employ after a dispute or a conflict in order to define the territorial boundaries of a newly formed state. The International Court of Justice explains the effect of this doctrine in the *Burkina Faso v. Republic of Mali* case:

> ... *the essence of the principle lies in its primary aim of securing respect for the territorial boundaries at the moment when independence is achieved. Such territorial boundaries may be no more than delimitations between different administration divisions or colonies all subject to the same sovereign. In that case, the application of the principle of* uti possidetis *resulted in administrative boundaries being transformed into international frontiers in the full sense of the term.*[6]

But all boundaries are artificial, in the sense that they do not necessarily contain a specific ethnic/indigenous group (Boggs, 1980). Hence, before acknowledging a specific critical date upon which the definition of a territory's boundaries was to be established beyond dispute, it would be necessary to examine the validity of such a rigid point of reference in order not to ratify the 'rights' of colonizer against indigenous communities (Castellino, 2005).

Nevertheless, had this doctrine been adopted from the start, that is *before* colonization, it would have been sufficient to protect indigenous peoples' title to the land where they lived, better than the doctrine of *terra nullius* could. The latter acknowledged the presence of indigenous peoples on certain lands, but viewed this occurrence as insufficient to ensure their possession of the territory.

TERRITORY AND TERRITORIAL INTEGRITY

Whatever the basis of indigenous peoples' entitlement to a specific territory, enclosed within certain borders according to history or to a treaty, the *condition* of the territory is at least as important as its boundaries for the health and the well-being of the inhabitants. International law protects the integrity of territories, although the expression refers to the borders or perhaps to the possibility of specific quantifiable harms. The classic case of protecting one country's territory from the harms arising from another country's industrial operations is *Trail Smelter*.[7] But in international law, perhaps the most cited and most influential case involves the legality of nuclear tests.

Nuclear weapons and the opinion of the World Court

> *The International Court of Justice has issued an advisory opinion of great weight on the legality of nuclear weaponry. It is the first time ever that an international tribunal*

has directly addressed this gravest universal threat to the future of humanity (Falk, 1998).

Before considering the International Court's opinion on this question, it is best to consider the context against which these weapons are developed and the international pleadings of Australia and New Zealand as part of that context. Nuclear power, in all its applications, represents one of the most hazardous products and processes on Earth (Shrader-Frechette, 1982). As such it is one of the clearest cases demanding immediate concern and legal action on several fronts: it is hazardous in the mining of its required materials and throughout the 'fuel cycle' (Draper, 1991; Shrader-Frechette, 1982); it is hazardous in all its uses, not only as a weapon (Shrader-Frechette, 1982); and it is especially hazardous in its disposal phase (Shrader-Frechette, 1993). Nuclear power is indeed 'risky business' from cradle to grave (Draper, 1991), and the results of its impact exhibit all the characteristic harms this work confronts: immediate harm to human health, delayed threats to health, life and normal function, and long-term harm to the 'diversity of life' (Wilson, 1992) and to its very survival, through direct and indirect (genetic) impacts (Colborn et al, 1996). Finally it is extremely and unpredictably hazardous through its disposal (Goodwin, 1980; Shrader-Frechette, 1993).

On the question of the legality of atmospheric nuclear testing, Australia and New Zealand instituted separate proceedings against France before the International Court (Ragazzi, 1997). Atmospheric nuclear tests clearly spread unwarranted radioactive material indiscriminately to any and all countries adjacent to the tests. Even France, who wanted to test, did not attempt to conduct such tests over its own soil. France must have recognized, as they defended their strategy, that the atmospheric tests were neither desirable nor risk-free. France claimed it needed to perform these 'last tests' in order to end atmospheric testing altogether. This declaration ensured that 'the International Court did not pronounce either jurisdiction or the merits of the cases, relying on the obligation undertaken explicitly by the French government'.[8]

But the importance of the case does not lie with the majority view expressed above. Rather, the four judges who wrote a forceful dissent (Judges Onyeama, Dillard, Jiménez de Arechago and Sir Humphrey Waldock) asserted that the 'object of the applicant States was to obtain a declaratory judgment' (Ragazzi, 1997) instead.[9] The pleadings in these cases show that the intentions of the states were not simply to stop France on this single occasion, but to make a universal point of principle. France, according to these pleadings, had violated important rights: the protection of New Zealand's sovereign rights to be free of radionuclear fallout and contamination. This was described as a right that belonged to 'all members of the international community' (Ragazzi, 1997).

Hence, especially for New Zealand, the obligation was *erga omnes*, and all states possessed correlative rights of protection. The fact that France (with China) had not been a signatory to the Treaty Banning Nuclear Weapons Tests in the Atmosphere, in Outer Space and Under Water (Moscow Treaty, 1963) was not relevant (Hossain and Chowdhury, 1984). Nevertheless, the additional fact that 104 states did become parties to the Moscow Treaty over the next ten years enabled Australia and New Zealand to argue that 'customary rule had gradually emerged' in the international community. New Zealand could also assert at the same time the *erga omnes* character of France's obligation (Ragazzi, 1997). Ragazzi 'infers' that the obligation is indeed *erga omnes* from the following arguments found in the pleadings:

... the obligation

(a) is stated in 'absolute' terms (the dictum refers to 'absolute' and 'unqualified' obligations);
(b) reflects a 'community interest' (the dictum refers to the 'concern of all States');
(c) protects fundamental goods, namely 'the security, life and health of all peoples' and the 'global environment' (security, life and health are also some of the basic goods protected by the four examples of obligations erga omnes given in the dictum);
(d) has a prohibitory content (like the four examples given in the dictum);
(e) is not owed to particular States, but to the 'international community' (the dictum refers to the 'international community as a whole'); and
(f) its correlative rights of protection 'are held in common' (the dictum provides that 'all States can be held to have a legal interest' in the protection of obligations erga omnes). (Ragazzi, 1997)

The 'dictum' here referred to is the one found in the *Barcelona Traction* case. This argument is of foundational importance because it introduces the principled approach sought later by the WHO in opposing the use of nuclear weapons.

The WHO submitted a question requesting an advisory opinion on 'the legality of the use by a state of nuclear weapons in an armed conflict', to the International Court of Justice, as follows: 'In view of the health and environmental effects would the use of nuclear weapons by a state in war or other armed conflict be a breach of its obligations under international law including the WHO constitution?'[10] Several states argued that the question went beyond 'the WHO's proper activities'. The court added (para. 10) that:

> *... three conditions must be satisfied in order to found the jurisdiction of the Court when a request for an advisory opinion is submitted to it by a specialized agency: the agency requesting the opinion must be duly authorized, under the Charter, to request opinions from the Court; the opinion requested must be on a legal question; and this question must be one arising within the scope of the activities of the requesting agency.* (Kindred et al, 2000)

Despite the interest and the competence of the WHO to assess and evaluate the health effects of the use of nuclear weapons, at first the court judged that the final condition had not been met because the WHO was not a state able to wage a war or enter into a conflict. Hence the UN General Assembly had to bring the question to the court once again. The court held that neither 'customary' nor 'conventional' international law authorizes specifically the use of nuclear weapons (by 11 votes to 3), that the threat or use of nuclear weapons is also not specifically permitted, and that:

> *... it follows from the above-mentioned requirements that the threat or use of nuclear weapons would generally be contrary to the rules of international law applicable in armed conflict, and in particular the principles and rules of humanitarian law; however, in view of the current state of international law, and of the elements of facts at its disposal, the Court cannot conclude definitively whether the threat or use*

of nuclear weapons would be lawful or unlawful in an extreme circumstance of self-defence, in which the very survival of a State would be at stake. (Speech of the president casting his vote to break the seven–seven tie)

This opinion, despite its ambiguous tone, was viewed as an important decision, and it shows the transition from state treaties as sole arbiters of the status of nuclear armaments, to an opinion whose history and background served to bring a normative issue to the forefront of public opinion. Falk (1998) traces the history of the movement that culminated in that request, from several groups in civil society, as 'the push to achieve elimination [of nuclear weapons] often merges with the view that weapons of mass destruction cannot be reconciled with international humanitarian law'. Falk shows how world opinion, as well as the work of many committed NGOs, prepared the ground for the very possibility of asking for an opinion from the time of the 1985 London Nuclear Warfare Tribunal, where those weapons were defined as 'unconditionally illegal' and hence that even a threat of their use would amount to a 'crime against humanity'.

The main point that emerges is that neither politics nor economic factors, nor even the advantage of groups of nuclear states, could be allowed to determine the use of these weapons. Hence, at first the UN General Assembly and the WHO referred a difficult question to the International Court, and although the question could be evaded because the WHO concern was 'health' (narrowly construed) and not the use of weapons, an opinion was later given. Implicit in both the original request by the WHO and the eventual opinion is the fact that, 'Nuclear weaponry, with its global implications, raises questions of legality that affect not just the citizenry of the nuclear weapons states, but the entire world' (Falk, 1998).

This position supports, once again, the *erga omnes* status of the question, at least in principle, given the careful phrasing of the Court's statements. Falk (1998) does not use this language in regard to either the question or the opinion itself, but adds:

Although not so formulated the radical element in this request was to transfer the question of nuclear weapons policy from the domain of geopolitics, where it had remained since the first attacks on Hiroshima and Nagasaki, to the domain of international law.

And if it has not transferred the question to treaty law, clearly both incomplete and insufficient to deal with this global threat, then Ragazzi's argument (1997) for placing its normative aspect among the few *jus cogens* norms generating an *erga omnes* obligation appears to be correct.

Ecological rights and human rights

The ingrained values of any civilization are the sources from which its legal concepts derive, and the ultimate yardstick and touchstone of their validity. This is so in international and domestic legal systems alike, save that international law would require a worldwide recognition of those values. It would not be wrong to state that the love of nature, the desire for its preservation, the need for human activity to respect the requisites for its maintenance and continuance, are among those pristine and universal values which command international recognition. (Weeramantry, 1997)

The role of ecological integrity in protected areas

Article 8(j) Each contracting Party shall, as far as possible and appropriate: Subject to its national legislation, respect, preserve and maintain knowledge, innovations and practices of indigenous and local communities embodying traditional lifestyles relevant to the conservation and sustainable use of biological diversity.[13]

The argument here concerns the interface between indigenous groups and their lands. The latter are not intended as any area, whether paved, built-up, open to commercial/industrial use or as a brownfield zone, but as naturally maintained ecosystems because 'The integrity of protected areas may be threatened by activities exercised within or beyond their boundaries' (de Klemm and Shine, 1993).

There are certain characteristics of individual reserves or parks, or as they are known in Spain, *parajes naturales* (de Klemm and Shine, 1993). These include their status as wilderness zones and the presence of protected ecosystems and species, that is, ecosystems where only traditional activities are permitted. But threats against the integrity of protected areas are not always fully proscribed in law. For instance, mining activities are forbidden, for the most part, in these areas, although 'exceptional' circumstances may lead to permits being issued, in combination with the obligation to ensure that mitigation measures be implemented (de Klemm and Shine, 1993).

This is a major problem, as it is easy for the ministries and governments of various countries to argue that economic activities carried out in certain areas, are 'in the public interest', although they are, invariably, only in the interest of the industrial complex undertaking the activities and, at most, some of the government officials who have authorized the activity.

In addition, 'Most protected areas are vulnerable to the effects of activities exercised outside their boundaries, in particular to those affecting the quantity and quality of the waters flowing into them' (de Klemm and Shine, 1993). In response to this common threat, most protected areas are also surrounded by buffer zones, where controls are applied to preserve the integrity of the core protected areas. These zones are normally viewed as part of the protected areas, as buffers are essential to the maintenance of biosphere reserves and all other areas of integrity (Karr, 2000; Westra, 1998).

This approach to the protection and maintenance of the integrity of any area is highly desirable; it represents the only way to preserve biodiversity and the natural systemic processes of that area. Hence, if these regimes are necessary to protect biodiversity, they are at least equally indispensable to protect traditional aboriginal lands and the indigenous groups that inhabit them:

> *indigenous human populations living on and from the land by traditional means, can still be considered as forming an integral part of the ecosystems concerned. When a protected area is established on such land, it should thus have as an additional objective the conservation of the particular culture, knowledge and way of life of the indigenous populations living within its boundaries.* (de Klemm and Shine, 1993)

In fact, the policy adopted by Parks Canada in 1979 accepts the preservation of tradi-tional resource uses by First Nations, while honouring their treaty rights (de Klemm and Shine, 1993). In this case, the interests of indigenous peoples and those of bio-diversity and conservation are interchangeable. The latter encompasses the diversity of ecosystems, the diversity of species, and genetic diversity within species (Article 2 of the Convention on Biological Diversity, cited in Bowman, 1996). This is so because although all humankind shares the basic need for 'nature's services' (Daily, 1997), in general, indigenous peoples have no way of substituting any natural services that become unavailable (such as healthy food or water), as do persons living in built environments, at least for a time. Their lands and waters are there to provide for all their basic needs, but they can actually do so only if the integrity and biodiversity of those areas is fully protected within and outside the core lands that belong to any specific group.

An aside on biological/ecological integrity

Ecological or biological integrity originated as an ethical concept in the wake of Aldo Leopold (1949) and has been present in the law, both domestic and international, and part of public policy since its appearance in the 1972 US Clean Water Act. Ecological integrity has also filtered into the language of a great number of mission and vision statements internationally, as well as being clearly present in the Great Lakes Water Quality Agreement between the US and Canada, which was ratified in 1988.

The generic concept of integrity connotes a valuable whole, the state of being whole, undiminished, unimpaired or in perfect condition. Integrity in common usage is thus an umbrella concept that encompasses a variety of other notions. Although integrity may be developed in other contexts, wild nature provides paradigmatic examples for applied reflection and research.

Because of the extent of human exploitation of the planet, examples are most often found in those places that, until recently, have been least hospitable to dense human occupancy and industrial development, such as deserts, the high Arctic, high-altitude mountain ranges, the ocean depths, and the least accessible reaches of forests. Wild nature is also found in locations such as national parks that have been deemed worthy of official protection. America, from Mexico to Alaska (Cooperrider, 1994; Noss, 1992) utilizes the ecosystem approach to argue the importance of conserving areas of integrity.

But the most salient aspect of ecosystem processes (including all their components) is their life-sustaining function, and not just within wild nature or the corridor sur-rounding wild areas, although these are the main concerns of conservation biologists. The significance of life-sustaining functions is that they ultimately support life everywhere. Gretchen Daily (1997), for instance, specifies in some detail the functions provided by nature's services, and her work is crucial in the effort to connect respect for natural systems integrity with human rights.

Arguments against the value of ecological integrity for public policy have identified the concept as stipulative rather than fully scientific (Shrader-Frechette, 1993). In a similar vein, even the concept of ecology has been criticized as insufficiently robust to guide public policy (Shrader-Frechette and McCoy, 1993). But ecological integrity is already a part of public policy, thus requiring consideration of its meaning and the role its inclusion should play in policy, rather than arguing for its rejection. Furthermore, to maintain that 'we need a middle path dictated in part by human not merely biocentric theory' (Shrader-Frechette, 1995) ignores how humans do not exist as separate to other organisms. Biocentrism is life-oriented, and this principle is increasingly accepted not only by science, but in the law.

The routine use of Karr's Index of Biotic Integrity (IBI) (1993) to reach general conclusions illustrates the ethical effectiveness of the scientific concept of ecological integrity in public policy. The law analyses a crime or victim under a particular set of circumstances. But public policy must abstract from specifics. Disintegrity (or lack of integrity) and environmental crime (Shrader-Frechette, 1995) are global in scope and need international forums and broad concepts to ensure that they will be proscribed and possibly eliminated.

In addition, there is mounting evidence to connect disintegrity or biotic impoverishment (Karr, 1993) in all its forms, from pollutions, climate change, toxic wastes and encroachment into the wild (Westra, 2000a) with human morbidity, mortality and abnormal functioning. International law has enacted a number of instruments to protect human rights (Fidler, 2000) and the WHO invited the Global Ecological Integrity Project (1992–1999) to consult with it. This collaboration eventually produced a document titled *Global Ecological Integrity and 'Sustainable Development': Cornerstones of Public Health* (Soskolne and Bertollini, 1999).

The ethics of integrity

Because of the global connection between health and integrity, and the right to life and to living (Cancado Trindade, 1992), a true understanding of ecological integrity reconnects human life with the wild, and the rights of the latter with those of the former. The ethics of integrity primarily involve respect for ecological rights (Taylor, 1998), without limiting these to the human rights that are the primary focus of the law. The main point of an ethic of integrity is that it is a new ethic (Karr, 1993), one founded on recent science demonstrating the interdependence between humankind and its habitats. Environmental ethicists may prefer to focus on one or the other aspect of this interconnected whole – biocentrism or anthropocentrism. While biocentrists accept the presence of humankind as such within the rest of nature, anthropocentrisms attempt to separate the two, in direct conflict with ecological science.

If it is argued that human health and function are both directly and indirectly affected by disintegrity (Soskolne and Bertollini, 1999), then no theory can properly separate one from the other. The strength of the proverbial canary-in-the-mine example is based on the fact that the demise of the canary anticipates that of the miner. Hence it is necessary to accept a general imperative of respect for ecological integrity. Onora O'Neill (1996) makes this point well:

> The injustice of destroying natural and man-made environments can also be thought of in two ways. In the first place, their destruction is unjust because it is a further way by which others can be injured: systematic or gratuitous destruction of the means of life creates vulnerabilities, which facilitate direct injuries to individuals... Secondly, the principle of destroying natural and man-made environments, in the sense of destroying their reproduction and regenerative powers, is not universalizable.

In addition, the vulnerability that follows the destruction of integrity links the concept to environmental justice. The principle of integrity together with appropriate second order principles would ensure, first, the defence of the basic rights of humankind (Shue, 1996), as well as second, the support of environmental justice globally, because it would ensure the presence of the preconditions of agency and thus the ability of all humans to exercise their rights as agents (Beyerveld and Brownsword, 2001; Gewirth, 1982b).

Ecological integrity is thus not an empty metaphor or a grand theory of little utility. It is a concept that is robust enough to support a solid ethical stance, one that reinstates humans in nature while respecting the latter, thus permitting clear answers in cases of conflicts between (present) economic human interest and (long-term) ecological concerns.

Ecological integrity and the law

It is reasonable to conceive of humanity as being morally responsible for the protection of the integrity of the whole ecosystem, and for that responsibility to be translated into such mechanisms that are cognizant of ecological thresholds (Taylor, 1998). Insofar as such responsibility is justified as a protection of human life and health, breaches of environmental regulations deserve not just economic penalties but criminal ones. Nevertheless, there is a growing parallel movement to recognize the intrinsic value of both the components and the processes of natural systems, not only in philosophy (Callicott, 1989; Leopold, 1949; Westra, 1998), but also in the law (Brooks et al, 2002).

A number of international legal instruments also reflect the emerging global ecological concerns, and thus include language about respect for the intrinsic value of both natural entities and processes. This point is illustrated by a project involving the justices of the worlds' highest courts, funded by the United Nations Environment Programme (UNEP). The project's biocentric goal, as outlined by Judge Arthur Chaksalson of South Africa, is one of the most important results of the Johannesburg meeting (also known as 'Rio+10'). The 2000 Draft International Covenant on Environment and Development incorporates the mandates of the Earth Charter (see Appendix 1), which was adopted by a United Nations Economic, Scientific, and Cultural Organization (UNESCO) resolution on 16 October 2003, in its language and includes articles on ecological integrity and the intrinsic value of nature.

Although the positions advanced in these international initiatives are present in law, economic interests often obscure the opposition between the basic rights of persons and peoples and the property rights of legal entities and institutions. In the process, courts tend to weigh these incommensurable values as though they were equal. But the right to life and the survival of peoples is not comparable to economic benefits or even the survival of corporate and industrial enterprises.

An additional connection arises from a consideration of ecological integrity, a complex concept that, after several years of funded work, the Global Ecological Integrity Project eventually defined in 2000 (Westra, 2000b). The protection of basic human rights through recognition of the need for ecological integrity, as Holmes Rolston (1993) acknowledges, is a step in the emerging awareness of humanity as an integral part of the biosphere (Taylor, 1998; Westra, 1998).

On the basis of the biocentric foundation for ecological integrity, it is necessary to move toward the twin goals of deterrence and restraint, as is done in the case of assaults, rapes and other violent crimes. Laws that restrain unbridled property rights represent a first target, but efforts should not be limited to action within the realm of tort law. The reason is obvious: economic harms are transferable, thus acceptable to the perpetrators of such harms, although the real harms produced are often incompensable. As Brooks and his colleagues (2002) indicate in reference to US law, science is now available to support appeals to interdependence:

> *Not only have conservation biology as a discipline and biodiversity as a concept become an important part of national forest and endangered species management, but major court cases reviewing biodiversity determinations have been decided.*

In addition, Earth System Science increasingly provides a 'multidisciplinary and inter-disciplinary science framework for understanding global scale problems', including the relations and the functioning of 'global systems that include the land, oceans and the atmosphere' (Brooks et al, 2002). In essence, the ecosystem approach and systematic science of ecological integrity have contributed support to what Cancado Trindade (1992) terms 'the globalization of human rights protection and of environmental protection.

As noted above, these ideals are contained in the language and the principles of the Earth Charter. The global reach of these ethics and charters, to be effective, must be supported by a supranational juridical entity such as the European Court of Human Rights. As the case for environmental or, better yet, ecological rights becomes stronger and more accepted in international law, the best solution, as suggested by Patricia Birnie and Adam Boyle (2002), could be to empower the UN. It might be desirable 'to invest the UN Security Council, or some other UN organ, with the power to act in the interest of "ecological security", taking universally binding decisions in the interest of all mankind and the environment' (Birnie and Boyle, 2002). Empowering the UN in this way would foster support for programmes based on the abundant evidence linking ecology and human rights and could become the basis for a new global environmental/human order (Westra, 2004a).

THE ECOLOGICAL AND TRADITIONAL CONNECTION BETWEEN INDIGENOUS PEOPLES AND BIODIVERSITY

> *Overlooked in virtually all accounts of the distribution of species and the structure of forests is the role of humanity. There is in fact a growing body of knowledge on how indigenous and local populations manage their natural resources and sustain them over time.* (Hecht and Cockburn, 1990)

Because of the historical and traditional interdependence between indigenous peoples and their lands, the present state of the Amazon forests, as well as that of the Arctic tundra, boreal forests and the like, are 'the outcome of human as well as biological history' (Hecht and Cockburn, 1990). The geographical distribution of biodiversity parallels the habitats of indigenous peoples in the world (Woodliffe, 1996; see also Burger, 1990).

Jim Nations (1988) argues that 'Wild genetic resources, that is, species of plants and animals and the variations within them, are now recognized as constituting the raw materials for future medicines, food and fuels'. Perhaps the most important aspect of biodiversity in developing countries is the role of medicinal plants in the health care of indigenous peoples. Of course the increased value of biological and plant material does not end with the uses indigenous groups make of those resources. Pharmaceutical giants such as Merck, Bristol-Meyers, Squibb, Smith-Kline and Glaxo and Pfizer have all entered into contracts with countries where areas of wild biodiversity still exist, such as China, Surinam, Peru, Argentina, Chile, Nigeria and Cameroon (Artuso, 1997).

The question then arises about the interaction between the large pharmaceutical companies and the indigenous peoples whose lands are home to the desirable and valuable medicinal plants. It is the respectful traditional practices of those groups that have ensured the continued flourishing of biodiversity in all its aspects. In some cases, large corporations have even entered into contracts that ensure advance payments and other royalty arrangements – Merck entered into such a contract with Costa Rica's Instituto Nacional de Biodiversidad, whereby 50 per cent of royalties was pledged to support Costa Rica's National Park Service (Artuso, 1997). In such cases, the role of government ministries and agencies should be to protect not only the valuable biodiversity, but also the indigenous peoples who are its *de facto* custodians.

In some sense, the knowledge of indigenous peoples, as well as the plants in their areas, should be under their exclusive control, but recent studies indicate that 'wild land biodiversity prospecting is currently operating in a "policy vacuum"' (Woodliffe, 1996). In fact, some have argued instead that these genetic wild resources, although conserved and nurtured by indigenous peoples, should be considered part of the common heritage of mankind (Sedjo, 1992).

Anil Agarwal (1992) concurs with this assessment, but argues that it should be based on a prior 'international system of income tax, so that wealth could be automatically transferred as a matter of right, and not just as aid and charity'. If this system were legally implemented and enforced, together with an international 'right to work', everyone, including all indigenous peoples would be assured of at least basic subsistence. In that case, it might well be fair and just to treat 'Third World biodiversity as … a global resource' (Agarwal, 1992).

It seems clear that the protection to which indigenous peoples are entitled and the rights they have impose corresponding obligations on everyone. It is a question of respecting human rights, but also a question of recognizing the unique position of these peoples to foster the conservation of life-saving biodiversity. This represents yet another strong reason to treat obligations to indigenous groups as obligations *erga omnes*.

Eco-crimes and international law: Applications to indigenous rights?

Environmental rights are human rights. Treaties that affect human rights cannot be applied in such a manner to constitute a denial of human rights, as understood at the time of their application. A country cannot endorse activities which are a violation of human rights by the standard of their time, merely because they are taken under a Treaty which dates back to a period when such action was not a violation of human rights. (Weeramantry, 1997)

Aside from the *Nuclear Tests* case that addresses directly the question of territorial integrity rights and the *erga omnes* obligations arbitrations that ensue, there are few other cases and arbitrations that seriously address environmental harms. But all cases ultimately tend to confirm that international conventions expressly recognized by some states are not enough, and that peremptory norms should guide and prescribe *erga omnes* obligations as the best way to mitigate and eventually eliminate the tragic consequences of environmental inaction and carelessness.

Hence, we need to consider the role of international custom and judicial decisions in order to confirm these conclusions. It is not sufficient to show that the nature of illicit environmental acts, or even the consequence of lawful acts affecting the environment can, and most often do, produce consequences much closer to large-scale attacks or crimes against humanity than to what might be expected from breaches of regulatory regimes. It is not even sufficient, although it appears to be necessary, to show the clear connection between environmental crimes and breaches of international instruments designed to defend human rights.

The Stockholm Conference consecrated the ideas among others, that (a) the environment is a global entity to be protected in its entirely (although this does not diminish the importance of particular rules applicable to different sources of pollution and to different components of the environment), and (b) environmental protection is a necessary condition of the promotion of peace, human rights and development. (Ragazzi, 1997)

We should reconsider briefly the three 'classic cases' that provide the best sources of international case law in regard to the environment, in addition to the *Nuclear Tests* case. The first of these, in chronological order, as well as in order of importance, is the *Trail Smelter Arbitration*,[14], where the Tribunal found that:

... no State has the right to use or permit the use of its territory in such a manner as to cause injury by fumes in or to the territory of another or the properties or persons therein, when the case is of serious consequences and the injury is established by clear and convincing evidence.

The language of the Tribunal's judgement is clearly dated, but one may want to apply the findings of this case, where the US justly sought compensation from Canada, to the present situation where, for instance, 'Global warming is a process that is no longer discounted in the international legal system, although the severity of its impact on the Earth is still debated' (Kindred et al, 2000), yet the present US government refuses to take responsibility for its own activities and ratify the Kyoto Protocol (to the United Nations Framework Convention on Climate Change, 1997).

The United Nations Framework Convention on Climate Change clearly defines 'climate change', and in Article 1.4 defines 'emissions': '"Emissions" means the release of greenhouse gasses and/or their precursors into the atmosphere and their interactions'. In principle then, the US refusal to curb its emissions runs counter to the principles and the letter of international law, completely ignoring the import (among other principles) of the Precautionary Principle (Article 15 of the Rio Declaration, 1992). Sharon Williams (1986) recognizes that the 'holding of the tribunal in *The Trail Smelter Case,* has today become an integral part of international environmental law and can be said to have widespread acceptance by states'. The language of the *Trail Smelter Arbitration,* however, is vague and imprecise, nor does it take into consideration state responsibility for the 'shared resources or the global commons' (Brunnée, 1993), as it considers *Trail Smelter* only as a civil case (see also Chapter 8).

The second classic case is the *Corfu Channel* case (Merits).[15] Although the case concerns Albanian responsibility for failing (or omitting) to warn British warships of the presence of mines in its waters, this is not, strictly speaking, an environmental case. But the language of the court can be integrated and extended to continue and support the point made in the *Trail Smelter Arbitration* about state responsibility. The judgement found the state (Albania) to be responsible, in these words:

> Such obligations are based not on the Hague Convention of 1907, No. VIII, which is applicable in time of war, but on certain general and well-recognized principles, namely: elementary considerations of humanity, even more exacting in peace than in war ... and every State's **obligation not to allow (knowingly) its territory to be used for acts contrary to the rights of other states.** (emphasis added)

This quote establishes that, first, humanitarian considerations are not limited to war circumstances, and second, that the *Trail Smelter* rule 'do no harm' also held in this case.

The third case, the *Lake Lanoux Arbitration,* completes the trilogy as support for the existence of customary duties to avoid causing trans-boundary environmental damage and to make reparation for such damage, should it occur (Mickelson, 1993).

Together, this trilogy of cases and arbitrations present the main elements in international environmental law that are neither domestic laws nor principles, rules or articles taken from various instruments. Using primarily the latter, Mickelson (1993) argues that the use of those documents 'perpetuates the notion that international environmental law has developed in a virtual vacuum', and that it is, for the most part, 'a decontextualized invocation of abstract principles'. Nevertheless, she also claims that this judgement is incorrect, invoking 'the rich body of material that does, in fact, exist'. I find this statement not to be supported by facts: a survey of much of the scholarly literature on the topic simply reveals different interpretations or analyses of the same basic cases. These interpretations are indeed 'rich' in theoretical arguments, but it is important to note that none of these cases is even remotely applicable to the grave environmental problems we face today. The only one that is truly environmental, the *Trail Smelter Arbitration,* at best involves economic damages to a specific agricultural community in a specific area. In addition, the independent research of the International Joint Commission, as well as other factual research upon which the arbitration was based, also cited insect infestations and climate variations as additional contributive causes to the problem (Mickelson, 1993).

The patterns prevailing in current problems are not present in *Trail Smelter.* That is, considerations of grave ecological disasters with global implications are absent from that arbitration, so that, in the final analysis, we are only left with one major principle, *sic utere tuo*, as a standard and guide arising from this 'case study'. Some of the major differences between the situation in the *Trail Smelter* and today's global problems are:

- a full comprehension of the scope of the harms imposed (such as the effects of disruptions of ecosystem functions on human health), beyond simple economic consequences;
- a full comprehension of the scale of the harms imposed (such as the effects on the ozone layer), with consequences affecting populations far removed from the location of the environmental hazard;
- an understanding of the possible mutagenic effects of the harm, such as changes in normal human functions and development, affecting even future generations;
- an appreciation of the substantive justice issues involved when environmental harms disproportionately affect certain populations more than others; and
- an appreciation of the need for the precautionary principle when evaluating an activity that might produce environmental harms.

Hence, we can conclude that not only is the case law meagre in regard to international environmental law, but it is almost irrelevant with respect to the real issues we face today. One could argue that there are, in addition to the few environmental cases and arbitrations, several international human rights cases, some involving aboriginal peoples,[16] where the ostensible primacy of human rights, both of the individuals and of peoples, are indivisible from environmental rights. These cases view the environment as a fundamental human right of peoples because it is basic to aboriginal cultures, not just in the physical sense of a necessary basis of all human life, as argued for the most part in this work.

Indigenous peoples are not states, although they are increasingly present and heard in international law (Anaya, 2004). So that in the sense I have applied, 'territorial integrity' is far more than the presence of borders or an area kept from the possible use of other national entities. It is the basis and the foundation of the basic rights of indigenous people, the very foundation of their right to survive both as individuals and as a people.

The question of collective indigenous rights

> *Indigenous peoples possess collective rights which are indispensable for their existence, well-being and integral development as peoples.*[17]

For the most part, international human rights instruments refer to individuals, with the paradoxical results that an aboriginal community intent on suing a corporation, for instance, requires that one or more of its members prepare the submission to a court of law, rather than allowing the community itself to speak officially through its representatives. The corporation, itself, an aggregate of far more diverse components, is viewed as one.

But the worst aspect of this approach is that the communication and collective aspects of indigenous rights are left aside. It is possible, according to Anaya (1999) and others (Newman, 2006), to understand the resistance of the US and others to the recognition of collective rights on political grounds, but their approach is no less harmful to aboriginal communities if their approach can be rationalized with reference to concerns about cold war issues and the like:

> *After a long interagency consultation, a 2001 US Security Council position paper on indigenous peoples, again referring to the concern of possible conflict with individual rights, indicated a preference for the intermediate concept of rights held by 'individuals in community with others', rather than by indigenous communities themselves.* (Newman, 2006)

In contrast, Article 27 of the ICCPR recognizes collective rights, as does also the government of Canada:[18]

> *... [a] further dimension of aboriginal title is the fact that it is held communally. Aboriginal title cannot be held by individual aboriginal persons; it is a collective right to land held by all members of an aboriginal nation.*

Both Australia,[19] and New Zealand[20] are equally committed to recognizing collective indigenous rights. This is, nevertheless, a difficult position to accept in general terms as the neoliberal ideal is one of maximum freedom and individual right of choice, without allowing many traditional moral and communitarian concerns to interfere with such choices. The emphasis is on 'my rights' rather than on 'my responsibility' (see Jonas, 1984), and this stark individualism also represents the fundamental tenet of capitalism, as I argue in Chapter 9.

That is why it is not only the US but also several of the affluent Western countries that hold the same or similar positions to the one noted for the US. This includes the UK's 'long-held position against the concept of collective human rights international law' (Newman, 2006). Whatever the political reasons that prompt the concern about the presence of collective rights in international law, the root cause is the undisputed and indisputable primacy of individual rights. Newman (2006) adds:

> *Saying that individual rights can also run up against other competing individual rights, and thus concluding that collective rights do not uniquely threaten to limit individual rights, does not limit individual rights further compared to what could have been the case without recognition of collective rights.*

I believe that Newman's concern shows that he is prepared to turn community and collective rights 'on its head', so to speak. As part of the general project of neoliberalism, it is the *individual* rights of natural and legal persons that not only 'threaten' but effectively obliterate community rights, and thus the rights of indigenous peoples, as we shall see clearly in the case law of Chapters 4, 5 and 6.

In defence of his position, Newman (2006) cites Buchanan (2004) and Kymlicka (1991), with his *real politic* effort to defend indigenous peoples by finding a way to convince non-indigenous powers 'in ways they will understand and respond to'. For both, it is important to fit indigenous peoples' discourse into the concerns of those who support the absolute primacy of individual freedom, a bizarre effort to reconcile opposites that does not seem to have worked in the past or to work today.

For instance, Lawrence Gostin (2004) (see Chapter 10) views this approach as fatal to the very existence of public health concerns, hence he sees the real danger of adopting, as a *starting* point, a position that endangers all of mankind in general, and, I argue, indigenous peoples in particular. In simple terms, not only aboriginal rights instruments, but also eco-footprint analysis (see page 221) have it *right*, as does much of the soft law we shall discuss below, including the Earth Charter. Aboriginal peoples are communities, their rights are appropriately collective and they do not deny but embrace the fact that they are also part of the community of mankind, as well as part of the community of life on Earth (see Earth Charter, Appendix 1).

They, and their understanding of what 'rights' mean are not the enemies of rights, properly understood. They simply represent the unavoidable counterpart of rights, that is responsibilities to their community, to future generations and to life on Earth. This is *their* starting point, and it is one I fully support in this and my previous work. To oppose the primacy of responsibility is to ignore the reality of morality and of science which, increasingly, indicates just how wrong and harmful the other 'starting point' is and has been. In the next section I consider a well-known case where this argument was brought to its full conclusion and presented successfully in the courts.

COLONIZATION, NEOLIBERALISM AND THE RIGHTS OF THE U'WA PEOPLE

Indigenous peoples are thus subjects of a special duty of care on the part of individual states and the international community, akin to the 'sacred trust' articulated in the United Nations Charter with regard to peoples of non-self-governing territories.[21]

There are two sources of consideration regarding indigenous rights: international law and domestic law. Although there are treaties and agreements between provincial (Canada) or state (US) governments, the federal governments of both countries, and native populations, international law standards influence all juridical decisions. Under international law, decisions taken to protect indigenous peoples may well be considered non-derogable obligations, governed by *jus cogens* norms. This is certainly true of all acts that can be considered genocide, and may also be true of the protection of the territorial integrity of national groups.

The protection model that addresses the biological/ecological rights of indigenous peoples also appeals to fundamental human rights, equally binding on all individuals as well as states. This is, in fact, the main appeal of international law as the best source of protection instruments. In contrast, treaties must be negotiated with the country in which the indigenous nation is embedded, and that approach does not always produce the best results for the indigenous groups.

The case concerns the U'wa's unrelenting resistance to neoliberalism's 'second conquest'.[22] Even without mobilizing armies, neoliberal policies have encouraged and supported 'the escalation of resource extractions'[23] that, I have argued, is a form of eco-violence as it is presently practised (Westra, 2004c). In other words, it is no longer a question of conquering a nation for their labour, but it represents a far more serious threat: 'The threat to the Indians is not this time one of slavery, but of expropriation of their lands and [the] total destruction of their way of life, *if not their persons as well*' (Maybury-Lewis, 1984, emphasis added).

The case of the U'wa people of Colombia combines the two strands arising from the previous section: first, the absolute dependence of indigenous peoples' lives on their territory; and second, the importance of international courts and legal instruments for the protection of that interdependence and their lives. It also demonstrates the need for a cosmopolitan reconstruction of human rights (to be discussed in the next chapter) (Anaya, 2004).

The U'wa are an indigenous people of 5000 members living in northeastern Colombia (Rodriguez-Garavito and Arena, 2005). Theirs was not the first effort of resistance in South America; for example, the Mayagnas in Nicaragua and the Huaorani, Secoya and Cofan in Ecuador have been fighting against Texaco (Rodriguez-Garavito and Arena, 2005). The 'global triad of modernity', comprising states, markets and Western ideology, has been the catalyst of the ongoing battles in support of indigenous peoples' 'trio of core demands: self-determination, land rights and cultural survival' (Brysk, 2000).

However, that 'trio' includes cultural integrity, but not the right to ecological/ biological integrity, despite the explicit, thorough and well-funded research of the WHO, the EEA and, in general, recent work in epidemiology, and abundant work from the 1980s in conservation biology. In Chapter 1 we also noted that international legal instruments call for the right to 'a clean and healthy environment'. This right was invoked on 22 March 2006 by the lawyers representing several Montana citizens (without specifying whether some might have been from local tribes), in a hearing before the Montana Supreme Court in Helena, Montana (Dennison, 2006).[24]

Lawyers for the polluting companies declared the right to be 'too vague and inconsistent', in fact 'essentially meaningless', and expressed the opinion that relying on laws 'for awarding damages' or for 'forcing cleanup' would make more sense. But Cliff Edwards, a Billings lawyer representing landowners in the case, responded that:

> We need it because we have it (in the Constitution) and we're entitled to it. I can't imagine a better policy of Montana public policy than this (as it was adopted at the 1972 Constitutional Convention). (Dennison, 2006)

The companies being sued include Asarco, for the pollution of soil and water by the Canyon Resources and the now defunct Kendall gold mine. Also, Texaco is appealing most of a US$41 million verdict against the company for groundwater pollution from their refineries' spills.

Of course, 'healthy environment' remains vague only when you do not refer the concept directly to the well-documented public health damages that follow upon these forms of pollution. The research of the WHO and many epidemiologists is quite explicit and precise, and the expression 'healthy' opens the door to the inclusion of that science, without waiting for the results of the present spills and pollution to directly affect the exposed populations, as cancers and other diseases may not develop for several years. Nevertheless Brysk (2000) is also correct when she adds that:

> *... indigenous concepts of land also encompass location as a source of cultural reproduction: territory as identity. This notion includes environmental consideration for land ('Mother Earth') viewed as a living organism whose existence and integrity must be respected.*

This view is indeed scientifically correct and generally accepted as a proper understanding of the relation between indigenous peoples and their lands. The latter has spurred 'transnational advocacy works' to integrate this position in the constitutions of South American countries. This was in fact done through the integration of indigenous rights in the constitutional frameworks of Nicaragua (1987), Brazil (1988), Colombia (1991), Mexico (1991), Peru (1993), Bolivia (1994) and Venezuela (2000) (Rodriguez-Garavito and Arena, 2005).

From the early 1970s, the U'wa started organizing to resist the infiltration of their territory. They pressed the Colombia government 'to recognize their collective entitlement to their land' (Rodriguez-Garavito and Arena, 2005). The U'wa enjoyed the constitutional right to consultation before any exploitation of their land could take place. In January 1995, the national office for indigenous affairs of Colombia organized a meeting with Oxy and Ecopetrol (the Colombian counterpart of Oxy, fully Colombia-owned), as well as the Colombian Ministry of the Environment and of Mining and Energy. The result was a joint communiqué acknowledging the U'wa's right to participate and modify the planned oil extraction project.

But on 3 February 1995 the Ministry of the Environment granted the licence for oil exploration drilling to Oxy, stating that the constitutionally required meeting had, in fact, taken place! The U'wa's response was a strong one: 'the U'wa announced that they would collectively commit suicide unless plans for exploration were halted' (Rodriguez-Garavito and Arena, 2005). They also issued a communiqué:

> *in view of a secure death as a result of the loss of our lands, the extermination of our natural resources, the invasion of our sacred places, the disintegration of our families and communities, the forced silence of our songs and the lack of recognition of our history, we prefer a death with dignity: the collective suicide of our communities.* (Rodriguez-Garavito and Arena, 2005)

International law and activism support the U'wa

> *After more than one and a half years of legal proceeding that slowed down both the U'wa political mobilization and preparations for oil exploration, in February 1997 the Constitutional Court ruled in favour of the U'wa. Invoking the Constitution and the ILO Convention No. 169, the Court concluded that indigenous collective rights stand on a par with individual human rights.* (Rodriguez-Garavito and Arena, 2005)

However, although this ruling opened the way for participation and actually guaranteed a new meeting time, the Council of State, in contrast, found that their constitution did not guarantee the right to participation to indigenous peoples and, on such procedural grounds, reversed the constitutional court's decision without even considering the *principles* and the material facts of the case beyond the procedural grounds (Rodriguez-Garavito and Arena, 2005).

A transnational advocacy network (TAN), together with many litigation-oriented non-governmental organizations (NGOs), such as the Earth Legal Defense Fund, the Rain Forest Action Network, the Italian Green Party and Spanish and British groups, put pressure on OXY to withdraw. The Organization of American States (OAS/Harvard Group) issued a report in September 1997 containing several recommendations, including:

- an immediate suspension of oil exploration in the territory under dispute;
- the granting of the long-standing petition of the U'wa to live in a unified reservation;
- the establishment of a two-phase consultation process, whereby negotiations would be conducted first to identify the limits of U'wa territory (outside of which the suspension of oil operations could be lifted) and then to develop measures to prevent harms to the U'wa that might result from renewed oil exploration;
- technical assistance to the U'wa to ensure that they are 'adequately prepared to evaluate and to decide on the issues under consideration' (MacDonald et al, 1998).

After several vicissitudes involving many indigenous groups as well as the U'wa, Oxy announced its withdrawal, and in late 2001, the ILO 'found that the new Colombian legislation violates the ILO Convention No. 169', as it does not establish the state obligation to consult with indigenous peoples before granting licences in their areas. In fact, Oxy had turned over its licence to the Columbian company Ecopetrol in 2002, and the latter was resuming prospecting in the area.

Thus, despite widening international support in the battle against Oxy, the U'wa won a battle but are still in a position to lose the war, as their fate is still hanging in the balance. Their case demonstrates the interface of politics and law and brought the rights of indigenous peoples to territory clearly to the forefront of regional and international consciousness (Rodriguez-Garavito and Arena, 2005).[25] Even more important, the U'wa people courageously stated the true position of all indigenous peoples and the life-altering consequences of the neoliberal 'second colonization'. From the point of view of my argument, the case clearly demonstrates that having a territory with certain borders and a certain number of square miles is not enough if the ecological integrity of the territory is not respected. The U'wa rightly felt they were losing their lands, even though no one attempted to change the size of their possession but only its natural conditions.

NOTES

1 UN Charter Article 2, para. 7.
2 See also Montevideo Convention on the Rights and Duties of States of 1934, www.yale.edu/lawweb/avalon/avalon.htm

3   See also Bernard Ominayak, Chief of the Lubicon Cree v. Canada, Comm. No. 167/1984, Human Rights Commission UN Doc. A/45/40, Vol. II, Annex IV.A., finding Canada in violation of article of the International Covenant on Civil and Political Rights because of state authorized natural resource extraction on indigenous traditional lands.

4   Conference on Yugoslavia, Badinter Commission Opinion No. 1, 29 November 1991 ILM 31, 1992: 1494–1497.

5   *Reference re Secession of Quebec*, 20 August 1998, SCR 2[1998], 281.

6   Frontier Dispute *Burkina-Faso v. Republic of Mali*, ICJ Reps. 1986, 586.

7   *Trail Smelter Arbitration*, US v. Canada 1931-1941 3 R.I.A.A. 1905.

8   *Australia v. France; New Zealand v. France* [1974] ICJ Rep. 253, at 267–70; 51.

9   ICJ Rep. 1974, 312 and 494.

10 Adv. Op.[1996] ICJ Rep. 66.

11 *Convention on the Prevention and Suppression of the Crime of Genocide* (1951), 78 UNTS 277.

12 See International Criminal Court Statute, Article 7.1(d) (g) and (h).

13 UN Framework Convention on Biological Diversity, Article 8(j).

14 *US v. Canada* (1931–1941), 3 R.I.A.A. 1905.

15 *UK v. Albania* (1949) ICJ Rep. 4, 17.

16 *Lubicon Lake Band v. Canada*, Communication No. 167/1984; or the ICCPR case Ilmari *Lansman et al v. Finland*, Communication No. 511/1992: Finland. 8 November 1994.

17 ECOSOC, *Commission on Human Rights*, 'Human Rights and Indigenous Issues: Report of the Working Group', Annex I, UN Doc. E/CN.4/2006/79 (22 March 2006), prepared by the Chairperson-Rapporteur, Luis-Enrique Chavez.

18 *Delgamuukw v. British Columbia* [1997] 3 SCR 1010.

19 Native Title Act, 1993, Aust. Cap. Terr. Laws §223(1).

20 Treaty of Waitangi, 1840.

21 UN Charter Article 73; see also Anaya, 2004, p. 186.

22 Ibid., p. 244.

23 Ibid.

24 See also www.missoulian.com/articles/2006/03/09/news/mtregional/news02.txt

25 See an International Court of Human Rights decision in the 2001: *Awas Tingni v. Nicaragua* case.

CHAPTER 3

Cosmopolitanism and Natural Law for the Recovery of Individual and Community Rights

INTRODUCTION: THE MEANING OF 'MINORITIES'

The non-arbitrary interference parameter apparently resembles the equally, at least primarily, negative rationale of Article 27 ICCPR, which states that persons belonging to ethnic, religious or linguistic minorities 'shall not be denied' the right to enjoy their own culture, to profess and practice their own religion, or to use their own language. At the same time, though, the hands off approach implied by the criterion of non-denial is measured against the backdrop of a marked interaction between individual rights and aspects of group protection. Irrespective of any positive action arguably attached to Article 27, this element is somewhat tentatively echoed by the reference in the provision to the communal exercise of rights. (Pentassuglia, 2006)

Territorial considerations, although prominent in international law, are not sufficiently developed to encompass current scientific paradigms. In a sense, current regulatory regimes are flawed; for example, offering the elderly or the poor unwholesome or harmful meals that would not appease their hunger would represent a flawed programme of 'assistance'. In addition respecting an indigenous nation's borders should include respecting the lands defined by those borders. Thus territorial considerations remain incomplete as forms of protection of indigenous rights, if all aspects of the territories in question are not protected in a way that permits them to function to provide 'nature's services' (Daily, 1997).

As we saw in the U'wa case, the unique relations between indigenous peoples and their territories renders the health and integrity of the land even more important and basic than its role as provider of life services when its unique cultural and religious features are acknowledged. These considerations support the emergence of a conflict between human rights (primarily understood as individually applicable) and group rights, when the latter do not coincide with either the state or with a specific legal aggregate (such as a corporate body). I am speaking of communities whose rights include those of individuals within their confines, but not necessarily the rights of the state within which they simply represent a minority. It is hard to define what, precisely, constitutes a 'minority', although it is indeed a meaningful concept in international law:

> *... the prevailing view is that it is possible to find some elements of the concept of minority endorsed by international law and therefore to determine the scope of application of the respective rules ratione personae.* (Pentassuglia, 2002)

In democracies, where 'equality' and 'equal treatment' for all are, at least in theory, the reigning bywords, it is hard to see how special or different treatment can be applied to individuals in certain groups without asserting that *they* are different in a pejorative sense. Nevertheless there are, traditionally, several definitions of 'minorities', starting with the two categories that apply to all such groups: first, 'minorities by force', that is, peoples who might offer to be fully integrated but are not allowed to do so; and second, 'minorities by will' or 'cultural integrity' (Claude, 1955). This dichotomy is best expressed in the definition proposed by J. A. Laponce (1960):

> *... a group of people who because of a common racial, linguistic or national heritage which singles them out from the politically dominant cultural group, fear that they either be prevented from integrating themselves in the national community of their choice or be obliged to do so at the expense of their identify.*

The UN Sub-Commission on Prevention of Discrimination and Protection of Minorities (1950), isolated several aspects of the concept of 'minorities' as their protection depends upon the full understanding of the notion:

- the stable ethnic, religious or linguistic peculiarities of the group, as to make them 'markedly different' from the rest of the population;
- their non-dominant position as national groups or sub-groups;
- the demand to preserve their own cultural identity; and
- their 'loyalty' to the state in which they live and whose members are citizens of the state (Pentassuglia, 2002)

These and later definitions combine objective and subjective elements and Pentassuglia (2002), for instance, adds several other components to the category of 'minorities': 'numerical size, non-dominant position, ethno-cultural distinctive characters ... and a "sense of solidarity directed toward preserving their own cultural identity"'.

There are several important points to consider. The first is that, according to the ICCPR, Article 27, belonging to a minority is not simply a matter of choosing a lifestyle or cultural preference that diverges from the majority. It is based on the traditional understanding of 'distinctness', based on 'ethnic, religious or linguistic communities' culture, practices and religion'. The main concern in international law is, therefore, to establish state obligations to maintain and respect the cultural identity 'for all ethnic/ religious minorities who strive to protect their identity, which include "the notion of 'implicit' will to preserve minority identity, so as not to make the subjective requirement too demanding, especially in relation to minorities living under undemocratic regimes"' (Pentassuglia, 2002).

This approach reinforces the difference between established indigenous/minority groups and more recent groups, such as migrant workers or refugees, whose intent may well be integration rather than the protection of distinct cultural identity. At least, their intent in this regard should be kept an open question. Hence, in this work, the arguments proposed will apply only to traditional minorities and indigenous peoples, not to any other newer group that call themselves 'minorities' in other senses.

The important difference, from our point of view, is that the traditional groups have a *sui generis* relation to the land, a form of physical and spiritual interdependence that renders necessary the preservation of ecological integrity in their territories in order to ensure the respect for their basic rights to biological integrity and normal function, as well as cultural integrity. No other groups qualify, so that our exclusion of others in this work is not discriminatory, but simply factual.

This factual aspect is clearly in evidence in the judgement of the Human Rights Court, in *Sandra Lovelace v. Canada.*[1] Sandra Lovelace had been prevented from returning to a First Nation to which she originally belonged, although she had indeed left to marry a non-band husband. She wanted to reclaim her First Nation rights after her divorce and the International Human Rights Court confirmed her right to do so because the domestic provision preventing her from doing so was unjustifiable (Kontos, 2005; Pentassuglia, 2002).

The fact that membership in a group is not simply a matter of choice or preference was confirmed by another case brought before the Human Rights Court, *R. L. et al. v. Canada.*[2] In that case, the members of a Canadian First Nation:

> ... *challenged the amendment made to Canada's Indian Act, in order to address the issues raised in* Lovelace, *on the ground that this amendment interfered with their freedom of association with others, since they could not themselves determine membership in their community.* (Pentassuglia, 2002)

The court did not deal with the merits of the case but simply judged the case to be inadmissible because all local remedies had not been exhausted. In general, however, the force of Article 27 was reaffirmed, and the possibility of equating minority rights exclusively with individual choice was rejected:

> *In general [the Court] ... indeed upheld the notion as reflected in the minority's treaties, that the individual declaration of affiliation with a minority group was to reflect a fact, not solely the expression of an intention or a wish.* (Pentassuglia, 2002)

FROM INDIVIDUAL MINORITY RIGHTS TO COMMUNITY RIGHTS

Rights based on biological integrity are clearly individual rights as are those related to health and normal function. In contrast, indigenous peoples 'minorities', in the sense of the term discussed in the last section are groups and, in fact, more than simply aggregates of individuals, a definition that would equally fit states, corporations and other disparate groups. For this aspect of their status and their rights, the presence of ecological integrity is absolutely fundamental, hence the coupling of 'biological/ ecological integrity' in the title of the third model of protection proposed in Chapter 1.

Community rights can best be found in the cosmopolitan aspects of human rights defended by Kant (1957; 1964; 1981) and Kantians. This is so not because Kant's doctrine has a particular affinity to indigenous groups, but because, in his time, a nation was much closer to a community than it is today, and the presence of small, distinct religious or cultural minority groups was not significant enough to violate his argument. This position acquires great importance, if we hope to transcend what Jose Manuel Pureza (2005) terms 'the three main assumptions of Grotian theory':

1   States are the only relevant actors in the world scene.
2   Respect for state sovereignty is the fundamental value in international relations.
3   Interstate relations are founded upon a logic of reciprocity, with which each state aims at maximizing its own individual interests and recognizes its partners' legitimacy to behave in the same way.

In contrast, Pureza (2005) analyses Kant in terms of 'three opposite characteristics' that emphasize: first, the major role individuals play; second, the presence of 'universally shared values (peace, self-determination, human respect)' that pose non-underogable obligations on the international community; and third, a sense of *ordre public* going beyond simple reciprocity.

This analysis shows precisely why indigenous/minority groups, although admittedly not Kant's explicit concern, fit much better within his theory than the rules governing globalization. However, Pureza does not appear to be prepared to grant Grotius the aspect of normativity that is strongly present in his thought, as we will see below, as it arises from its natural law roots (Falk, 1998). Nevertheless Kant's normativity is indeed the better path toward a supranational form of government that may attempt to mitigate or even eliminate the harms wrought by globalization.

Kant for supranational eco-justice and human rights

> *A global system of a plurality of more-or-less sovereign states, whose inhabitants' lives are restricted for many purposes to their own state, can injure many lives. Even if each state were more or less internally just, and they rarely are, states may injure those whom they exclude; and a system of states may systematically or gratuitously injure outsiders by wars and international conflict and by economic structures that control and limit access to the means of life.* (O'Neill, 1996)

There is a basic difference that emerges in this passage between globalization and cosmopolitanism. While the former is primarily procedural in its structures and primarily influenced by powerful, market-oriented powers, the latter is based primarily on substantive moral principles of justice that include but also transcend the economic realm and rely on Kantian principles. States may or may not be fully just within their own borders but, even at best, they may well injure those outside their borders by exclusionary practices and these are direct injuries (O'Neill, 1996). Trans-boundary pollution and disintegrity provide indirect injuries instead. This is a form of indirect injustice as 'destroying parts of natural and manmade environments injure those whose lives depend on them'. In addition, 'the principles of destroying natural and man-made environments, in the sense of destroying their reproductive and regenerative powers is not universalizable' (O'Neill, 1996). Ecological and biological integrity is precisely what O'Neill terms 'regenerative and reproductive powers', or true sustainability:

> *Environmental justice is therefore a matter of transforming natural and man-made systems only in ways that do not systematically or gratuitously destroy the reproductive and regenerative powers of the natural world, so do not inflict indirect injury.* (O'Neill, 1996)

In O'Neill's terms, moral principles represent the 'blueprint' and the 'specifications', which define the 'product' to be eventually produced. In a similar sense, strategies based upon principles are not, as such, the strategic tools to use in order to achieve just aims, but they define what forms such tools might take. O'Neill (1996) argues that 'The move from abstract and inconclusive principles of justice toward just institutions, policies and practices is analogous to moves from design specification towards finished product'.

The possession of fundamental, inalienable rights for all humanity finds its strongest expression in Kant's philosophy. His categorical imperative defends human dignity and the infinite value of each human life, so that the Universal Declaration of Human Rights (1948), the UN Charter (signed 1945, amended 1965, 1968, 1973) and all other international legal instruments that take a strong position in defence of human rights, originate from Kantian moral theory (Kant, 1964; 1981). But Kant also wrote on 'perpetual peace', and he saw a 'league of nations' as 'the ideal of international right' (Cavallar, 1999; Kant, 1957). It is not very common to find appeals to Kantian theory today, in law or even in political thought. But it is in Kant that one can find both strong support for human rights and the move to focus beyond the state as the ultimate source of legitimacy, to a vision of cosmopolitanism and constructive peace that comes quite close to the vision that animates the UN Charter.

In Kant's theory, reconciliation is achieved between individual rights and universalism, as instantiated not only through international laws, but through cosmopolitanism. In 1310 the Italian poet Dante Alighieri advocated a 'universal monarchy'. Kant knew that a monarchy may not foster respect for individual autonomy and freedom that are foundational to human dignity and thus to his moral theory (Cavallar, 1999). According to Kant (1957):

> *There is only one rational way in which states coexisting with other states can emerge from the lawless condition of pure warfare. Just like individuals, they must renounce their savage and lawless freedom, adapt themselves to public coercive laws, and thus form an international state.*

In this passage we find almost a premonition of the direction that will be taken by public international law. From a consideration of international legal instruments, at least three points emerge:

1   The rule of law is the goal for individuals, states and beyond.
2   Public international law should be the final arbiter of what is just; it should provide the connection between individuals, single states, and the so-called 'international state' or supervening regulations and laws, when required.

3   The reason for going beyond single states and allowing these to have the ultimate power in all matters, is to enable states to transcend warfare, as the goal of 'perpetual peace', indicated in Kant.

Kant sees a 'world republic', rather than a single monarchy that might give rise to a 'soulless despotism' that 'leaves no room for rightful or lawful freedom, or public coercive laws' (Cavallar, 1999).The 'finished product' of this work, or a strategy toward just and ecologically sensitive institutions may not yet be achievable, but at least there emerges a prototype of what the 'finished product' may look like and what it may achieve.

In this section we are still at the 'blueprint' and 'specification' stage. In contrast to the procedural thrust of liberal governance, with its avoidance of moral absolutes or of any clear commitment to a specified 'common good', beyond the economic advantage of the most powerful groups, states and institutions, cosmopolitanism recognizes the porousness of borders, despite their logic of inclusion and exclusion. It recognizes the existence of non-derogable obligations beyond borders so that its scope includes 'distant strangers and future generations' (O'Neill, 1996). Cosmopolitanism based on Kantianism can supply the principles and also the guidelines that are largely absent from even the best among the advocates of liberal democracy, as the roots of injustice are seldom sought out by these thinkers:

> *The idea that our economic policies and the global economic institutions we impose make us causally and morally responsible for the perpetuation and even aggravation of world hunger, by contrast, is an idea rarely taken seriously by established intellectuals and politicians in the developed world.* (Pogge, 2001)

Rawls' (1999a; 1999b) work distorts this basic reality: 'like the existing global economic order that of Rawls' Society of Peoples is then shaped by free bargaining' (Pogge, 2001). I return to the strategies required to overcome 'free bargaining' below, but for now, the main point is that every practice that bears the prefix or qualifier 'free' is, *ipso facto* not so in the universal sense: 'free' to pursue harmful practices does not render those who are harmed 'free'. It can be considered an obstacle to global justice, not a constructive component of it, as, for instance, in Rawls' liberalism in his work on justice (1999a) and in *The Law of Peoples* (1999b). These works emphasize and support the very lack of substantive, principled approaches that must be transcended because they support globalization with all its inherent injustices (Pogge, 2001).

The alternative to globalization here proposed is a form of Kantian cosmopolitanism, an approach that embodies the respect for near and distant persons and future genera-tions as well. In contrast, the principles that Rawls embraces and that support 'fairness', are said 'to be internal to liberal societies' (O'Neill, 1996), hence, at best, they attempt to mitigate some of the 'evil' fostered by liberalism, but without any attempt to reach all the way to the destructive foundation on which these theories and practices rest. This 'pattern of derivation shows that inclusive principles of indifference to and neglect of others also cannot be universalized' (O'Neill, 1996).

Hence, in order to proceed from 'blueprints' to specifics, we must ensure that our starting point is compatible with and supportive of our final aim: a Kantian form of cosmopolitanism provides such an initial 'blueprint'.

Pureza (2005) views the doctrine of the 'common heritage of mankind' as the approach to the community of humankind. I am not entirely convinced by this argument, but I will discuss it further in the final chapter of this work. What is important at this point is to discover what specific principles, beyond the respect for individuals, might help the transition from that form of respect to the respect for a community, a group that is neither a nation nor a simple aggregate of diverse individuals. Pureza (2005) argues that in 'the second age of the common heritage of mankind', there should be 'no privileged political targets'. But, while we can applaud his quest for 'social and ecological' forms of sovereignty, the point is moot when we need to find an appropriate way to 'privilege' groups or, at least, to find the legal basis required to justify their treatment as particular, and indeed as unique.

That is why we must return to the other two protection models discussed in Chapter 1: the cultural integrity and self-determination models. Even taken together, these two models are certainly necessary but not sufficient to fully characterize the kind of protection required by indigenous peoples: the biological/ecological integrity approach is required to separate traditional indigenous groups that are fully and explicitly protected in international law by *erga omnes* obligations, imposed on the states that house them.

As we saw, the mere wish to be a member of an indigenous group or tribe is insufficient to allow a person to acquire membership. But self-determination and culture both play a pivotal role, combining with the individual Kantian rights expressed in cosmopolitanism, to provide an additional justification for special status. In conclusion, these groups possess:

- individual human rights beyond the general rights engendered by citizenship in the state where they reside;
- these rights, and the corresponding non-derogable obligations of both their state and of the international community, are based on their culture and self-determination in a special way that includes first of all a special relation to their land;
- that relation manifests their uniqueness and imposes special obligations *erga omnes* on the international community to extend respect and full protection to their territory, beyond the protection required for other areas and other citizens;
- hence 'community' in this special sense, emerges as the result of joining culture and self-determination to the integrity of their specific territory.

Self-determination and culture may suffice to define other minorities, but while necessary, they are not, as such, sufficient for the indigenous/tribal peoples that are the focus of this work. For example, another traditional group worth special cultural features and the need for self-determination, the Roma or gypsies in Europe, have no particular legal or other form of attachment to a specific territory, and one of the features of their culture is precisely the practice of moving freely from place to place. In contrast is a group that fits our definition well, the Sami of Finland and Norway.[3] In that case, the Supreme Administrative Court of Finland (nos 692 and 693, 31 March 1999) ruled against mineral exploration of their territory because of its effects on reindeer herding, which would have violated the Sami's cultural rights protected under Article 2 of the Finnish Constitution (see Anaya, 2004).

NATURAL LAW AND INDIVIDUAL AND COMMUNITY RIGHTS: THE 'WRONG TURN' AFTER GROTIUS

A just law is a man-made code that squares with the moral law or the law of God. An unjust law is a code that is out of harmony with the moral law. To put it in terms of St Thomas Aquinas: an unjust law is a human law that is not rooted in eternal law and natural law. Any law that uplifts human personality is just. Any law that degrades human personality is unjust. (King, 1990)

In order to best understand natural law, we must start by considering the laws of nature and their foundational role in natural law, according to Aristotle. Nature is central to Aristotle's argument in the *Politics*, written around 340 BC. This is routinely accepted by Aristotelian scholars:

Aristotle conducted his study of things human in the fields of politics and ethics (and also of logic, poetry and oratory), side by side with a study of things natural (physics, medicine, and general biology). (Barker, 1973)

In addition, his 'inclination towards the Ionic "becoming" – the genetic doctrine of phusis' (Barker, 1973) ensures that nature will be and remain foundational for all his arguments, from the admiration he evinces for the beauty of perfected forms, to the presence of design in nature (Aristotle, 1968 [c. 350 BC]). Governance, citizenship and the polis itself were discussed with reference to natural standards (of size, of completeness and the like). In the same sense, the constitution of the state will provide its 'essence', the explanation of its identity as a 'quasi-juridical person' (Barker, 1973). The constitution is analogous to the natural laws governing physical organisms (Artistotle, 1900 [c. 340 BC]).

Like all natural entities, the state has two main ends (in this case, not just one end), for the association it represents. Aristotle starts with the basic 'natural impulse', according to which 'men desire to live a social life'; the other end is represented by the common interest: 'The good life is the chief end, both for the community as a whole and for each of us individually. But men also come together, and form and maintain political associations merely for the sake of life' (Aristotle, 1900 [c. 340 BC]). Hence, the *essential* nature of a state and the laws that regulate it, exist for the sake of maintaining life, social association and the good life (Barker, 1973). This simply re-elaborates the theme clearly stated in Book I of the *Politics*, that 'every polis exists by nature', and that the 'nature of things consists in their ends or consummation', as 'the end, the final cause is the best' (Aristotle, 1900 [c. 340 BC]). The polis exists 'by nature' and man is meant 'by nature' to live in a social environment.

If we consider the modern liberal democratic state, we find something that is in direct conflict with the Aristotelian view of 'the state'. It does provide association, so it satisfies at least one condition Aristotle finds essential to the nature of the state. But note that the other two 'ends' or reasons why men join together in political association are missing or under threat. In glaring contrast with the Aristotelian emphasis on the state's support of the common good, or the happiness that is based on the 'natural end of man' as a moral ideal, in modern times even a token quest for that sort of good has been completely eliminated from present political institutions (Westra, 1998).

Thomas Aquinas, nature and natural law

As we move to consider natural law in Thomas Aquinas, we necessarily pass from antiquity to the Middle Ages, a very different historical period. Yet it would be simplistic to assume that the difference is simply one of adding Christianity to Aristotle, or eliminating from his doctrine whatever is contrary to Christian thought. We need to understand how the concept of natural law evolved, as it did not leap a thousand years from the great philosopher to a great philosopher/theologian, without maintaining some sort of continuity. We find the thread of this continuity quite early in the definition attributed to a Roman jurist, Domitius Ulpianus (circa 170–228 AD): *Jus naturale est quod natura omnia animalia docuit* (natural law is that which nature taught to all animals). This definition was also adopted by Justinian in the *Corpus Juris Civilis* (Crowe, 1974). Ulpian was known as a 'great name' in Roman jurisprudence and, unlike other contemporaries, he distinguishes clearly between the 'natural law' and the '*jus gentium*'. Gaius (180 AD) instead 'distinguishes only two kinds of law, the *jus civile* and the *jus gentium*, the latter being the work of natural reason' (Crowe, 1974).

What nature teaches animals, freely translated from Ulpian, is 'to reproduce, (Ulpian adds, "that is what we call marriage"), to educate one's offspring, and the like' (Crowe, 1974). *Jus gentium*, is the law used by humans, which is different 'because it is held in common solely by human beings'. Finally, there is civil law. This division, surprisingly, was the one preferred by Aquinas, rather than Isidore's two-way division between *jus naturale*, incorporating whatever is natural to mankind, and is thus common to all nations and civil law. The former is natural because it is 'independent of human conventions' (Crowe, 1974).

Eventually Bonaventure (circa 1217–1274), who did not write specifically on laws, adopted Ulpian's definition in his own *Commentary on the Sentences*. The tripartite definition can be roughly translated as follows: in the first sense, natural law represents what is found in both Gospel and laws; in the second sense, it is the law common to all nations, and it is mandated by right reason; and finally, in a third sense, it encompasses what is most appropriately what nature teaches all animals.

There is no need to pursue further the history of natural law, interesting and varied though it is. The main point, at least according to Ulpian, Bonaventure and Aquinas, is the relation of nature, as non-human, that is a firm component of a true understanding of natural law. Nature remains the standard, the starting point and basis to help us understand what natural law might mean when we apply it to humankind. It is implicitly acknowledged that man and non-human animals (to insert the use of modern terminology) have several common characteristics: they are created and they are subject to identical or similar biological laws, so that a Cartesian split between nature and human reason becomes impossible. We are connatural with whatever is alive, though it might not be possessed of reason, at least insofar as we are considered as biological beings. The presence of biological nature is, thus, ensured in this conception of natural law.

I have briefly traced the role of the laws of nature, and of the concept of nature in natural law doctrines, from ancient philosophy through the Middle Ages, looking at Aristotle and Thomas Aquinas. I have shown the presence of several important principles linking morality and law through nature and to nature. If we are to understand the direction our laws should take today, in order to help correct the inability of modern governance to enact laws and regulations that are environmentally sound and that protect citizens, we should reconsider the doctrine of natural law.

We found a number of principles and arguments tying the historical, powerful natural law doctrine to nature, its processes and its laws. Particularly important, yet mostly absent from today's understanding of the proper role of governance and the law, are the following:

● The connaturality of human and non-human life, with the clear acknowledgement that the same laws and processes apply to both.
● Therefore, the legal and regulative part of modern governance should equally reflect that reality in its mandates.
● Because of this reality, it is wrong, at least in principle, to act in ways that prevent the actualization of natural entities, according to their own natural unfolding. To prevent such entities from reaching their final form cannot be done routinely, as it is morally suspect (as well as prudentially suspect, according to environmental ethics and the precautionary principle).
● Objections aimed at discrediting the validity of natural law can be answered, and the common attacks on it from analytic philosophy can be refuted.

In the final analysis, whether implicitly or explicitly, much of the content of natural law, its core meaning including the value and importance of natural laws and functions, is present in today's civil and criminal laws. Of course, it is not fully understood and the debt to past traditions is seldom acknowledged or accepted. It is, therefore, imperative to re-examine and clarify the full import and meaning of natural law doctrines so that their implicit message can be rendered explicit.

No doubt this brief excursion into natural law helps to clarify its biological or 'animal' aspects, and hence to show that it is not a question of 'construction' of ideas about what it is to be human; rather it is a question of scientific observation, albeit only at the scientific level possible in 300 BC. Harris (1990) names one of the values and the related rights that natural law supports in Aquinas' formulation as:

> *'Biological Values', including life and procreation, both of which support the right of self-defense, in turn foundational for the rules of* jus ad bellum *and* jus in bello, *and the natural inclination 'to engage in sexual intercourse and to rear offspring'.*

These values do not attempt to make a statement about human choices, they simply observe what is true in the animal world and accept those basic tenets as typical of the animal part of rational animals, or humans. What can be learned from this simple exposition is that, whatever is inimical to the support of human life in its natural unfolding, is morally wrong and unjust, as Ken Saro-Wiwa recognized when he referred to 'genocide' and 'ecocide' in the same paragraph with regard to the life-threatening conditions forced upon the Ogoni by the complicity of their own government and the actions of Royal Dutch Shell Oil (Westra, 1998).

According to Aquinas, that complicity would be sufficient to delegitimize the military government. Barker (1973) summarizes the legal implications of natural law as follows:

the doctrine that law is the true sovereign and that governments are the servants of the law; the doctrine that there is a fundamental difference between the lawful monarch and the tyrant who governs by his arbitrary will: the doctrine that there is a right inherent in the people by virtue of their collective capacity of judgement to elect their rulers and to call them to account.

Harris (1990) names another of the values stemming from Aquinas as 'characteristically human values', listing 'knowledge and sociability' under this category. The first clearly implies the right to education and to the pursuit of knowledge, including religious knowledge. The second implies the right to associate with others and form communities (Harris, 1990). War is permitted as a just extension of self-defence, to the defence of one's community and rightful state. But when the state is radically unjust, then the obligation is to disobey and not to be in any way complicit in its wrongful aims because the state's legitimacy is lost when the 'common good' is not served by its rulers. Speaking of man's obligation to obey a 'prince', Aquinas says clearly, 'if he commands what is unjust, his subjects are not bound to obey him'.[4] Essentially, the relations between community and individual are emphasized in natural law, as is the pivotal role played by the laws of nature. Only through natural law, may individuals and communities be reconciled and understood in ways that complement one another.

It is partially a function of the doctrines of both Aristotle and Aquinas, but also in part, as we noted in the cast of Kant, the fact that in earlier times, before the advent of migrations, colonization and conflicts that created a constant stream of refugees, that ensured the presence of a Eurocentric perspective that made it a lot easier to identify a 'people' with the citizenry of a small nation mostly composed of an homogeneous group. Thus the complementarity that may be observed between individuals and communities is unequivocally based on the physical laws of nature as well as in the rational characteristics of humankind, and can never become identified with various aggregates of peoples such as corporate entities or even states.

Hence, the 'wrong turn' of Emmerich de Vattel (1872), who obscured the true sense of natural law because he believed that it would be sufficient to simply apply natural law to the relation between states, rather than to individual humans (Anaya, 2004). In contrast, states are aggregates that lack all the principal characteristics of human persons and of specific communities, thus resulting in a total misunderstanding of both natural law and of the concepts of individuals and communities within it. In defence of de Vattel, one must concede that he is motivated by excellent reasons, and that the difficulties inherent in his 'turn' may not have been clearly visible to him at the time.

For instance, he sees a 'nation' as a homogeneous group of citizens, and colonization as fully appropriate on behalf of sovereigns. The latter would attain both 'the domain' of a country (thus allowing the sovereign to receive necessities from it and to dispose of it), and 'the empire' or his right to govern it entirely as he sees fit. Starting with the establishment of a country, de Vattel (1872) says:

The earth belongs to mankind in general; destined by the Creators as their common habitation, and to supply them with food, they all possess a natural right to inhabit it, and derive from it whatever is necessary for their subsistence, and suitable for their wants.

His point is that, with the numbers of humans constantly growing, the Earth at the time was no longer capable of providing for humankind spontaneously, so that various nomadic tribes had to give way to groups practising proper cultivation to improve yield (de Vattel, 1872). Appropriating uninhabited lands is one thing, but in the presence of 'Indians', these may need to be lawfully 'confined' because, according to de Vattel, they had no need of the 'vast lands' over which they roamed. Thus it is not their lack of certain forms of governance or their specific culture that makes it appropriate to limit their rights to territory, but the fact that they had much more than they could use to survive well.

Nevertheless, he finds admirable the actions of the Puritans who, despite possessing a charter from their sovereign, bought the land from the 'Indians' (as did the Quakers later, led by William Penn) (de Vattel, 1872). Among the rights following upon the conquest (or purchase) of the land, like all nations, the conquerors had the right to keep themselves 'alive' by perpetuating themselves through 'propagation', for which women are necessary, and – if these should be unwilling to accede to such requests of marriage – the nation's peoples have the right to carry them off by force (de Vattel, 1872)!

This brief overview of some of the rights of nations according to de Vattel is probably sufficient to give the flavour of his work and its somewhat anachronistic tenets, despite the presence of its natural law background. In Chapter V of his work, 'Of the Observance of Justice Between Nations', we come closer to the spirit of his position and the somewhat reasonable causes of his 'wrong turn', as I have termed it. He argues that, 'The obligation imposed on all men to be just, is easily demonstrated the law of nature'; but although it is not legally binding on all nations, 'All nations are therefore under a strict obligation to cultivate justice toward each other, and to observe it scrupulously, and carefully abstain from everything that may violate it' (de Vattel, 1872).

It is clear then, that de Vattel's concern is *not* to suppress or diminish individual rights, but to use the strongest principle in his arsenal to ensure that *nations*, too, like individual humans, be bound by natural law's commands to ensure that justice be present in all their decisions and activities. He goes even further, anticipating the gist of *erga omnes* obligations when he states:

> To form and support an unjust pretension, is only doing an injury to the party whose interests are affected by that pretension; but to despise justice in general, is doing an injury to all nations. (de Vattel, 1872)

Therefore, I would like to propose that perhaps de Vattel himself may have been guilty of a 'wrong turn' as much as his interpreters might have been too hasty in their reading of his doctrine, or at least the motives that animated his thought. Nevertheless, granting individual rights to legal entities like states, may also be seen as the precursor of granting them to corporate legal individuals, a wrong turn from which we are all suffering today.

The origin of indigenous rights in international law and the role of natural law

> *The jurisprudential starting point of the rights of peoples is a direct assault upon the positivist and neopositivist views of international law as dependent upon state practice and acknowledgement. In this regard, the rights of peoples can be associated with the positivist conception of natural law which, at the very birth of international law were invoked by Victoria (sic) and others on behalf of Indians being cruelly victimized by the Spanish conquistadores.* (Falk, 1988)

Natural law is basic to human rights of indigenous peoples, in direct contrast with the prevailing 'statism'. Crawford (1987) reinforces this belief in his work on 'The Aborigine in comparative law':

> *The first thing to notice is statism. Discussion of Aborigines takes place against the background of the division of the world into states or state areas and the assumption that primary human collective, above the family, is the state.*

By dissolving peoples and communities into individuals within states, and by identifying the latter's interests with those of the former, positivism ignores and in fact eliminates indigenous communities and groups, as well as the individuals themselves, from consideration in international law.

As we saw in the previous section, natural law is based on a series of principles that use human nature as foundational, hence it has no obvious application to states or other aggregates. In fact, Thomas Aquinas explicitly contrasts the rights of individuals against inappropriate laws enacted by a state, thus clearly showing that states are not the ultimate authority and nor can they be substituted for individuals and indigenous communities.

Unjust laws are even more likely to appear when the 'governed' are far from the governing body, both geographically and in other senses. This is the situation encountered by Spain and Spanish colonizers in relation to the indigenous peoples inhabiting the Americas. The problems presented by such a 'conquest' are well described in the work of the Spanish school and natural law scholars such as Bartolme De Las Casas and Francisco de Vitoria. The 'Spanish School of International Law' (Scott, 1934) provided the point of origin for international law:

> *... the discovery of America gave rise to a modern law of nations... the Spanish School came into being and passed on within the course of a century, but it has to its credit the modern law of nations.*

Natural law, the treatment of the theological/juridical work of De Las Casas and de Vitoria, was the basis of the universalization of international law (Brierly, 1963). This is also the argument of Marks (1990–1991), and it is fully supported by our earlier analysis of natural law in the work of Aquinas.

The first point to consider is that these early scholars disputed the classification of the 'conquered' lands as *terra nullius* and argued for establishing indigenous rights in law. In addition, de Vitoria 'proclaimed a "natural community of all mankind, and the universal validity of human rights"' (Stone, 1965). De Vitoria, and especially De Las Casas, argued that indigenous peoples were not 'barbarians', and therefore they did not fit Aristotle's understanding of 'natural slaves'. In contrast, they argued, these people, although unable to read or write, had laws, religion, a good form of governance, and held most values that were dear in the home country. Hence colonialism (or the 'first conquest') could not be justified, although de Vitoria's position is somewhat softer because it allows for colonization *if* that appeared to benefit the indigenous peoples themselves (thus unfortunately providing a first step toward ensuing paternalist domination).

In any case, from its promising beginning as defender of indigenous rights, natural law has only remained as one of the sources of international law recognized today. Natural law supported individual rights, but it also served to empower rulers (as part of the natural order), as these are, like everyone else, subjects of the natural law (Marks, 1990–1991). From the point of view of our argument, one of the most important issues is captured in De Las Casas's understanding of indigenous rights. As Marks (1990–1991) argues:

> *his wide view of such rights to encompass material security, cultural integrity and political autonomy, [which] make his doctrine comparable with modern notions of self-determination and assertion of indigenous rights.*

The most important concept in this passage is that of 'material security'. This notion is not a component of today's views on indigenous rights, although 'cultural integrity' and 'political autonomy' (or 'self-determination') certainly are. I propose therefore that 'material security' might be translated into 'biological/ecological integrity' or the latter viewed as its basis, as argued in Chapter 1, and it can be understood as the historical precursor of my 'third model' perhaps.

Although De Las Casas does not fully define 'material security' to my knowledge, the notion should involve the life and physical security of individuals and groups; precisely what modern science has proven to be the function of biological and ecological integrity. Hence, those who view the natural law beginning of individual rights as incapable of providing guidance in today's modern world, neglect to take into consideration this important and fruitful beginning.

In times when the global presence of so many different peoples and cultures is obvious to all, it is almost viewed as reactionary to attempt to draw the (admittedly) fine line between tolerance and acceptance on one hand, and repression or even 'imperialism' on the other. Yet even in the times of the Roman stoics, the thrust to cosmopolitanism was present, in the same sense that commonly accepted practices, including slavery, were at least viewed as necessarily limited and constrained by principles of justice (Lauterpacht, 1950). In those cases, long before the *Magna Carta*, the primacy of law and rationally recognized moral principles (not simply religious observances) were deemed to be superior even to the will of 'kings'. Lauterpacht (1950) notes these advances and says that 'By the end of the Middle Ages, the substance of what proved to be the doctrine of the natural rights of man was well established'.

But the question raised by Baxi (2001) is whether in today's multicultural world it is even possible to use absolute principles originating in one age in another where quite different cultural realities are present. For instance, because the present concern with eco-violence and eco-crimes is the fruit of practices that rapidly multiplied, became magnified and incrementally hazardous since the Second World War (Carson, 1962), we cannot expect to find anything in natural law to accommodate these phenomena. In a sense, eco-violence (an evil), like multiculturalism (a good), is an emergent phenomenon that is not obviously or clearly covered by the provisions of international human rights legal instruments. As far as multiculturalism is concerned, there is an abundant literature on the topic in relation to human rights. For instance, Jennings (1987) notes that:

> ... as more and more aspects of international law reach down through the states to corporations to other legal entities and to individuals, so international law has more and more to take into account and allow for differences of municipal law, differences of legal tradition, and differences of culture.

But to acknowledge these developing issues, and, in the case of eco-violence, these 'emergent risks' (Hiskes, 1998) does not necessarily require abandoning previous principles of natural law in their support of human rights.

FROM NATURAL LAW TO *ERGA OMNES* OBLIGATIONS FOR THE DEFENCE OF INDIGENOUS PEOPLES

> *The protection of the environment is likewise a vital part of contemporary human rights doctrine, for it is a* sine qua non *for numerous human rights such as the right to health and the right to life itself. It is scarcely necessary to elaborate on this, as damage to the environment can impair and undermine all the human rights spoken of in the Universal Declaration and other human rights instruments.* (Weeramantry, 1997)

Weeramantry's (1997) opinion defends the right to treat the environmental reasons advanced by Hungary to justify its non-compliance with the original treaty with Slovakia to build a dam diverting the River Danube, as an obligation *erga omnes*. But he appeals to universality by presenting a scholarly dissertation on how all countries, from the time before Christ to modern times, considered environmental concerns to be the common rights of humanity, but also considered them to be their international obligations.

The examples in Weeramantry (1997) include the 'royal edicts' dating from the third century BC in Ceylon:

> *Mahinda, son of the Emperor Asoka of India, preached to him a sermon on Buddhism which converted the king. Here are excerpts from that sermon: 'O great King, the birds of the air and the beasts have as equal a right to live and move about in any part of the land as thou. The land belongs to the people and all living beings; thou art only the guardian of it. [This sermon is recorded in the Mahavamsa, Chap. 14]'.*

'Do no harm' is the basis of all morality, from ancient Greece onwards. In Buddhism, no harm can be caused to others, hence '*sic utere tuo ut alienum non laedas*' is present in all laws and moral principles. Weeramantry (1997) adds:

> '*Alienum*' *in this context would be extended by Buddhism to future generations as well, and to the other component elements of the natural order beyond man himself, for the Buddhist concept of duty had an enourmously long reach.*

Other examples confirm the universality of these principles of respect and conservation: from sub-Saharan Africa, where two ancient cultures, the Sonjo and the Chagga (Tanzanian tribes), had created complex networks of 'irrigation furrows' in order to convey water from mountain streams to the cultivated fields. The maintenance of these furrows was the sacred responsibility and duty of all citizens (Weeramantry, 1997). Weeramantry's historical survey ranges far afield in place and time in order to demonstrate the *timelessness* and the universality of environmental concern and obligation, supporting laws and customs entailing sustainable development long before the concept became a modern byword. In essence, the traditions of peoples everywhere show that 'environmental rights are human rights' (Weeramantry, 1997).

Weeramantry's (1997) historical survey, however, does not show that different cultures chose these principles, and that, therefore, they represent legitimate sources of international law. It demonstrates instead that all peoples, universally *recognize* the existence and the acceptability of these beliefs, hence they are far more than the modern articulation of principles arising from a European country (Sweden), were Gro Brundtland led the contemporary articulation of 'sustainable development' principles.

Similarly, natural law in its original formulation embodies principles and beliefs that can be found in many civilizations, hence it is well able to provide *not* the latest word on human rights, but the best *starting point* for a comprehensive and non-partisan understanding of human rights, imperative in our complex and changing world.

Therefore if we lose the template or standard provided by universal moral principles, we retain no ground from which to argue about the difference between different mores and unacceptable action. The right to wear a turban, to refuse certain foods or to wear a veil must be respected as different cultural mores; but the 'right' to segregate according to colour or race, the 'right' to eliminate minorities perceived as threatening, or the 'right' to practise painful, non-consensual mutilations on girl-children, all fly in the face of basic morality, whether founded in natural law, which proclaims the basic equality of all, regardless of colour or ethnic origin, or Kantian belief in the respect due all humans (Westra, 1998). On what ground, or with what voice, are we to say to a cultural group or to any people, that their accepted practices are in fact genocidal (Schabas, 2000) or represent attacks on the human person (Bassiouni, 1996) and are therefore unacceptable, although they are accepted in their community? If we cannot discriminate between acceptable and unacceptable practices on principle, we have little else to use to proscribe what some groups are prepared to do.

Ragazzi (1997),[5] discussing human rights in relation to obligations *erga omnes* (through the examples provided in the *Barcelona Traction* case), lists: 'acts of aggression', 'acts of genocide', 'protection from slavery' and 'protection from racial discrimination'. Ragazzi (1997) states:

In giving the examples of the outlawing of genocide and the protection from slavery and racial discrimination, the International court wrote that obligations erga omnes may derive, in general, from the principles and rules concerning the basic rights of the human person.

Ragazzi (1997) adds that, according to Fitzmaurice (1950), '...a principle is something which underlies a rule, and explains or provides the reason for it'. Hence it is important that the principles be preserved and used as standards, even as the circumstances that provide the background for our activities may be in constant flux. In sum, embracing ethical relativism would admit and permit far more negative decisions as legal and just than it would eliminate. It seems clear that if the Aristotelian background of natural law principles is fully understood, as is the development of natural law from ancient Greece to the Middle Ages, from Aquinas to Grotius, there are several points that may help rather than hinder the protection of human rights internationally. Some of these are:

1   the 'basic rights' to subsistence and physical security (Shue, 1996);
2   the right to a safe 'habitat' or environment that would not hinder the 'natural' development and biological function of all humans (Shue, 1996);
3   the right to 'social' living, the right of all humans to live in a community that fosters their 'common good';
4   the right to the acquisition and pursuit of knowledge, including religious knowledge;
5   the right to a form of government that ensures (1), (2) and (3) above, so that the common good of all is protected;
6   the right to rebel against any form of governance that does not respect and protect the rights listed in (1) to (5) above.

The sixth and final point, needs much more discussion because, like ecological degradation, the presence of diverse ethnocultural groups and their rights as 'peoples' are anachronistic from the standpoint of natural law, although, I believe, they are compatible with it. Hence, peoples' rights is the topic of the next section.

COSMOPOLITANISM AGAINST GLOBALIZING 'COLLATERALISM' AND THE RECOVERY OF INDIGENOUS RIGHTS

Although natural law precedes cosmopolitanism historically, and it may even be considered to be stronger than cosmopolitanism in defence of indigenous rights, Kantian cosmopolitanism is undisputedly against neoliberal globalization. In a world where the WTO is the most powerful court, and the ecological footprint harm perpetrated by globalizing trade can be considered a weapon of mass destruction wielded by the North against the South, it is imperative to appeal to non-derogable rights that are not open to be bypassed in favour of any trade deal, even when the latter may be based on signed treaties.

Kant bases his concept of human dignity, hence human rights, on free agency, and I have argued for the importance of the preconditions of free agency, based on the right to be free from environmental harm (Westra, 2006). The point is that no one can develop normal agency, the ability to think, to be a self-directed person, unless the preconditions necessary for his/her normal development are present and protected (Westra, 2004b).

Hence, although Kant did not address specifically environmental or public health concerns, the basic sense of his doctrine presupposes autonomous individuals (hence, individuals that have developed normally, rather than having any aspect of their development arrested or interfered with by multiple exposures) (Westra, 2004b). Hence, I have argued that the protection of the preconditions of agency is an absolute requirement of the respect due to all human beings. Kant's emphasis on 'autonomy' for individuals also lends itself well to the 'self-determination' model of protection of indigenous peoples.

For all these reasons, Kant's cosmopolitanism joins natural law in support of individual rights, especially in their just fight against globalization with its prevailing logic of economics over and often against life. It is a familiar story: as the power of states recedes and is all but eliminated by the domain of trade groupings (WTO, North American Free Trade Association and the like), there is very little left to protect vulnerable people in general, and indigenous peoples in particular, from the phenomenon that Sheldon Leader (2004) terms 'collateralism'.

Leader argues that although the WTO, IMF and other economic organizations have a specific purpose (outlined in the documents that define those organizations), and that therefore their choices are functional as they reflect those goals, they still consider human rights. Nevertheless, there is conflict between what he terms 'civic principles' or 'responsibilities' and the 'functional imperatives' of those organizations (Leader, 2004).

Civic principles guide the conduct of states, in contrast with the function imperatives of economic and trade organizations, according to Leader (2004). But the analysis ignores the fact that, for the most part, powerful states, and in fact all of them in various manners, are allied to economic institutions and complicit with them in their harmful dealings. If they are the powerful states of the North, they *count on* trade organizations to expand and support their power, and foster their economic goals. If they are the weaker states of the South, they need and actively court the goodwill of economic organizations in order to survive as states.

In both cases, the most vulnerable people are the poor, globally, and indigenous populations. Both are victimized both by trade organizations *and* by the application of 'civic principles' by states. The first conquest was conducted brutally by powerful states, and the principles of natural law were involved to attempt to mitigate its deleterious impacts. But the 'second conquest', whereby states and trade and economic organizations form an almost unbeatable 'unholy alliance', can only appeal to Kantian principles of the absolute value of life, for the respect for all human beings, in order to counteract both economic functionalism and the current amorality of today's states and their 'civic principles'.

FROM COMMON MORALITY TO INTERNATIONAL LAW IN DEFENCE OF INDIGENOUS PEOPLES

> *3. The Committee is conscious of the fact that in many regions of the world indigenous peoples have been, and are still being discriminated against, deprived of their human rights and fundamental freedoms and in particular that they have lost their lands and resources to colonists, commercial companies and State entrepreneurs. Consequently the preservation of their culture and their historical identity has been and still is jeopardized.*[6]

Most of this chapter has been devoted to a discussion of moral principles and morally supported political principles. Some of the most basic legal principles existing in defence of indigenous people are to be found in the work of the Committee on the Elimination of Racial Discrimination (CERD). But that work, and indeed that document, is fairly recent (1997), whereas the principles upon which it is based can be traced far back both in morality, in the sense of respect for the dignity of human beings (Beyerveld and Brownsword, 2001), and in the law.

An exemplary case of this moral principle, together with the aspiration to see it enshrined in international law, is the *Le Louis* case.[7] On 11 March 1816, the *Queen Charlotte* cutter captured a French ship, *Le Louis*, that had sailed from Martinique, destined for Africa and back. *Le Louis* was seized and taken to Sierra Leone, where the Vice-Admiralty Court heard the pleadings of the case, to the effect that *Le Louis* was clearly fitted and intended for the slave trade from Africa, that the slave trade was contrary to both the Treaty of 20 November 1815, between England and France (abolishing the slave trade) and the laws of both countries, as well as the 'law of nations', and that the crew of the *Queen Charlotte* was duly empowered to search the French vessel. The court also relied on an earlier case of *The Amedie*:[8]

> *in which it is laid down generally by the Superior Court that the slave trade is* prima facie *illegal, and that the burden of proof is on the claimants to shew (sic) that the laws of their own country permit such a traffic.*[9]

However, Sir William Scott in his judgement, despite his horror at the 'trade' involved, took quite a different position, as he argued:

1   that the search and seizure were both illegal according to the law of nations, as the slave trade is not considered a crime internationally, as piracy is, which alone grants leave to anyone to seize and search vessels on the high seas in peacetime;

2   that because of that illegality, the fruits of the search should not have been admitted in evidence, and the force used in the search and seizure that led to the death of five persons and many injuries, could not have been legal in itself;

3 that even if, under the British Slave Trade Act, slave trading were indeed illegal, *Le Louis* was a French vessel with French documents and a French Master, thus it remained unclear at that time whether any applicable legislation supported the condemnation of the slave trade (initially made by Bonaparte, but after the latter's exile to Elba, also adopted by the King of France). The note of the British Minister to Prince Talleyrand (the French King's minister) elicited only the information that 'His Most Christian Majesty' had issued 'directions' to the effect that 'the traffic should cease for the present time everywhere and forever', but a formally promulgated law appeared to be missing at that time,[10] and was apparently only formalized in 1817.

This is a highly instructive case, because slavery, the ultimate form of racial discrimination, was viewed with unquestionable distaste and even disgust by the judge and the court, but in the final analysis it was not possible to condemn the vessel's activities, and free the slaves, while condemning the ship's master as well as his country, as there was no law expressly forbidding that activity at the time. Sir William Scott said:[11]

> *I must remember that in discussing this question, I must consider it, not according to any private moral apprehension of my own (if I entertained them ever so sincerely) but as* the law *considers it.*

He added that to simply consider the state of laws at the time (from one perspective, without the presence of a 'United Nations', or the possibility of enforcing *erga omnes* obligations), had he attempted to condemn and punish the practice through violent acts, would be:

> *... to force the way to the liberation of Africa by trampling on the independence of other states in Europe; in short, to procure an eminent good by means that are unlawful; is as little consonant to private morality as to public justice.*[12]

What is obvious in this case is that the common morality of the day, at least in England, viewed slavery as akin to piracy, a practice that rendered those who followed it *hostes humanis generis* (enemies of humankind), thus open to seizure and attacks on the open seas even in times of peace. Yet the lack of a specific law forced a judge who strongly believed in the wrongness of the slave trade to argue that it was hard to term it a 'crime', as it had historically been practised from ancient times to date and was even permitted in British colonies.

At any rate, one can judge the vast gulf that separates almost universally held moral principles from the legal codification of those principles into international law. The slave trade has been abolished for a long time, but racism and ethnically motivated attacks are alive and well in all regions of the world, as we shall see in the case of law discussed in the next chapters. Hence the thrust of this work is to see the physical reality of the harms against indigenous communities acknowledged in law. It is incredible that we are still, in some sense, placed in the position of Sir William Scott, viewing a crime he abhorred being committed and being unable to enforce the punishment in the law of the time of an act that his conscience told him unequivocally was against both morality and justice.

The connection between environmental injustice and racism is clearly in place in CERD (see Appendix 3). The UN Human Rights Committee expects periodic reports from all countries that are signatories; it is the most relevant treaty for the rights of indigenous peoples, together with the International Covenant on Civil and Political Rights (ICCPR). The latter is intended to secure the cultural integrity of indigenous peoples, 'including cultural attributes linked to land use, economic activity and political organization' (Anaya, 2000).

Hence the UN Committee's reporting requirements clearly support the environmental justice for which I am arguing in this work. CERD now considers reports on indigenous peoples' rights, 'within the general framework of the non-discrimination norm running throughout the Convention on the Elimination of All Forms of Racial Discrimination' (Anaya, 2000), and the fact that the convention acknowledges the connection between land use/cultural integrity and racial discrimination, demonstrates that CERD is one of the instruments that has not yet been used to its full potential in international law for the protection of indigenous rights.

Racial discrimination, like slavery, is part of the totally unacceptable consequences of present-day economic activities, thus the emphasis of CERD on the principle of self-determination for indigenous peoples is a necessary, though insufficient, approach to their protection. Unless the harms that befall them are clearly understood in all their implications, especially as environmental and health related, even full internal self-determination within indigenous communities will do nothing to restrain the attacks perpetrated by those activities *outside* their lands. In 1993, CERD adopted 'early warning measures' or 'urgent procedures' to ensure that preventative action might help to better protect indigenous peoples:

> *Under this mechanism, efforts to prevent serious violations of the [convention against racial discrimination] would include ... Early warning measures to address existing structural problems from escalating into conflicts... and urgent procedures to respond to problems requiring immediate attention to prevent or limit the scale and number of serious violations of the convention.*[13]

CERD, however, interacts only with states, whereas it is – for the most part – non-state actors that are responsible for the unjust treatment to which indigenous peoples are subjected. Nevertheless, it is indeed the state's responsibility to protect all people within its borders, including indigenous communities. I return to this topic in Chapter 9.

For now, we note the similarities between one of the gravest forms of racial discrimination, the practice of slavery (including abductions and trafficking of those unfortunate people), and the present grave attacks against land-based minorities that include (as we shall see in Chapter 5), deportation, forced labour (akin to slavery), torture and other forms of racial discrimination. Despite the fact that we are no longer in the 18th or 19th centuries, the courts continue to lack the appropriate instruments needed to translate into practice the quest for justice that is their obligation and their mandate.

CONCLUSIONS

The three chapters of Part One were intended to set the stage for the argument of the whole work and its main points: first, the fundamental necessity for ecological and biological integrity to be enforced in order to protect the rights of indigenous peoples to individual and collective survival; and second, the genocidal results that ensue when this first necessity is not upheld and defended. The first chapter addressed the significance of the existing models of indigenous peoples' protection, the second focused on the meaning and role of ecological integrity and added a brief survey of some of the law regarding their rights.

The third chapter traced the historical background of the laws and principles that have led to the present situation facing aboriginal peoples. In Part Two, it will be important to move from principles and arguments for more desirable outcomes (*lex ferenda*), to *lex lata*, and the reality of some representative cases where indigenous peoples attempt to fight legally for their own protection and for environmental justice.

NOTES

1   Communication No. 24/1977, Views of 30 July 1981, [1981] Annual Report, p. 166; [1983] Annual Report, p. 248.
2   *R. L. et al v. Canada*, Communication No. 358/1989 views of 5 November 1991, [1992] Annual Report, p. 358.
3   See the Administrative Court of Finland, Nos. 692 and 693, 31 March 1999.
4   *Summa Theologiae*, bk. II. pt. I, Q. 104, A. 6, reply obj. 3 in Aquinas (1988 [c. 1260]).
5   See also IJC Reports 1970, p.32, para. 34.
6   Committee on the Elimination of Racial Discrimination (CERD), general recommendatins (XXITTI) concerning indigenous peoples, adopted by the UN Committee on the Elimination of Racial Discrimination at its 1235th meeting, on 18 August 1997. UN Doc.CERD/C/51/misc.13/Rev.4 (1997).
7   *Le Louis*, 2 Dods. Rep. 210; it is 'the sentence of a Vice-Admiralty Court, condemning a French ship for being employed in the slave trade, and for forcibly resisting the search of the King's cruisers, reversed – No British Act of Parliament, a commission founded upon it, if inconsistent with the law of nations can affect the rights or interest of foreigners'.
8   1 Dods. 84.
9   *Le Louis*, 2 Dods. 211–212.
10   ibid., 237–259.
11   ibid., 247.
12   ibid., 257.
13   *Prevention of Racial Discrimination, Including Early Warning and Urgent Actions Procedures: Working Paper Adopted by the Committee on the Elimination of Racial Discrimination*, UN GAOR 48th Sess., Supp., No. 18, UN Doc. A/48/18, Annex III, para. 8.

PART TWO

Selected Examples from Domestic and International Case Law

CHAPTER 4

Indigenous Peoples and Minorities in
International Jurisprudence and the
Responsibility of the World Bank

THE CASE OF THE *AWAS TINGNI V. NICARAGUA*

[The case of the Awas Tingni v. Nicaragua*]... is the first legally binding decision by an international tribunal to uphold the collective land and resource rights of indigenous peoples in the face of a state's failure to do so.* (Anaya and Grossman, 2002)

On 31 August 2001 the Inter-American Court of Human Rights held that the state of Nicaragua, by allowing a foreign company the rights to log within the community's land, had violated the rights of the Awas Tingni community. The Dominican-owned company, Maderas y Derivados de Nicaragua, S.A. (Madensa) was granted about 43,000 hectares of land for their logging operation in 1993, but under pressure from the World Wildlife Fund (WWF), the Nicaraguan government agreed to ask that Madensa suspend these operations until environmental regulations could be put in place (Anaya and Grossman, 2002). Although lawyers from the Iowa Project (Indian Law Resource Center), at the request of the Awas Tingni community, asked that all concessions be revoked as unconstitutional according to Nicaraguan law, the government attempted 'to have the constitutional defence "cured" by securing a *post hoc* ratification of the concession by the Regional Council' (Anaya and Grossman, 2002).

Eventually and through another legal action, the concession was cancelled. Despite this important success, however, the question of the Awas Tingni's land tenure had not been addressed, let alone resolved. The community and their legal representatives presented their case to the Inter-American Court of Human Rights and the case was decided on 31 August 2001.[1]

There were two main problems to granting title, according to Nicaragua. The first was the fact that the listed members of the community were no more than 300 or 400 people, and even the more recent census only established the number of 1000 members, thus too few to require a deed to the number of hectares requested by the legal representatives, Dr Anaya and Dr Acosta, in 1993:

The State, in turn, has argued that the extent of the territory claimed by the Mayagna [Sumo] is excessive, bearing in mind the number of members of the Community

> *determined by the official census, and that the area claimed by the Community is not*
> *in proportion to the area it effectively occupies.*[2]

In addition, the second problem was the claim by Nicaragua that their main village had only been established in 1940, hence contradicting the community's claim to traditional historical occupation, whereas other indigenous groups had similar land claims in that general area (Anaya and Grossman, 2002). The witnesses before the Inter-American Court stressed how vital the land, in all its variety, was for 'their cultural, religious and family development', and that territory was not only necessary for their hunting and fishing activities (as agreed by the community, based upon their conservation goals), but also the territory included several sacred hills and places where fruit trees grew. Their people were accustomed to walking through those areas in silence, 'as a sign of respect for their dead ancestors, and the great Asangpas Muijeni, the spirit of the mountain, who lives under the hills' (Anaya and Grossman, 2002). According to the testimony of Rodolfo Stavenhagen in *The Mayagna (Sumo) Awas Tingni Community Case*:

> *Indigenous peoples are defined as those social and human groups, culturally identified*
> *and who maintain a historical continuity with their ancestors, from the time before the*
> *arrival of the first Europeans to this continent.*

Stavenhagen adds that the historical continuity can be established not only through their self-identification, but also through the use of a pre-Hispanic language they speak.

Under Article 25 of the Constitution of Nicaragua (1995), indigenous peoples have the right to 'juridical protection', hence to prevent the group's access to the judiciary represents an act of discrimination. In fact, Article 25 affirms that states are obliged to offer all legal remedies against 'acts that violate their fundamental rights' and, under Article 5, the existence and rights of indigenous peoples are reaffirmed. Article 5 guarantees political pluralism and the respect for the sovereignty of all nations and states Nicaragua's strong opposition to discrimination: 'Article 5... [Nicaragua] is opposed to any form of discrimination, and it is anticolonial, anti-imperialist, anti-racist and rejects all subordination of one state to another state' and furthermore, Article 89 adds:

> *The Community of the Atlantic Coast have the right to maintain and develop their*
> *cultural identity within national unity; to their own forms of social organization and*
> *to manage their local affairs according to their traditions.*[3]

Nicaragua was responsible for violations of the Awas Tingni community relationship with the lands and natural resources under a 'combination' of breached articles of the American Convention: Articles 4 (the right to life); 11 (right to privacy); 12 (freedom of conscience and religion); 16 (freedom of association); 17 (rights of the family; 22 (freedom of movement and residence); and 23 (right to participate in the government).[4]

In this case, then, the doctrine of *uti possidetis* (see Chapter 2) would appear to be appropriate because the traditional presence of the Awas Tingni in the same area strengthens their interdependence with *those* lands and no others. But, although in 1998 the government of Nicaragua drafted a bill, 'Organic Law Regulating the Communal Property System of the Indigenous Communities of the Atlantic Coast and the Bosawas', to implement the sections of the constitution to formally provide legal instruments 'to regulate and provide borders for indigenous lands', that bill had been adopted as law after 2001.

Aside from granting monetary compensation to the community, the court unanimously decided that Nicaragua should create 'effective mechanisms for delineation, demarcation and titling of property of indigenous communities', pursuant to Article 2 of the American Convention on Human Rights. The court also decided unanimously that the state:

> ... *must abstain from any acts that might lead the agents of the state itself, or third parties acting with its acquiescence or its tolerance, to affect the existence, value, use or enjoyment of the property, located in the geographical area where the members of the Mayagna (Sumo) Awas Tingni Community live and carry out their activities.*
> (Constitución Politica de la Republica de Nicaragua)

Therefore, as well as the groundbreaking judgement upholding the collective land rights of an indigenous group, this judgement breaks new ground by ensuring that a state should not be allowed to 'acquiesce to' or to 'tolerate' activities that may affect 'the existence, value, use or enjoyment' of the newly allocated lands.

In Chapters 1 and 2, the lack of buffer zones to protect the integrity of the indigenous lands was discussed; without them, the land's 'existence', 'value' or 'use' are affected so that it no longer provides the same services or permits the same enjoyment to the community. Although the particular point in the court's decision refers explicitly to the period *before* the 'delimitation, demarcation and titling of the corresponding lands' could be carried out, the *principle* supporting the argument remains the same, once the scientific evidence is understood.

If it is wrong to affect the 'existence', 'value' and 'use' of the lands through possible activities that might affect the land's natural functions and services, then, if it can be demonstrated (as it has been), that industrial or extractive activities, just outside the established borders have the same deleterious effects, then those activities should be equally forbidden for the same reason.

The court's decision was based neither on the tenets of conservation biology, nor on those of public health. But the principle upon which it based its decision (point no. 4 of the judgement), may well be adapted to reflect both. The understanding of the 'protection of indigenous territories' can and should incorporate the science developed since the 1970s, demonstrating beyond doubt the effects of industrial/ extractive activities beyond the borders of a specific territory, unless the territory is protected by a properly sized corridor or buffer zone. In this case, Nicaragua had not fulfilled its international obligations, 'because of the particular acts and omissions of legislative, executive, and judicial agencies that, in the aggregate, resulted in failure to protect indigenous land rights'. The Inter-American Court of Human Rights found that Nicaragua has 'an inadequate legislative and administrative framework to address land titling procedures', as well as an inappropriate way of allowing logging in traditional lands, without indigenous consent (Anaya, 2000).

BEYOND CORPORATE ACTIVITIES:
INDIVIDUAL CHOICE V. CULTURAL INTEGRITY

The 1988 case of *Ivan Kitok v. Sweden* (Anaya, 2000) stressed the cultural integrity rights of an indigenous people without, however, involving any corporate enterprise or foreign individuals. The case demonstrates the interdependence between cultural and ecological integrity, although the former is its main focus, as Article 27 of the ICCPR's main focus is on culture and not ecology.

Ivan Kitok, a Swedish citizen of Sami ethnic origin (half-Sami), requested his right to participate in the traditional cultural activities of his people. He claimed that he belonged to a Sami family that had practised reindeer breeding for 100 years, and 'On this basis the author claims that he has inherited the "civil right" to reindeer breeding from his forefathers as well as the rights to land and water in Skatium Sami Village.[5]

Kitok here refers to the fact that, in order to protect the reindeer breeding programmes, both the Lapp Swedish Crown and the Lapp bailiffs have decided that a Sami who has engaged 'in any other profession for a period of three years ... loses his status and his name is removed from the rolls of the Lappby, which he cannot re-enter unless by special permission' (para. 2.2). Hence this is not a case of an indigenous group against either a state (except for the fact that the rules are promulgated by the Swedish state) or a transnational corporation. The conflict is between a Sami and the Sami group, that is, it is a conflict between individual and group rights. The case of *Lovelace v. Canada* faced a similar problem: the right of one woman, belonging to a First Nation of Canada, but forbidden to return by her own group (according to the Indian Act), after marriage to an outsider and a period of absence. The UN Committee on Human Rights decided against Canada in favour of Lovelace (see Chapter 3).

But in the Kitok case, the very real possibility of exceeding the carrying capacity of Sami lands puts an entirely different spin on an apparently similar question:

> *The pasture areas for reindeer husbandry are limited, and it is simply not possible to let all Sami exercise reindeer husbandry without jeopardizing this objective and running the risk of endangering the existence of reindeer husbandry as such.[6]*

Of the estimated 5000 Sami who live in the Samby (Sami land) at issue, only 2000 are actually Samby members, whereas the others are 'assimilated', in conflict with Article 27 of the International Covenant on Civil and Political Rights. Of the total Sami population of about 15,000 to 20,000, most have no special rights under Swedish law (although they do have some language rights, as they are either half-Sami or they have been assimilated) so that only a small number enjoy specific hunting and fishing rights. In addition, the half-Sami population is forced to pay 4000 to 5000 Swedish krona in order to belong to the Sami association. In the three main states where Sami people still exist – that is, Sweden, Finland and Norway – and the Kola Peninsula region of Russia, they represent a small percentage of the population. One of the larger Sami groups, 20,000 living in Sweden, still represents only 2 per cent of the population. Only 10 per cent of the Sami in all countries are presently involved in their traditional occupation of reindeer herding.[7]

Kitok comments that 'the important thing for the Sami people is solidarity among the people (*folksolidaritet*), and not industrial solidarity (*narigssolidaritet*)'. The 1964 Royal Committee wanted to make the 'reindeer village' (renby), 'an entirely economic association', as the large reindeer owners were favoured: they had a new vote for every 100 reindeer. But reindeer herding is essentially a cultural activity, and Article 27 of ICCPR states:

> *In those States in which ethnic, religious or linguistic minorities exist, persons belonging to such minorities shall not be denied the right, in community with other members of their group, to enjoy their own culture, to profess and practice their own religion or to use their own language.*

The Human Rights Committee decided that 'a restriction upon the right of an individual member of a minority must be shown to have a reasonable and objective justification to be necessary for the continued viability and welfare of the minority as a whole' (Morse, 2002). Hence Kitok was permitted to graze and farm his reindeer, hunt and fish, but 'not as of right'.

What makes this case particularly interesting is that it makes the cultural integrity/ecological integrity of the group primary, and the right to self-determination secondary, as was argued in Chapter 1. Cultural integrity is based upon indigenous territorial rights, and these are inseparable from their 'ecological integrity'. Indigenous peoples are *defined* by their special relation to the land, as this aspect of their culture is inseparable from what gives them their uniqueness and their special rights. Thus the possibility of an indigenous group denying this tradition and choosing options that are deleterious to their cultural background, and hence to their identity, must be considered, as was argued in Chapter 1.

In Fort McMurray, Alberta, there is presently a First Nation that has entered into a lucrative business arrangement with Shell Oil in order to participate in the present oil sands boom in that province. This decision negates most of the major aspects of their identity (see Chapter 1), based upon which they are enjoying a special status in international and domestic law. Yet some have argued[8] that to take into consideration such decisions takes away their basic human rights to freedom of choice and to 'self-determination', and 'This seems paternalistic and inconsistent with other bundles of property rights afforded to other entities (e.g. States) in international law, and therefore a double standard' (Sandler, 2006). Sandler (2006) suggests that perhaps individuals 'cannot violate their own rights', but – at least from a Kantian point of view – this is certainly not true; people are not morally allowed to sell themselves into slavery, sell their body parts, or allow themselves to be dehumanized.

It is important to note that individual rights and group rights may be different too. Also, indigenous peoples have special community rights, beyond those each of the members may have as an individual. Hence the claim advanced here is that the *community* as such, cannot make choices that contradict their essential identity, upon which their special status and rights are based, and retain those rights. In fact, as noted here, even a single group member cannot choose ways that might jeopardize the community's survival and thus their rights.

In principle (though not necessarily in the law) the First Nation at Fort McMurray should retain the individual rights of the members as those of all human beings, and their corporate rights as any other business entity, but perhaps they should not claim any special rights that accrue to them as an indigenous community while they continue their industrial operations. In law, they are defined by their unique interdependence with the land, and the respect for it that is both traditional and mandatory in their culture. If they choose to ignore that aspect of their identity, their identity could and should be brought into question, and their rights might be differentiated according to the different spheres within which they operate.

ENTITLEMENT AND HISTORICAL OCCUPATION

Native communities still occupy the bottom rung of the ladder of economic and social status in the countries in which they reside. Their physical and spiritual survival is threatened by outside encroachment – private and sometimes public action. There is, however, a clearly discernible trend toward legal recognition of the special spiritual bond between indigenous peoples and their lands, the demarcation and legal guarantee, if not return, of lands of traditional indigenous use, and a recognition of Native Title conferring right to at least use of the resources of nature in the traditional communal ways (hunting, fishing for example). (Sandler, 2006)

Several issues have emerged in our discussion of indigenous rights: all are related, but they are characterized by emphasis on diverse problems. Territorial integrity is a major problem, and so is the protection of ecological integrity and of biological integrity and public health. Then there is the problem of the limits of self-determination and the importance of cultural integrity. In addition, we can also consider another problem related to territory: the question of title, something we discussed briefly when we considered the conquest of North America and the concept of *terra nullius*. The first case to be considered is in North Africa, the *Western Sahara* case; the second is the *Mabo* case from Australia.

Western Sahara advisory opinion (16 October 1975)

The General Assembly of the UN had requested the court to give its advisory opinion on two questions: first, 'was Western Sahara (Rio de Oro and Sakriet el Hamra) at the time of the colonization by Spain, a territory belonging to no one (*terra nullius*)?'; and second, 'what were the legal ties between the territory and the Kingdom of Morocco and the Mauritania Entity?'.

Most important is the court's answer to the first question: Western Sahara was not *terra nullius* at the time of the Spanish conquest. Hence, at the time of Spain's withdrawal and the 'decolonization' of the area, it is necessary to discover the original political situation before the conquest. Both Mauritania and Morocco wanted to have their own chosen *ad hoc* judge sitting in the proceedings (paras 1–13, Advisory Opinion) to support the existence of early 'legal ties' between the indigenous tribes and their countries. For instance, Morocco claimed 'sovereignty' on the grounds of alleged immemorial possession of the territory and the uninterrupted exercise of authority (paras 90–120).

Morocco wanted the court to take into consideration various documents produced in support of the allegiance of various tribes to the Sultan of Morocco, 'through their caids or sheiks, rather than on the notion of territory' (Wiessner, 1999). But these documents, at best, indicated that 'a legal tie of allegiance existed at the relevant period between the Sultan and some, but only some, of the nomadic peoples of the territory' (Wiessner, 1999).

The 'Mauritanian entity' also claimed a connection to the tribes at the relevant period, based on their earlier political authority over both emirates and tribal groups. Mauritania also proposed the notion of a 'people' or 'nations' for the inhabitants at that time. They claimed to have 'legal ties' with them, but these 'ties' were also judged to be insufficient to determine the status of the area's indigenous peoples. In contrast:

> *The Court stressed that self-determination, the overriding principle in the decolonization of the Western Sahara, required regard for the freely expressed wishes of the peoples of the territory, notwithstanding their character or political status immediately prior to colonization.* (Wiessener, 1999)

In fact, this advisory opinion recognized the presence of 'native title' on the 'basis of historical use and occupancy'.[9] Hence a 'title' of sorts was present for the nomadic tribes of the area, based on their lengthy association with the lands subsequently taken over by Spain. Hence the historical roots of the Western Sahara's indigenous peoples were sufficient to confer upon them the title they sought to those lands after Spanish decolonization.

Mabo v. Queensland: Native title and the Australian High Court

> *... this means that if traditional nation title was not extinguished before the Racial Discrimination Act came into force, a state law which seeks to extinguish it now will fail.*[10]

The issue before the Australian High Court was the Queensland Coast Island Declaratory Act 1985 (The Queensland Act), that purported 'retrospectively' to abolish 'the rights and interest of the Miriam people of Murray Island', and to have the traditional lands revert to the Crown instead. The plaintiffs (Miriam Peoples or Murray Islanders), now own and have both proprietary and usufructuary interests 'in relation to the land, seabeds, reefs and fishing waters of the Murray Islands'. The Murray Islanders are a distinct indigenous group and section 9(1) of the Federal Racial Discrimination Act states that:

> *... it (is) unlawful for a 'person to do any act' involving racial discrimination which has the purposes or effect of nullifying or impairing the recognition, enjoyment or exercise of any human right or fundamental freedom in the field of public life.*[11]

In addition, 'Section 109 of the Constitution... resolves any conflict between competing laws in favour of the paramountcy of the Commonwealth law; to the extent of that inconsistency the State law is inoperative'. Thus section 3 of the Queensland Act, declaring that the lands in question were 'freed' from all previous right claims and became simply 'wastelands of the Crown' cannot stand.

The Racial Discrimination Act's section 10 also aims at eliminating discrimination in all legal instruments (Commonwealth, state or territory law), so that persons of all races, colour, national or ethnic origins must be permitted to enjoy the same rights under conditions of full equality, a position also held by the International Covenant on the Elimination of all Forms of Racial Discrimination, Article 5(d), which includes the right to own property, as well as the right to inherit.

The presence of Murray Islanders in their lands from time immemorial is not in question, thus the Queensland Act is invalid and unable to impair the traditional rights of these peoples on three separate grounds: first, 'As a matter of construction', as it cannot extinguish the specific rights of a people; second, 'As a matter of power', as there are limits to the power of Queensland on how to deal with Crown lands and to deprive people of their property rights; and third, 'As a matter of inconsistency', as it is inconsistent with the provisions of section 9 of the Racial Discrimination Act of 1975, as well as section 10(1), that ensures the continuation of traditional rights.[12]

Brennan (CLR at 120-1),[13] adds a very important point regarding racial discrimination. He argues that 'The dominant theme that runs throughout the Convention, is equality before the law'. But depriving the Murray Islanders of their rights, even to allow their lands to become the property of anyone else, without discrimination, does not correct the 'inequality', because 'a deep sense of injustice may remain'.

Formal equality in law is not the same as 'effective and genuine equality'. Equality in law precludes discrimination of any kind, 'whereas equality in fact may involve the necessity of differential treatment in order to attain a result which establishes an equilibrium between different situations'.[14] This is the sort of correct argument that has been advanced in defence of quotas and other anti-discrimination procedures in the workplace and elsewhere in North America.

Hence the most important consequences of the resolution of this case are: first, no domestic or regional law may impair basic international human rights and promote instruments in direct conflict with such rights; and second, formal, procedural 'equal treatment' is insufficient to support the human and community rights of indigenous peoples, as they represent a *sui generis* case, and they require special treatment under conditions of substantive justice instead.

Aboriginal land rights in Australia

Echoing the pattern of the Canadian judiciary, however, the Australian High Court followed several opinions upholding the environment-related rights of indigenous peoples with a series of opinions severely curtailing those rights.[15]

Three years after the *Mabo v. Queensland* decision, discussed above, the court returned to the same or similar issues, in *Wik Peoples v. Queensland* (Manus, 2006). The question was, once again, Aboriginal rights regarding 'pastoral leases granted by the government to non-indigenous lessees':[16]

If the government had entered into leases that extinguished native title, the appellants argued, those leases were illegal and a breach of the sovereign's fiduciary duty to the tribe as its trustee. (Manus, 2006)

The majority of the judges in the case concluded that pastoral leases could coexist with the kind of land uses Aboriginal peoples practised, hence demonstrating the court's acceptance of the specific ties of Aboriginal peoples to the land and their environmental rights (Manus, 2006).[17]

Nevertheless, after the amendment of the act in 1998, subsequent cases do not follow the lead of *Mabo* and *Wik*. In *Ward*,[18] for instance, and in *Yorta Yorta*,[19] the tribal peoples hoped that the court would declare their right to 'exclusive possession' of their territories, the right 'to speak for' the lands, and the right to protect 'culture knowledge related to it'.

It is interesting to note that although the court recognized the spiritual/religious relation between Aboriginal people and their land, and also acknowledged that it amounted to 'a protective dominion or stewardship over its environment'[20], it reached a conclusion quite different from that hoped for by the local tribes. The court argued that this 'spiritual' relation had to be 'translated' into 'non-indigenous legal rights and interests'.[21]

This approach runs counter to that of the Canadian courts which, increasingly, accept oral histories and other indigenous witnesses as equivalent to other more formal legal histories. The Australian court treated native title as a 'bundle of rights', implying that each needed to be proved separately and each could be extinguished by the Crown (Manus, 2006). Even more damaging than this understanding by the court is the formal interpretation of the relation between Aboriginal people and the land one finds in *Yorta Yorta*.

Various government policies and activities, both legal and illegal, had conspired in several ways to force the alteration or elimination of Aboriginal traditional practices, from the removal of local children from their families, to the near elimination of the use of tribal languages, to the interference with the right to perform traditional ceremonies. The court, however, concluded that their present lifestyle and practices did not have 'a continuous existence and vitality since sovereignty' (Manus, 2006).

It seems to be particularly offensive to an indigenous group that a government should first allow and support activities that destroy the integrity of a group's territories and their cultural identity by negatively affecting the lands and declaring their cultural and religious practices forbidden, then look at the group's current lifestyle and declare that there is no 'continuity' between traditional ways and their present practices in their 'adapted' form.[22] Nevertheless, at the time of the British settlement of Australia in 1788, the land was viewed as *terra nullius*, that is, 'the land was treated as if it had been vacant or desert so as to be available for claim by any nation that established settlements upon it'.[23]

This understanding implied that the 'Aboriginal people were so primitive that their occupation was inconsequential' (Morse, 2002). Hence, Aboriginal peoples there had to battle to demonstrate from the start that they were human beings with rights. The fact that they presently have the same rights as other Australians, therefore, is an indication of great progress, although they have neither 'sovereignty' nor other special rights.

The High Court, in the Mabo decision, found that:

> ... *the common law of this country recognizes a form of native title which in cases where it has not been extinguished, reflects the entitlements of indigenous inhabitants, in accordance with their laws and customs, to their traditional lands.* (Morse, 2002)

Thus, the Mabo case was by no means the final word on Aboriginal rights. The Racial Discrimination Act of 1975 (according to sections 9 and 10) provides that, '... if Aboriginal people are deprived of certain rights by discriminatory laws, then those rights are not lost' (Stephenson, 2004). The Native Title Act (1993) codifies the fact that the common law in Australia 'recognizes native title', rather than creating it (Stephenson, 2004). As noted in *Yorta Yorta* (Stephenson, 2004), the 'bundle of rights' of Aboriginal groups was determined as 'a matter of fact' by reference to the traditional laws, customs and practices of the particular indigenous community,[24] thus avoiding a decision enshrining a clear definition of native title rights.

In conclusion, although clear progress has been made by Aboriginal communities in Australian law, grave problems remain, given the apparent lack of an overarching protective principle or instrument and the *ad hoc* treatment of indigenous rights.

Ongoing environmental issues in Oceania

The interface between harmful commercial practice and lax laws and incomplete indigenous rights instruments is a problem much in evidence, although some other areas appear to promote much stronger respect for traditional ways and knowledge. The *Final Report* of the International Marine Project Activities Centre Limited (IMPAC) lists numerous case studies intended to study local practices, cultures and the interface between Aboriginal groups and the environment:

> *Many government regulations in the Pacific, however, apply management concepts and models developed elsewhere or by international processes and do not properly take into account the customary practices and traditional knowledge – even though there is a high degree of congruence between the local customary systems and these other models.* (IMPAC, undated)

The harmful Western practices emerge as one reviews the numerous case studies presented by various participants in the work, including attacks on biodiversity that are acknowledged to also be attacks on traditional legal and policy regimes. An example from Papua New Guinea touches on some of these issues:

> *PNG is a biodiversity 'hot spot' and has the second largest variety of species in the Pacific with 40,000 square kilometres of reefs; it hosts 7% of the world's biodiversity. Major threats of this exceptional biodiversity include logging, mining, destructive fishing and subsistence practice methods, and industrial and natural disasters.* (Henao and Genolagani, undated)

This case study also cites the 'mining policy' funded by the World Bank, and the inclusion of biodiversity in local protocols, but the authors lament the lack of implementation. Another interesting aspect of the ongoing accommodation between local governments and indigenous communities is the newly adopted 'six feet law', 'stating that the first six feet depth of the land belongs to the customary owners, while the land under this burial limit, belongs to the State' (Henao and Genolagani, undated).

The differences between Western and customary forms of governance are also emphasized in a case study on Palau in Micronesia. In villages ruled by traditional chiefs, conservation was achieved by declaring moratoriums (*buls*):

> *Breaking buls was a serious misconduct and would bring shame and dishonour to the lawbreaker. The role of Taboos on food (e.g. eagle spotted ray) was and still is important in marine resources management, as it could lead to the effective protection of endangered species.* (Ridep-Morris, undated)

The use of taboos is also important in Vanuatu, although they have now been incorporated in the newly enacted Environmental Management and Conservation Act (2003) (Nar, undated).

The inclusion of aboriginal values in local law is also present in New Zealand, although the Western laws on which local regulations are based tend to separate 'sectors like plant, land, water and fishes', in contrast with traditional Maori values and management practices (Havemann, undated). This case study also raises a different question: what is the difference, if any, 'between indigenous and place-based peoples?', a question also raised in Chapter 1 by a scholar researching African peoples. No answer is proposed here. Another unanswered question is how to protect traditional knowledge from exploitation, as '99 per cent of traditional knowledge is used commercially by outside users' in Pacific countries (Evans-Illidge, undated).

The usurpation of both traditional knowledge and of marine biodiversity itself by outsiders remains a grave problem:

> *Marine resources are of great importance in the Fijian communities, historically, culturally, and economically. People are identified by the land, animal, sand, fish that they traditionally own – so they are strongly identified with the environment which is of great importance in their culture.* (Tuivanuavou, undated)

Authors and researchers in the area view the establishment of more 'taboo sites' (*goligolis*) as an increasingly viable manner of achieving effective site/species protection. Despite significant recent increases in their numbers, these sites are not supported by government instruments but only by NGOs (Tuivanuavou, undated). In addition, even 'taboos' are insufficient for marine protected areas (MPAs), as the issue of the 'eco-services' provided by these areas, to benefit both local and larger communities, must also be considered:

> *... different ecosystems should be regarded as a whole as land and sea are intimately connected for conservation management. MPAs can only be successful if the watershed is also managed. Vanuatu for instance is trying to manage the islands as a whole instead of sectionalizing.* (Tuivanuavou, undated)

The findings of the IMPAC report were considered by the World Conservation Union (IUCN) Secretariat for the Commission on Environmental Law. It created a Specialist Group on Indigenous Peoples and Environmental Law, which met in December 2002 for the first time in Gland, Switzerland (Craig, undated). In general, the report indicates a very impressive approach to the marriage of customary law, traditional knowledge and state laws. It also recognizes the importance of traditional knowledge for the conservation of biodiversity, and for the protection of 'natures services' (Daily, 1997), as well as the need to combine traditional knowledge with recent scientific research, particularly in the field of ecosystem management.

It is regrettable that the merging of these harmonious strands cannot be found in many other locations, where confrontation, rather than mutual understanding and complementarity, seem to be the rule as the only form of interaction between indigenous peoples and the legal regimes of the countries they inhabit. What is clearly missing is a full understanding of the human rights dimension of their environmental plight. Craig Scott (2001a) notes:

> *An Aboriginal community may have certain rights within Article 27 of the ICCPR related to land and natural resources because of the way the environment ties into their cultural community survival needs. Some of these rights may have a property rights dimension. These are still human rights even if there is no general (non-treaty) right to property in international human rights law and even if most other communities cannot make exactly the same claim because they do not have a similar mix of cultural, spiritual, and economic ties to the land base and resources.*

Aboriginal land rights in New Zealand

> *We, the hereditary chiefs and heads of the tribes of Northern parts of New Zealand, being assembled at Waitangi, in the Bay of Islands, on this 28th day of October, 1835, declare the independence of our country which is hereby constituted and declared to be an Independent State under the designation of the United Tribes of New Zealand.[25]*

The situation in New Zealand is quite different than that of Australia regarding indigenous peoples. There are now estimated to be over 60,000 Maori in New Zealand, or more than 15 per cent of the total population (Morse, 2002). The Maori consider that anyone who 'self-identifies as Maori' has met the test, as there is no government-sponsored test to identify members of the group. The Maori's own institutions foster language retention for children, and New Zealand schools offer at least partial instruction in the Maori language, so that many aboriginal peoples go on to higher education today, and English and Maori languages now have equal status:[26]

> *Maori chiefs eventually negotiated the Treaty of Waitangi (1840) in both languages, and ... it has also come to symbolize once again the partnership and commitment to mutual understanding between the two cultures. (Morse, 2002)*

In 1975, the Treaty of Waitangi Act was adopted and the Waitangi Tribunal was established, with the mandate to examine disputes, defend the appropriate interpretation of the treaty, and to make practical recommendations to the government. Although the tribunal cannot make binding judgements, the government has, in fact, accepted all the solutions proposed by the tribunal in various disputes (Morse, 2002).

Regarding their traditional territories, fisheries, rather than hunting and trapping, have been the major concern of the Maori:

> *For over one hundred years, Maori had argued before the Crown, the Waitangi Tribunal and the courts that the guarantee of 'full, exclusive possession ... of their fisheries' contained in the Treaty of Waitangi had never been given effect.* (Stavenhagen, 2002)

The Treaty of Waitangi's Fisheries Deed of Settlement of 1992, had the Crown paying NZ$150 million, so that Maori could 'purchase half a share in Sealord Products Ltd (New Zealand's biggest fishing company) holding 27 percent of the New Zealand fishing quota' (Stavenhagen, 2002). Hence Maori appear to be more integrated in the general and economic life of New Zealand than many aboriginal groups in other countries. In contrast, Morse (2002) says:

> *... from the vantage point of total land quantum that is currently in the hands of or dedicated to the exclusive use of original owners of the land, then Australia has the best record by far, even though its courts had failed to accept the application of the common law doctrine of aboriginal title to the nation until 1992. Nordic treatment of the Sami would then deserve the worst rating with New Zealand a close second.*

In addition, CERD has been working with New Zealand on the implications of the Foreshore and Seabed Act of 2004. Rodolfo Stavenhagen (2002) explains:

> *Both foreshore (the area of land between the low and high tide marks) and seabed have long been a part of Maori environment, culture, economic activity and way of life, basically for marine farming and small scale sand mining, more recently for tourism.*

The problem arose because, according to New Zealand, the 'government understood that foreshore and seabed in New Zealand was generally owned by the Crown', an understanding based on existing legislation and domestic case law (1963 *Ninety Mile Beach* case) (Stavenhagen, 2002). But the New Zealand government subscribed to CERD and claimed that the Foreshore Act was intended 'to preserve the public foreshore and seabed in perpetuity as the common heritage of all New Zealanders and to recognize the rights and interests of individuals and groups in those areas' (Stavenhagen, 2002).

In Chapter 10, we will return to the implications of using the 'common heritage of mankind' regulatory framework as a possible strategy to be used in defence of the rights of aboriginal peoples. In this case, it seems the act was used by the government of New Zealand for a purpose contrary to that goal. Nevertheless more research is necessary to assert whether the position of Maori in New Zealand is one of progress and advancement, or whether this is a case of assimilation, which remains essentially a form of elimination of aboriginal communities. Stavenhagen argues (2002), in a section entitled 'The Challenge: Reducing Inequalities' that 'Maori are highly integrated into the wider national economy at all levels and made a significant and vital contribution to it, as workers, owners, investors and consumers'.

There are, however, racial inequalities that 'continue to exist in health, housing, employment, education, social services and justice' (Stavenhagen, 2004). While it is highly desirable that any gaps between Maori and other New Zealanders be eliminated, it remains unclear whether Maori will retain their existence as a people when that gap has been closed.

PRECEDENTS IN LAW: THE *TRAIL SMELTER ARBITRATION* ON ENVIRONMENTAL HARMS

> *[U]nder principles of international law, as well as the law of the United States, no State has the right to use or permit the use of its territory in such a manner as to cause injury by fumes in or to the territory of another or the **properties** or **persons therein**, when the case is of serious consequence, and the injury is established by clear and convincing evidence.*[27] (emphasis added)

No one can dispute the importance of the *Trail Smelter Arbitration*, although the extent of its influence over international environmental jurisprudence is the subject of much debate. The facts are well known. Consolidated Mining and Smelting Company had established the Trail Smelter for the extraction of sulphur from the fumes (McCaffrey, 2006). The International Joint Commission (IJC) (Canada and US) started by making an 'exhaustive examination' of the facts (Read, 1963), thus placing itself above all recent courts dealing with pollution harms, none of which had the desire or the foresight to actually investigate the claims of harm brought to them by various indigenous groups.

In fact, the IJC's report recommended the drastic reduction of emissions in order to ensure that no trans-boundary harm would ensue (McCaffrey, 2006). Nevertheless, no health study was even considered in order that 'serious consequences' to human health might be properly assessed. The US was prepared to delve into other cases that might indicate the correct procedures to follow when sovereignty (or 'quasi-sovereignty') might collide (McCaffrey, 2006). Many years later, Principle 21 of the 1972 Stockholm Declaration on the Human Environment separated the references to sovereignty and to harm in its formulation. In addition, it did not qualify the severity of the harm required to trigger legal mechanisms:

> *States have, in accordance with the Charter of the United Nations and the principles of international law, the sovereign right to exploit their own resources pursuant to their own environmental policies, and the responsibility to ensure that activities within their jurisdiction or control, do not cause damage to the environment of other states or of areas beyond the limits of national jurisdiction.*[28]

It is unclear, from the point of view of justice and fairness, why 'sovereignty' permits any country to harm its own environment, as the consequences of environmental harms are seldom confined within borders anyway. The consequences of environmental harms affect territories and people worldwide, and climate change is an excellent example of this (see Chapter 8 and the discussion of global warming and the Nunavut people in the Arctic).

The second aspect of this principle is even more important, but, as listed, it is equally incomplete. It relates to the question of the true import of 'environmental damage'. It is a great improvement over the *Trail Smelter* principles, in that 'damage' is here not qualified by 'severe', 'significant' or other limiting characteristics. But it is still insufficient, and it was with scant justification in 1972 (and absolutely none in this century), that environmental harms or damage were still not linked to the health and normal function of human beings – not only those facing immediate exposure in the area, but also those far removed, such as in the Arctic regions. Nevertheless, the obligation to a state's own citizens is not clearly articulated in law. For those living in other states, the IJC refers to the duty of protection beyond one's borders, as it was apparent, for instance, in the *Corfu Channel* case,[29] where that state duty is explained as 'not to allow knowingly its territory to be used for acts contrary to the rights of other States'. Similarly, the *Gabcikovo-Nagymaros Project* (Hungary v. Slovakia), 1997, ICJ 7, para. 53 (September 25) argued for:

> *The existence of the general obligation of States to ensure that activities within their jurisdiction and control respect the environment of other States or of areas beyond national control is now part of the corpus of international law relating to the environment.*

Yet even this formulation, clearly arising from the tradition of *Trail Smelter*, over 50 years after it, refers to the 'environment' as a separate entity, without recognizing the connection between humankind and their habitat (Westra, 2004a). However, the case represents a great improvement over its precedent in *Trail Smelter*. In Judge Weeramantry's dissenting opinion (1997):

> *Environmental rights are human rights. Treaties that affect human rights cannot be applied in such a manner to constitute a denial of human rights, as understood at the time of their application. A Court cannot endorse activities which are a violation of human rights by the standards of their time, merely because they are taken under a treaty which dates back to a period when such action was not a violation of human rights.*

Hence, even applying the precedent of *Trail Smelter* to modern cases, as Weeramantry argued, that case 'could not operate as precedent on the basis of environmental norms as though they were frozen in time when the Treaty was entered into' (Weeramantry, 1997).

THE ROLE OF ECONOMICS IN INDIGENOUS PEOPLES' ISSUES

The main debates in the jurisprudence pertaining to indigenous peoples fall into at least five major categories: first, the question of territorial integrity and that of title to their lands and resources; second, the impact of economic/industrial (especially extractive) activities on traditional practices, and on ecosystem and human health; third, the lack of protection available to indigenous communities by local governments; fourth, the power of the World Bank Group and the IMF, and the limits of the guidelines under which they operate in relation to indigenous peoples; and fifth, the question of 'consultation' v. 'consent' to the extractive/industrial activities.

As the literature on *Trail Smelter* acknowledges (Handl, 2006), both *Trail Smelter* itself and other cases involving indigenous groups arise primarily from conflicts between environmental/human rights, and the economic thrust of industrial operations aimed at 'developing' or 'expanding' the present economic basis of their operation, either in general, in some remote location, or in various developing countries. Essentially, it is consistently the economic motive, viewed as both ultimate and determinant, that initiates most disputes. But the extractive/mining operations that are most dangerous are not, for the most part, the effort of an individual company. The funding required to bring about these large projects requires solid outside financing, and most often a coalition of corporate persons. Hence the World Bank Group and the IMF are in an ideal position to commit to and enforce the strongest regulations for the protection of the indigenous peoples at risk.

In order to examine the root of the problems we are discussing, I start by reviewing the fourth and fifth issues listed above in order to pinpoint one of the causes of the major problems discussed, the *sine qua non*, almost, of the hazardous operation we have examined.

The World Bank, indigenous peoples and the problem of consent

The first, second and third issues listed above are closely related, as we shall see below. In Chapter 3 the importance of 'collateralism' was considered and in Chapter 2 I attempted to define eco-footprint crime. In both cases, the harmful/criminal activities are the effects, or perhaps the 'side effects', of corporate/industrial activities, primarily but not exclusively mining and other extractive operations. For the most part, it is these large-scale activities that result in eco-footprint crimes, that is, that give rise to criminal activities such as grave breaches of human rights, beyond the obvious overuse of local resources to the detriment of indigenous peoples and their lands.

Large-scale activities by transnational corporations based in wealthy Northern countries tend to be supported by the IMF or the World Bank Group, both of which are ostensibly committed to the alleviation of poverty, especially in developing countries. The World Bank has prepared studies and developed policies since the early 1980s, intended to 'mitigate harms to indigenous groups' through the projects they finance (Goodland, 1982; MacKay, 2005). But we cannot expect too much from these documents. At best those of the Bank state that it 'should avoid unnecessary or avoidable encroachment onto territories used or occupied by tribal peoples'. It also rules out involvement 'not agreed to by tribal peoples, requires, guarantees from borrowers that they would implement safeguard measures and advocates respect for indigenous peoples' rights to self-determination' (MacKay, 2005).

Compliance with the first Operational Manual Statement produced by the Bank (OMS 2.34) in 1982 was slow. The 1986–1987 first review of implementation of the policy, four years after it had been adopted, found that only 2 of 33 World Bank Group projects substantially complied with the policies (MacKay, 2005), leading to ongoing critiques by indigenous peoples and NGOs. The major lack of compliance with the policy prompted a revision and update of OMS 2.34, so that in 1991 the Operational Directive 4.20 on Indigenous Peoples was adopted.[30]

This document represents an improvement on the previous manual as it requires indigenous input for all projects, as well as respect for indigenous lands and resource rights; it also demands that local domestic legislation be strengthened (MacKay, 2005). Nevertheless the requirements of OD 4.20 were still judged to be insufficient, largely due to limited compliance by both the Bank and its borrowers with those requirements. Internal evaluations continued to note that newer drafts under discussion had to respond, minimally, to indigenous demands that their internationally mandated rights be respected, that is:

> ... *their right to free, prior and informed consent, recognition and protection of terri-torial rights, self-identification (as the fundamental criterion in determining the peoples covered by the policy), a prohibition of involuntary resettlement, and respect for indigenous people's rights to self-determination.* (Griffiths, 2003a; see also Griffiths, 2003b)

Even if the policy prescriptions of the instruments of the World Bank were sufficient to reflect the mandates of the UN Permanent Forum on Indigenous Issues, the results of the applications of those policies, 'were not satisfactory in the energy, mining, transportation and environment sectors, which comprise 65% of Bank commitments'.[31] However, even if their intentions were the best, there are several problems that the World Bank projects encounter: some are formal and internal; others are external and contingent, as we shall see. But the role played by the Bank cannot be underestimated when we consider the jurisprudence that involves indigenous groups. In order to fully appreciate both its policies and the respective applications of those policies, it might be useful to start with the 'Preambular Paragraphs' of OP 4.10 (MacKay, 2005), which is the document presently in use:

> *Para. 1 states that the document 'contributes to the Bank's mission of poverty reduction and sustainable development by ensuring that the development process fully respects the dignity, human rights, economics and cultures of indigenous peoples'*

This statement is neither fully defensible as 'true' as it stands, nor does it represent a clear plan of action of the Bank's future projects. In addition, in the same paragraph, we find that 'the borrower must engage in free prior and informed consultation ('FPICon') with indigenous peoples', and that this mandate is valid for both projects where the Bank is the sole lender and where it is simply one of several (World Bank Group, 2004). Further, the Bank will 'include measures to avoid potential adverse effects', or, if 'not feasible', it will 'minimize, mitigate or compensate for such effects'.

The second paragraph of this document, however, does 'recognize that indigenous peoples' cultures and identities are inextricably related to traditional lands and resources' (MacKay, 2005), and thus that these people will be exposed to risks and impacts beyond those to which other groups would be exposed. In contrast, indigenous peoples 'play a vital role in sustainable development' so that special (and increasing) recognition must be given to their rights.[32]

In the next section, I consider more closely these preambular requirements, both through the internally generated position of the World Bank and through the conflicts that arise from those requirements.

Internal issues within the World Bank: Consent or consultation? The meaning of 'free', 'prior' and 'informed'

'Consent' is a concept that is clear to understand. It should mean that the indigenous group in question should be able to veto a project that, after a period of discussion, information gathering and consultation, it finds it cannot approve. When we turn to 'consultation' instead, we find a truncated approach to the broad 'community consensus' each project is intended to secure. That is the main difference between free, prior, informed consent (FPIC) and free, prior, informed consultation (FPICon). The former implies an ongoing process requiring the latter.

Both consent and consultation need full prior disclosure of information presented in terms and in a language that are fully understandable by the people affected by the decision. Nor is the 'broad community support' clearly defined: 'It is a general principle of law that consent is not valid if obtained through coercion or manipulation' (MacKay, 2005). Given the inequality present in processes involving indigenous peoples and powerful and wealthy corporations and their lenders, at least some level of manipulation can be assumed. In addition, neither the 'community support' nor the 'freedom' of the final decision is ever monitored by established mechanisms. The sequencing itself is unclear; when is the support to be secured? Probably, the intention is to seek it after the borrower has submitted a proposal to the Bank. At that stage there must be a clear interplay between the Bank, the borrower and the country where the specific indigenous group lives. I return to this topic in the next section.

For now it is sufficient to mention that various countries' domestic law defines their own requirements for FPIC.[33] The process of consultation is therefore basic and necessary, but it is insufficient and the concept is by no means equivalent to 'consent', a far stricter requirement. The effective switch from one term to the other is reminiscent of the industry-led initiative by chemical companies to engage in 'consultation' with the general public affected by their hazardous operations in North America. The result of such a process of 'consultation', based on all parties sitting around a table while the affected people voiced their concerns, usually resulted in some public relations efforts but no real change, making it is easy to be cynical about the possibility of tangible change ever resulting from 'consultation' alone. In fact, the whole process could be termed simply a public relations operation, even in countries like Canada where people's human rights are somewhat better developed and enforced than they are in other areas where indigenous peoples live (Westra, 1994a).

One needs to understand the basic imbalance between such different groups with disparate interests, and, most of all, with entirely different powers, to see these exercises for what they really are. Indigenous peoples have been clear on what they want: their right to express FPIC.[34] The World Bank Draft Indigenous Peoples Policy Draft is criticized because it does not incorporate previous recommendations by indigenous peoples, because it confuses consultation with effective participation and '... it fails to recognize the right to free, informed prior consent' (McKay, 2005). The affected groups clearly understood that 'FPICon resulting in broad community support' is not the same as FPIC, so that the manipulation involved in making the latter appear to be like the former is an action that 'lacks any basis in international law'.[35]

What is offered is, at best, a nebulous goal such as 'development'. But most indigenous groups want to be left alone to live their lives in the traditional ways they have practised since time immemorial, and not to 'develop' in some forced and foreign direction. For instance, an indigenous Mayan group in Guatemala, the Sipakapa of San Marcos, live peacefully, practising agriculture and animal husbandry. In 2005, Montana Exploradora, a subsidiary of the Canadian/US Transnational corporation Glamis Gold, received US$45 million from the World Bank Group to exploit an open pit gold mine in their area.[36] The original video with English subtitles, demonstrates clearly the vast gulf between the arguments and proposals of the mine representatives, and the responses of the local people. In the final analysis, the people's 'no' should have meant just that. ILO Convention No. 169 and even the Constitution of Guatemala demand consultation with the indigenous peoples; the result was not consensus but a resounding 'no' to the project, but that was not respected and the exploration and work continued. While the Guatemalan courts are still to pronounce themselves on the topic, in April 2006 the open pit mine was in full operation, resulting in highly toxic cyanide ponds and the heedless use of the scarce local water for industrial activities. In the video, the people ask 'what is *our* advantage?'. The answer to this question remains unclear, while the damages inflicted emerge clearly, and the courts deliberately proceed at a slow pace as the corporation continues with its unwanted and harmful 'development'.

Some have argued that it is wrong to: first, view the World Bank Group as a fully homogeneous group, inherently inimical to any policy of respect for human rights and ecological integrity;[37] and second, as incapable of influencing domestic laws in a way that 'facilitates norm internalization' (Sarfaty, 2005).

Sarfaty (2005) does present evidence of the presence of agreements between various 'parties' within the World Bank, and she emphasizes the conflict that exists between environmentalists (as a 'second class' group) and anthropologists on one side, and the economists on the other. Nevertheless, the Bank Group is a unitary body, making important decisions through its own international decision-making processes. In fact this process and unitary decision-making define it as a legal entity (Westra, 2004a). The presence of internal conflicts, even if proven, is only meaningful up to a point. It parallels the case of accused persons speaking of their own internal conflicts leading to a criminal act; interesting mainly to psychologists, and useful at the penalty stage of trials, but essentially *not* fully exculpatory.

The second point of Sarfaty's (2005) argument about how the World Bank shapes domestic law, actually makes the weight of responsibility resting on their collective shoulders even clearer. Some of the positive aspects of this reality are the topic of the next section.

An aside on corporate/institutional decision-making

The legal and moral status of the corporation should be discussed in the context of *mens rea* requirements for assaults/convictions in corporate crimes. To sum up, briefly, corporations are indeed legal persons, and there are several theories that address the meaning of that terminology (Chick, 1993; French, 1984). For our purpose, it is sufficient to mention three major positions to predicate corporate intentionality: fiction theory, legal aggregate theory, and the position that is taken to be most appropriate, corporation's internal decision structure (French, 1979). Fiction theory has its roots in Roman jurisprudence, but its main flaw is that, in relying on the description of 'legal fictitious persons', it ignores the biological existence of real persons, as well as, by implication, of any others. Legal aggregate theory recognizes the biological reality of persons and grants priority to these legal subjects, while treating corporate persons as purely derivative, and identifying them only with 'directors, executives and stockholders' (French, 1979). In so doing, however, aggregate theory supporters are choosing arbitrarily where to ascribe responsibility, and make it impossible to distinguish between a group (or mob) and corporate reality.

A case in English law demonstrates the difficulties embedded in the first two theories. In *Continental Tyre and Rubber Co. Ltd. vs. Daimler Co. Ltd.* (1915) (K.B., 893), a company whose directors and shareholders were German subjects and residents, was incorporated in England and carried on its business there. The question was whether Continental Tyre should be treated as an English subject and could bring suit in an English Court (while Britain was at war with Germany). The Court of Appeals' majority opinion (five to one) was that, 'the corporation was an entity created by statute', hence that it was 'a different person altogether from the subscribers to the memorandum, the shareholders on the register' (French, 1979). Hence, the corporation's biological composition may not be identical to its true 'personhood' or its intentional structure.

It is also worthy of note that not all who are subjects of rights can in fact be the administrators of rights, and infants, foetuses, animals, future generations and eco-systems are relevant examples of entities that have been declared at one time or another to have some rights, although it has never been argued that any of these could administrate their own rights (Stone, 2000). If we accept a non-specific description of a person, such as the subject of a right, we can at least make the following claims: first, biological existence is not always necessary to personhood; and second, the subject of a right is 'the noneliminatable subject of a responsibility ascription' (French, 1979).

Responsibility is the necessary correlative of a right. In this sense, it goes beyond simply being the one (or the corporate person) who performed an action. We must address the question of intent. For corporations and institutions, the corporate internal decision-making (CID) structure is the locus of the intentionality we intend to establish. Through the CID structure, corporate power is deployed, setting in motion a series of actions flowing from a central, hierarchically made decision, but involving the 'acts of biological persons who ... occupy various stations on the organizational chart of the corporation' (French, 1979).

An advantage of this approach is to be able to maintain corporate responsibility while also, at the same time, retaining the ability to consider varying degrees of intent or of desire to bring about a certain result, the product of corporate ordered activities. French's (1979) argument strongly supports corporate responsibility and, because of its inclusivity, could easily be extended to other institutional bodies, as long as these are also possessed of 'internal decision-making structures'. Can French's argument help to redefine the *mens rea* question? French assumes the presence of intentionality; would that impose a heavier burden upon regulatory offences cases? Perhaps we can argue that the CID structure approach *implies* intentionality as corporate activities are performed by subjects of rights in all cases where an action has been performed or omitted. But neither institutions nor corporations may be free to be the subjects of rights without accepting the corresponding full responsibility toward all other right holders, be they individual or corporate.

In other words, once a corporate body has been distinguished from a mob or an aggregate, and is, in fact, *defined* by its structure, then it is clear that its very nature is to be capable to intentional agency; that is the root of its 'personhood'. In addition, because it is not a biological entity, it can also be argued that such persons are not capable of the emotions that characterize individual biological entities. Corporate persons then, can only rationally intend whatever activity they choose; such actions cannot be the result of sudden impulses or passions (provocation), fear for its own life (self-defence) or addiction (intoxication). Neither mental disorders nor automatism or any other syndrome is possible. Hence, in a sense, by claiming to be persons, yet admitting they are not individual biological persons, corporations may represent the clearest examples of pure purposefulness or desire to bring about certain results, including the activities whose results are the physical elements of an *actus reus*.

If this line of argument is accepted, the court's burden of proof in regard to the mental element of a corporate fault will be substantially reduced and simplified. Once the physical elements of the fault are present, and after they can be causally connected to the corporate person, the mental states that connote its agency are limited to variants of intent, and may range from the purposeful desire to bring about a certain result, to the certain knowledge that the result will occur, to the probability or possibility (recklessness) that a result might follow.

But corporations do have aims, goals and purposes, as do institutions (and many of these are even codified in their statements of intent or codes of practice). Thus, the only conclusion one can draw is that, for the most part, and barring sabotage or people acting outside the corporate perimeter on their own, whatever corporations actually do is something they decided, planned out and fully intended to accomplish. That guarantees the responsibility of the perpetrators. Chick (1993) argues that the US has had a long time to define and regulate corporate rights in relation to constitutional law. However, he adds: 'it was only through the acceptance of one particular corporate personality, the 'aggregate theory', that American courts even decided that corporations were entitled to claim constitutional rights' (Chick, 1993). But aggregate theory is not correct, and that is why it is not generally accepted as the best way to understand corporate personality and function. The reasoning employed in order to link corporations and constitutional protection is that individuals, those who compose the corporation, should not lose constitutional guarantees because they join together in a lawful association. I find this argument to be incoherent: if the lawful association is to provide the associate with a new entity, with legal personality and corresponding rights, then it is not logical to argue that the new body is nothing but an aggregate of persons and nothing more. If the newly formed association is *one*, rather than as French (1979) argued, a mob or a heap with no unitary defining characteristics, then there appears to be no grounds for requiring special status for it, any more than it would be to require and demand such status for a crowd.

French (1979) is correct in saying that to enjoy some rights (and legal status), something more is required than a mass of individuals. There has to be something that makes many into one, at least in one respect. He found this unifying element in the CID structure of the corporate/institutional body. It is not sufficient to say that each component part of the association has rights and duties, true though it is. There are simply no grounds for additional legal status and personality, unless we can identify something that serves to unify the corporation. The CID structure provides unity through purpose and therefore provides that ground. However, the additional entity, as it acquires the right to be and to act like single individuals, single citizens, has duties and obligations.

It is possible to argue that corporate personality theories have been manipulated and are still discussed from the standpoint of political ideals (Romano, 1984). But what remains clear is that in order to be one person there must be something to permit such terminology, as an undirected crowd or mob has no status as such beyond that of the individuals that comprise it. On that basis, therefore, the CID structure theory of corporate personality can be accepted as the most accurate. To sum up:

- We cannot accept diminished responsibility of any sort for an action because, as a separate unit different from its human components, I can never claim defences or mitigating circumstances based on human frailties and emotions.
- Based on similar reasons, the lack of human features, we need not claim for it the status of 'vulnerable accused' in courts of law, and seek for it corresponding Canadian or other legal protection (Sheehy, 1982).
- Having been accorded independent status and rights in the law, this will entail corresponding duties and responsibilities; individual purposes cannot be pursued without considering the rights of others as imposing on individual freedom. So too the corporation must assume full responsibility for all its activities and their results.

The World Bank's influence on domestic laws?

It is vital to understand fully the role of the World Bank in the projects supporting extractive industries before turning once again to the case law, and this brief section will provide some additional information. As most of the cases I consider pit a domestic or international court against a multinational corporate body funded by the World Bank, it is clear that the 'community support' required, let alone the mandated 'consent' are hardly, if ever, present. Nevertheless it is a fact that:

> *Transnational legal process, one of the leading theoretical approaches to international law, can help explain the increasing importance of nonstate actors like the World Bank in enforcing international norms such as human rights.* (Sarfaty, 2005)[38]

Harold Hongju Koh (1996) describes transnational legal processes as 'the theory and practice of how public and private actors, nation states, international organizations' and others, interact to 'interpret, enforce and ultimately internalize rules of transnational law'.[39] In fact, we noted in the *Awas Tingni* case, in this chapter, the importance of the input of non-state actors into the process, which eventually helped that indigenous group to prevail, at least for now, against corporate projects. So it would not be correct to think of international law as simply the relation between states, when NGOs, transnational corporations and bodies such as the World Bank, may wield such power in their affairs, and even influence international tribunals in their decisions.

So, what is the role the World Bank Group may play? First, the World Bank can impose a 'policy conditionality', that is, 'a set of requirements and preconditions that the recipient country is expected to meet in order to receive financial assistance'.[40] But in its 1992 Wapenhaus Report, 'the Bank's Operations Evaluation Department acknowledged the one-sidedness of negotiations between the Bank and borrower countries' (Sarfaty, 2005).[41]

When loans are extended to corporations rather than to countries, the situation is even more complex. Sarfaty (2005) suggests that the Bank's policy on environmental assessment, for instance, has inspired guidelines for both private sector donors and other development groups such as the Asian Development Bank, the European Bank for Reconstruction and Development, and the Inter-American Development Bank. Yet Sarfaty acknowledges that 'the Bank's institutional practices diverge from its written policies' and notes that 'domestic political factors' also play a significant role in the Bank's decision-making.

In is undeniable that the Bank plays an important role with developing countries' legal and policymaking regimes, and that this role represents an integral part of 'transnational legal processes', but, of the three phases of these processes, 'interaction, interpretation, internalization', the Bank, at best, is active at the 'interaction' level (Koh, 1996), and even this 'interaction' does not appear to play a role with corporate borrowers. In general, the Bank's own culture rewards efficiency and the quantity of loans over quality, and protracted consultations and dialogue with indigenous peoples may contribute to neither. In addition, the Bank's Articles of Agreement, stating that the Bank shall not interfere in the political affairs of any member, and even more significant, that 'only economic considerations shall be relevant to decisions',[42] do not prioritize human or ecological rights considerations, or even special treatment of indigenous peoples. Even when guidelines for appropriate conduct are present, 'punishments imposed by the Bank for failing to meet Bank conditions lack moral legitimacy' and, as mentioned, a 'loan approval culture prevails' (Sarfaty, 2005).

Another problem is that, at best, requirements for FPIC or FPICon tend to apply only to 'recognized' or 'titled lands', thereby excluding approximately three-quarters of the lands that traditionally are owned and are presently claimed by indigenous peoples, as is the case in Guyana or Australia (MacKay, 2005). Because many indigenous groups do not presently hold legal title to their lands and some may not even occupy traditional territories because of 'forced severance',[43] a criterion that excludes all these peoples cannot be just.

The Bank's OP 4.10 requires paying special attention to 'customary rights' and to the 'cultural and spiritual values that indigenous peoples attribute to their lands and resources'.[44] When the commercial exploitation of natural resources is at issue, the required 'broad community support' is left undefined, although para. 18 of the same document demands it, and the history of displaced peoples, despoiled land and depleted resources does not encourage the belief in any positive outcomes when the Bank supports projects related to extractive industries (MacKay, 2005).

Hence the expected 'trickle down' effect of desirable language in the World Bank Group's documents, intended to inform the domestic laws of state borrowers, or the areas where commercial projects are funded, is no more successful than the economic 'trickle down' effect ever was. The Bank's primary intent remains strongly financial, and the 'collateralism' of environmental and indigenous concerns fosters – at best – some interaction with borrowers regarding norms, but the internalization of better norms is not clearly in evidence anywhere.

A further grave problem exists, which unfortunately has grave consequences for indigenous peoples, as the result of corporate activities in general, even beyond the ones funded by the World Bank Group. Robert Goodland (2003) explains:

> *Agencies trying to fight poverty should also redress today's asymmetry between all the many strong protections for capital vs. the few and little-enforced protections for labor. The WBG [World Bank Group] and governments are often both stakeholders in extraction. Governments' role as regulator of industry and protector of its citizens may conflict with its need for receipts from extraction. Governments, abetted by extractive corporations on occasion, and often supported by the WBG, have been strengthening national mining and hydrocarbon codes for about a decade in order to protect multinational corporations, and to promote investment in the extractive sector. Oil, gas and mining legislation has been changed in line with WBG advice in more than 70 countries over the last 20 years. People affected by extraction – indigenous peoples and civil society in general – have been penalized by such mining codes, and their rights have been reduced. The harming of indigenous peoples in Australia, Canada and the USA is being repeated in developing countries (sometimes with WBG support).*

Although the World Bank Group's chief economist has emphasized that 'the principle of equality underlies poverty reduction', the Bank has not explicitly acknowledged human rights requirements as basic to poverty reduction. In 2000, the Bank committed itself 'to the Millennium Development Goals including direct poverty reduction, and is phasing out its lending for big infrastructure projects including mines and dams' (Goodland, 2003). UN organizations are more fully and explicitly committed to human rights, but the World Bank Group is slowly evolving in the same direction, and it even intervened directly in three recent cases involving gross human rights violations (Goodland, 2003).[45]

THE WORLD BANK'S INSPECTION PANELS

> *2. The Bank recognizes that the identities and cultures of Indigenous Peoples are inextricably linked to the lands on which they live and the natural resources on which they depend. These distinct circumstances expose Indigenous Peoples to different types of risks and levels of impacts from development projects, including loss of identity, culture and livelihoods as well as exposure to disease.[46]*

Before leaving the topic of the World Bank's interface with aboriginal communities, we need to consider the presence of the inspection panels that can in fact provide a forum for the complaints of affected peoples regarding any project supported by the Bank. All projects seeking funding start with a project concept review (as of July 2005). Several problems emerge even at the conceptual planning stages. For instance, I question whether the Bank's commitments to: '(a) avoid potentially adverse effects on the Indigenous Peoples' communities'; or '(b) when avoidance is not feasible, minimize, mitigate or compensate for such effects', are even possible or logically sound.

When the vital importance of biological/ecological integrity is factored into the project and taken seriously into consideration, then the 'mitigation' or 'compensation' aspects appear to be nothing but empty rhetoric. What is mitigation in oil extraction or mining, against the background of epidemiological research that demonstrates a high percentage of cancers, deformed births and other serious diseases and impairments, as the outcome of these projects (Grandjean and Landrigan, 2006)?

If, say, 50 per cent of the population is presently affected (now and in the foreseeable future) is a reduction to 40 per cent acceptable as mitigation? And what can possibly compensate for the persistent ill-health, organic dysfunction and premature death of children (Westra, 2006; Licari et al, 2005)? Finally, what is the meaning of 'when avoidance is not feasible'? An unfunded project seems to be the obvious answer to the 'feasibility' of avoidance.

Turning now to the question of 'identity' (paras. 3 and 4), the document is more helpful, starting with a definition:

> *4. For the purposes of this policy, the term 'Indigenous Peoples' is used in a generic sense to refer to a vulnerable, social and cultural group, possessing the following characteristics in varying degrees:*
>
> *1 self-identification as members of a distinct indigenous cultural group and recognition of this identity by others;*
> *2 collective attachment to geographically distinct habitats or ancestral territories in the project area and to the natural resources in these habitats and territories;*
> *3 customary cultural, economic and social, or political institutions that are separate from those of the dominant society and culture; and*
> *4 an indigenous language, often different from the official language of the country or region.*

It is also important to note that, although the 'project preparation' requires 'screening by the Bank to identify whether Indigenous Peoples are present in, or have collective attachment to, the project area', when we turn to 'a social assessment by the borrower', given the borrower's interest in securing funds, her impartiality is, at best, in question. Equally problematic is 'a process of free, prior, and informed consultation'. This requirement means little unless the final term is changed to 'consent' (as argued above), and the reference to 'broad community support' is clearly defined.

Nevertheless the World Bank has undertaken to remedy any lacunae that may arise in the process through inspection panels; 40 of these have in fact been reviewed from 1996 to January 2007. It is useful to review two of the 'investigation reports' arising in response to the 'requests' of indigenous groups. The first is the most instructive as it includes both the request and the report itself, dealing with forests in Cambodia; the second is only at the request stage and concerns the forests of the Pygmies of the Democratic Republic of Congo.

Cambodia: Forest concession management and control pilot project

> *7. The requesters claim that through a flawed design and poor implementation the Bank promoted the interests of the logging concession companies rather than those of the people.*[47]

This passage indicates the tone of the whole request, as it details, 'among other things, human rights abuses and illegal logging of resin trees', with no attempt to correct any of this on the part of the Bank. The request also cites:

> *... noncompliance with Bank policies and procedures, including safeguards policies such as OP/BP 4.10 on Environmental Assessment, OP/BP on Natural Habitats, OP/BP 4.36 on Forestry, OD 4.20 on Indigenous Peoples, and OPN 11.03 on Cultural Property.*[48]

Clearly most of the problems cited were in conflict with the required 'social assessment' by the borrowers, with the addition of only a '19-day consultation period', insufficient to permit the forest communities informed input, let alone fully informed consent.[49] The main purpose of the subsequent investigation (approved by a panel, with Chairperson Professor Edith Brown-Weiss and others visiting Cambodia from 12–19 March 2005) was procedural, that is, intended 'to establish whether the Bank complied with its own policies and procedures in ... the Project'. Nevertheless, besides the expected review of all documents and procedures, the second part of the investigation was an 'in-country fact-finding visit'.[50]

It is imperative right at the outset to understand the interface between forests and Cambodia's society, and to be aware of the threat to the 13 million hectares, or about 73 per cent of the country's forests and that since the mid-20th century, more than a million hectares or over 10 per cent has been lost to deforestations.[51] Forests represent the only livelihood available to indigenous communities, as well as the basis for a strong cultural and religious interest. However, Cambodia's forests also represent a great untapped source of income for the Cambodian government and its concessionaires: 'The value "on the stem" of the average mature tree in Cambodia of the 1990s was at least US$50. The value converted to lumber and plywood would have been US$250 or more'.[52]

In addition, while indigenous peoples do not, normally, work in the timber industry, a great percentage of them owns resin trees,[53] which net them an average of over US$300 per year per family, an income loss that would be hard to bear for indigenous communities if the country succumbed to the lure of immediate profits:

> *The immediately available commercial values of timber could make an important and desperately needed economic contribution to the country, but the unsustainable exploitation of timber conflicts directly with the survival strategies of the rural poor, with conservation of biodiversity.*[54]

Some involvement of indigenous communities in the long-term permits (or concessions) operating in certain areas might have been an option, but the government of Cambodia which owns the forest land, was not eager to relinquish control to any local group.[55] Against this background, the panel found that most of the Bank's efforts in the 1990s were on industrial logging, so that 'there remains a large agenda for further policy analysis and development related to agro-forestry, wood energy production, biodiversity conservation and human resources development'.[56]

The Bank, in fact, had not recognized the tensions existing in Cambodia between profitable forest activities and the rights of local communities. For instance the right to tap resin trees is a legal usufruct right entrenched in law for indigenous peoples. Funded by the Asian Development Bank, Fraser's (2000) work states:

> One of the major criticisms of the forestry sector is that for too long its primary focus has been the sustained supply of wood products from forests in processing facilities, and that inadequate attention has been given to the needs of forest-dependent communities, to the broad hydrological and soil conservation functions of forests, their conservation value and the broader significance in cultural and other terms.

In the case of the World Bank, in addition to the persistence of this attitude, there has also been a lack of 'emphasis on using the potential of forests to reduce poverty'.[57] The latter is particularly inappropriate, as one of the project's objectives was 'to demonstrate and improve the effectiveness of a comprehensive set of forest management and operational guidelines and control procedures in forest concession areas'.[58] Hence, the Bank was in the position to truly help develop the terms of reference for the required guidelines, together with the United Nations Development Programme (UNDP)/Food and Agriculture Organization (FAO) mission that same year.[59] Although the 'main aim of the loan was to support a legal and regulatory program on the basis of which long-term concessions were to be granted', the staff generally viewed it as a 'technical assistance project', an outlook that could not address the 'total systems failure' (Fraser, 2000) that was occurring at many levels, including large-scale corruption.[60]

The Bank indeed had policy guidelines that exclude commercial logging,[61] and it could be argued that in fact it adhered to its own policies. However, the panel acknowledges that, given 'the rampant forest destruction and community abuses' present prior to their loan, a more thorough investigation and a far more precautionary approach would have been indicated.[62] Finally, the project did not have adequate levels 'of local involvement, community consultation, and social-environmental assessment'.[63]

After reviewing the situation, the Bank concluded that the project should have received far more supervision to ensure that it could develop towards a 'broadly based constituency'.[64] Thus, in response to the request, the Bank ensured the 4 million hectares of land under concession were cancelled[65] and an additional 1 million hectares of concessions are currently under review. Hence one can see significant, though limited, success in redressing grievances, some of which may take a long time to be satisfied. It will not be easy to regrow the forests that have been cut.

At least, unlike other mining and extractive projects, the impact on the health and normal function of the affected indigenous groups was not as significant. However, the impact of the deforestation allowed by the improper functioning of the original project was not calculated in terms of the corresponding climate change, and was not taken in consideration when assessing damages.

Indigenous Pygmy organizations and the Pygmy Support Organization in the Democratic Republic of Congo: Another request

If zoning of these forests were to be carried out, as the Bank's current actions and failings appear to indicate, without consulting the indigenous peoples, without taking their interest into account, and after the new forest concessions have been allocated, this operation would result in:

1. *The violation of their right to occupy their ancestral lands;*
2. *The violation of the integrity of their traditional lands;*
3. *The violation of their right of access to their traditional lands and the resources found thereon;*
4. *The violation of their right to manage their forests and the resources located therein, in keeping with their traditional knowledge and practices;*
5. *The violation of their cultural spiritual values.*[66]

The request submitted to the World Bank Inspection Panel on 30 October 2005 has not yet been followed by the report of the investigation as it is ongoing at this time. It is number 37 of the 40 requests presently listed by the Inspection Panel.[67] It is worthy of note that only four of the listed requests have been denied by the Bank, and only in the earlier years, that is, 1994–1998.

The request of the Pygmy peoples starts with a list of failures: the failure to list the Emergency Economic and Social Reunification Support Project (EESRSP) as a Category A project; the failure to conduct an environmental assessment; and the failure 'to implement OD 4.20' despite the presence of Pygmy peoples in the area.[68]

The objective of the project as an 'energy recovery loan' includes reforms to areas controlled by rebels. It was meant to 'lay the foundations for reunification and economic stability throughout the country'. In addition, it was to ensure implementation of forestry reforms, a forest zoning plan, and intended to separate different areas for rural development, sustainable production and environmental protection.[69] To give additional substance to the Pygmy peoples' claim, in August 2002, a Forest Code was adopted in the Democratic Republic of Congo.[70]

Hence, it seems that the Bank should have considered and reviewed very seriously the Pygmy people's term 'the fallacious principles of the Forest Code',[71] as well as ensured at least full consultation with the indigenous peoples. Neither apparently was done, and the Forest Code itself, according to the request, is based on the Forest Law of Cameroon (1994), and, like that document, it ignores both the traditional rights of the indigenous groups in the area and 'the boundaries of their traditional territories'.[72]

The Bank's own 'Preparation of a Forest Zoning Plan, Draft Terms of Reference', states:

Consult a wide range of stakeholders: villages, territorial and district capitals, economic agents, etc. with a view to designing, and assessing the feasibility of various zoning scenarios. Particular attention will be paid to consultations with Pygmy groups by taking into account the distinctive characteristics of their nomadic or semi-nomadic lifestyle.

The problems in this situation are akin to those arising in Cambodia: no consultation and little understanding of, or even interest in, the interests and the traditional rights of indigenous peoples, and a project originally intended to help foster sustainability, later resulting in unwanted support for logging concessions instead.

The result of the lack of supervision and control on the part of the Bank is the violation of the rights of the Pygmy peoples noted above. The ensuing damage would lead, in their estimation, to:

1 the destruction and/or loss of their natural living environment;
2 the elimination of their means of subsistence;
3 an imposed, even forced, change to their lifestyles; and
4 serious social conflicts.

The plight of the Pygmy groups, although not fully investigated and researched at this time, echoes the plight of indigenous peoples all over the world; to destroy their habitat for various industrial activities is a crime against humanity (or should so be defined). The lack of clear intent to eliminate should not excuse or diminish the guilt and culpability of perpetrators and complicit governments.

Perhaps the Bank needs to tighten up both its follow-up procedures and the conceptual and regulatory framework within which it operates. Witness the undefined concept of 'consultation', or 'broad support', or the lack of the simple requirement of 'consent'. It is, however, to the Bank's credit that a majority of the requests for redress brought to it are investigated, and that some of the most egregious injustices are redressed. If a somewhat inappropriate comparison is allowed, the Bank appears to do better than the US courts in Alien Torts Claims Act (ATCA) jurisprudence in many cases.

Nevertheless, the effects of deforestation not only on local indigenous groups, but also on coastal peoples everywhere, or on Arctic peoples though global warming, are never considered, despite the widespread availability of scientific information, ecological and biological in particular. For extractive industries, the same 'wilful blindness' is apparent about the expected health results, so that the consequences are ignored for the most part by both civil society and governing bureaucracies.

CONCLUSIONS

This chapter has reached across Europe, North and South America, Africa, New Zealand and Australia, to touch upon some representative cases that deal with native title, self-determination and justice. In all cases, the import of the area's ecological integrity is central. In addition, I considered the influence on subsequent jurisprudence and laws of the classic *locus* of international environmental law, the *Trail Smelter Arbitration*. Its ongoing influence on international environmental instruments cannot be denied, but, it must be acknowledged, its major flaws have not been corrected in the 60-plus years since its emergence.

We also considered some of the other classic cases normally cited in court decisions dealing with environmental damage. The *Corfu Channel* case, for instance, is also too general to offer specific guidance. In contrast, the well-known dissenting opinion of Judge Weeramantry, in the *Gabcikovo-Nagymaros Project*, offers much greater hope for the future instead.

Nevertheless, any hope is dashed when one considers the uneven power that, for the most part, stands behind both corporate individuals and governments, that is, the power of and the support for the economic motive, a power that can never be matched by the resources of aboriginal groups. The main sources of this support come from the World Bank Group and the IMF, especially for the largest (and most hazardous) projects.

Hence, given the difficulty in ascribing full criminal responsibility to non-human legal entities, I briefly described Peter French's CID structure theory, and the application of that theory to our problem, in order to show clearly how 'intent' can and should be ascribed to a legal entity. In fact, I argued that their 'intent' is particularly clear and strong, as it is not open to the mitigating presence of emotions, alcohol abuse or any other human weakness.

It will be particularly important to keep in mind the significance of 'intent' as we continue to argue for the presence of genocide in the cases discussed in Chapter 5, as well as in Chapter 7's analysis of genocide itself.

NOTES

1   *The Mayagna (Sumo) Awas Tingni Community Case* – Series C, No.79 [2001] 1A CHR 9 (31 August 2001).
2   www.worldii.org/int/cases/IACHR/2001/9.html, p. 16.
3   Constitución Politica de la Republica de Nicaragua, Managua, 9 January 1987.
4   ibid., 54.
5   *Ivan Kitok v. Sweden*, Communication No. 197/1985, CCPR/C/33/D/197/1985 (1988).
6   Communication No. 197/1985, submitted under the Optional Protocol of the International Covenant on Civil and political Rights, Article 5, Para. 4, no. 2.
7   ibid., para. 4.3.
8   Citing the *ratio decideni* of *Lovelace v. Canada*, No. 24/1977.
9   Abopoz VIIX:108.
10 *Mabo v. Queensland*, 83 ALR High Court of Australia, (1992) 175 CL.
11 *Mabo and Another v. State of Queensland and Another*, 83 ALR 14, Breenan J.
12 ibid.
13 ibid.
14 ibid.
15 ibid.
16 W*ik Peoples v. Queensland* (1996) 187 CLR 1.
17 See also *Native Title Act*, 1993, 223; later, however, amended as *Native Title Amended Act*, 1998, 2B.
18 *Western Australia v. Ward* (2002) 213 CLR 1.
19 *Yorta Yorta Aboriginal Community v. Victoria* (1998) 1606 FLR (Austl.).
20 *Western Australia v. Ward* (2002) 194 ALR 538; Manus, 2006.
21 ibid.
22 *Yorta Yorta*, 214 CLR 444; see also Manus, 2006.
23 *Yorta Yorta*, 214 CLR 435.

24   *Aboriginal Community v. Victoria* (2002) 194 ALR 538.
25   The Declaration of Independence of New Zealand, 28 October 1835, Article 1.
26   The Maori Language Act of 1987.
27   *Trail Smelter Arbitration*, 35 *American Journal of International Law*, 6 84 (1941 at 716).
28   Report of the UN Conference on the Human Environment, UN Doc. A/CONF.48/14/Rev.1
     at 3 (1973), adopted 16 June 1972.
29   *Corfu Channel* (U.K. v. Albania) 1949 ICJ 4 (April 1949).
30   World Bank (1991).
31   World Bank Group, 'Implementation of Operational Directive 4.20 on Indigenous Peoples:
     An independent desk review', 10 January 2003, OED Report No. 25332.
32   United Nations, Report of the World Summit on Sustainable Development, 26 August – 4
     September 2002 at 10, Article 25, UN Doc. A/CONF.199/20/Corr.1, at 10, Art. 25.
33   See for instance, Aboriginal Lands Rights (Northern Territory) Act, 1976 B42(6) 77A
     (Austl.); Philippines Indigenous Peoples Rights Act, 1997, B3(g), 59.
34   Indigenous Peoples Statement at the 19th Session of the United Nations Working Groups on
     Indigenous Populations, 29 July 2001; at www.forestpeoples.gn.apc.org/briefings.html
35   Comments on the World Bank Management Response to the Final Report of the Extractive
     Industries at www.eireview.info/doc/P%20ManRes-short.sig.doc.; see MacKay, 2005.
36   *Sipakapa No Se Vende*, Video Documentary Caracol Production, Guatemala, 2005, at www.
     sipakapanosevende.org
37   See for instance the ECA Watch, Jakarta Declaration for Reform of Official Export Credit
     and Investment Insurance Agencies, at www.eca-watch.org/goals/jakartadec.html; the
     guidelines address questions of environmental reviews to 'benchmark projects ... against
     the safeguard policies published by the World Bank Group' especially when they involve
     involuntary resettlement or 'indigenous peoples and cultural property', Sarfaty (2005).
38   See also Press Release, Friends of the Earth et al, 'Memorandum on Canisea Project
     Violations of World Bank Safeguard Policies' (17 October 2002) at www.bicusa.org/bicusa/
     issues/misc_resources/338.php
39   See also Koh (1997).
40   Operations Policy and Country Services, World Bank, Review of World Bank Conditionality:
     Issues Note 4 (2005).
41   See also World Bank (1992).
42   Article of Agreements of the International Bank for Reconstruction and Development, Art.
     IV, 10, 60 Stat. 15 1449, 2 UNTS at 158.
43   OP 4.10 para. 4.
44   OP 4.10, para. 16.
45   The three instances involved were: (a) allegations of slavery on Myanmar's Yadana gas pipeline
     led the World Bank Group to drop the Thai component the day before board presentation;
     (b) Bank President Wolfensohn personally interceded against gross mistreatment of critics
     of the Chad–Cameroon oil pipeline, managing to spring the leader of the opposition,
     Ngarledjy Yorongar, out of a torture chamber and to exile in Paris in May 2001; (c) President
     Wolfensohn called Chinese Premier Zhu Rongji to free two researchers imprisoned while
     investigating the Group's fiercest controversy, the Western Region Project. This was a major
     improvement in the Bank's position on slavery as a non-economic, sovereignty or political
     issue, therefore off limits to World Bank Group discussion.
46   OP 4.10, July 2005, 'Indigenous Peoples'; I am grateful to Serge Selwan of the World Bank
     for the information provided on inspection panels used in this section. Additional critique
     and interpretation is entirely my own.
47   Credit No. 3365-KH and Trust Fund 26419 – JPN; Report No. 35556, 30 March 2006.
48   ibid.

49 Request, no. 12, p. 3; in their Response, at no. 16, the management argued that the 'Bank made it's Phnom Penh office available for disclosing the forest management plans', an obviously poor choice as 'forest peoples' would be highly unlikely to travel to town to receive explanations.
50 ibid.
51 ibid.
52 ibid.
53 ibid.
54 ibid.
55 ibid.
56 ibid.
57 ibid.
58 ibid.; note also that in 1996 the Cambodia Forest Policy Assessment recognized that the concessions had been operated in an unsustainable manner, and recommended a 'precautionary approach to logging'.
59 ibid.
60 Global Witness, 'Taking a Cut. Institutionalizing Corruption and Illegal Logging in Cambodia's Aural Wildlife Sanctuary', London, 2004, 'Project', para. 145, p. 42.
61 OP 4.36, 1 (d): 'The Bank does not finance commercial logging operations or the purchase of logging equipment for use in primary tropical moist forests'.
62 ibid.
63 ibid.
64 ibid.
65 ibid.
66 ibid. IV Rights and interests likely to be affected and possible damage.
67 Listed as 37. Democratic Republic in Congo: Transitional Support of Economic Recovery Credit Operation (TSERO) and Emergency Economic and Social Ramification Support Project (EESRSP), November 19, 2005.
68 'Request', p. 2.
69 ibid.; see also World Bank, EESRSP, Technical Annex, Report No. T7601-ZR, p. 29.
70 President of Democratic Republic of Congo, Law No. 011, /2002 on the Forest Code, www.radiookapi.net
71 ibid.
72 ibid.

CHAPTER 5

The United States and Indigenous Peoples: Some Recent ATCA Jurisprudence

THE US AND INDIGENOUS PEOPLES: AN INTRODUCTION

Wounded Knee, the Trail of Tears, the Siege of Cusco, these words, vessels of meaning, capture only a fragment of the history of suffering, actual and cultural genocide, conquest penetration, and marginalization endured by indigenous peoples around the world. (Wiessner, 1999)

It is perhaps unrealistic to expect a nation that started with the brutal conquest of indigenous peoples to totally reverse its policies and practices even today, long after the 'legacy of conquest'. In contrast, the government of the US extols the Declaration of Independence, so that self-determination and beliefs in the natural rights of peoples to secede are viewed as basic. The federal government eventually established a 'trusteeship' over Indian lands.[1]

The Indian Nations' relation to the US resembles that of a ward to his guardian, thus Indian tribes were considered 'domestic dependent nations'. This position made it relatively easy to conclude treaties with the Indian as 'subjects of international law', until 1891, when the US Congress discontinued the practice. Nevertheless several instruments were enacted to extend the rights of 'Indian self-determination', including the *Indian Child Welfare Act* of 1978;[2] *The Indian Tribal Government Tax Status Act*;[3] *The Indian Self-Determination and Education Act* of 1975;[4] *The Indian Tribal Justice Act* of 1993,[5] and others.

US President Bill Clinton not only appointed a native leader, the Honorable Ada Deer, as Head of the Bureau of Indian Affairs, but he explicitly pledged to respect tribal sovereignty (Wiessner, 1999) in a statement to Indian leaders present at the White House:

This then is our first principle: respecting your values, your religions, your identity, and your sovereignty. This brings us to the second principle that should guide our relationship with the tribes and become partners with the tribal nations. I don't want there to be any mistake about our commitment to a stronger partnership between our people. Therefore, in a moment, I will also sign an historic Government directive that requires every executive department and agency of Government to take two simple steps: first, to remove all barriers that prevent them from working directly with tribal governments, and, second, to make certain that if they take action affecting tribal trust resources, they consult with tribal governments prior to that decision.[6]

However, the US Supreme Court judgements have not always dealt fairly with indigenous and tribal peoples, especially in recent times.[7] Against this somewhat sketchy background we need to consider the numerous cases tried by US tribunals under ATCA that involve serious complaints advanced by indigenous peoples against US corporations. It is important to note that US courts are also connected to inter-American laws, regional laws and international laws. Equally important, although ATCA cases involved torts and liability rather than principles of human rights or crimes against humanity, nevertheless because of the nature of the complaints brought to these tribunals, they are based precisely on issues that should mandate *erga omnes* obligations.

SOME RECENT CASES TRIED UNDER ATCA IN VARIOUS US JURISDICTIONS

All these cases involve 'egregious human rights violations', perpetrated by multinational corporations based in the US against local peoples and their communities, even when indigenous status is not present. An example is *Doe v. Unocal Corp.*[8]

The law and corporate responsibility: *Doe v. Unocal Corp.*

The case dates back to 1992, when Unocal Corporation acquired a 28 per cent interest in a gas pipeline project in Myanmar (Burma) (Harrington, 2002). One of the main questions in the case is whether the project actually hired the Myanmar military to facilitate their operations, as some of Unocal's own employees suggested. The plaintiffs, villagers from the area where the project was taking place, alleged that they had been forced 'to serve as laborers on the project', with threats of violence, and that, in order to protect the project's security, the military:

> *subjected them to acts of murder, rape and torture. One plaintiff testified that, after her husband was shot for attempting to escape the forced labor program, she and her baby were thrown into a fire resulting in injuries to the woman and death of her baby.*
> (Harrington, 2002)

Two groups of villagers brought action for human rights violations against Unocal and the project (under the ACTA).[9] The treatment to which the villagers had been subjected was termed by the Ninth Circuit, the 'modern variant of slavery' (see Chapter 3), and Unocal's role, a form of aiding and abetting, to say the least. Unocal's earlier response that the plaintiffs were barred from bringing this action by the 'act of state doctrine', was not accepted by the Ninth Circuit (Harrington, 2002).

Although this case is not directly related to environmental harms, it is in many ways similar to the *Saro-Wiwa* case, in that the nefarious alliance between corporate crime and egregious human rights violations are clearly present, and so is the corporate support for the role of the military to ensure citizens' compliance through rape, murder, torture and terror. Scholarly writings on this case are divided on whether the concept of slavery should have been introduced by the Ninth Circuit, as forced labour is also proscribed in both national and international law. Tawny Aine Bridgeford (2003) argues that the Ninth Circuit was practising judicial activism in this case. Andrew Ridenour (2001) instead argues that the use of slavery is entirely apt in this case.

Ridenour's concern is that municipal law should not be considered to determine when acts are brought before the courts under ATCA, as section 1350 of the Judiciary Act of 1789 (the Alien Torts Claims Act) permits federal district courts to hear claims by aliens for torts committed 'in violation of the law of nations'. When we consider the import of ATCA's history, it is evident that an act intended to deal with matters of liability must deal exclusively with criminal matters instead: 'Crimes such as genocide, slavery, summary executions, and torture [which] have been universally held by courts as violations of contemporary *jus cogens* and thus subject to liability under ATCA' (Ridenour, 2001).The meaning of *jus cogens* was addressed in passing in Chapter 1 and is discussed in detail in Chapter 7. In essence, violations so defined, according to *Barcelona Traction*, must be of norms that are 'universal, specific and obligatory';[10] hence, they must be of a character *beyond* even the general concerns of customary international law. For the most part, international treaties are enacted for the interests of their signatories (Bridgeford, 2003), and derogation from their mandates does not entail penalties other than economic or procedural, although customary law evolves over time 'to include offenses that the international community universally prohibits' (Bridgeford, 2003).

Ridenour (2001) remarks on the odd coupling of criminal and tort law in ATCA: 'While these violations are criminal in nature, international law allow states to fashion remedies under universal jurisdiction, which the United States has done in a civil form through ATCA.' Ridenour's important article was written in 2001, and in 2002 the International Criminal Court of Rome came into force. Eventually, perhaps, ruling under ATCA will form the basis for additional criminal prosecutions best suited to these crimes of universal jurisdiction that, like genocide, piracy, the slave trade and war crimes, extend beyond the scope of state action.

The main point for our argument is that, although 'no court had found a corporation liable for a violation of *jus cogens* under ATCA' (Ridenour, 2001) until this case, a test for conspiracy (under US 1983) is that 'both public and private actors share a common, unconstitutional goal' and hence fit the Principles of Nuremberg as well (see Chapter 1) (Ramasastry, 2002). This is the incalculable importance of this case: not only to show a clear example of corporate liability, but also to establish the foundations for a possible eventual criminal prosecution, based on *jus cogens*, for the violations of which corporations were found liable.

Harrington (2002) notes that not only were human rights directly violated in Myanmar, but that, in addition, 'Myanmar's rich pool of diverse natural resource is currently being exploited for the benefit of the military'. He adds that 'heightened standards could translate into a victory for the environment', at least if US corporations could be forced 'to adhere to US standards', even when operating abroad. Given that US standards on the environment, while better than those of most military regimes, whether in Nigeria or Myanmar, are hardly a guarantee of a 'victory for the environment', it seems to me that the threat of criminality (albeit a remote one, as the US is not a signatory of the International Criminal Court), might better serve to indicate to corporations of all countries the full extent of their responsibility.

Extractive industries and ATCA cases: Environmental and health harms

> *Citizens of Peru and Ecuador brought class action suits alleging that defendant oil company polluted rain forests and rivers in their countries, causing environmental damage and personal injury.*[11]

This case is typical of this kind of jurisprudence and it has a long history that led to an unsuccessful appeal.[12] Texaco's oil operation in Ecuador was initiated in 1964, when Texaco Petroleum Company (TexPet) began oil explorations and drilling in the Oriente region of eastern Ecuador.[13] A petroleum concession was initiated in 1965 for a 'consortium' whereby TexPet was part owner with Gulf Oil Corporation and, in 1974, the Republic of Ecuador (PetroEcuador) joined in with a 25 per cent ownership. Eventually Gulf Oil relinquished its shares to TexPet and the latter operated a trans-Ecuadorian oil pipeline and continued to operate the consortium's drilling activities until 1992. At that time PetroEcuador took over that aspect of the operation and finally, in 1999, TexPet left the consortium entirely in PetroEcuador's hands.[14]

The plaintiffs brought a suit against Texaco in 1993, as Texaco's activities had 'polluted the rain forests and rivers' in both Ecuador and Peru, and those polluting and harmful activities were 'designed, controlled, conceived and directed ... through its operation in the United States'.[15] The indigenous peoples sought to recover damages, citing 'negligence, public and private nuisance, strict liability, medical monitoring, trespass, civil conspiracy and violations of the Alien Tort Claims Act, 28 USC § 1350'.[16]

These requests were appropriate redress for contaminated water and environment, for the restoration of hunting and fishing grounds, for both medical and environmental monitoring funds, and the establishment of standards for future Texaco operations as well as 'an injunction restraining Texaco from entering into activities that risk environmental or human injuries',[17] all appeared reasonable and appropriate.

These details are vital to a full understanding of the specifics of the case as well as an appreciation of these proceedings in general. Note the *substantive* claims based on indisputable scientific evidence, some of which has been presented briefly in earlier chapters, and the extensive research that supports this sort of claim (in relation to extractive industries' operations) can be found in the work of the WHO and in that of many epidemiologists, public health and cancer specialists, among others (see Epstein, 1978; Soskolne and Bertollini, 1999; Westra, 2006; WHO, 2002; Licari et al, 2005).

But the US court's responses are, once again, typical of the courts' analyses in this sort of claim: they do not answer any of the claims made with counterclaims, and they do not even attempt to dispute the factual issues as set out by the plaintiffs. But the logic of their responses is flawed. *Forum non conveniens*, for instance, is based on the 'fact' that too many witnesses should be brought in to testify, speaking various languages and dialects. But the injuries and diseases the plaintiffs name are well-known consequences of chemical and toxic exposure, not some obscure symptom that needs to be personally verified by someone who 'saw' the development of the disease, an almost impossible feat for illnesses such as cancers. Not only are certain diseases well documented as following upon certain exposures, but their treatment is equally well known, and no member of an indigenous community can be better informed about both illness and treatment than scientists and practitioners at local universities and hospitals, or the WHO itself. In fact, the corporation could not say that *their* operation did not and could not result in the harmful consequences the claimants outlined. When the extractive operations are pursued in the usual way, one can and should expect the resulting harm, both ecological and biological.

The certainty of this expectation renders the resulting injuries more than unexpected 'collateral' harm; it adds the knowledge of the relation between the cause (extractive operations) and the harm itself. I have argued that it is this aspect of 'eco-crime' that ensures the presence of a significant mental element, and hence facilitates or should facilitate the transition from environmental regulatory breaches to 'eco-crime' (Westra, 2004a). When this knowledge is ignored in regard to indigenous peoples and groups, because it is clearly more than an unexpected externality, the ensuing effects of extractive practices are very close to genocide or attacks against the human person, and I return to this topic in Chapter 7.

This aspect of ATCA jurisprudence, together with the details of the responses offered by Texaco, and the court's assessment of those responses, sheds a different and much clearer light on the proceedings. These were some of the major issues discussed, instead of the material/factual complaints themselves:

1 Texaco's motion to dismiss on grounds of *forum non conveniens*, accepted by Judge Rakoff.
2 Texaco's motion to dismiss because of 'international comity'.
3 Texaco's motion to dismiss because the Republic of Ecuador was not joined and neither was PetroEcuador; Judge Rakoff believed both would be 'indispensable partners' in order for the court to assess the relief sought (and because the Foreign Sovereign Immunities Act, 28 USC & 1603(b) and 1604, 'prevented the assertion of Jurisdiction on either').
4 Class disputes and common damages would require 'large amounts of testimony with interpreters, perhaps often in local dialects, (which) would make effective adjudication in New York problematic at best' (Westra, 2004a).
5 These cases have 'everything to do with Ecuador and nothing to do with the United States' (Westra, 2004a).
6 'Environmental torts are unlikely to be found to violate the law of nations' (Westra, 2004a).
7 The United States has no special public interest in hosting an international law action against a US entity that can be adequately pursued in the place where the violations occurred' (Westra, 2004a).

Hence, the reasons for the suit were not even addressed, only the reasons why a US court should not be involved. Nor are such arguments separate and thus sufficient to rebut the harms listed by the plaintiffs. First, point six is factually incorrect, and that error is in fact the main reason for this work, and much of my previous work and that of the scientists I cite (Westra, 2004a; 2006): 'environmental torts' are not simply that. For the most part, 'environmental torts' entail gross breaches of human rights to life, to health, to normal function, as well as to 'family life'. These rights and their violations are routinely addressed by international courts and the European Court of Human Rights, hence they do indeed 'violate the law of nations'.[18] Hence, to simply provide a misdescription of the situation, without providing adequate support for the validity of that interpretation is insufficient to prove one of the major claims of this US court.

Another counter-example to the approach taken by the US court on point four might be the international jurisprudence regarding nuclear tests.[19] In that case, the courts decided on the issue *without* requiring individual witnesses, either from the area in question or from any other area that might have been affected by nuclear weapons (say Hiroshima or Nagasaki survivors), to demonstrate the harm that would result from exposure to radioactivity. The effects of nuclear weapons were judged to be given, that is universally accepted harms would ensue, hence the court judged there was an *erga omnes* obligation to desist from those tests because of the possibility of inflicting harm on both New Zealand and Australian citizens.

While the harms that result from exposure to the practices of extractive and mining industries are perhaps less catastrophic and immediate that those produced by a mushroom cloud, the long-term effects of exposure to carcinogens and other toxic substance that are part of those practices parallel those resulting from radiation exposure and today are equally well researched. That said, it is worth repeating, neither the court nor Texaco itself even attempted to refute the plaintiffs' claims, and as we noted, the procedural answers that were used instead are based on mistaken facts and misunderstandings.

Similarly, neither 'comity' (point two) nor the fact that the relief sought should have been shared by Ecuador (point three), are really applicable, when the gravity of the harms perpetrated are fully understood. Bilateral obligations are superseded by *erga omnes* obligations instead. Nor are the claims acceptable that these cases 'have everything to do with Ecuador' (point five) and have no 'public interest' (point seven) for the US. The 'collateralism' inherent in business-as-usual practices, I have argued, is as harmful to human rights as any other attack on human life, including the better-known 'disasters', such as Bhopal and Seveso. In all these cases, the countries of origin of the hazardous operation did not succeed in avoiding their responsibility by saying that the citizens of India or Italy should bear the burden of redressing the harms that had occurred (Westra, 2006).

In sum, even the appeal to procedural matters in order to avoid altogether the consideration of real reasons advanced in the plaintiffs' claims should fail, as the factual material (hence scientifically provable) elements of the crimes committed by Texaco are implicitly denied by the court's assessment of the case. Nevertheless, the *forum non conveniens* doctrine is the first step to overcome, that is the first question asked on 'whether a court having jurisdiction may decline to exercise it' (Scott, 2001a). The question is closely tied to whether local remedies have been exhausted, but it is often employed as a way of escaping the *responsibility* to provide a forum against multinational corporations (MNCs):

> *One important reason* forum non conveniens *doctrine is so susceptible to being employed to remove human-rights related suits against MNCs from Northern courts is the ease with which judges in home states of MNCs persist in thinking in highly parochial terms about whether the home state has an interest in being the venue for global justice against its national MNCs* (Baxi, 2001).

Forced relocation, war crimes and genocide: *Bancoult v. McNamara*

> *The plaintiffs in this case are persons indigenous to Chagos their survivors or direct descendants... they bring this action against the United States and various current and former officials of State and the Department of Defence ('the individual defendants'), for forced relocation, torture, racial discrimination, cruel, inhuman and degrading treatment, genocide, intentional infliction of emotional distress, negligence and trespass.[20]*

Although the Chagos Archipelago comprises 52 islands administered by the British government, it is leased to the US, and the US is responsible for the islands under the British Indian Ocean Territory (BIOT) Agreement. In the late 1960s and early 1970s, the whole Chagos population was moved to Mauritius and the Seychelles, to allow a US military facility to settle in their space. The original inhabitants were not allowed to return, and were offered no compensation to help ease their transition into a new environment and the loss of their homes.

Those who had not left were forced on 'overcrowded ships for Peros Banhos and Salonen, from whence they eventually were taken to Mauritius and Seychelles'.[21] The US Congress went ahead with the construction of a military basis on Diego Garcia island, despite hearings where multiple human rights violations were detailed, from the lack of relocation assistance, to harsh removal conditions that caused injuries to the survivors, including miscarriages, and eventual living conditions that include poverty, unemployment and other deprivations.[22]

Before the judgement proper could be decided, the 'individual defendants' all claimed that they had been obeying superior orders, based on 'the statutory immunity granted to the Federal Officers under the Federal Employee Liability Reform and Tort Compensation Act'.[23] Yet the gravity of the effects of the forced removal bring to mind the language of the Nuremberg Principles, hence the international law's denial of such claims of immunity. In Canada, organization crime is addressed in Bill C-45, now part of the Canadian Criminal Code as an amendment to section 22.1. The main changes effected to the Criminal Code are as follows:

> *S 1.(1) extends the definition of 'every one', 'person' and 'owner' to include 'an organization'. In turn, 'organization' means,*
> *(2) (a) a public body, body corporate, society, company, firm, partnership, trade union or municipality, or*
> *   (b) an association of persons that*
> *   i)   is created for a common purpose,*
> *   ii)   has an operational structure, and*
> *   iii) holds itself out to the public as an association of persons...*

Here, and in the amendments to section 22.1, Bill C-45 ensures that a wide array of actors within an organization may be viewed as responsible for an offence, 'whether by act or omission'. It also ensures that if the prosecution is required 'to prove fault, other than negligence' (section 22.2), then senior officers or representatives may manifest the requisite 'mental state' also by '(c) knowing that a representative of the organization is or is about to be a party to the offence, or does not take all reasonable measures to stop them from being a party to the offence'. The bill also adds a section (217.1) to define 'the legal duty to take reasonable steps to prevent bodily harm', on the part of anyone who is in the position to direct and order how work is to be done.

In addition, several sections deal with making or causing to be made false statements with respect to the financial conditions of the organization (section 362.1(c)), or in general, committing fraud or causing it to be committed. For the sake of the present purposes, I will limit my observation and my discussion to the aspects of Bill C-45 that are directly relevant to this work, thus to eco-crime rather than white collar crime in general.

The expanded definition of organizations is of cardinal importance in cases where the authority, other responsible senior party, or those directed by the senior individuals 'depart markedly from the standard of care' (5.22.1) that could reasonably be expected, and could be found to be provincial or federal officials. There is no case law yet to determine whether this interpretation might eventually be part of the positive developments arising out of Bill C-45, and of course 'depart markedly' from the standard of care does not define the 'standard of care' itself or what, precisely, a 'marked' departure from a non-specified form of behaviour might be. In fact it may be the case that the standard of 'due diligence' (also largely undefined), which has been the expected test, is not different from the standard included or implied by the changed wording of Bill C-45.

Another important point worthy of attention is that after section 718.2, the act now provides section 718.21 on 'organizations' and the 'factors regarding the offence' that must be taken into consideration in sentencing. Some of the most interesting of these factors, in relation to our main concern, are:

> (a) any advantage realized by the organization as a result of the offence;
> (b) the degree of planning involved in carrying out the offence, and the duration and complexity of the offence;...
> (g) whether the organization was or any of its representatives were convicted of a similar offence or sanctioned by a regulatory body for similar conduct;...
> (j) any measures that the organization has taken to reduce the likelihood of it committing a subsequent offence.

Briefly, the first factor cited shows that economic advantage renders the offence graver; the second parallels the premeditation aspect as it renders a homicide committed by an individual, a murder instead; planning may also include 'conspiring', something that has become a crime in itself according to the Nuremberg Charter. Previous crimes are now admissible at sentencing; (g) recognizes that an organization does not require the same constitutional (charter) protections as does the individual offender, at least implicitly. The commitment not to repeat the crime (j) also allows a degree of official intervention that is not possible with individual persons.

Even if the individual defendants are eliminated from the action (justly or unjustly), that leaves the US as the sole defendant. However, all those who knowingly perpetrated the actions involving the Chagos indigenous population violated the tenets of international law:

Pursuant to the Alien Tort Claims Act, 28 USC & 1350 ('ATCA'), the district courts shall have original jurisdiction of any civil action by an alien for a tort only committed in violation of the law of nations or Treaty of the United States.[24]

Other issues used to rebut the plaintiffs' claims were the fact that 'they had failed to exhaust their administrative remedies', despite the fact that they were not allowed to return to their home base, now a US military basis (in Chagos), nor to the other islands, where the UK itself was not likely to offer an impartial forum after entering into an agreement with the US that led to the very actions in question.

Another issue was 'the judicial expertise' of the court, as it was required to pass judgement on US policy:

> *Neither our federal law nor customary international law provide standards by which the court can measure and balance the foreign policy considerations at play in this case such as the containment of the Soviet Union in the Indian Ocean thirty years ago, and today the support of military operation in the Middle East. The court concludes that it is ill-equipped to review the conduct of the military operation challenged in this case, because they implicate foreign policy and national security concerns.*[25]

Essentially, if the US government's political branches made a decision 30 years earlier, the court was not prepared to second guess that decision today.[26] Of course, even if the court was not prepared to question either the decision of the US government at the time those decisions were made, or the reasons for those decisions, the way those decisions were carried out appears to remain untouched by this argument. Even if a country's political or other decision cannot be judged under ATCA, 'Article 2(3) of the Torture Convention explicitly states that "An order from a superior official or public authority may not be invoked as a justification for torture"' (Steiner and Alston, 2000). Torture is forbidden by *jus cogens* norms, and so is genocide, so that appealing to this article appears to be appropriate, and I address this question below.

This point was also made clearly in the *Filartiga v. Pena Irala* case.[27] In that case, the US Supreme Court recognized that the law of nations:

> *... may be ascertained by consulting the work of jurists writing professedly on public law; or by the general usage and practice of nations, or by the judicial decisions recognizing and enforcing the law.*[28]

Nevertheless, it must be acknowledged:

> *Unlike the criminal remedy, there is no treaty that clearly obliges or even authorises courts to take jurisdiction over civil actions respecting torture committed abroad with the exception of the US, there is no domestic legislation in any other country that expressly grants courts jurisdiction with respect to these matters.* (Terry, 2001)

Because ATCA permits individual citizens to sue for torture and other such injuries, without the far more complicated requirements of initiating a criminal action for the International Court of Justice or International Criminal Court, this avenue appears to remain the preferred one of claimants in various venues:

> *While it is premised on the principle that victims of torture much be compensated, its true role in many cases is admittedly symbolic: the third country tort remedy provides recognition for, and emotional vindication of, the victims of torture and places moral and political pressure on rights abusing governments.* (Terry, 2001)

Beanal v. Freeport-McMoran Inc. and Freeport-McMoran Copper and Gold Inc.: Torture and cultural genocide

> *Beanal's first amended complaint alleges that Freeport has committed environmental torts, human rights abuses, and cultural genocide.* (para.4)[29]

This case sues corporate bodies, but from the results obtained since 1997 and even earlier, one wonders about the effect such judgements have on the actions of the corporate bodies involved. It seems apparent that the 'symbolic' aspect of the court's decisions is somewhat lost, and the reduction of *jus cogens* acts to torts implying liability that may be compensated (at worst) hence resulting in costs that may well be internalized, are not having an appreciable effect on corporate behaviour. Translating crimes into acts that are open to monetary compensation (and no further effect on chief executive officers and firm's other officers) reduces what should be *erga omnes* obligations not to do harm to acts that courts find apparently less serious than insider trading or other stock/accounting-related acts (as is apparent from the recent Enron judgement).

Tom Beanal is a leader of the Amungme Tribal Council of Lambarga Adat Suku Amungme (LEMASA). As such, he filed a complaint against Freeport-McMoran Inc. and Freeport-McMoran Copper and Gold Inc. ('Freeport'). He describes the human rights abuses and harmful environmental practices of Freeport as they affected himself as well as others in his group. The practices included: 'torture, detention, surveillance', the 'deliberate, contrived and planned demise' of the Amungme culture, due to various human rights and environmental violations including 'contamination of the natural waterways, as well as surface and ground water sources, deforestation, destruction and alteration of physical surroundings'.[30]

The details describe repeated acts of torture, including kicking with military boots, beating with fists and rifle butts, starvation, shackling and keeping in uncomfortable positions. Other examples describe victims 'forced to stand in Freeport containers which reeked of human faeces', and 'indigenous peoples ... detained with their eyes taped shut ... subject to repeated beatings by Freeport security personnel'.[31] These acts are not simply proscribed by specific treaties, they are committed in violation of the 'law of nations'. In fact the Alien Tort Statute § 1350 states that 'the alleged violation must be definable, obligatory (rather than hortatory) and universally condemned'.[32] Hence the issue is whether the plaintiffs can assert that Freeport has failed to meet its *erga omnes* obligation. In contrast, Freeport's response is that 'state action is required to violate international law'; as state action is not involved, Freeport adds, it is not possible to claim that the law of nations has been violated.[33]

Nevertheless, genocide, one of the categories alleged by the plaintiff, violates international law, whether undertaken by a state or non-state actor (Restatement § 404 also asserts that 'universal jurisdiction exists over specified offenses, as a matter of customary law'). This is a central claim in most cases involving indigenous peoples and determines the extent to which the concept of genocide is applicable.

Because of the interdependence between indigenous or tribal peoples including the Amungme tribes and their lands, forced relocation, for instance, or any corporate operation that displaces an indigenous group or 'destroys natural habitats and causes dislocation of the populations', may be said to result in 'the planned demise of a culture',[34] and can be described as 'eco-terrorism'.

I return to consider the full import of genocide in Chapter 7. But it is important to note the explicit appeal to one of the two presently recognized and accepted approaches to the protection of indigenous communities, that is, the protection of 'cultural integrity'. The main issue is the relation between the protection of indigenous groups like the Amungme and their lands. Open pit mining involves the use of harsh chemicals to process the metals once these have been extracted, and the damage to environmental and human health is truly incalculable and often irreversible.

An example from the Australian courts reinforces this point. In the *Ok Tedi* case[35] BHP eventually settled the considerable claim (Aus$400 million) and the motion to dismiss because the doctrine of *forum non conveniens* was not followed by BHP.[36] Such cases demonstrate some progress toward holding corporate bodies accountable for human rights abuses grounded in environmental harms. In the case we are considering in this section, a similar trend emerges as well:

> *The fact that Freeport is itself not a 'state' does not preclude its liability for violations under the law of nations, since state actors, not merely the state itself, can be held liable for such violations.*[37]

Although Beanal could not ultimately prove the 'symbiotic relationship' between Freeport's employees and its security guards and the Indonesia military,[38] not only are governments expected to punish crimes within their borders, not aid and abet them, but there is a long history of extractive industries' practices in securing military or paramilitary support from the country where their activities take place. This happens in many areas including, as noted, South America and Nigeria, among others.

In this case, Beanal alleged that, 'Freeport maintains, i.e. feeds, transports, pays and equips, Indonesia military personnel on the premises'.[39] Finally, despite the copious and entailed claims of environmental damage from mismanagement of the tailings drainage, 'resulting in sulphide oxidation and leaching', and a long list of other environmental torts, the court could not discern an 'international tort' sufficient to permit redress under ATCA.[40]

The court only found three international environmental law principles: the polluter pays principle; the precautionary principle; and the proximity principle. And it added that 'none of the three rises to the level of an international tort'.[41] This assessment totally ignores the *Trail Smelter Arbitration*, which is perhaps the best known and foundational case of international environmental law, and the *erga omnes* obligations it supports.

The conclusion that Beanal has 'failed to allege an international environmental tort' while it affirms that 'corporate policies ... however destructive, do not constitute torts in violation of the law of nations'[42] is a clear example of the far-reaching results of ignoring the science related to the case, such as epidemiology, public health, medicine and toxicology, as well as ecology and biology. The proposed model of 'biological/ecological' protection was designed to correct this lacuna, which should have been addressed by the Judges Portal initiated by Justice Arthur Chalkalson of South Africa, after the Agenda 21+10 meeting, intended to prepare judges to understand the implications of the cases they are called to adjudicate (Westra, 2004a).

The Presbyterian Church of Sudan, Rev. John Gaduel, Nuer Community, Development Services and Others v. Talisman Energy Inc. (1): Extra-judicial killings, war crimes and genocide

> *Talisman, a large Canadian energy company, collaborated with Sudan in ethnically cleansing civilian populations surrounding oil concessions located in Southern Sudan in order to facilitate oil exploration and extraction activities.*[43]

This is a case where the gross human rights violations, from forced displacement to killings, can be described as genocide because these acts were all directed at the specific ethnic and religious groups in the south of Sudan (footnote no. 2 of the case addresses the meaning of 'ethnic cleansing' as a literal translation of a Serbo-Croatian term: it is a euphemism for genocide).

Historically Sudan was a 'collection of small independent kingdoms and principalities'.[44] After a period of Egyptian, then British rule, Sudan became independent in 1956. Nevertheless, the Arab-controlled northern part reinstituted *Sharia* law and even transferred some of the judges to the Christian south, where Christianity and indigenous religions were practised. In fact, that government, according to the plaintiffs, pursued:

> *... a war of genocide against the population in the southern part of the country (Amended Complaint at p. 14). This genocide which Plaintiffs also described as a* jihad *or holy war, is purportedly aimed at the forced Islamization of the south, and has resulted in approximately two million deaths and the displacement of four million people.*[45]

Against the background of this ongoing conflict and the accompanying human rights violations, first Chevron, then Arakis Energy Corporation (later 'Talisman') (a Canadian company), were accused of collaborating fully and deliberately with the government of Sudan in its genocidal activities:

> *In exchange for oil concessions, the government promised to clear the area around the oil fields of the local population. The oil companies agreed to invest in the infrastructure, such as transportation, roads and airfields and communication facilities, to support exploration, and the government would use the infrastructure to support its genocidal military campaign of ethnic cleansing against the local population.*[46]

The targeted inhabitants were the Dinka and the Nuer people, Christians or practitioners of traditional indigenous religions. The plaintiffs detail the various forms taken by this 'ethnic cleansing' or, as it was also put, 'to provide a *cordon sanitaire*' to facilitate the exploration and extraction of oil: murder of civilians (including women and children), destruction of villages and the enslavement of surviving civilians.[47] These details were provided by a number of affected parties, also by the Presbyterian Church of Sudan and some of its pastors.

Aside from the usual requests to dismiss the plaintiffs' motion, based on *forum non conveniens*, as was repeatedly argued in most of the ATCA cases we have considered, Talisman also alleged that the court would have no jurisdiction, as well as other grounds such as the 'act of state' doctrine. But the Alien Tort Claim Act was indeed expected to deal with all torts 'in violation of the law of nations', which is understood to be synonymous with international law. In fact, *Filartiga* served to catapult 'a largely overlooked statute in the limelight as a means of vindicating rights under international law'.[48] ATCA became the best-known vehicle to deal with *jus cogens* violations of *erga omnes* obligations.

Talisman insisted that: first, corporations are not legally capable of violations of international law, despite the wealth of precedents; and second, that the reach of international law was limited to the states and those acting under state law, despite the presence of the Genocide Convention, which states that 'Persons committing genocide or any of the other acts enumerated in Article 3 shall be punished whether they are constitutionally responsible rulers, public officials or private individuals' (Article 4). In addition, common articles of the Genocide Convention do not support Talisman's contention. There are several references to *Wiwa*,[49] because the two defendants in that case were private corporations. In light of the fact, *Wiwa* clearly extended the decision in *Kadic* to apply the ATCA to the acts of corporations that constitute *jus cogens* violations.[50] Corporations were sued under ATCA in *Jota*, *Wiwa*, *Tachiona v. Omugabe*,[51] and *United States v. FMC Corporation*,[52] extending criminal liability to a corporation for violating the Migratory Bird Treaty Act. As we saw in *Doe v. Unocal Corp*,[53] the US Ninth Circuit court recognized explicitly that a corporation could be sued under ATCA, and 'The court, citing *Kadic*, held that because the complaint alleged *jus cogens* violations (including rape, torture and summary execution), no state action was necessary and Unocal could be held liable'.

The plaintiffs' complaint in the case of Southern Sudan also involved similar *jus cogens* violations, so Talisman's claims to the effect that corporations could not be found to be acting against the law of nations cannot stand, according to both ATCA's principles and according to the precedents in law. Talisman also adduced (a) *forum non conveniens*, and (b) the 'political question', as obstacles to the ATCA trial. On (a) the court responded that neither Sudan nor Canada were better as alternative forums. The affidavit of Dr Abdel Rahman Ibrahim al Khalifa explains in detail why, according to the Sudanese judicial system, a fair trial in that country would be impossible, especially because of the reduced rights of various groups: 'these reduced rights include a total lack of legal personality for plaintiffs who practiced traditional African religions, and diminished testimonial competence for Christians'.[54]

Canada fares no better as a trial choice, according to the testimony of experts in both Alberta and Ontario. In Alberta, the court would '*prima facie* apply the *lex loci delicti*, or the law of the place where the activity occurred', and in this case, that would be *Sharia* law, thus defeating the purpose of seeking a different forum for the violations of human rights of the indigenous Christian groups.[55]

If the case were to be tried in Ontario, according to the affidavit of Christopher D. Bredt,[56] as for Mr Foran's affidavit, *jus cogens* violations of the law of nations are not even mentioned, and the focus remains on Canadian domestic rather than international law. The court remarked that 'Genocide may quantitatively be the same as a large number of murders, but it is qualitatively different, and this difference is recognized by the fact that the act enjoys special status under international law'.[57]

Finally, the court noted that 'Canada does not have a well placed class action procedure'.[58] Because of these reasons, the plaintiffs' choice of forum should be respected.

Talisman's request to dismiss because the action raised non-justiciable political questions was also found to be without merit. The questions raised were not political and internal to Sudan, rather the issue was whether Talisman violated international law. Thus, the court denied Talisman's motion to dismiss the plaintiff's Amended Complaint on 19 March 2003.

THE QUESTION OF CORPORATE RESPONSIBILITY

Aside from the repeated appeals to *forum non conveniens* (sometimes successfully argued by corporations), appeals to excluded parties (often the nations where the activities took place), and even to 'political questions', two major issues stand out: first, whether the alleged 'torts' rise to the level of acts committed against the 'law of nations', and whether they are indeed breaches of *jus cogens* norms; and second, whether corporations *can* be charged under these categories at all.

The first question is a basic one requiring a detailed multidisciplinary discussion (see Chapter 7). The second question, while clearly a complex one, is basic to the whole issue of indigenous peoples' rights, and should be addressed here. Although corporations are charged with multiple attacks on indigenous groups that are better considered under the categories of attacks against the human person and genocide, even of war crimes, the question of their responsibility for each and every attack, that is, on the criminality of their activities, hence the question of *mens rea*, should be considered first.

Corporate accountability and the problem of intent

Political theory, moral principles and the national legislative framework ensure that ministries and other government bodies have a duty of care, a responsibility for the citizens in the regions they govern. This, however, is not true of corporate bodies, especially the powerful MNCs who operate at many levels and in many countries, under diverse jurisdictions. As we noted, it is extremely difficult even to characterize their hazardous activities as crimes although, when these crimes are perpetrated, multi-nationals operating in various countries cannot claim state immunity, unless they are true representatives of their countries in their foreign operations.[59]

The question of corporate responsibility in regard to indigenous peoples will be re-examined in Chapter 9. But it is undeniable that the corporations' legal personhood gives them the same rights as individual, natural persons, although the extent of the protection to which they are entitled has been increasingly debated. In *R. v. Wholesale Travel Groups Ltd.* ((1991) 3 SCR 154), Cory J argues that the charter was primarily intended to protect 'vulnerable members' of society, hence, no corporate institution, especially one provided already (legally) with 'limited liability,' should be able to appeal to the charter for protection. In essence, the charter's primary focus is the protection of individual rights, an intensely and particularly 'liberal' focus, according to Chick (1993) and the sources he cites:

Those who take the view that individual rights must always come first, and ... must take precedence over collective goals are often speaking out of a view of a liberal society which has become more and more widespread in the Anglo American world. (Taylor, 1992)

I have argued that liberal democracy, as presently implemented in Western affluent countries, has failed to protect even the citizens in the nations where it prevails, let alone those who, though geographically or temporally removed from decision-making institutions, are bearing the gravest risks (Rees and Wackernagel, 1996; Rees, 2000; Westra, 1998). This is true because collective and community rights are not respected, nor are the natural systems and processes on which we depend for life and health. The protection of the common good is neither an institutional nor a corporate priority in the environmental context. The same is true in the area of employee's rights for workers employed in risky businesses, and it is constructive to compare the two (Draper, 1991).

A well-known Canadian mining disaster can be analysed in a similar way as the legislative framework for the protection of the workers is as lacking as that intended for the protection of citizens from environmental harms. In their discussion of the *Westray Mine* disaster, Harry Glasbeek and Eric Tucker (1993) point out the repeated, unpunished disasters brought about by unconstrained corporate activities. Among several points worthy of note, some could be repeated for the eco-violence in Walkerton, where E. coli spread through the community because of the contaminated water supply, causing around 3000 cases of serious illness and at least 7 deaths (Westra, 2004a, Chapter 4). For instance:

1   *Invariably, the inquiries reveal that the deaths and injuries are attributable, at least in part, to violations of existing mine regulations;*
2   *This finding inexorably leads to statements of firm resolve that there will be no recurrences, no more violations, no more disasters. But, as the records show, these oft-asserted goals are never realized.* (Glasbeek and Tucker, 1993)

The assumptions underlying these glaring breaches of human rights are that somehow the employing corporations, the law-dispensing institutions, and the affected workers are all working towards similar or at least compatible goals (Glasbeek and Tucker, 1993). This is both untrue and indefensible on the basis of evidence. There is no deep and substantive consensus between corporate owners and their employees, although the latter, especially in male-dominated industries, tend to frown on manifesting any concern about workplace safety and risk as not 'manly'.

A risky business (Draper, 1991), such as a corporation disposing of capacitors laden with PCBs (Westra, 1994a) or the nuclear industry attempting to site a waste disposal facility against the citizen's will in Nevada (Schrader-Frechette, 1993), are viewed by the men in the community as a possible source of employment and the risk involved is considered an acceptable part of doing their job, even viewed as a 'heroic exercise of manly confrontation', itself understood as a test of toughness, rather than an unwarranted and unconsented risk to be avoided (Glasbeek and Tucker, 1993). In all these cases, workplace/health concerns and eco-violence/health concerns, are treated in a similar manner, both in the public mind, and by the boardrooms and the institutions that could control such risks.

We should question our acquiescence in the context of our liberal democratic political system as we reconsider the corporate/institutional 'facilitator' who enables and supports the risks and condones the harms. One of the major causes of our unthinking support of 'business as usual' is the tranquilizing effect of marketing and advertising campaigns, within the context of what I have termed 'the failure of liberal democracy' (Westra, 1998). Homer Dixon (1994) shows democracy's failings:

> *If you only have procedural democracy in a society that's exhibiting environmental stress and already has cleavages, say ethnic cleavages, then procedural democracy will tend to aggravate these problems and produce societal discord, rather than social concord.*

The same point can be made about economic cleavages, rampant in a capitalist system whose openly avowed goal is increased production, increased profits, and not global justice, conservation and respect for the natural systems on which their very activities depend.

FROM *MENS REA* IN DOMESTIC CRIMES TO CORPORATE ACCOUNTABILITY IN INTERNATIONAL LAW

> *Human Rights Watch establishes a special unit on corporations and human rights; in 1999 it issued 2 lengthy reports, one accusing the Texas based Enron corporation of 'corporate complicity' in human rights violations 'by the Indian government', and another one, accusing Shell, Mobil and other international oil companies operating in Nigeria of cooperating with the government in supporting political opposition.* (Ratner, 2001)

Steven Ratner (2001) argues that international law should 'provide for human rights obligations directly on corporations', and that corporate duties should also extend to the elimination of their complicity with states that may be viewed 'as the prime source of human rights abuses'.

The background to the present situation originated when European states left their colonies and the process of decolonization started. It was to be based on the sovereignty and equality of all states, and any relation with the former colonial power had to be based on a clear choice by the people of the territory (Ratner, 2001).[60] The most important document for that period was the *Charter of Economic Rights and Duties of States*, emphasizing the obligations of the North to the South.[61]

But human rights law is not limited to state interaction, and the presence of both the ICCPR and the ICESCR, as well as treaties on women's and children's rights, and covenants against racial discrimination and torture, all contributed to diminish the inviolability of state sovereignty, as the legality of intervention replaced the former duty of non-interference in the internal affairs of individual states (Ratner, 2001).

Although states had tried to limit the power of MNCs in the 1980s and early 1990s, the increasing spread of globalization in the 1990s gave rise to a counter-reaction with a strong emphasis on corporate rights (Ratner, 2001).[62] The reality is that multinationals are becoming 'more embedded in the economy of the host states than ever before' (Ratner, 2001) but, while governments have obligations to their citizens under human rights law, the question of the corporations' duties under international law has not been fully clarified (Ratner, 2001), especially in developing countries, where indigenous peoples are often based. These impoverished states are far more interested in foreign investment and trade than in protecting their citizens and ensuring compliance with domestic or international law. The corporate position was that 'The citizenry's human rights were the government's responsibility, not theirs. In short, the race to the bottom was on' (Ratner, 2001).

When we consider the interface between powerful corporate actors and indigenous communities under the category of international law, the problem of *mens rea* recedes in importance. The states have been retreating from their duties to foster their own economic interest so that the corporations have taken on a direct role vis-à-vis the communities, not as one or another individual with clear human rights. Yet, ultimately, it is indeed individuals who are harmed both singly as part of groups. Because of the laxity of states in enforcing existing laws, whole territories are in fact given controls over vast tracts of indigenous traditional lands (Howard, 1994; Ratner, 2001).

Human rights violations: Torts and crimes

> *The inadequacy of state responsibility stems fundamentally from trends in modern international affairs, confirming that corporations may have as much or more power over individuals as governments.* (Ratner, 2001)

It is commonplace to affirm that many corporations have budgets and economic powers in excess of those of many developing countries (Strange, 1996). Even without turning to developing nations and indigenous groups, one sees the subtle and widespread power MNCs wield, even in a developed country like Canada. Monsanto corporation, for example, offered funds to the University of Toronto for a 'research institute', and the result was that they were accused of effectively muzzling dissenting voices that might have arisen against their policies and practices, as exemplified in the *Percy Schmeiser* case in Saskatchewan.[63] (*Monsanto (Canada) Inc. v. Schmeiser* [2004] 1 S.C.R 902).

Of course when we turn to areas like the Colombian rainforest, Indonesia or Sudan, those governments have relinquished any protective role they might have originally had over their citizens' rights, hence they have little incentive to restrain the corporations who are willing to provide economic incentives in exchange for laissez-faire attitudes on the part of the governments in question. Often, rather than curtailing corporate practices, governments are complicit in their activities. Ratner (2001) proposes three possible approaches to ameliorate the situation:

1   *to continue to focus exclusively on state encouraging it eventually to control such enterprises;*

2   *to enforce obligations against individuals;*

3   *or to identify and prescribe new obligations upon those private entities in international law and develop a regime of responsibility for violations they might commit.*

It seems that the first option is somewhat unrealistic, especially given the retreat of the state to which I have alluded and the clear disinterest on the part of most states to hamper or restrain corporate activities. But both the second and third options seem to offer a better avenue to the protection of human rights in general, and of those of indigenous peoples specifically. Aside from genocide, attacks against humanity, and war crimes, the UN Commission of Experts for the former Yugoslavia concluded that there are several acts that could fall under the Convention on Genocide (especially Article 2):

> *murder, torture, arbitrary arrest and detention, extra-judicial executions, rape and sexual assaults, confinement of civilian populations in ghetto areas, forcible removal, displacement and deportation of civilian populations, deliberate military attacks or threat of attacks on civilians and civilian areas and wanton destruction of property (Final Report of the Commission of Experts Established Pursuant to Security Council Resolution 78 (1991), May 27, 1994, UN Doc.S/1994/674, at 33; note that the commission defined 'ethnic cleansing' as 'the rendering of an area ethnically homogenous by using force or intimidation to remove persons of given groups from the area').* (Ratner and Abrams, 2001)

Many of the corporate activities described in the cases discussed thus far include several of the acts that Ratner and Abrams (2001) believe could and perhaps should be covered by the convention. In addition, Article 2 specifies 'ethnic, racial and religious groups' as those against whom those acts must be committed in order to qualify as acts covered by the convention, although the terms 'ethnic' and 'racial' are sometimes viewed as interchangeable, many disagree on the possibility of a distinction between the two.[64]

At any rate, despite these debates, protected groups are explicitly covered by the convention, and those who attack them cannot claim, as many try unsuccessfully to do, such defences as 'superior orders', 'duress', lacking a moral choice and 'necessity', which are no longer permissible after Nuremberg (Ratner and Abrams, 2001). The question of corporate accountability has not been fully answered in these brief remarks. But one may also consider historical precedent. At one time the slave trade was a 'global' business activity tolerated by many states, while it was strongly condemned by others. Those who worked to eliminate the practice, 'convinced governments to conclude a series of treaties that allowed states to seize vessels and required them to punish slave traders' (Ratner, 2001). The classic case is *Le Louis*, and it is instructive to read a representative passage, as Sir William Scott attempts to explain why resistance to the slave trade should be normatively required, thus anticipating the existence of *jus cogens* norms in international law:

Piracy being excluded, the Court has to look for some new and peculiar ground: but in the first place a new and very extensive ground is offered to it by the suggestion, which has been strongly pressed, that this trade, if not the crime of piracy, is nevertheless crime, and that every nation and indeed every individual has not only a right, but a duty to prevent in every place the commission of crime. It is a sphere of duty sufficiently large that is thus opened out to communities and their members. But to establish the consequence required it is first necessary to establish that the right to interpose by force to prevent the commission of crime commences, not upon the commencement of the overt act, not upon the evident approach towards it, but on the bare surmise grounded on the mere possibility.[65]

Sir William Scott is addressing the issue of slave trading, in terms that tend to place the action in the realm of emergent, if not present, *jus cogens* norms (Ragazzi, 1997). He ends his judgement by admitting that, as it is not as yet the established practice of all states, and even less 'international law' to view the slave trade as a crime, it cannot be so considered, despite the fact that most would agree with his moral position against slavery and the slave trade (see Chapter 3).

But the point made in this passage is that we need to appreciate the activity to be proscribed first and foremost in its true nature (in our case, viewing corporate activity as a crime), before we can even start to place it in the appropriate legal context that attacks human rights.

The second important point emerging from *Le Louis* is the need for a clear international norm, one that has accepted the corresponding *erga omnes* implications. *Le Louis* shows without a doubt the problems that arise when a universal moral norm conflicts with a treaty or state practice, or is not at a certain time fully operative in either context. The strong beliefs of most people, their revulsion in the face of an activity (such as the slave trade) that ought to be proscribed everywhere, is insufficient, unless a treaty exists with signatories from all countries globally, the 'delict' is raised to the status of crime, or the activity is viewed as impermissible in customary law.

But, even aside from moral principles that are explicitly constitutive of international law (in contrast with municipal law), state responsibility in the international context demands more than fines. First, what is the meaning of 'state responsibility'?

'State responsibility' simply put is the name public international law gives to the normative state of affairs which occurs following a breach by a state of one of its international legal obligations (whether that obligation derives from treaty law, customary law or other recognized sources such as 'general principles' of law). (Scott, 2001a)

This description sounds essentially similar to a breach of domestic regulatory obligations in some ways. For both domestic and international law, for the most part, damage must be demonstrated before it can be decided that a violation has occurred. But further obligations, beyond compensation, are present when we move from domestic to international law:

The breach of a (primary) rule of international law triggers certain secondary obligations. These are commonly considered to include duties to: 1) discontinue the act; 2) apply national legal remedies; 3) re-establish the situation existing before the act in

question or, to the extent that this is possible, pay corresponding compensation; 4)
provide guarantees against repetition. (Brunnée, 1993)

In essence then, there are three further obligations beyond no. 2, 'apply national legal
remedies', that accrue to the state, when this is viewed from an international, trans-
boundary perspective. One of the questions raised by this approach is whether the well-
established principle *nullum crimen sine lege*, while still foundational, acquires perhaps
a special meaning when applied to international criminal law (Ratner and Abrams,
2001), as scholarly writings seeking to advance justice are often used to promote the
achievement of this goal.

A recent example emphasizes this point. In June 2006, France's railways (SNCF)
were found liable 'for the wrongful dispatch, by cattle car' of Jewish people to 'Drancy',
a holding camp near Paris, prior to their shipment to Auschwitz. One family was
successful in the case, winning the equivalent of Can$85,000 in the judgement. This is
the first time that a French court had charged a French government agency, viewing it
as complicit in the horror of Nazi crimes (although the case's judgement was reversed
in 2007, based on the doctrine of 'superior orders') (Marrus, 2006). In this case there
is a crime not established in the law of the time, but one that simple justice may force
us to accept as such.

NOTES

1   *Cherokee Nations v. Georgia*, 30 US 5 Pet., 17 (1831).
2   *Indian Child Welfare Act* of 1978, 25 USC § 1901 (1978).
3   *Indian Tribal Government Tax Status Act*, 26 USC § 7871 (1982).
4   *The Indian Self-Determination and Education Act* of 1975, 25 USC § 450 (1975).
5   *The Indian Tribal Justice Act* of 1990, 25 USC § 2901 (1990).
6   Clinton, William J., Remarks to American Native and Alaska Native Tribal Leaders, 29 April
    1994, 30 Weekly compilation of Presidential documents, No. 18, 941, 942 (9 May 1994).
7   See Chief Justice Marshall 'opinions' in *Worcester v. Georgia* 31 US (6 Peet.) 515 (1832);
    Employment Div., Dept. of Human Resources v. Smith, 494 US 872 (1990).
8   *Doe v. Unocal Corp.*, 2002 WL 3.D 63976 (9th Cir. 2003).
9   *ATCA*, 28 USC 1350 (2002)), the Ninth Circuit reversed the original verdict; *Doe/Roe v.
    Unocal Corp.*, 110 F. Supp. 2d 1294, 1306 (CD Cal. 2000).
10 *Filartiga v. Pena-Irala*, 630 F.2d 876, 881 (2d Cir. 1980).
11 Maria Aguinda and others including the *Federation of the Yagua People of the Lower Amazon and
    Lower Napo v. Texaco, Inc.*, 303 F 3d 470; 2002 US App. LEXIScl6540; 157 Oil and Gas Rep.
    333, 16 August 2002.
12 *Aguinda v. Texaco, Inc.*, 1945 F. Supp. 625 (SDNY 1996); *Aquinda v. Texaco, Inc.*, 142 F. Supp.
    2d 534 (SDNY 2001); *Jota v. Texaco, Inc.*, 157 F 3d 153 (2d Cir. 1998).
13 ibid.
14 ibid.
15 ibid.
16 ibid.
17 ibid.
18 *Guerra v. Italy* (116/1996/735/932), 19 Feb. 1998; *Lopez-Ostra v. Spain* (1995) 20 HER 277m
    (1994) ECHR 16798/90.

19   *Nuclear Tests* case, Australia v. France; New Zealand v. France (1974) ICJ Rep. 253.
20   *Bancoult v. McNamara*, 370 Supp. 2dl. US Dist., LEXIS 27882 (21 December 2004 decided).
21   ibid.
22   ibid.
23   Westfall, Federal Employees Liability Reform and Tort Compensation Act of 1988, Fub.L. No. 100-694, 102 Stat. 4563 (1988) (codified at 28 USC && 2671-2680).
24   ibid.
25   ibid.
26   ibid.
27   *Filartiga v. Pena-Irala*, US Court of Appeals, 2d ct, 1980 630 F 2d 876.
28   *United States v. Smith*, 18 US, 153, 160–161, 5 L. Ed. 57 (1920).
29   *Beanal v. Freeport-McMoran, Inc. and Freeport-McMoran Copper and Gold, Inc.*, 969 F. Supp 362; 1997 US Dist LEXIS 4767 (April 1997 decided).
30   ibid.
31   ibid.
32   Citing *Filartiga*, 630 F.2d at 881.
33   ibid.
34   ibid.
35   *Dagi; Shackles, Ambeu; Maur and others v. the Broken Hill Proprietary Company Ltd. and Ok Tedi Mining Limited* (No. 2) [1997] Victoria Reports [VR] 428, where plaintiffs in the area of Papua New Guinea complained about the toxic pollution into a river and flood plain from an Australian copper mine operation (BHP). In this case, 'the judge held he *did* have jurisdiction over certain cases of action related to negligence' (Steiner and Alston, 2000; see also Scott, 2001a).
36   ibid.; see also *Sequinha v. Texaco*, 847 F. Supp. 61 (SD Tex. 1994); *Sequinha v. Texaco, Inc.*, 945 F. Supp. 625 (SDNY 1996); *Ashanga v. Texaco, Inc.*, SDNY Dist. No. 94 Civ. 9266 (13 August 1997); *Jota v. Texaco, Inc.*, 157 F. 3d 153 (2d Cir. 1998).
37   ibid., Restatement § 207.
38   ibid.
39   ibid.
40   ibid.
41   ibid.
42   ibid.
43   *The Presbyterian Church of Sudan, Rev. John Gaduel, Nuer Community, Development Services and others v. Talisman Energy, Inc.*, 244 F. Supp. 2d 289:2003 US Dist. LEXIS 4085:155 Oil and Gas Rep. 409, 19 March 2003, decided.
44   ibid.
45   ibid.
46   ibid.
47   ibid.
48   ibid.
49   *Wiwa v. Royal Dutch Petroleum Co.*, 226 F. 3d 88 (2d Cir. 2000).
50   ibid.
51   *Tachiona v. Omugabe*, 234 S. Supp 2d. 401, No. 00 Civ. 6666 (VM), 2002 WL 317 9018 (SDNY 11 December 2002.
52   *United States v. FMC Corporation*, 572 F. 2d 902 (2 Cir. 1978).
53   *Doe v. Unocal Corp.*, 2002 US App. LEXIS 19263, Nos. 00-56603, 00-57197, 00-56628, 00-57195, 2002 WL 3103976 (9th Cir. 18 September 2002).
54   ibid.
55   Affidavit of F. Fran, paras. 15–16.
56   ibid.

57 ibid.

58 *Derensis v. Cooper and Lybrand Chartered Accountants*, 930 F. Supp. 1003, 1007 (DNJ 1996).

59 ILC Draft Articles on Jurisdictional Immunities of States as adopted at 43rd Session, 1991, and recommended to UN General Assembly, Article 10, 30 It. Lg. Mt. 1554 (1991).

60 GA Res. 2625, Declaration on Principles of International Law Concerning Friendly Relations and Co-operation Among States in Accordance with the Charter of the United Nations, UN GAOR, 25th Sess., Supp. No. 28, at 121, 124, UN Doc. A/8028(1970); *Western Sahara*, 1975 ICJ 12, 39 (1 October), noting the legal status of 19th century territories.

61 *Charter of Economic Rights and Duties of States*, GA Res. 3281, UN GAOR, 29th Sess., Supp. No. 31, at 50, UN Doc. A/9631 (1974).

62 *Development and International Economic Co-operation: Transnational Corporation*, UN ESCOR, 2d See., UN Doc. E/1990/94 (1990); Draft United Nations Code of Conduct on Transnational Corporations, UN ESCOR, Spe. Sess. Supp. No. 7, Annex II, UN Doc. E/1983/17/Rev. 1 (1983).

63 *Monsanto (Canada) Inc. v. Schmeiser* [2004] 1 SCR 902.

64 *Convention on Genocide*, UN GAOR 6th Comm. 3d Sess. 75th mtg. at 115-116 (UN Doc. A/633 (1948).

65 *Le Louis*, 2 Dodson Rep. 238, Judgement – Sir William Scott at 248.

CHAPTER 6

First Nations of Canada and the Legal and Illegal Attacks on Their Existence

Genocide is a new word for an old tragedy. The term, coined only in the twentieth century, describes the decimation of a people, of a nation... We most commonly think of genocide as synonymous with the Nazi Holocaust, the loss of six million or more lives, or in the context of the Chinese Communist extermination of eighteen to twenty million dissidents. The term also describes the North American Native experience. (Strickland, 1986)

FIRST NATIONS OF CANADA AND SOME LEGAL POLICIES OF ELIMINATION

It seems that North American indigenous peoples fare no better than those in developing countries in the face of Western conquest and economic interests. Strickland (1986) argues for another 'conquest' long before the 'second conquest' by transnational and multinational enterprises, and long after the violence vested by Spaniards and others on the hapless tribes of North America. He sees this conquest as one where the rule of law prevailed, but its aim was to deprive native peoples of their 'Indianness', their pride and their culture. He cites Alexis de Tocqueville:

The Spaniards were unable to exterminate the Indian race by those unparalleled atrocities which brand them with indelible shame, nor did they succeed even in wholly depriving it of its rights; but the Americans of the United States have accomplished this two fold purpose with singular felicity, tranquilly, legally and philanthropically, without shedding blood and without violating a single great principle of morality in the eyes of the world. It is impossible to destroy men with more respect for the laws of humanity. (de Tocqueville, 1945 in Strickland, 1986)

One of the most disconcerting aspects of the legal forms of genocide of North America's aboriginal people is one that is not described in any of the instruments that specify what constitutes genocide; it is 'genocide by assimilation' (LaVelle, 2001). The main tools of assimilation, at least in Canada, were the 'residential schools', where children were removed from their families and communities for the sole purpose of 'eliminating their Indianness', or as the Report of the Royal Commission on Aboriginal Peoples[1] describes it:

> *... the children, effectively re-socialized, imbued with the values of European culture, would be the vanguard of a magnificent metamorphosis: the 'savage' was to be 'civilized', made fit to take up the privileges and responsibilities of citizenship.*

In an atmosphere of general disrespect for the individual rights, their community, their tradition and history, these children were 'educated' in surroundings that were 'quite unfit for human habitation' for the most part. There was tuberculosis in the schools, and the conditions of heating, drainage and ventilation were appalling. In addition, the food was of poor quality and limited quantity, so that their needs for a healthy and varied diet were not met. Neglect and harsh punishment were endemic (Westra, 2006). But although these would appear, *prima facie*, to be the sort of issues often found in poorly funded and supervised state institutions, there were certain aspects that were unique in this situation. General disinterest, even criminal negligence, although they are definitely crimes, do not rise to the level of genocide, as do these deliberate attacks on the very essence of what it is to be Indian. Thus there is the intent, openly stated in earlier times, to eliminate the essential features of their tradition and culture, a thing that made them a distinct people, even though there was no specific intent to kill individual Indian children. It seems that the defining conditions of cultural genocide (see Chapter 7), if nothing else, are present.

SUI GENERIS LAND-BASED RIGHTS

> *Aboriginal title encompasses the right to choose to what uses land can be put, subject to the ultimate limit that those uses cannot destroy the ability of the land to sustain future generations of Aboriginal peoples.*[2]

The question of aboriginal title, and the difference between 'ownership' and 'possession' based on continued occupation and the use of traditional lands at the time of sovereignty, rather than the first time of contact,[3] clearly shows the centrality of land to the aboriginal way of life. It is ironical that, although that centrality to their survival as a people is acknowledged, their consent to any use of their land may 'even' be required in some cases, and, when their title is infringed, 'fair compensation will ordinarily be required'.[4] But anything that is taking place in aboriginal people's traditional areas that affects their lands is more than likely to affect their present and future survival. In that case we are looking at incompensable harms, not harms that can be 'fairly compensated'. The special relationship between First Nations and the land is the topic of the next section, as I consider the historical background of the Canadian government's policies regarding their aboriginal peoples.

Historical and traditional background to current First Nations issues

> *Nations or Tribes of Indians ... should not be molested or disturbed in the possession of such Parts of our Dominions and Territories as not having been ceded to or purchased by Us, are reserved to them ... as their Hunting Grounds... We do ... strictly enjoin*

and require, that no private Person do presume to make any purchase from the said
Indians of any lands reserved to the said Indians...; but that if, at any time any of
the said Indians should be inclined to dispose of the said lands, the same shall be
Purchased only by Us in our Name, at some public meeting or Assembly of the said
Indians.[5]

After the Constitution Act of 1982, specifically after the adoption of section 35(1) of that act, aboriginal rights or title cannot be extinguished without the consent of aboriginal peoples (Ulgen, 2000), despite ongoing settlement treaties disputes (Asch and Zlotkin, 1997).

Prior to European occupation, and after the Treaty of Paris (1783), which ended the war between Britain and France regarding Canada, the aboriginal peoples did not sign treaties giving Europeans the power to decide their fate. In fact, as noted above, the Royal Proclamation of 1763 was intended to protect the land rights of aboriginal people in the region. However, before the Constitution Act of 1982 proclaimed that consent was needed before native rights could be extinguished, the situation was somewhat unclear. The Crown had a 'fiduciary duty',[6] so that its power regarding indigenous peoples was limited by its obligation to observe 'the principles of recognition and reconciliation' (Ulgen, 2000; Hogg, 2005). The Crown has the obligation to ensure that there are limits to its sovereign power, in order to protect aboriginal peoples.[7] The aboriginal peoples once had sovereignty over the lands they occupied historically and the Crown did not avail itself of the categories of *terra nullius*, discovery or conquest, recognizing that these were organized native societies already present there (Ulgen, 2000).

As we will see, the 1990 case of *Sparrow v. The Queen* provides a clear statement of the obligation of the Crown regarding the protection of indigenous environmental rights. The case appears at first to be a fairly trivial one, as it deals with native fishing rights and the fact that 'the net restriction in the Band's License violated Section 35' (Manus, 2006). The court pointed out that 'An existing aboriginal right cannot be read so as to incorporate the specific manner in which it was regulated before 1982'.[8]

Yet, while 'the taking of Salmon was an integral part of their lives',[9] and indeed the Indians of all bands had 'a constitutionally protected, existing aboriginal right to fish' (Manus, 2006), there are, I believe, good and compelling reasons to view Sparrow's actions in a critical vein.

Questions raised by the court were many; among them, whether the new restrictions 'reduced the Musqueam fish catch to levels below that needed for food and ceremonial purposes', and 'whether the net length restriction caused the Musqueam to spend undue time and money per fish caught', both of which are not the most important consideration in the light of dwindling natural resources (Manus, 2006). The importance of *Sparrow* cannot be overestimated both for what it says and for what emerges from the discussion.

The significance of *Sparrow v. The Queen*

This case provided what was later termed the 'Sparrow test', an approach that reappeared in any number of subsequent cases:

The first step in this test is to determine whether there was a prima facie infringement of an Aboriginal right. If an infringement is found, the Court would then determine whether it was justified. There are two steps to the justification determination in the Sparrow test. First, the Court would ask whether the objectives of the legislation were 'compelling and substantial'. If there answer is yes, the infringement moves to the second stage, where the Court asks whether the Crown has fulfilled its fiduciary duties to the First Nation, by implementing the legislation in a manner consistent with the honour of the Crown. (Imai, 2001; see also Hogg, 2005)

This test appears to be strong enough to withstand the attacks on First Nations' rights by corporate bodies intent on securing logging, fishing or other rights. Nevertheless other 'rights' or objectives may be introduced into the argument, as providing equally compelling objectives, beyond the rights of aboriginal peoples. For example, these objectives might include 'the economic and cultural needs of all people and communities in the Province'.[10] Imai (2001) notes that recently the Supreme Court of Canada has been prepared to allow more and more 'compelling and substantial' reasons for infringement, so that just about any 'resource development activity' may be allowed to pass the test.[11] Unrestrained resource development on the part of either First Nations or corporate legal persons should be carefully examined from the ecological standpoint.

The problem is that the absolute importance of ecological integrity, of retaining lands in their natural state, has not been incorporated in the law of Canada (or any other country for that matter). But it is essential to maintain biodiversity in the region (Noss, 1992; Noss and Cooperrider, 1994), but also to ensure the continuance of its natural systemic processes, hence the presence of 'nature's services' (Daily, 1997). This basic necessity applies to all humans, but its absence produces particularly severe results for First Nations and all aboriginal peoples who may not possess the temporary protection against environmental degradation that economically stronger groups possess, and that enables the wealthier groups to misunderstand the role and nature of such essential services to existence. First Nations are, in a sense, the 'canaries' that show first and most clearly the results of the harms we are perpetrating on our habitat.

Their rights, like those of all indigenous peoples, are collective rights (Kapashesit and Klippenstein, 1991), and the right to social, cultural and economic survival are necessary, but not sufficient (see Chapter 1; see also Scott, 2001b). Essentially, the most important right these groups have is the right to their lands in their natural condition, in perpetuity. Hence, when economic activities dictate the way 'tracts taken up' are to be used, without any reference to ecological considerations, there will be 'no appropriate approach to preserving First Nation resources' (Imai, 2001). Neither courts nor Canadian judges, nor even First Nations' advocates can be relied upon to understand and respect the conditions required to maintain indigenous peoples' lands in the way that will ensure both the survival and the cultural needs of future generations. These are protected by treaty rights and, in the final analysis, by their constitutionally guaranteed rights supported by the 'honour of the Crown'.

But cases are tried singly by the courts, and it is impossible to fully understand the implications of the harms perpetrated by the infringements of those land rights. According to Imai (2001):

> *Unless there is a macro picture of the resources and territory needed, it would be very difficult to decide on a micro level whether a particular 'taking up' would result in an infringement of a treaty right.*

This is no longer a legal question; it is a scientific one that should be based on ecology. What is required then is the total respect for the integrity of the First Nations' traditional lands and even, as I proposed earlier (see Chapter 1), an appropriately sized buffer zone around these lands, and a careful and thorough analysis of the ecological footprint of any and all commercial activities proposed. For First Nations, the basis for this conclusion is found, first, in the Great Law of Peace of the Haudenasaunee, and the widely accepted 'seven generations rule'; but also, second, in the *sui generis* relation they have to their lands, the very foundation of the culture and lifestyle. Essentially then, aboriginal title manifests three basic differences from other forms of property under common law:

1 The title can only be surrendered to the Crown if that is the wish of the community; this may also happen if the people want to use their land in ways that are incompatible with their traditional ways;[12]
2 The title arises from the prior occupation of lands, namely, their 'historical occupation before the assertion of British sovereignty'; the 'occupancy requirement' is sufficient to demonstrate the connection to a specific parcel of land for their distinctive culture;
3 Aboriginal occupancy refers not only to the presence of aboriginal peoples in villages and to previously settled areas, *but also to the use of adjacent lands and even remote territories used to preserve a traditional way.*[13]

COLLECTIVE RIGHTS AND ABORIGINAL LAND MANAGEMENT: RESPECT FOR AND OBLIGATIONS TO NATURE

In Chapter 1 the basic requirement of ecological and biological integrity, and the need for an additional buffer zone to ensure that the territories of First Nations are properly protected was defended. The history of aboriginal rights and title in Canada, including the 'inherent limitation' that characterizes such title, was discussed earlier in the chapter:

> *For example, land used primarily as hunting grounds may not be used in such a way as to destroy its value by being used for strip-mining. If a group claims title by virtue of a special relationship to the land, the land may not be used in such a way to destroy this relationship, by turning it into a parking lot.*[14]

Equity requires *a fortiori* that others should abide by the same policy that has been imposed on First Nations. If the First Nations must abide by environmental limitations to their right to self-determination, then commercial interests, eliminated *a priori* from dealing directly with First Nations for their lands (as only the Crown retains that privilege, should the First Nations so desire), have an even clearer, non-derogable obligation to abstain from using their lands in ways that clearly contradict both the Canadian Constitution and international agreements. For instance, United Nations Draft Declaration on the Rights of Indigenous Peoples (UNDD) (Article 25) states:

> *Indigenous peoples have the right to maintain and strengthen their distinctive spiritual and material relationship with the land territories, waters and costal areas and other resources which they have traditionally owned or otherwise occupied or used, and **to uphold their responsibilities to future generations in this regard.*** (emphasis added)

The concept of intergenerational equity is as entrenched in international law as that of intragenerational justice, for both environmental and ecological rights are foundational (Brown-Weiss, 1990; Westra, 2006). This double requirement renders the attacks on First Nations' children and their 'Indianness' particularly heinous.

The environmental component of First Nations' rights is still being debated in the courts:[15]

> *And yet, the foremost factor in the survival of tribal cultures in nations with common law court systems may be the courts' willingness to accept as part of its judicial role a responsibility to both recognize and impose the sovereign obligation to understand, value and preserve the environmental interests of native populations.* (Manus, 2006)

These obligations reflect more than the requirements of legal instruments and the constitution. They reflect the reality of aboriginal treatment and use of their lands. This is something technologically 'advanced' societies have forgotten or ignored, resulting in the present global ecological situation.

First Nations environmental ethics and their collective rights

> *The Koyukon people are strongly influenced to harvest only as much as they can use and to use everything that they harvest. Among the Koyukon, reverence for nature, which is strongly manifested in both religion and personality, is unquestionably related to conscious limitation of use.* (Nelson, 1982)

Governed by social custom, taboos and strict regulations, most aboriginal peoples, such as the Cree for instance, 'do not kill more than they need, for fun, or for self-aggrandizement, although they are fully aware of their ability to do so' (Kapashesit and Klippenstein, 1991; see also Feit, 1982). In general, aboriginal hunters are regulated through 'rotational hunting' and by shifting the consumption from one animal to another, as well as other seasonal considerations to ensure sustainability (Feit, 1987). Their practices emphasize 'reciprocity and balance' in their relation with the natural world, of which they deeply believe they are a part. Hence aboriginal environmental ethics are deeply embedded in their culture and in the social fabric of their community, and many environmental philosophers have noted this important fact, especially

Callicott (1989b). But the best way to understand that connection starts with the famous work of forester Aldo Leopold (1949), who defines right conduct as that which 'tends to preserve the ecological stability, *integrity* and beauty of the biotic community, and wrong as it tends otherwise'.

First Nations and the land: Our forgotten bond

It is not necessary for indigenous peoples living a traditional lifestyle to work out an explicit environmental ethic because their essential 'Indianness' or the accumulated beliefs of their communal life incorporate precisely the outlook required for sane environmental policies, outlining the 'principle of integrity' as the basis for an environmental ethic (Westra, 1994a). In addition, however, their tradition incorporates a spiritual role for nature that is unique, as it is not present in either environmental ethic literature or in ecological science (Kapashesit and Klippenstein, 1991). In fact, their approach represents the one way today's societies may still halt or at least moderate the environmental catastrophe that is upon us (see, for example, Gore, 2006) as:

> *Aboriginal ecological management systems are distinct and largely independent from a modern Western state. Aboriginal ecological management systems are based on local knowledge and structures, and derive legitimacy from their traditional origin.* (Kapashesit and Klippenstein, 1991)

From keeping track of the number and conditions of beaver lodges, to establishing 'hunting bosses' charged with controlling where to hunt and how much could be taken, aboriginal practices manifest both scientific understanding of and respect for communal resources (Kapashesit and Klippenstein, 1991; see also Chapter 8). Had the affluent societies of the Western world been governed by such principles, we would not be facing what I have termed 'the final enclosure movement', as the commons and even the common heritage of mankind, are almost entirely non-existent today (Beyerveld and Brownsword, 2001; Westra, 2004b).

The reciprocity with non-human animals and all of nature, and the intimate bond First Nations share with both, is something that modern liberal individuals have long since cast aside, as our economics are based on an impossible and unfair 'growth' ethic. Ever-larger takings from nature, without any consideration for human and non-human life, and even less for the vulnerable people that try to cling to that nature, such as indigenous groups or future generations (Westra, 2006), manifest the violently oppressive aspects of our ecological footprint.

The neoliberal goals of an expansive economy and ever-increasing power are based on not recognizing limits to growth and to enrichment, no matter how unjust and at what cost. Ultimately, 'appropriating' resources indiscriminately leads to a general biotic impoverishment that will affect first, and most obviously the 'canaries', or those who have neither the protection afforded by better economic conditions nor the luxury of being able to move elsewhere. Eventually, as epidemiology increasingly shows, we are all affected, albeit in different ways. Neither attackers nor victims can fully sever the natural bond we all have to the Earth. It might help us to learn from indigenous peoples, who are the only communities presently fighting to protect that bond.

THE PROBLEM OF 'FROZEN RIGHTS' AND BORROWS' CRITIQUE OF THE ABORIGINAL RIGHTS TEST

In ways that we may not fully recognize or appreciate, native Canadians represent our society's only deep historical links to the land, consolidated over millennia. If their land is now our land as well, their relationship with that land is particularly worthy of our understanding and respect. (Slattery, 1987)

We must understand and respect First Nations' relations with the land, and those relationships must also be respected through entrenchment in the law for their protection. But some question this entrenchment and the effects that follow upon it. John Borrows (1997–1998) terms aboriginal rights based on their traditional relationship to the land 'frozen rights'. The Constitution Act, 1982, section 35(1) states that 'The existing aboriginal and treaty rights of the aboriginal peoples of Canada are hereby recognized and affirmed'. Tests for defining the import and scope of aboriginal rights may be found in *Van der Peet*,[16] under ten headings intended to specify what constitutes a 'distinctive culture'. Borrows (1997–1998) isolates the following:

1   'the perspective of Aboriginal peoples themselves on the meaning of rights at stake';
2   'the tradition, custom or practice being relied upon to establish the right';
3   'the centrality of the practice to the group claiming the right';
4   the practice under consideration 'integral to a distinctive culture' that has 'continuity with activities which existed prior to the arrival of the Europeans in North America';[17]
5   the evidence offered should be accepted even if 'it did not conform precisely with evidentiary standards in private litigation';
6   aboriginal rights are not 'general and universal, but related to the specific history of the group claiming the right';
7   the practice contains 'independent significance to the community';
8   aboriginal rights involve the 'distinctive nature of the aboriginal practice';
9   'a distinctive practice does not derive solely as a response to European influences' and it 'can arise separately from the aboriginal group's relation to the land';
10 the right may arise from the prior social organization and distinctive culture of aboriginal peoples'.

Borrows (1997–1998) finds several aspects of the *Van der Peet* test problematic. His critique includes issues that seem to diminish rather than enhance the content of aboriginal rights in some way. The starting point ought to be the two principles that are internationally recognized to be basic to the protection of indigenous rights: 'self-determination' and 'cultural integrity', and the implication of those principles. The first thing to note is that these are two *equal* domains but they are interconnected, and both are collective in nature. Hence, for instance, individual self-determination is not part of the protected basis upon which aboriginal communities can rely. Several cases appear to bring into question individual choices: the right to fish using 'contemporary implements' for instance, although fishing is certainly an activity that was practised since time immemorial. As Borrows (1997–1998) notes the Musqueam 'always fished for reasons connected to their cultural and physical survival'.

The court also acknowledged that those rights could be enjoyed equally by fishing in a more contemporary manner than by using more traditional ways. But the conflict between aboriginal activities 'integral' or 'distinctive' to the culture at the original time of first contact with Europeans, and one of the activities they seek to pursue in modern times, persists. For example, the establishment of casinos and gambling places is a fairly recent kind of activity, with no 'continuity' with pre-contact culture (Borrows, 1997–1998). Nor is that practice 'central' to any group's distinctive culture, or even part of any distinctive aboriginal national identity; 'incidental practices, customs and traditions cannot qualify as aboriginal rights through a process of piggybacking on integral practices, customs and traditions'.[18]

But it is modern-day aboriginal people who come before the courts with current problems and issues, hence it seems unfair to 'freeze' any aboriginal rights to those present several centuries ago, from both substantive and procedural points of view. In other words, equity considerations suggest that both evidentiary rules and subject matter in each case ought to incorporate first and foremost the indigenous point of view today, and Borrows (1997–1998) emphasizes this approach.

Nevertheless it seems that not every aspect of the 'essentialism' practised by the courts should be judged as inappropriate. The existence of land-based cultures of aboriginal peoples is not an outmoded 'frozen' form of their rights but a basic and fundamental aspect of their existence as *a people*, totally aside from individual preferences or non-collective choices. Therefore, this is not only a 'Western, non-aboriginal perspective', it is a basic foundation of their rights in international law, the best and strongest argument that aboriginal groups can advance for their own protection. The emphasis on different hunting or fishing techniques or equipment, or whether or not a casino on reserves is appropriate and should be permitted ought not to be judged solely from the standpoint of antiquated choices and lifestyles.

The Crown's obligations: Local issues or fundamental principles?

> *But, at the least, the following sorts of regulations would be valid: (1) regulations that operate to preserve or advance section 35 rights (as by conserving natural resources essential to the exercise of such rights); (2) regulations that prevent the exercise of section 35 right from causing serious harm to the general populace or native peoples themselves (such as standard safety restrictions governing the use of fire-arms in hunting); and (3) regulations that implement state policies of overriding importance to the general welfare (as in time of war or emergency).* (Slattery, 1987)

The most important point to keep in mind is emphasized by the wording of section 35(1) and the underlying principles dating back to the Royal Proclamation of 1763 and re-emphasized in *Delgamuukw*, *Sparrow* and other cases.[19] The Crown's fiduciary duty and the aboriginal peoples' right to their lands are based on *principles*, not on specific examples. They are universally valid, despite the attempts found in some cases to restrict and specify them as 'distinctive' or specific to this or that national culture, as we noted in the *Van der Peet* test.

The cases deal with individual hunters or fishers, or others involved in specific forms of trade. The universally valid rights they all share represent the Crown's non-specific obligation: it is the *sui generis* land-based rights discussed above, rights to the land that will not impair 'the ability of the land to sustain future generations of aboriginal peoples'.[20] The Crown's fiduciary duty is not a temporary contract, as neither section 35(1) nor any other instrument dealing with these issues states time limits to those obligations, nor is the duty owed only to one or another nation. That duty, by its very nature, demands respect for the integrity of the land, in perpetuity. That in turn requires, as I argued in Chapter 1, protection of the land from both internal and external threats, starting with the addition/protection of a buffer zone to ensure the existence of bio/ecological integrity, on which alone future generations' rights can depend. In addition, that fiduciary duty should have strong *negative* as well as *positive* components. The negative protection should be exercised by denying firmly the individual economic rights of natural or legal persons who would pursue their own interests at the expense of the health, safety and integrity of indigenous peoples.

The question should not be, was a casino part of pre-confederation Indian lifestyles, but can the casino be built in a way that is less deleterious to the environment than other enterprises, and can it be built in a way that does not have an adverse impact on the health and integrity of aboriginal lands in the area? Conversely, a case involving land leased for a golf club[21] should involve more than the more obvious issues discussed in the case: lack of information, lack of consent by the band, and the concomitant breaches of fiduciary duty of the Crown, as well as breaches of trust and agency. The main issue should have been the presence of the 'inherent limit' for aboriginal enterprise, no matter who approved the deal. Although this might be viewed as a paternalistic approach, it is instead one of respect for their uniqueness that depends on ecologically sound choices. Golf clubs are among the most hazardous areas on earth, as the amounts of pesticides, fungicides and other chemicals involved in keeping their 'greens', sound the death knell for the area's integrity and multiply the cancers and other grave diseases of nearby inhabitants.

If the Crown has a fiduciary duty to protect the integrity of Indian lands and the supporting lifestyle these lands can provide for present and future generations, then that obligation cannot give priority to the interests of individuals or collectives inside, or even right outside Indian lands, without contradicting its own proclaimed intent. Hence any project or proposed activity within or outside the lands where aboriginal peoples reside, ought to be judged *first* from that point of view. If it is not, then the commitment to ensure the lands for *all* Indian generations is meaningless. The scientific research available in support of this argument is uncontroversial, and both lawyers and judges sitting in courts ought to be prepared to assess cases and situations in the light of that knowledge (Westra, 2006; WHO, 2002; Licari et al, 2005).

Returning for a moment to Slattery's (1987) summation of the Crown's obligations listed above, his first point supports the conclusions advanced here. The second point is equally important: the harms suffered by the proverbial 'canary in the mine' are only the portent of what will befall the miners, unless they cease their activity immediately. The same is true in this case: the harms perpetrated on aboriginal populations by disregarding ecological and epidemiological evidence of the effects of hazardous industries, are more visible *first* in non-mobile populations that live directly on the land. But it is also a foregone conclusion that all humans will be adversely affected in some measure. Hence policies concerned with the general welfare (point three) could simply learn to comply with the basic tenet of the proclamation and of the Constitution Act. The duty of protection exists for all citizens (Westra, 2006), and the implied commitment to future generations of aboriginal people should support a reconsideration of all general welfare policies in order to protect all people in Canada.

ENVIRONMENTAL RACISM: A BRIEF INTRODUCTION

... the current environmental protection paradigm has institutionalized unequal enforcement, traded human health for profit, placed the burden of proof on the 'victims' rather than on the polluting industry, legitimated human exposure to harmful substances, promoted 'risky technologies' such as incinerators, exploited the vulnerability of economically and politically disenfranchised communities, subsidized ecological destruction, created an industry around risk assessment, delayed cleanup actions, and failed to develop pollution prevention as the overarching determinant strategy. (Bullard, 2001)

Robert Bullard is arguably the best-known social scientist and expert on environmental injustice regarding African American communities in the US. But the initial problems cited in the paragraph above, although aimed at the problems faced in urban minorities in his country, also represents a good introduction to the topic of traditional indigenous communities in Canada and elsewhere. In passing, it is worth noting that 'environmental justice' is part of regularly taught courses at US universities from Harvard to Auburn, Alabama, whereas, at least until 2000, when I was in the ethics field as a professor in Canada, the University of Windsor was one of the few Canadian universities that offered such a course (from 1995 to 1999, I taught a very popular course entitled, 'War, Terrorism and Environmental Racism', for the philosophy department of that school).

In the US, the literature and research on environmental racism, or environmental justice, regarding African Americans is well established, and it emphasizes the multiple problems afflicting those citizens in various states, especially, but not exclusively, in the southern US. Repeatedly, the problems arise when corporate individuals pursue their interests and those of their shareholders at the expense of vulnerable, impoverished populations of colour. For the most part, the rationalizations offered by large companies assured African Americans and the general public that the siting decisions regarding hazardous facilities were purely motivated by economics, not race, from Chicago's 'toxic doughnut' (Gaylord and Bell, 2001),[22] Titusville, Alabama and Browning-Ferris Industries (Westra and Lawson, 2001), 'cancer alley', Louisiana (Wrigley and Shrader-Frechette, 2001), and Halifax, Canada (McCurdy, 2001). However, there is a vast difference between these citizens and the indigenous communities in Canada. Both are affected by decisions based on environmental racism, but the former would like nothing better than to be integrated within the general community, a very hard goal to achieve for a poor visible minority; the latter want to be respected and recognized in their difference and uniqueness instead, and 'integration' in their case, is an existing and constant danger to their existence as a people.

Environmental racism refers to harms perpetrated in and through the environment, which affect disproportionately populations of colour. It includes both procedural and geographical inequities. Speaking of the problem in the US, Bullard (2001) argues that:

> *The geographical distribution of both minorities and the poor has been found to be highly correlated to the distribution of air pollution, municipal landfills and incinerators, abandoned toxic waste dumps, lead poisoning in children and contaminated fish consumption.*

Some of the categories emphasized in Bullard's writing fit equally well with indigenous traditional communities. There are serious lacunae in the regulatory framework regarding both of these communities, in Canada as well as in the US, which include problems of procedual equity, geographical equity and social equity (Bullard, 2001). According to Bullard (2001), the following are the five principles (without some of the details that pertain primarily to other populations) of environmental justice:

1   the right to protection;
2   the prevention of harm;
3   the need to shift the burden of proof;
4   laws should obviate the proof of intent; and
5   equities must be redressed.

Keeping in mind these principles, we can now return to the Canadian situation, first, to the 'settlement' of a case that demonstrates why Bullard's analysis is also applicable to Canada: the Grassy Narrows and White Dog case. Finally I end this chapter with a somewhat dated case study that incorporates not only environmental racism, but also several other issues exclusively relevant to the Canadian indigenous peoples' scene, the 1990 *Oka* case (Wellington et al, 1997).

The Grassy Narrows and White Dog Reserves of Northern Ontario

> *... the settlement and the events leading up to it provide a striking example of the fragility of Canadians' environmental rights in the face of environmental wrongs. Access to justice has been difficult to achieve for victims of environmental catastrophes. The substantive, procedural and evidentiary rules in private environmental actions appear biased in favour of the polluter.* (West, 1987)

The first point to note is that even a 'mediated settlement' is, at best, a fought and won measure based on laws intended to *prevent* the occurrence of multiple harms. The case involves methyl mercury pollution, contaminating the English-Wabigoon River system downstream from Dryden, Ontario:

> *Two pulp and paper plants in the area, the Dryden Paper Company Ltd., and Dryden Chemicals Ltd., both subsidiaries of Reed Paper Ltd., of England, used mercury cells in sodium chloride electrolysis to produce caustic soda and chlorine.* (West, 1987)

The harm from mercury pollution is not a new discovery, as alternative technologies had already been discovered in the 19th century (Charlesbois, 1977); also, scientific evidence about the toxic effects of methyl mercury poisoning have been known since the early 1960s (West, 1987). In fact, the Ontario government had sent a team to the Japanese courts.[23]

In Chapter 8, I discuss the effects of various chemicals, especially pollution from oil production, not only on human physical health, but also on brain and character development and behaviour, in relation to the *Lubicon* case, as well as the Arctic area of Nunavut (the information for those cases comes from research by the WHO, as well as the November 2006 groundbreaking article by Grandjean and Landrigan in the *Lancet*). In this case, similar effects were observed in the Ojibway communities because the ravages of mercury pollution affect all aspects of the health and the life of the inhabitants. West (1987) lists some of the grave problems they encountered:

> ... *in the years immediately preceding and following the pollution, the unemployment rate quadrupled from twenty percent to eighty percent.... Statistics indicated increases in violence, alcohol-related deaths caused by pneumonia, exposure, and suicide.*

In addition, what emerged was 'the link between mercury poisoning and the increase in deviant and violent behaviour' (West, 1987; see also Charlesbois, 1977; Troyer, 1977). Nor is the mercury poisoning a thing of the past. Recent research[24] focuses on mercury poisoning occurring at Thunder Bay and elsewhere and is an example of current scientific information on this problem in Ontario (see table below):

Ontario mercury cell chlor-alkali plants: Operation dates and release of mercury

Location	Plant	Date mercury cells opened	Date mercury cells closed	Years in operation	Operational Hg release in tonnes*
Sarnia	DowChemical Canada Inc.	1948	1973	25	317.73
Cornwall	ICI Ltd.	1935	1995	60	196.13
Sarnia	DowChemical Canada Inc. III	1970	1973	4	71.73
Marathon	American Can of Canada Ltd.	1952	1977	26	62.11
Hamilton	Canadian Industries Ltd.	1965	1973	8	51.47
Thunder Bay	DowChemical Canada Inc.	1966	1973	8	43.30

Note: *Does not include mercury released in solids
Source: After Tripp and Thorleifson (1998)

43.30 tonnes of mercury that was released by Dow Chlor-Alkali plant in Thunder Bay, right next to Fort Williams First Nation, puts into perspective [the Grassy Narrows case]: the Chlor-Alkali plant at Dryden (which mercury poisoned Grassy Narrows and White Dog people) only released 10 tonnes of mercury.

In addition, scientist Michael Gilbertson recently retired from the International Joint Commission and in 2006 submitted a PhD thesis entitled 'Injury to health: A forensic audit of the Great Lakes Water Quality Agreement (1972–2005) with special reference to congenital minamata disease'.

The scientific evidence has been available for years, yet in 1985 when the federal Department of Indian affairs contacted Mr Justice Emmett Hall (former Supreme Court of Canada Justice), who visited Grassy Narrows and studied a '211 pages legal brief prepared for the Indian Bands by Robert Sharpe, a University of Toronto professor and expert in such litigation' (West, 1987), what emerged persuaded him not to recommend going to trial. He believed that the results of the complex and time-consuming litigation would be uncertain, hence that the best interests of the Ojibways would be served by 'a negotiated settlement outside the court system' (West, 1987).[25]

There is no question about the connection between mercury pollution and the diseases that follow upon that poisoning, yet Mr Justice Hall was correct in stating the following, among his many concerns, in his affidavit:

> *(vi) I was concerned about the Plaintiff's ability to establish their claim that mercury poisoning posed a potential hazard to the health of the unborn because of mercury induced genetic damage in one or both parents.*
>
> *(vii) In general, I was concerned about the likelihood of legally establishing the link between mercury pollution and health damages because the symptoms of mercury poisoning, such as tremor, ataxia, and sensory abnormality are also the symptoms of conditions such as alcoholism. . .[26]*

Hence, to ensure some degree of success for the First Nations involved, Mr Justice Hall decided to negotiate a settlement outside the court system. Because of the problems existing in the evidentiary and regulatory framework in environmental cases, 'the Ojibways Bands really did not have an alternative to settlement', and the Can$14 million they received, helped them cope with the problems they were facing, although, to be sure, 'no level of compensation exists which can ever redress the harms caused by the poisoning' (West, 1987).

The problem, as we have noted repeatedly, is not linked only to this case; it is a systemic problem, endemic to Canadian regulatory legislation. 'Canadian plaintiffs must rely on inadequate common law remedies for a number of reasons' (West, 1987). These reasons include: first, the reliance of environmental law on English common law tort system, 'a system geared to furthering the interests of industrial enterprises'; second, 'group disputes and collective rights do not fit comfortably into the traditional framework of tort litigation'; third, 'nuisance' action is incapable of accommodating modern scientific realities; fourth, 'the Canadian Judiciary is reluctant to play an active role' to address environmental degradation and human rights; and fifth, the question of the 'burden of proof borne by the victims in environmental tort litigation' is an 'important insurmountable hurdle' (West, 1987).

Most of the problems listed here are clearly a part of the general difficulties faced by all cases involving environmental racism. West (1987) argues that the US judiciary is better equipped to accommodate environmental court cases but the analysis of the US situation in the work of Bullard (2001) points to the contrary, and we also noted in Chapters 4 and 5 that cases tried in the US under ATCA are similarly affected. Both countries, as well as international law in general, have not accepted the direct causal link with health present in these cases:

> ... *in environmental litigation a direct line for the health problems must be established, there is a tendency for some courts to confuse scientific and medical questions with legal questions, where they arise in a legal context.* (West, 1987; see also Catrilli, 1984; Large and Mitchie, 1981)

In addition, I have argued that the whole concept of 'torts' and compensation for environmental injuries is legally insufficient and morally inadequate (Westra, 2004a). The envionmental attacks directed at vulnerable people should be considered crimes and proscribed accordingly. Aside from possible compensation to the victims, if harms occur they should be treated as the violations and homicide that they are. Further, the idea of closing cases with compensation may give some relief to the victims but does little or nothing to restrain the criminals who can easily pass the expense along to consumers, or claim it as a legitimate business expense.

Like other ongoing, economically driven issues, the whole idea of not addressing these grave problems through prevention but only *after* the fact, and only as torts, should be revised completely. One is reminded of the huge campaigns mounted everywhere to find the 'cure' for cancer, despite the fact that Samuel Epstein published in 1978 a thorough indictment of that approach as he explained the role of the 'dirty dozen' environmental practices that must be eliminated to achieve prevention of cancer instead (Epstein, 1978). Of course those who are presently ill must receive treatment, but the fact that treatment is available should not blind us to the fact that most cancers are extremely profitable for pharmaceutical companies and others, whereas prevention would be economically harmful to both pharmaceuticals and chemical companies (Grandjean and Landrigan, 2006; Tamburlini, 2002; WHO, 2002; Licari et al, 2005).

Hence, rather than compensating for the harms, strong environmental regulatory regimes would eliminate the suffering of countless people, such as those in the Grassy Narrows and White Dog in the 'line of fire' from such operations. I return to the possible role of the WHO and other public health considerations in Chapter 10. For now, it seems that racism is alive and well in the cases we have considered, and that, in Canada, the indigenous peoples bear most of the brunt of it. The American experience demonstrates how often the use of 'brownfields' and other apparent economic considerations, mask environmental racism. Such racism wears many masks, such as business requirements or economic rationality for decisions that are either based on it, or help to perpetuate it in the future, like the continuation of using polluted areas for more polluting businesses, thus perpetuating brownfields in areas where the lack of land value makes further hazardous sitings a 'good' proposition, not only now but in the future. The next case describes and discusses several other related issues as well as environmental racism.

ENVIRONMENTAL RACISM AND STATE TERRORISM AT OKA: A CASE STUDY[27]

This is a case study about environmental racism, recently emerging as a 'new' issue in the US and in countries in the South. Environmental racism is a form of discrimination against minority groups and countries in the South, practised in and through the environment. It involves such practices as the siting of hazardous or toxic waste dumps in areas inhabited primarily by people of colour, or hiring African Americans or Native Americans to work in hazardous industries, or even exporting toxic waste to impoverished countries (Westra and Lawson, 2001). However, the problem acquires a new 'face' when it affects the aboriginal people of Canada. In their case, questions about environmental racism cannot be separated from issues of sovereignty and treaty rights, and this is clearly not the case for either urban or rural African Americans and nor is it true of American Indian people. In the US, Native Americans are 'regarded in law as "domestic dependent nations" with some residual sovereign powers. In Canada the majority of First Nations people seek recognition under the Constitution of Canada of an inherent right to self-government'.[28]

This difference is extremely significant as it injects an additional component of violence, repression and state terrorism that is largely absent from cases affecting visible minorities in the US, where even violence takes on quite different connotations and has no component of national self-defence (Westra and Lawson, 2001). This additional component of Canadian 'difference' emerges clearly in the discussion of the Oka confrontation below.

Environmental racism is not a new phenomenon, but it is a new issue to some extent as it was targeted by the Clinton administration; Clinton signed an 'Executive Order' on 11 February 1994 to make environmental justice for minorities a specific concern for the Environmental Protection Agency (Bullard, 2001).

The Mohawks at Kahnawake and Kanesatake, and the confrontation at Oka, Quebec, summer 1990

In order to understand the events culminating in the summer of 1990, several complex issues underlying the conflict must be understood. These are: first, the position of the Mohawks and their forms of government, as well as that of the Canadian government; second, the environmental issue and the demands of the township of Oka; and third, the chronology of the actual events and confrontations. All three issues are discussed in turn.

The federal government, the 'Indian Act' and Mohawks' governance

Mohawk communities in Canada total 39,263 persons, including Kanesatake, Kahnawake, Akwesasne and another four tribes. The Kanesatake community totals 1591 persons and the Department of Indian Affairs funds their total budget for education costs. Status Indians are eligible to attend both elementary and secondary schools off the reserve.[29]

Nevertheless the 'status of Kanesatake with respect to the land does not fit within the usual pattern of Indian reserve lands in Canada': they are Indians within the meaning of the term under the Indian Act, live on Crown Lands (since 1945) reserved for their use (within the meaning of section 91(24) of the Constitution Act of 1867), but they do not live on lands clearly having status as an Indian Act Reserve.[30]

The reason for this anomaly can be traced to the 1717 Land Grant by the King of France, and to seigneurial grant at Lac de Deux Montagnes given to the Ecclesiasticals of the Seminary of St Sulpice. The Sulpicians' mandate was 'the purpose of protecting and instructing the indigenous people (a policy reflecting the ethnocentrism and paternalism of that time)'.[31] This led to continuous disputes between the Mohawks at Kanesatake and the Sulpicians over land sales and management. In fact, the Sulpicians asked France's king for a second land grant 'to provide a greater land base for the Indians', and this, too, was granted in 1735. The Indians were told that the land would revert to the Sulpicians only in the event that the Indians would decide to leave. But the Sulpician's 'tutelage' and paternalism quickly turned to tough-minded abuse. The Indians were allowed to build houses and grow crops, but they could neither sell land nor wood or hay without explicit permission. They could be brought to trial for cutting wood for snowshoes, house repairs or firewood, and despite the Indians' repeated petitions to the King of France and, after his defeat by the British, to all those in power, their miserable conditions and the exploitation of their lands continued unabated. The Sulpicians explained their position by saying that, without strict controls, the 'savages' would return to their 'natural laziness' (Pindera and York, 1991).

A French native of the region, turned Methodist missionary, records many instances of inhumane cruelty and mistreatment of Indians on the part of the priests. When Amand Parent returned to establish a small Methodist church at Oka in 1872, the Sulpicians felt he taught the Indians to behave 'above their station', and he too encountered ill-treatment and hostility. In 1875, the church was torn down by Crown order because it had been erected without permission with wood from the seigneury (Parent, 1887). In 1936, the Sulpicians, blatantly disregarding the original French mandate, sold much of the land to a rich Belgian, Baron Empain, who in turn resold it in 1950.

Canadian government records note continuing disputes, which at times led to confrontations in the area. In 1912, a decree of the Privy Council (then the highest court of appeal for Canadian cases), officially deprived the Mohawks of any rights in respect to the lands 'by virtue of aboriginal title'.[32] As the seminary continued to sell off lands, the federal government attempted to put a stop to the controversies by purchasing the rest of the Sulpicians' lands in 1945, without consulting the Mohawks. These lands, however, were interspersed with 'blocks' of land privately owned by the municipality of Oka (Begin et al, 1990).

The Mohawks, meanwhile, continued to advance their claims on separate, but related, legal grounds:

1   *territorial sovereignty flowing from status as a sovereign nation;*
2   *treaty rights;*
3   *the Royal Proclamation of 1763;*
4   *unextinguished aboriginal title under common law;*
5   *land rights flowing from the obligations imposed on the Sulpicians in the 18th century land grants by the King of France.* (Pindera and York, 1991)

The federal government believed that the issues were settled by the Privy Council Order of 1912, and that the claims were weakened by the fact that the Mohawks have not been continuously in possession of the land since time immemorial, as 'land use by natives and non-natives is also recorded'. These land users included some white settlers, as well as other native tribes. However, the federal department also described the Mohawks at Oka as descendents of some of these other groups who had been in possession, that is the Iroquois, Algonquians and Nipissings. In fact the federal government attempted to purchase additional land to give the Mohawks at Kanesatake a 'unified land base', from 1985 up to the time of the Oka conflict.

Additionally, the Canadian government requires certain specific forms of Indian governments in order to recognize Indians' sovereign nation status. The Mohawks at Oka have a long history of debate about their own forms of governance. They belong to the Six Nations of the 'Iroquois Confederacy' (the other five are Oneida, Onondaga, Cayuga, Seneca and Tuscarora), and are governed by the 'Great Law of Peace' (Kayanerakowa) or the 'Longhouse System'. But the Department of Indian Affairs (under the Indian Act), supports the act's election system of band councils. Instead, Chief Samson Gabriel wrote in 1967 that the Longhouse was the only form of legitimate Mohawk governance. As Chief Gabriel put it:

> *We recognize no power to establish peacefully, or by the use of force or violence, a competitive political administration. Transactions of such groups in political and international affairs is very disturbing to the Six Nations 'Iroquois Confederacy Chiefs'.* (Pindera and York, 1991)

In essence, there is a direct connection between any possible progress on land rights, native sovereignty or self-determination, and progress on the issue of Mohawk leadership or governance. The Department of Indian Affairs may permit the application of the Indian Act 'on an interim basis', until some appropriate alternative local form of government policy can be established. If the Mohawks could not agree on the forms of leadership and governance appropriate to their tribe, then the Department of Indian Affairs could refuse to consider their claims because no local (native) governance policy was firmly established, as required.

The environmental issues and the demands of the Oka township in 1990

The previous section details the political and ideological controversies that led to the violence at Oka:

> *The controversies included conflicts over divergent native ideologies about self-government and about the historical residence of other tribes in the disputed area, which was viewed by some to invalidate any native land claim on the part of the Mohawks.* (Begin et al, 1990)

Before turning to a narrative of the events of the summer of 1990, it is necessary to show the role environmental issues played in the racism and the violence of the events that followed the dispute. The municipality of Oka 'legally owns the clearing in the Pines and calls it a municipal park' (Begin et al, 1990), but the Mohawks argue that the land is theirs, and that they never sold it or gave it away, hence they do not recognize that ownership claim. The Pines have been part of the Kanesatake territory for over 270 years. About 100 years ago, the fine and sandy soil of the crest of the hill overlooking Oka was severely affected by deforestation and in danger of being washed away by the rains. The Mohawks, together with the Sulpician fathers, planted thousands of trees in the unstable sand. That area is now known as 'the commons', at the very heart of the 800 hectares of Mohawk settlement. Thus the Mohawks' approach to dealing with the Pines was ecologically sound, and it is easy to understand their dismay at the later turn of events. They believed that the original 'Lake of Two Mountains' seigneury (including the parish and the town of Oka), was their property. Yet they had to watch powerlessly as housing and recreational developments, including a golf course, continued to erode what they took to be Mohawk lands, in order to benefit the rich newcomers.

A small graveyard, the Pine Hill Cemetery, holds the bones of dead Mohawks at Kanesatake, the parents and grandparents of the warriors who were to fight for the Pines in 1990. It is placed between the Oka golf club's driveway and its parking lot. The Mohawks have cherished the Pines since they were planted, and they organize a careful clean-up of the area every year. But in March 1989, Oka's mayor, Jean Ouellette, unveiled his plans for the expansion of the golf club. A strip of 18 hectares of forest and swampland near the clearing in the Pines was to be bought and leased to the club in order to add nine holes to the golf course. The mayor did not consult the Mohawks as he believed he had the law on his side; the government had 'consistently denied the Mohawk land claims for 150 years' (Pindera and York, 1991). When an angry citizen demanded to know why the township had been faced with a *fait accompli*, instead of being consulted before the fact, and why the Indians had not been consulted, Ouellette responded with a shrug and said, 'You know you can't talk to the Indians' (Pindera and York, 1991). Many citizens were outraged by the mayor's attitude; 900 signed a petition opposing the project, which was perceived not to be in the interest of the general public as well as being environmentally unsound.

The Pines' soil is sandy, so erosion and shifting sands on the hillside would again become a continuing threat, if the painstakingly planted and nurtured trees were to be cut. At one time, in the 19th century, the sand had threatened to bury the town, and that formed the rationale for the planting of the pines themselves. Moreover, there are two additional environmental problems that are not even mentioned in the literature describing the Oka incident: first, the Indian 'world view' about land and their respect for natural entities and laws; and second, the particularly hazardous nature of the envisioned project.

Native world views (basic to all Indian groups in North America) involve respect for nature and all the creatures with which we share a habitat. Disrespect and wasteful use of anything on Earth is unacceptable to Indians as a people, totally aside from personal preferences or even personal or group advantage (Sagoff, 1988). This represents a basic belief, a value akin to a religious one, and not to be confused with political beliefs about sovereignty or self-governance.

Further, even aside from the issue of shifting sands and deforestation, or of religious and traditional beliefs, the enterprise, namely a golf course, for which deforestation was planned, is often a significant source of environmental contamination, in spite of its benign green appearance (Pimentel, 1993). Lise Bacon, environmental minister at the time, could neither help nor intervene because the law did not require an environmental impact study for a recreational project in the municipality. But although golf courses are much in demand when they are adjacent to better housing developments, as well as for the sport for which they are created, their perfect manicured appearance depends heavily on fungicides, pesticides and other chemicals that are hazardous to wildlife, ecosystems and human health (Pimentel, 1991; 1992).

Hence, aside from the question of Mohawks' rights in regard to First Nations' sovereignty, the people of the Pines were correct in their opposition to the development, and so were the other objectors who protested on environmental grounds based on the value of life-support systems and the inappropriateness of siting a hazardous, chemically dependent operation near a fragile ecosystem on which the Mohawks depended. (Westra, 1994a; 1994b). The Mohawks' lifestyle requires a healthy, unpolluted habitat, even more so than other Canadians, because their world view entails particularly close ties to the land, and their traditional reliance on hunting and fishing self-sufficiency demands it. As a people and as a separate nation, they have the right to live according to their religious beliefs, without being second-guessed or overruled by others. Even if they were not viewed as a separate nation and a separate people according to the Canadian Constitution, but simply as any other Canadians, they would have the right to live according to their own convictions. But the respect due and normally accorded separate ethno-cultural or religious groups was not accorded to the Mohawks. They were treated in a way which did not accord them either the respect due to them as free and equal citizens, or the respect due to citizens of a separate sovereign nation (that is, as people who were not subject to Canadian laws on their own territories). This lack of understanding and respect led to the ongoing hostility and the racism demonstrated through the events of the summer of 1990.

In this case, the racism was and is perpetrated in and through the land; it manifested itself in the careless attempt to impose environmental degradation and ecological disintegrity, hence it can be termed appropriately a form of environmental racism, but one which showed a unique, specifically Canadian 'face'.

The chronology of the events and the confrontation at Oka

In early March 1990, the township council pressed for proceeding with plans for the golf club expansion, against a background of vacillations from Ottawa about appropriate forms of governance. The Mohawks, although disagreeing among themselves, were united in their opposition to the council and the mayor of Oka. In essence, although the Mohawks had always maintained that even the blocks that had been sold off to the township were part of their territory, there was a lot of disagreement on the question of compliance with the Indian Act. The Department of Indian Affairs demanded that 'traditional or band custom councils' be used to pass band resolutions and to administer funds from Ottawa, and that some sort of democratic elections be used.

The Longhouse form of government was the Mohawks' traditional way, involving clan mothers whose role was 'to listen to the people of their clans and counsel the Longhouse chiefs' (Pindera and York, 1991). When word spread about a possible early start to the project, a camp was set up in the clearing in the Pines to alert band members through an 'early warning system'; this was the start of the occupation on 10 March 1990. As word spread through Kanasatake, more and more people came to see what was happening and then decided to stay. Signs were erected near the edge of the golf course in French and English, saying 'Are you aware that this is Mohawk land?' (Pindera and York, 1991).

Although many Mohawks did not take the occupation seriously, others started to spend more time at the camp each day as they returned from work or from school, and some initiated a night shift armed with sticks, branches and axe handles for protection. After Earth Day on 22 April 1990, when the Mohawks traditionally cleaned up the forest area of garbage and debris, more and more Mohawks joined the camp. They were armed and erected the Warrior Flag and set up barricades of cement blocks a few metres back from Highway 344, and pushed a large fallen log across the northern entrance of the Pines (Pinder and York, 1991).

In May, the Akwesasne war chief, Francis Boots, made his first trip to the Pines in response to requests from a Longhouse chief's son for a patrol vehicle, a supply of two-way radios and money for gas and groceries (Pindera and York, 1991). Although not everybody was in favour of being armed, eventually a consensus was reached for resistance. On 7 May, a Mohawk representative was allowed to address the council of Oka citizens; he pleaded for peace rather than confrontation, but the mayor insisted there was no room for negotiations or discussions: the land belonged to the township. Premier Robert Bourassa and the Quebec public security minister were approached by the mayor, who asked them to send the police to dismantle the barricades. Bourassa responded: 'I don't want to send anyone to play cowboy over the question of a golf course'. The Provincial Minister of Aboriginal Affairs, John Ciaccia, was sent to negotiate, but he was not given the power to significantly affect the outcome of the discussions, beyond initiating a dialogue.

On 5 June, the municipality adopted a resolution: they proposed a moratorium on construction, but only if the barricades were lifted. The Mohawks refused, and Curtis Nelson of the Longhouse met with the Federal Minister of Indian Affairs, Tom Siddon, in Parliament in Ottawa on 21 June. Nelson and other Mohawk representatives intended to press their land claims, but they hoped for some 'limited jurisdiction' and hence they refused to discuss the barricades, and left.[33]

The municipality decided to seek an injunction against the Mohawks; at their meeting with Tom Siddon on 28 June, they compared the barricades to 'a state of anarchy'.[34] Further, when the municipality sought the help of the Surete de Quebec on 10 July, their request read, in part:

> ... we ask you therefore to put a stop to the various criminal activities currently taking place ... and to arrest the authors of the crimes, so that we can proceed with establishing the recreational use of the occupied land.[35]

On 11 July, the police decided to intervene and, although before that date 'the use of arms by First Nation people' was unprecedented, this time an armed conflict developed. The police had backed away from confrontation up to that time. When the police attacked and opened fire, the warriors, who had been quietly joining the resistance for the past several months retaliated and gunfire was exchanged. Corporal Marcel Lemay of the police was fatally wounded and rushed to hospital. To this day, it is unclear who hit him, as the recovered bullet could have come either from a police gun or from a warrior's gun. Eventually an inquest decided that it had been a Mohawk gun that had killed him but, since the only evidence submitted and accepted at the inquest was that of the police themselves, the result must remain uncertain (Pindera and York, 1991).

When a lawyer for the Kanesatake band in Montreal was told by the Mohawks that the police were getting ready to attack again, he made 'forty-five calls in four hours' trying to reach someone with the power to stop the attacks. He finally reached Premier Bourassa, who, when told of the police officer's death, cancelled the second raid (Pindera and York, 1991).

From 13 July, a new strategy was initiated: the police would not permit supplies, food or medicine to enter the occupied lands, and even the Red Cross had to wait 24 hours before being permitted to enter. Indian women who attempted to go to the town to shop for groceries were jeered at and jostled. On one occasion, the police arrived barely in time to prevent a beating by an angry crowd. They had to leave without the food they had purchased. A Human Rights Commission official attempted to enter the roadblock to observe conditions at the camp, but he was refused, in glaring violation of the Quebec Charter of Rights and Freedoms. The Indians' survival was in fact dependent on the cooperation of other bands who brought in food and other necessities by canoe, under the cover of night and across the dense brush. Attempted negotiations continued to be stalled and the Mohawks issued a revised list of demands on 18 July. That list read:

> *Title to the lands slated for the golf club expansion and the rest of the historic Commons; the withdrawal of all police forces from all Mohawk territories, including Ganienkeh in New York State and Akwesasne, on the Quebec, Ontario and New York borders; a forty-eight hours time period in which everyone leaving Kanesatake or Kahnawake would not be subject to search or arrest; and the referral of all disputes arising from the conflict to the World Court at the Hague.* (Pindera and York, 1991)

Their demands also listed three 'preconditions' before further negotiations: free access to food and other provisions; free access to clan mothers and spiritual advisors; and the 'posting of independent international observers in Kanesatake and Kahnawake to monitor the actions of the police' (Pindera and York, 1991). Eventually talks were arranged in a Trappist monastery, la Trappe, at Oka, where the monks had been supportive of the Mohawks and had sent food and supplies for the warriors and their families. At this time, the Mohawks argued for their position on sovereignty. Loran Thompson, a Mohawk representative, showed his Iroquois Confederation passport, 'complete with Canadian customs stamps from occasions when (he) had crossed the Canadian/American border', hence he had proof that Canadian officials had accepted them as a separate nation. The Mohawks also explained the major political principles that govern them: 'The Two Row Wampum' Treaty (originally a treaty with the Dutch), and the 'Great Law of Peace'. The former supported peaceful but separate coexistence with non-Indians, as a canoe and a boat can both travel down the same river, provided each crew rowed their own boat only and did not attempt to straddle both. According to the treaty, any Mohawk who would submit to any other government would be treated as a traitor. The Great Law of Peace also supported separate sovereign status and non-submission, and it recommended not bearing arms and preferring peace.

Unfortunately, although the Mohawks were perceived as patriots whose cause was valid even by some of the soldiers who eventually replaced police at the barricades, their situation placed them in 'vicious circle'. If they were not recognized as a separate nation, they could not bear arms in their own defence or in support of their territorial claims. But without arms, some argue, 'they will not be able to affirm their rights as a nation' (Pindera and York, 1991) or to protect disputed territories until negotiations and peaceful talks could help rectify the problem.

At the Mohawks' request, international observers were allowed into the Pines, and it is very important to hear their comments:

> 'The only persons who have treated me in a civilized way in this matter here in Canada are the Mohawks', said Finn Lying Hjem, a Norwegian Judge. 'The army and the police do nothing. It's very degrading... degrading to us, and perhaps more degrading to the government who can't give us access'. (Pindera and York, 1991)

When Premier Bourassa asked the international observers to leave, they warned Quebec and Canada of the 'dangerous precedent' that had been set by arbitrarily breaking off talks. After many fruitless weeks of barricades and occupations, while the Mohawks' case became the cause for all First Nations people, no progress was made on any of their demands. Eventually the warriors, under pressure from the soldiers, decided to 'disengage' and accept the word of the Canadian government that their land claims would be seriously considered. The warriors were taken off in police vehicles, each with several plastic handcuffs, as they showed they could easily break one handcuff with their bare hands. As a last gesture of defiance, a Mohawk warrior society flag was smuggled onto the bus and waved at onlookers as the police took them away.

This, unfortunately, was not the end of either violence or racism. Many of the warriors were badly beaten by the police during 'interrogations'. Some were roughed up as they were arrested and charged with 'rioting and obstruction of justice'. As well as Corporal Lemay, two Mohawks died. One, an elderly man, died of heart failure after a stone-throwing mob attacked him at the outskirts of town; the other was poisoned by tear gas and died later.

It is noteworthy that the Canadian Army (which eventually replaced the police) had only been used once before in Canadian history against domestic rebels (in the 1970 Quebec Liberation Front crisis). The crisis at Oka was described in the Canadian press as 'the greatest ever witnessed in Quebec, Canada, even North America' (Pindera and York, 1991). Finally, more than ten months after the end of the conflict, disciplinary hearings were held 'to examine the conduct of eight senior officers of the Quebec police, and of 31 junior officers, during the Oka crisis', (no information is available about the outcome of these hearings) and neither Quebec nor Canada showed any desire to improve relations with the people of the First Nations of Canada, even after the conflict, although the situation is substantially different today.

Environmental racism, environmental justice and terrorism: The Canadian difference

In this section, I define and describe environmental racism in general, and relate the specific position of the Indians of Canada's First Nations to environmental racism so that the difference in their case becomes clear. I also discuss the interconnectedness of the land issue and the environmental questions in relation to territorial rights. I argue that the position of the First Nations required them to take a stand and even to take arms, and that the response of the provincial government could be fairly characterized as state terrorism.

Environmental racism

Environmental racism can be defined as racism practised in and through the environment. It refers to environmental injustice whereby, for example, toxic and hazardous waste facilities and are frequently located in or near poor non-white communities. Speaking of the US, Bullard (2001) says, 'If a community is poor or inhabited largely by people of colour there is a good chance that it receives less protection than a community that is affluent or white.' This is a recurring situation because in the US environmental policies 'distribute the costs in a regressive pattern, while providing disproportionate benefits for the educated and the wealthy' (Bullard, 2001) in wealthy white neighbourhoods. This disparity has been institutionalized and has lead to disregard for, and ultimately to ecological violence perpetrated against, people and communities of colour.

Furthermore, although both class and race appear to be significant indicators of the problems outlined, 'the race correlation is even stronger than the class correlation' (Bryant and Mohai, 1990; Gelobter, 1988; United Church of Christ Commission for Racial Justice, 1987). What is particularly disturbing about this trend, is that the ecological violence that is amply documented and which targets vulnerable and often trapped minorities, is not a random act perpetrated by a few profit-seeking operations that could perhaps be isolated and curtailed or eliminated, but that it is an accepted, institutionalized form of 'doing business', taken for granted by most and ignored by all.

This institutionalized pattern of discrimination is an anomaly in a world that is committed to 'political correctness', at least officially and in the so-called 'free world' (Freedman and Narveson, 1994). For instance, both in Canada and the US, neither government institutions nor corporate bodies would deliberately promote or practise hiring in an openly discriminatory manner, or explicitly advocate segregation in housing or education. Although both women and minorities often feel that covertly discriminatory practices or 'glass ceilings' exist both in business and government, which prevent them from achieving their full potential, still these difficulties are not openly fostered by institutions.

Yet the practice of placing hazardous business operations such as dump sites and other waste facilities in the 'backyards' of minority groups is practiced regularly, with no apology. It is described as a purely economic decision with no consideration for the unjust burdens it may place on individuals and affected communities who are often too poor and weak to fight back (Gewirth, 1982; Rawls, 1999b). Similarly, when the US Environmental Protection Agency uses its 'superfund' and other means to ameliorate acute problems in white neighbourhoods long before it even acknowledges or attempts to respond to environmental emergencies in black ones, then it appears that environmental racism is practised almost by rote, with little fear of retribution. Bullard (1994) argues that:

> *The current environmental protection paradigm has institutionalized unequal enforce-ment; traded human health for profit, placed the burden of proof on the 'victims' rather than on the polluting industry; legitimized human exposure to harmful substances; promoted 'risky' technologies such as incinerators; exploited the vulnerability of communities of colour.*

The same practice of ecological destruction happens overseas, by the countries of the North and the West in relation to the countries of the South and East. Toxic dumping and other unfair burdens are routinely imposed on countries whose leaders are often all too willing to trade off the safety of their uninformed and unconsenting disempowered citizens for Western hard currencies. Those who may respond that no racism is involved, as the hazardous transactions simply reflect economic advantage and 'good business sense', ignore the fact that most often the perpetuation of brownfields is founded on various forms of earlier segregation and racism.

In the global marketplace, this approach has been termed the practice of 'isolationist strategy' (Shrader-Frechette, 1991). In this case, the restraints and controls that busi-nesses may employ in their home countries are not carried on in interactions with countries in the South. Relying on several arguments such as 'the countervailing benefit argument', 'the consent argument', 'the social progress argument' and 'the reasonable possibility argument', the isolationist strategy replicates many segregation arguments and thus cannot be acceptable from the moral standpoint (Shrader-Frechette, 1991).

Unfortunately, often poor communities cannot fight off the harm that threatens them insidiously through environmental contamination. When they actually try to do so, however, especially in present times and in the better-educated and better-organized countries of North America, they may reach a favourable outcome. For instance, in a recent case in Titusville, Alabama, a community group decided to fight Browning-Ferris Industries, who intended to site a waste-transfer station in their neighbourhood. The area was already legally the site of 'heavy industry', but garbage was to be excluded, according to the ownership ordinance. It was also one of the few areas where African Americans had been able to buy property in the city of Birmingham, so that the whole community was and is one of colour. In this case, the community was exposed to a lengthy legal battle, and even police violence, as they demonstrated in the park between Birmingham's City Hall and its Civil Rights Institute. In the end, the city won against the company, and the infamous facility, already built, stood empty as late as November 1994, when I visited at the invitation of the community leader, Whitly Battle, and the lawyer, David Sullivan. In this case, the perpetuation of brownfields in one specific area indicates the institutionalized intent to burden disproportionately citizens of colour with society's hazards, without consent or compensation (Greenpeace, 1995; Westra and Lawson, 2001).

Examples of this kind of problem could be multiplied, although citizens' victories are rare indeed. From toxins in Altgeld Gardens in Chicago (Gaylord and Bell, 2001), to radioactive waste in Louisiana (Wigley and Shrader-Frechette, 2001) and predominantly in the southern US (Bullard, 1994), the story can be repeated again and again with slight variations, and with the black communities regularly the losers. But it is not only the urban minorities that are so targeted; their rural counterparts fare no better. 'Geographic equity' does not exist in North America any more than it does in countries in the South.

Environmental racism and First Nations: Human and religious rights to self-defence

Recently there has been growing support for the defence of minority groups against the ecological violence perpetrated against them. The 'First National People of Colour Environmental Leadership Summit' was held in October 1991 in Washington DC. It united many grass-roots groups and inspired them to seek governmental and national support for strategies to eliminate the rampant environmental racism practised against them (Bullard, 1994–1995). In this section, I argue that the case of Canadian First Nations is quite different in several senses from what has been described above, although it remains environmental racism. Their case is unique because health and safety are not their only concern. Natives require high levels of environmental quality to meet both physical and spiritual needs. They need the land they inhabit to be free of toxic and chemical hazards so that various species of animal and fish, which are part of their traditional diet, do not suffer or disappear; but they also need spiritually to be able to live in a way that is consonant with their world view. This is grounded on respect for all living things with whom they share a habitat.

It can also be argued that the native traditional world view is so much a part of their deeply held values and beliefs that it can be considered a religion common to most Indians in North America. Quite aside from the issue of status as a separate nation discussed above, Mohawks respect for their own ecologically inspired lifestyle should be treated as a constitutionally protected right to freedom of religion under the Canadian Charter of Rights and Freedoms. In fact, the 'Great Law of Peace', which forms the basis for the Oka warriors' ideology, does not separate 'church' and 'state': 'it provides a complex combination of spiritual and political rules... It is the rule book of an entire way of life... it forms the thesis of a modern theocracy' (Pindera and York, 1991).

Hence the rights of the Mohawks to their traditional ways can be supported on the basis of freedom of religion, even before considering their separate national status. Unlike other minorities, these religious rights and freedoms are inseparable from environmental protection. Finally, this approach to ecological protection for large areas of wilderness is necessary for global sustainability, and the Indian traditional way is close to the mandate to 'restore ecosystem integrity', which forms the basis of Environment Canada's 'vision' statement and a host of other regulations and mission statements around the globe (Westra, 1994a; 1995).

In sum, ecological concern is everyone's responsibility, but traditional American Indian 'attitudes' towards nature appear to be particularly apt to support an environmental ethic (Callicot, 1989; Rabb, 1995). These attitudes also provide yet another reason why the Indians ought to have been permitted the peaceful enjoyment of their territory, and why their wishes in relation to the land ought to have been respected. The priests at St Sulpice were twice granted lands on behalf of the Indians, with express instructions to administer them of their behalf. In fact their second request explicitly cited the Indians' needs and lifestyle as the basis for requesting larger areas from the King of France. The priests' needs or their economic advantage were never cited. Their role was not that of owners, but of caretakers and managers of the granted territories. Hence it would be unfair to penalize the Mohawks for the repeated sale of lands that were meant for their sole use and enjoyment. The lands were exploited, mismanaged and sold inappropriately and illegally, and in clear violation of the mandate from either the King of France or that of England (Pindera and York, 1991).

Land, environment, territorial rights and native identity

I have argued that the police of Quebec, federal government officials, and the residents and bureaucrats of Oka, can all be 'charged' with environmental racism. To prove this, it is not necessary to demonstrate specific intent on the part of any one person or group, as environmental racism may be perpetrated through carelessness, self-interest or greed. It is sufficient to show that the practice is accepted and even institutionalized in a way that does ecological violence to a specific community or group of colour. I have also argued that in this case the Indians' historical and legal claim to independent nationhood, as well as their traditional lifestyle, culture and religious beliefs, all contribute significantly to their right to take a stance against environmental racism. The same combination of factors renders their resistance, their unshakable position and even their bearing arms potentially justifiable on moral grounds. Moreover, if their position is morally defensible, then their activities should not be viewed as crimes against the law, but as self-defence, conscientious objections, and affirmations of religious and cultural self-identity. That in turn makes the actions of both police and government in support of ecological violence and repression possible forms of state terrorism. It is this particular situation and combination that makes environmental racism distinctly Canadian in this case, as I argue below.

As the cultural self-identity argument is based on the understanding of the Indians as a people, one might ask, what makes a 'people', other than law or custom? Do citizens involuntarily form associations, or is it their choice that makes them a community or a nation? Is it the case that common allegiance to a state constitutes a nation or people? On what grounds, then is national identity to be founded? According to Henry Sidgwick (1878), legitimate government rests on the consent of the governed, hence the 'voluntarist' model of what constitutes a nation, 'derives from the rights of individuals to associate politically as they choose' (Gilbert, 1994). But it is hard to understand what makes a specific association worthy of recognition, other than the exercise of the citizens' collective will, as people willingly form associations that may be less than worthy of respect (for example, the Ku Klux Klan). Another approach may be to appeal to a national character, emphasizing shared characteristics that might constitute a national identity. Gilbert (1994) terms this 'the ethnic model of nationality'. But to view nations as species of 'natural kinds', is to subscribe to racist theory with the pitfalls we have all learned in Nazi and fascist times (Gilbert, 1994). But there are other, better ways of conceiving of national identity: 'culturalism', for example, provides a useful model. This approach cannot rely exclusively on religion, which usually transcends national borders and hence language; common practices and aspirations, possibly even territory are required as well (Gilbert, 1994). Even someone's upbringing is constitutive of the national identity of individuals. Wil Kymlicka (1991) also discusses the parallel conception of 'communitarianism', that is, viewing nations as groups living a common life in accordance with their own rules, hence this 'community' view or 'cultural view' (Gilbert, 1994), is also relevant to establish national identity. As Kymlicka (1991) points out, 'cultural membership affects our very sense of personal identity and capacity'.

First Nations people in general and Mohawks at Oka in particular can claim national identity, based on what Gilbert (1994) terms 'culturalism', as well as their biological heritage. Kymlicka (1991) speaks of a 'cultural heritage' for all Indians in Canada. This supports the Indians' claim that they are a 'people', and that they can therefore demand to be treated as such:

> *'All peoples have the right to self-determination' declares the first article of the United Nations International Covenant on human rights. That is to say, they have the right to independent statehood.* (Gilbert, 1994)

If this is the case, then certain other rights follow from it, for example, 'their right to throw off alien occupation, colonial status or absorption into some other state' (Gilbert, 1994). Furthermore, at Oka it seems that not only were the Mohawks treated unfairly, so that some suffered harm as the cost of increased benefits to others (an immoral position); they were also treated unjustly (an illegal action), because they were wronged through discrimination:

> *Discrimination mistreats individuals because they are part of a certain group, so that the primary object of mistreatment is the group of which they are a part.* (Gilbert, 1994)

But Gilbert's (1994) discussion, which is primarily about possible explanation and justification for terrorism in certain circumstances, is intended to deal with the situation between Israel and Palestine and that between Ireland and England. Hence, it cannot apply precisely to our case, although, as we have seen, many parallels can be drawn.

What is required then, is to understand the specific way in which racism and discrimination is practised against Indians in Canada that distinguishes their situation completely from that of African Americans in the US and minorities in countries in the South. As we argued earlier, the intent of the Executive Order by which President Clinton established an Office of Environmental Justice, was to eventually eliminate all practices that excluded black communities from the environmental protection and concern that favoured white communities, granting them not only defence against environmental threats, to some extent, but also redress in the case of problems or accidents, both of which were not equally available to communities of colour.

African Americans want to be included within the larger community. They want to avoid the *de facto* segregation to which exclusionary practices condemn them. They can argue that in housing, job seeking and schooling, segregation is not legally permitted at this time; thus, as I suggested earlier, environmental racism constitutes a 'last frontier', or the only area within which racism is not only tolerated, but neither criticized nor discouraged or punished as such by the law.

The interest in avoiding this form of racism is equally as true for Indians as it is for blacks. But the forms of 'discrimination', aside from those which involve the environment, are quite different for Canadian Indians; they are in fact opposite to those that affect blacks. Any 'colour-blind' interpretations of the law are inappropriate for Indians; it is integration that is viewed as a 'badge of inferiority' by Indians, not segregation.

Hence, simply granting Indians the same rights as all Canadians is not only insufficient, but essentially wrong. Kymlicka (1991) writes that 'The viability of Indian communities depends on coercively restricting the mobility, residence, and political right of both Indians and non-Indians'. It is therefore a necessary component of the Indians' rights and liberties to deny non-Indians the right to purchase or reside on Indian lands. A *fortiori* then, the right to adversely affect and pollute or otherwise ecologically affect these lands should be equally impermissible. Hence the activities of non-Indians in lands adjacent to Indian lands, must be consonant with a 'buffer zone' (as it is for instance in Man and the Biosphere areas surrounding a wild 'core' zone (see Westra, 1995).

In the concluding section, I defend the Mohawks' actions as morally defensible and discuss the government's interventions as motivated by environmental racism supported by terrorist attacks.

Conclusion: National identity, environmental racism and state terrorism

On the account presented in the last section, the cause of the Mohawks at Oka can be defended as just on moral grounds; environmentally and culturally they were clearly under attack. Those responsible for the circumstances in which they found themselves were guilty not only of racism but of environmental racism. The final question that must be asked at this point is whether the Mohawks were justified in taking up arms, and whether the police and the army were justified in the way they handled the warriors after the 'disengagement'. The Mohawks are not the first or even the only people who have resorted to civil resistance and even violence in defence of the environment. What makes their acts different and in fact unique, has been described above.

In contrast, those chaining themselves to trees at Clayoquot Sound in British Columbia came from all over Canada, and could have in fact come from anywhere in the world in defence of the common cause: protecting the environment. The Indians also shared this generalized concern, as I have shown, through their concern for the forest in relation to the township. The Mohawks were also motivated by other, specific reasons. These were: first, the way their identity as a people is dependent on a certain place, so that any attack on either its size or its environmental quality and integrity must be construed as an attack on their identity; and second, the spiritual and religious components of their need for the land, which go beyond our own acknowledged need for wild places for various reasons (Westra, 1994a).

Hence, the Indians' defence goes beyond ecological concern in a general sense. It becomes a case of self-preservation. That makes bearing arms for that purpose more than a simple criminal act, as some claimed. The paradigm or model, according to which the Mohawks activities must be viewed, is not that of breaking the law or that of committing crimes. The closest model is that which fits other bi-national territorial disputes, such as those between Ireland and Britain, or between Israel and Palestine, where, as Gilbert (1994) has argued, border disputes are not open to democratic decisions based on votes. Neither Israelis nor Palestinians can democratically decide on the location of a specific border affecting their two nations. The only avenues open to these national groups, as to the Irish, in their territorial dispute, is either to declare war, or to attack or respond to violence through terrorist attacks outside a formal war situation.

Therefore these acts cannot be simply defined as 'random violence' or as crime, because significant differences exist. The perpetrators announce their intention to stand their ground or to fight, and they publicize their political motives explicitly, in contrast with the hidden and furtive activities of criminals. Hence, the Mohawks' use of force must be viewed, and perhaps justified, in terms of terrorism, not random violence. It is important to note that they resisted and defended, but did not launch violent attacks beyond their own territories. In fact, all their interactions and negotiations with the representatives of the Canadian government or the township were characterized by reasoned arguments, the repetition of their claims and the reasons for those claims, coupled with the sincere desire to achieve and maintain peace. They bore arms for self-defence, not attack.

I have argued elsewhere (Westra, 1990) that often even terrorist aggressive violence may be defensible in principle, though not in its practical expression, and I have called defensible violence of this sort, a form of 'whistle-blowing', as it calls attention to some grave injustice. The extent of the injustice and the discriminatory treatment, neither of which were random occurrences but rather formed a historical pattern on the part of the Canadians, has been discussed above. Their perpetration justifies, I believe, resistance on grounds of self-determination. Their resistance then becomes analogous to that intended to throw off foreign occupation (Gilbert, 1994).

The events may be described, using Gilbert's felicitous expression, as an 'ethical revolution' (1994). Such a revolution is typically based on a 'different conception of the state and the community'; it is an 'inspirational aspect of violent change', which might be of two kinds: 'ethically conservative', or 'ethically radical' (Gilbert, 1994). The former appeals to values that the resisting group shares with the majority, including its opponents, but which are not properly implemented. The latter, 'makes its case on the basis of a change in the values themselves' (Gilbert, 1994), and is persuasive because it demands a change of values. The Mohawks' case seems to fit the second model. They can be seen as 'ethical revolutionaries', as people who 'seek to change the criteria for membership of the political community' (Gilbert, 1994).

They were criticized for not using democratic means to state their grievances and get redress, but their grievances were not of the sort that can easily be settled by democratic means. This is because the very core of their complaint was that the Mohawk nations was not viewed as an equal, viable political community, responsible for decisions affecting their people and their land. It is here that the parallel with terrorism becomes even clearer.

International terrorism is most often concerned with territory and political equality. But claims to self-determination should be 'made within existing borders', an impossibility when the very extent of the territory within those borders is at issue (as argued earlier), and when the dissenting and protesting group is in a clear minority position. But in that case, the group seeking redress that is, as in this case, at the same time environmental, territorial and concerned with national independence, has no democratic recourse, no peaceful voice through which to make its claim other than perhaps attempting a 'sit-in' to gain national and international attention. It seems as though it must resist, even while seeking peace. And if its arguments and claims are not heard and respected, its only recourse is to resist attack and bear arms. Note that they were indeed resisting peacefully, and only turned violent when violently attacked.

What is the state to do in response to such a position? Should it respond with force and attack? But then can we not charge it with hypocrisy and view its actions as open to a *tu quoque* argument (Gilbert, 1994). It is not sufficient, as we have seen, to say that government force must intervene to 'punish crime', as the Indians are not breaking a law to which they are legitimately subjected. On the contrary, their claim is that law is not their law, that state is not their state, and its values are not theirs. In this, the Canadian constitution appears to support their position. When weighing the forms of violence (that is the Indians' and the state's), there seems to be little cause to view the former as 'wrong', the latter as 'right', from the moral standpoint.

The stronger the moral case for the Mohawks, the weaker, morally, the case for the 'legal' repression and violence they had to endure. While the reasons for supporting the Indians' position at Oka are many and defensible, only one possible reason can be given in support of the army's intervention (Gilbert, 1994). The state has the authority to enforce the law and to punish crimes. But is the state's violence against those who are not subject to its laws (or whose major claim for resistance is that they are not), morally better than their opponents' resistance? When we compare even terrorists' action 'seeking to gain power, and those of the agents of the State in seeking to retain it', there may be no moral reason to term the former 'criminal' and the latter 'punishment of crime' (Gilbert, 1994). This is particularly the case, when there was no violent attack on the part of the Mohawks, and the main reason for their resistance was to protest the assumption that they were in fact subject to those laws.

It is also clear that the other alternative – that is, the presumption that while the Mohawks belonged to a separate, sovereign nation, Canada could bear arms against them as a form of warfare – is not appropriate. Rules of war demand that if violence is to be part of a just war, then the war should first be openly declared. This is the reason why terrorism is not precisely warfare, whether it is practised by dissenting groups or by the state itself. State terrorism, therefore, refers to violent responses to terrorism on the part of a government. It is often the alternative preferred to simply treating terrorists as criminals (that is, as innocent until proven guilty, using restraints but not violence against them, and so on). Although a violent response is often employed, this use of state power is hard to justify as anything other than retaliation.

State terrorism involves warlike intentions that are impeded by constraints from issuing an open war. These constraints are characteristically political rather than military, reflecting political inhibition from resorting to war (Gilbert, 1994). However Gilbert adds that normally 'internal State terrorism' does not have the 'warlike aims' of 'acquisition and control of territory'. It seems that the Oka situation instead manifested precisely this aim; perhaps then it represents an atypical form of state terrorism as it has the added component while manifesting many of the usual ones as well. As Gilbert outlines and defines state terrorism, the provincial government's intervention through the police and, particularly, through the army appears to fit under this heading. The state, of course, purports to be operating 'within the framework of the law, which it presents itself as upholding' (Gilbert, 1994). But if its legal framework is 'unable to resist terrorism', the state may simply 'resort to the covertly warlike operations which constitute state terrorism' (Gilbert, 1994). Yet, lacking an openly declared war, 'the ordinary rules of civil life' should guide the state's acceptable intervention. Armed attacks on dissenting citizens of another country (or even of one's own), or beatings as part of 'interrogation' or 'capture', are not the way the state ought to deal even with hardened criminals or serial killers, before or after sentencing. Hence the state denounced the Mohawks as criminals during the crisis but only belatedly treated them as such after their cases came to court. Throughout the crisis, a state of war appeared to prevail, giving additional credence to the Mohawks' claim to sovereignty and national independence, something that is already legally true in Canada for people of the First Nation in general.

It is clear that the federal government cannot have it both ways: either their attack on resisting Mohawks is war – in which case a proper declaration of war, the recognition of their independent nationhood and adherence to the rules of war are mandatory – or it is not. Further, over and above these formal requirements, from the moral standpoint only a war of self-defence (from an actual attack, not from dissent) may be viewed as a just war (Westra, 1990). Or we might accept the other alternative, that the state is viewing their resistance as criminal. It has been shown that this does not appropriately describe the government's response. Unless a criminal is actually attacking a police officer, for instance, drawing fire against him is not a permissible, legal response. As explained earlier, the Mohawks were standing their ground, not even fleeing from the law; and 'if terrorists are denied due process of law, the same acts are criminal' (Gilbert, 1994).

To start shooting prior to trial and conviction of specific individuals, is to deny them due process. Had they even been convicted criminals or killers, retaliation in kind is not appropriate, particularly in a country with no capital punishment. And, it must be kept in mind, no one was ever found guilty of murder. Those who were considered the 'worst offenders' were perhaps Ronald Cross (nicknamed 'lasagna') and Gordon Lazore. Helene Sevigny (1993) reports on the actual sentencing:

> Sentence 'Sa Majesté la Reine vs. Ronald Cross et Gordon Lazore' Province of Quebec, District of Terrebonne, No. 700-01-000009-913; Judge B.J. Greensberg, Superior Court, Criminal Division, St Jerome, 19 February 1992. The two were found guilty of half of their charges, primarily attacks with 'arms' such as baseball bats. The case was appealed on 20 February 1992. On 3 July 1992, the other 39 Mohawks that were originally taken from the barricades and detained, were acquitted. (author's translation)

The Mohawks' well-founded message and their fight against racism in all its forms, including its environmental aspect, has been around for a long time, as has the Indians' effort to have their cause and their reasons heard. Gilles Boileau's (1991) indictment of the 'lords wearing cassocks' ('les seigneurs en soutane'), presents a detailed historical account of the difficulties the Mohawks had to endure:

> The 'Messieurs' and all others must recognize that the Mohawks have a right to 'their dignity and our respect,' and it is high time that Oka should be recognized primarily as Indian land.

In conclusion, the Oka case combines several unique features specific to the Canadian political scene. It manifests aspects of environmental racism, as the ecologically inappropriate choices of a non-Indian majority were to be imposed on the Mohawks without regard for their traditional lifestyles. At the same time, this imposition infringed their right to self-determination and their constitutional status as a First Nation. Finally, the case shows the inappropriate use of force and the employment of state terrorism in response to the Mohawks' position, which, I have argued, is defensible on moral, environmental and legal grounds.

It is clear that not everyone will readily agree to the strong, land-based obligation here proposed, but many do defend the ultimate importance of unextinguished aboriginal title (Asch and Zlotkin, 1997). The peoples in original Indian societies were strong on sharing, cooperation and good faith, all aspects missing from the dealings involving European newcomers.

Treaties that require the extinguishment of aboriginal rights cannot be based on: first, true collaboration; because, second, they are incompatible with the understanding of aboriginal rights in section 35 of the Constitution Act, 1982; third, they are incompatible with the Crown's fiduciary duty; fourth, they are incompatible with international human rights instruments and are not consistent with the prohibition against racial discrimination; fifth, asking aboriginal peoples to give up their rights would be 'equivalent to asking Canadians to give up their Canadian citizenship'; and sixth, these policies can only be viewed as ethnocentric (Asch and Zlotkin, 1997).

Jim Antoine, Chief of Fort Simpson Dene Band puts it well:

> We are a real part of the land. Our roots are connected into the land. But if you want to extinguish your aboriginal rights and title to it, then you are cutting off those roots. You are cutting us off from the land, and we are floating.[36]

This paragraph is consistent with the major premises of this work; that is, the primacy of the right to biological/ecological integrity of indigenous peoples and First Nations, and the role its absence plays in furthering the ongoing elimination of such people, as peoples, even without a clear genocidal intent on the part of the perpetrators.

CONCLUSIONS

Part Two discussed a number of representative cases, all of which support the main contention of this work: the basic need for the protection of both ecological and biological integrity, and the recognition of its lack as a crime resulting in genocide for the affected aboriginal communities. The contrast between the complaints (the 'facts' in the court cases) of indigenous groups worldwide and the court decisions responding to those complaints repeats the argument of this work. In general, neither the quantitative nor the qualitative aspects of indigenous territories are respected, and the resulting biological and cultural harms to those communities are extensive.

The courts continue to ignore the full import of environmental harms to indigenous peoples despite the laudable 2002 initiative of Justice Arthur Chaskalson, of South Africa (and UNEP), to initiate the 'Judges Portal', intended to promote environmental knowledge and understanding for all judges globally, so that they might better be able to decide on the cases brought before them.

Today, science in general, and public health and epidemiology in particular, have forged ahead of anything found in domestic or international instruments, upon which judges might depend for the cases they are asked to decide. When legal scholars of impeccable reputation are called as expert witnesses, they too are hampered by the limited array and reach of international environmental and human rights instruments. However, those who would be able to speak with an authoritative voice, and as totally independent, are the scientists of the WHO, and these experts are, unfortunately, never called to testify. We shall return to this lacuna in the final chapter of this work.

In the next part, I confront the claim of genocide here advanced head-on, both in its meaning and in the possibility of applying it in the jurisprudence, before turning to a paradigm case, that of the Arctic people of Nunavut in Canada, where several aspects of genocide emerge clearly.

NOTES

1   *Report of the Royal Commission on Aboriginal Peoples: Looking Forward Looking Back* (Vol. 1), 1996, RCAP, www.ainc-inac.gc.ca/ch/rcap/sg/sg28_e.html#99, 'Residential Schools'

2   *Delgamuukw v. British Columbia* [1998] 1 CNLR 14, 11 December 1997, Lamer C. J. (Cory, MacLachlin and Major J. J. Concurring) para. 21.

3   ibid.

4   ibid.

5   Royal Proclamations, 7 October 1763, (1985 RSC Appendix II, No. 1, in part.

6   Reorganized in 1984 in *Guerin v. Canada* [1984] 2 SCR 335.

7   *Sparrow* [1990] 1 SCR. See also Hogg (2005, pp621–621).

8   ibid.

9   ibid.

10 *Halfway River First Nation v. British Columbia* (Minister of Forests) (1999) 178 DLR (4th) 666 716; see Imai, 2001, p. 18.

11 *R. v. Gladstone* [1996] 2 SCR 723; *R. v. can der Peet* [1996] 2 SCR 507.

12 *Delgamuukw v. British Columbia* [1998] 1 CNLR 14, 1997: Per La Forest and L' Heureux-Dube' J.J.: 'Aboriginal title is based on the continuous occupation and use of the land as part of the Aboriginal peoples' traditional way of life.'

13 ibid, emphasis added; however, in *R. v. Marshall* and *R. v. Bernard* (2005), The Supreme Court of Canada seems to pull back from this position.

14 ibid (*Delgamuukw v. British Columbia*).

15 *Marshall v. The Queen* [1993] 3 SCR 456; infra Part I A.2.c.

16 *R. v. Van der Peet*, 137 DLR 4th 289, 9 WWR1 (Can. 1996); *R. v. Gladstone* , 137 DLR 4th 648,9 WWR1 1996.

17 *Van der Peet*, 137 DLR 4th 289; see also *Pamajewon*, [1996] SCC.

18 *Van der Peet*, para. 40.

19 *Delgamuukw v. British Columbia* [1998] 1 CNLR 14, 11 December 1997; *R. v. Sparrow* [1990] 1 SCR 1075.

20 *Delgamuukw v. B.C.* [1998] 1 CNLR 14, para. 21.

21 *Guerin v. Canada* [1984] 2 SCR 335.

22 Clarice Gaylord was Bill Clinton's first appointee to the EPA office of Environmental Justice, by Executive Order No. 12898 in 1992, to redress inequities in the way EPA addressed environmental harms in white communities and communities of colour.

23 See the *Toyama Itai-Itai* case, 635 Hanji 17 (Toyama District Court, 30 June 1971); the *Niigata Minamata* case, 642 Hanji (Niigata District Court, 29 September 1971); the *Yokkaichi Asthma* case, 672 Hanji 30 (Tsu District Court, Yokkaichi Branch, 24 July 1972); the *Kumamoto*

Minimata Disease case, 696 Hanji 15 Kumamoto District Court, 20 March 1973; reprinted in J. Gresser, K. Fugikura and A. Morishima, *Environmental Law in Japan*, 1981.

24 Hummel, J. H. W. from links; see also the Madison Declaration on Mercury Pollution, www.unbc.ca/assets/media/2007/03_march/madison_declarationon_mercury_pollution_with_non-technical_summary.pdf

25 See also Mr Justice Hall's 'Affidavit' before the Supreme Court of Ontario, NO. 14716/77, no. 13.

26 ibid.

27 Adapted from Wellington et al (1997) with permission from Broadview Press, 1997.

28 *Fifth Report of the Standing Committee on Aboriginal Affairs, House of Commons*, Canada, May 1991.

29 ibid.

30 ibid.

31 ibid.

32 *Corinthe v. Seminary of St. Sulpice.*

33 ibid.

34 ibid.

35 ibid.

36 Transcript of the Public Hearing of the Royal Commission on Aboriginal Peoples, Fort Simpson, Northwest Territories, 26 May 1992.

PART THREE

Justifying Genocide: Principles and Reality

CHAPTER 7

Genocide and Eco-crime: The Interface

INTRODUCTION

Suppose that you are wandering across the tundra and you find an infant all alone in the snow. The infant is incapable of discourse. And there is no one to conduct discourse for her. And yet she has the same human rights as everyone who is capable of discourse. There, in the snow, whether she is in Canada in 2006 or Antarctica in 2000 BC, the infant has all the human rights that anyone has in any community with any social conventions. These claims run contrary to much rights talk. (Endicott, 2005)

The previous chapters have reviewed some of the law relating to the interaction between indigenous peoples and MNCs, and the states that facilitate and most often support their activities. Given the gravity of the harms perpetrated against indigenous populations, we ought to set aside for a moment legal conventions and instruments, and ask first the basic questions: do they have human rights, whether or not they can argue for these rights and regardless of their locations and the social conventions present in those locations? Do they have the right to life? To the conditions that support life? To bodily integrity?

The 'infant in the snow' appears to be a case where neither discourses nor conventions are needed to ensure full human rights, and corresponding absolute obligations to whoever might happen upon her: truly obligation *erga omnes*, simply based on her humanity. Hence the sort of attacks described in the case law we have discussed are based upon that position: indigenous peoples' rights are and should be non-derogable, and the continued attacks on their lives, health and existence as peoples ought to be treated like the international crime that it is, genocide

INDIGENOUS PEOPLES
AND THE CRIME OF GENOCIDE

In 1944, Lemkin provided a rich and complete definition of genocide:

Genocide is directed against a national group as an entity, and the actions involved are directed against individuals, not in their individual capacity but as members of the national group.

He also distinguished between different forms of genocide. Based upon his work, Pentassuglia (2002) specifies various forms:

> ... *taking examples from Nazi practice, 'political genocide', 'social genocide', 'cultural genocide', 'economic genocide', 'biological genocide', 'physical genocide', 'religious genocide' and 'moral genocide'.*

Hence indigenous people do not only possess the right to life individually, but they do so in an extended, richer sense, as a group as well. In fact, the biological and physical integrity of groups is clearly dependent on both their individual and communal dimensions. Genocide is a primary example of an obligation *erga omnes*.[1] After reviewing the ATCA jurisprudence, the argument to elevate attacks on indigenous peoples, singly and collectively, from torts to international crime should not be too hard, as each of the cases discussed contains realistic, often first-person accounts of the material facts involved. In some cases, the non-state actors perpetrating the crimes attempt to evade responsibility by claiming that international law only applies to states, hence it cannot touch them. But William Schabas (2001) reminds us that:

> ... *at the end of the Rome Conference in July 1998, the* Financial Times, *the prestigious British business daily, published an article warning commercial lawyers that the treaty's accomplished liability provisions 'could create international criminal liability for employees, officers and directors of corporations'.*[2]

In this chapter, I consider those aspects of the crime of genocide that are most relevant to indigenous peoples, starting with the components of the crime itself.

Genocide: The question of intent

> *From a legal policy perspective, it is especially noteworthy that the magnitude of problems of traditional groups all over the world ... still awaits a comprehensive treaty response, and many of them still struggle for recognition and appropriate protection at home.* (Pentassuglia, 2002)

One of the possible causes of this anomaly lies in the economic/trade orientation of most legal instruments that presently deal with the issue, and with the powerful interests that militate against a serious consideration of indigenous peoples' rights. Another possible answer, albeit a partial one, may be found in the 'intent' requirement that forms an integral part of the crime of genocide, cited in almost every one of the cases discussed in Chapters 4 and 5.

The problem of *mens rea* in general in international crime was introduced in Chapter 5. *Mens rea* is basic to all serious crimes, and it is certainly required for the act of genocide. In that earlier discussion, the focus was on the responsibility of both states and corporations. The starting point now should be the definition of *mens rea* in Article 30(2) and (3) of the Rome Statute of the International Criminal Court:

2. For the purpose of this article, a person has intent here:
(a) In relation to conduct, that person means to engage in the conduct.
(b) In relation to a consequence, that person means to cause that consequence or is aware that it will occur in the ordinary course of events.
3. For the purpose of this article, 'Knowledge' means awareness that a circumstance exists, or that a consequence will occur in the ordinary course of events. 'Know' and 'knowingly' shall be construed accordingly.[3]

In addition, the Chapeau of Article II (Physical and Biological Genocide) of the Genocide Convention emphasizes the required 'intent': the proscribed acts must be deliberate, and they have to be 'committed with the intent to destroy a national, racial, religious or political group, on grounds of the national or racial origin, religious belief, political opinion of its members'. That said, it remains to consider the meaning of 'intent', 'knowledge', 'awareness' and related concepts, in the context of the cases we have discussed in the previous two chapters.

The first problem is that the clear statement of intent required by the definition of genocide is hard to prove, as Bullard (2001) has argued in his indictment of environmental racism. Yet it is an unavoidable component of genocide. Schabas (2000) adds: 'But in cases that cannot be described as purely accidental, the accused's mental state may be far from totally innocent and yet not egregiously evil. To quote Racine (1946): "[a]insi que la vertu, le crime a ses degrés".'

And murder itself has many categories that may render it more or less heinous, as they are considered at the sentencing stage. For genocide, Article V of the convention imposes an obligation to 'provide effective penalties for persons guilty of genocide or any of the other acts enumerated in Article III'.[4] Because 'international law now frowns upon capital punishment' (Schabas, 1997), the maximum sentence that can be imposed is life imprisonment (Schabas, 2000), and it is clearly impossible to impose that penalty on legal individuals who, with the complicity of states, are the most likely to perpetrate genocide upon indigenous peoples in peacetime.

In fact, one of the most salient characteristics of genocide is that it cannot be committed by a single (natural) individual. It requires a large-scale operation and planning as Lemkin (1944) also argued. Case law also speaks of 'widespread and systematic' crimes,[5] or of involving a 'plan or policy'.[6] Hence, although the hatred or at least the deliberate intent to destroy or eliminate a group (in part or as a whole) may be hard to prove, the 'planning' aspect of *mens rea* must be in place, as it is for 'crimes against humanity'.[7] Unlike murder (a crime that may not be premeditated but that could occur spontaneously in a variety of circumstances), for genocide, a widespread 'systematic policy or practice' must exist.[8] And in that case, it is hard to see how it can be argued that the main element of the crime is not present. It is certainly present in the corporate crimes we have discussed in the review of ATCA jurisprudence; at the very least, those acts demonstrate recklessness as to the result of those acts, or 'wilful blindness', as I have argued elsewhere in that regard (Westra, 2004a). Glanville Williams (1961) puts it best, 'The rule that willful blindness is equivalent to knowledge is essential and is found throughout criminal law'. It is telling that even when the specific intent cannot be established 'the act remains punishable but not as genocide. It may be classified as a crime against humanity or it may simply be a crime under ordinary criminal law' (Schabas, 2000).

Although Bassiouni (1979), for example, believed that genocide was not committed by the US regarding their aboriginal populations, in 1995 a special reporter of the Commission on Human Rights took the opposite position, stating, 'the history of the United States of America is closely bound up with the ... genocide of the Indians that [was] openly practiced from the seventeenth century to the nineteenth century'.[9]

Premeditation and intent in corporate genocide

In Chapter 5, at least two of the cases discussed 'genocide' and 'war crimes': *Bancoult v. McNamara*[10] and *Presbyterian Church of Sudan, Rev. John Gaduel and others v. Talisman Energy Inc.* It will be instructive to revisit those cases in order to better understand the sequence of events leading to the alleged crimes. Starting with the latter, Arakis Energy Corporation (later 'Talisman') sought to secure oil concessions from the local Sudanese government. Eventually a deal was struck, but it was worth repeating the language taken from the case, in part:

> *The oil companies agreed to invest in the infrastructure, in transportation, roads and airfields and communication facilities to support exploration, and the government would use the infrastructure to support its genocidal military campaign of ethnic cleansing against local populations.*

The following sequence, therefore, suggests itself. First, the oil company reaches a corporate decision, a free and informed one, to extract oil from a specific location. Second, the corporation decides on the infrastructure required to facilitate their operation. Third, it negotiates with the Sudanese government on that government's requirements to ensure that both the first and second steps can proceed to their mutual satisfaction. In this instance, they agreed that a *cordon sanitaire* was to be provided 'to facilitate the exploration and extraction of oil' (see Chapter 5).

I believe that such a sequence of events would not require an appeal to 'wilful blindness' in lieu of knowledge, as the terms of the deal had to be explicit. Premeditation, intent, knowledge and complicity, all would arguably be present. The events did not occur by chance, through ignorance or on the spur of the moment. They were not even 'collateral damage', or unintended results, as Sudan's intentions would have been apparent. The acts that resulted would therefore have been planned and orchestrated, part of a campaign to treat indigenous and Christian lives as purely collateral to the successful execution of Talisman's plans.

In fact one can add crimes taken from the list of 'other acts' of genocide described in Article III of the convention: 'conspiracy, direct and public incitement, attempt and complicity' and many of these categories merit additional discussion:

> *Yet complicity in genocide should hardly be viewed as being less serious than genocide itself. The accomplice may well be the leader who gives the order to commit genocide, while the 'principal offender' is the lowly subordinate who carries out the instruction. In this scenario, the guilt of the accomplice is really superior to that of the principal offender.* (Schabas, 2000)

This is indeed the case in Talisman; it does seem very likely that without Talisman's proposal and infusion of cash and expertise, the Sudanese government would not have had the means to perform the 'ethnic cleansing' they subsequently undertook. Talisman neither possessed nor provided the fundamental hatred, but their role remains pivotal nevertheless. Nor did the 'incitement' and 'conspiracy' remain inchoate (or incomplete); the genocide was completed as expected and foreseen, and Talisman was able to establish its business operation without the need to comply with the international law requirement regarding securing consent from indigenous peoples (see Chapter 4). Thus the desire to obliterate a people did not have to be a motive for Talisman, but this does not ameliorate their total lack of consideration for the humanity, dignity and needs of specific indigenous groups. Arguably, this was as grave as hatred would have been because they showed corporate negligence, wilful blindness and total unconcern.

In Chapter 5, Peter French's CID structure was discussed, in order to demonstrate the ability of legal entities to devise plans and carry them out as a *whole* – aside from the plans and goals of the individuals that comprise the corporation – and their lack of any mitigating circumstances, because a CID structure cannot have been maltreated or abused in its 'forming years', be subject to emotions today, or to sudden provocation (Westra, 2004a). Thus, lacking clear extenuating circumstances to diminish their culpability, and presenting instead what appear to be full calculation and intent, incitement and planning complicity as well as the economic rewards reaped from the completion of the operations, corporate legal entities appear to possess all the necessary requirements to be viewed as fully responsible for the crime of genocide.

The other case, *Bancoult v. Robert McNamara*, includes the war crimes of forced relocation, cruel, inhuman and degrading treatment, and genocide. It is particularly important to establish the presence of one or more international crimes, in this case, given the court's conclusion that Bancoult had 'failed to allege an international environmental tort' and also given their additional statement that 'corporate policies ... however destructive, do not constitute torts in violation of the law of nations' (see Chapter 4). The corporation, Halliburton, was alleged to have supported the Indonesian military and to have fostered 'a symbiotic relationship' between them and its own security guards and employees. (The appeal to cultural genocide is no less grave than the actual genocide that best describes the results of the listed corporate activities, but it might be better grounded in indigenous peoples' rights law, and I return to it below.) Aside from the presence of an otherwise notorious corporation, Halliburton, and the presence among the defendants originally cited of Robert McNamara, Donald H. Rumsfeld and others from the US Department of Justice, this is a case where the US government was instrumental in bringing to fruition a plan to place a military base 'in the middle of the Indian Ocean', in the Chagos Archipelago, with the complicity of the British government. It is impossible to claim that there was no intent, planning or complicity present.

In order to set up a military base, the first step envisioned was to remove the local indigenous population: 'During the late 1960s and early 1970s, the Chagos population was forcibly removed to nearby Mauritius and Seychelles to make way for a US Military facility.'[11] The whole operation started in 1964 when the governments of Britain and the US 'entered into secret negotiations to establish a United States military facility in the Indian Ocean'.[12] Note that the two governments also 'conducted a survey and concluded that the construction of a military base in Diego Garcia would require the displacement of the indigenous population living in the island'.[13]

There are a number of problems in the handling of this case under ATCA, and with the resulting judgement, especially the question of the 'individual defendants', and the court's conclusion that, 'this case raises a nonjustifiable political question as to the potentiality of embarrassment and multifarious pronouncements by various departments on one question'.[14] But at this time, the main concern is to demonstrate that not only was genocide committed as well as war crimes, but that intent and premeditation were also present, even if the court cannot 'second-guess the initial and continuing decision of the executive and legislative branches to exclude civilians from Diego Garcia'.[15] Aside from raising additional questions about whether the actions of the US executive and legislative branches are thus to be considered to be acting outside the law, it is hard to deny that planning intent and knowledge were indeed present.

CONSPIRACY, COMPLICITY AND 'OTHER ACTS' OF GENOCIDE

Aside from the twin issues of knowledge and intent, there are 'other acts' of genocide that are also clearly in evidence in *Bancoult v. McNamara*, especially 'conspiracy' and 'complicity'. In fact, the court also refuses to assess 'whether it was proper for Britain and the United States to enter an agreement for the construction of a military base in Chagos thirty years ago'.[16] Nevertheless the British themselves condemned their own involvement in 2001 when the British judiciary considered the legality of the 1971 Immigration Ordinance in the case *Regina (Bancoult) v. Secretary of State for Foreign and Commonwealth Affairs and Another.*

That judgement recognized that removing the population of Chagos, even though it was done 'pursuant to the 1971 Immigration Ordinance', was carried out for military considerations, although the manner in which it was carried out 'was not conducive to the peace, order and good government of the British Indian Ocean Territory'.[17] Thus, whatever could and should be said about the *results* of that joint operation, the fact that it was the product of premeditation and previous (joint) planning cannot be denied. 'At common law, a conspiracy is committed once two or more persons agree to commit a crime, whether or not the crime itself is committed' (Schabas, 2000). This planning and agreement among parties, in fact, are essentially parts of the crime of genocide: 'By its very nature, the crime of genocide will inevitably involve conspiracy and conspirators' (Schabas, 2000). The Charter of Nuremburg tribunal itself recognizes not only genocide, but also conspiracy as a separate and distinct crime.[18] The International Military Tribunals acknowledged that even in cases when there is a ruler or a dictator in power, a plan that demands the collaboration of many fits the definition of common planning and could well be a form of conspiracy (Schabas, 2000). A 'criminal organization' could be considered a form of conspiracy:

> A criminal organization is analogous to a criminal conspiracy in that the essence of both is the co-operation for criminal purposes. There must be a group bound together

and organized for a common purpose. The group must be formed or used in connection with the Charter.[19]

Not only are the 'other acts' related to genocide, but also 'crimes against peace', and 'Offences Against the Peace and Security of Mankind'[20] include conspiracy, complicity and direct incitement (Ratner and Abrams, 2001). However various courts interpret conspiracy and complicity in various ways. The *Tadic* case[21] concluded that an accomplice is guilty if 'his participation directly and substantially affected the commission of that offence through supporting the actual commission before, during or after the incident' (Ratner and Abrams, 2001). Yet a grave problem remains: although related acts take place routinely as do other crimes such as acts of physical torture, most courts do not consider that corporations could be guilty, even when they perform the crimes, or incite and facilitate them: 'Transnational and multinational corporation's vis-à-vis indigenous peoples provide further evidence of human rights violations perpetrated by non-state actors' (Birch, 2003). Although these difficulties persist in international law, a recent Canadian amendment to the Criminal Code (7 November 2003) adds special considerations to the way corporate crime is understood, as noted in Chapter 5.

Holding MNCs responsible under international law: Some public health considerations

The Canadian Criminal Code Amendment discussed in Chapter 5 is only one small step in the right direction. From the date of its inclusion in the Criminal Code, to my knowledge, there have been no cases tried under section 21.

In February 2001, a symposium entitled 'Holding Multinational Corporations Responsible Under International Law' was presented at the University of California, and several of the panellists addressed various aspects of the question posed here. Many of the presentations addressed specifically the way indigenous peoples were treated under ATCA. Richard Herz (2001) argued that:

> *The primary hurdle in seeking to apply the international norms protecting cultural rights under the ATCA is* Beanal v. Freeport McMoran. *There the US District Court for the Eastern District of Louisiana rejected a cultural genocide claim, because it found the Genocide Convention does not prohibit the destruction of a culture. The US Court of Appeals for the Fifth Circuit affirmed holding that a cultural genocide claim was not actionable under the ATCA because cultural rights are neither sufficiently specific nor universally accepted. Both decisions were wrong.*[22]

Herz's statement is supported by the fact that, although the Genocide Convention debated the issue, it did not ultimately accept 'cultural genocide', but remained with the 'physical destruction of a people' instead (Herz, 2001). Subsequent treaties *do* protect cultural rights (see for instance the ICCPR and the ICESCR). In addition, the Stockholm Declaration (1972) defends 'the right to an environment adequate for survival', and the 'right to a minimally healthy environment' exists as well under customary international law (Herz, 2001). Unfortunately, even if we accept Herz's assessment of the *Beanal* judgement and concur with his position, this does not help to move forward on the vexed question of corporate accountability under international law. Nevertheless, Article IV of the convention states:

> *Persons committing genocide or any other acts enumerated in Article III, shall be punished, whether they are constitutionally responsible rulers, public officials or **private individuals**.* (emphasis added)

The article does not single out 'natural individuals', hence it should include legal individuals, for example, corporations, especially since, according to Article I, 'genocide, whether committed in time of peace or in time of war, is a crime under international law'. If legal entities such as corporations or other organizations are included as 'private individuals', then all harmful and criminal aspects of the 'second conquest' should be included, driven as they are by economic advantage without any other considerations.

Recently, the connection between corporate products, processes and activities was emphasized by Wiist (2006):

> *Many public health professionals are aware or have been involved in public health problems and issues related to corporate products, services or practices. Freudenberg described a wide variety of products and practices of what he termed 'disease promoting corporations'. Included are products such as tobacco, unsafe motor vehicles, expensive medications, guns, alcohol and certain foods.*

The undeniable effect of these products and practices, at least in developed countries where some regulatory regimes exist to impose restraints, is quite different from the effects of the same corporate quest for profit maximization and the externalization of costs in developing countries, in the absence of legal restraints. Normally public health addresses specific products, companies or, at most, a certain industry, such as big tobacco. The research of the WHO is outstanding in that regard, and they have recently published comprehensive collections of scientific materials, especially regarding children's health (WHO, 2002; Licari et al, 2005; see also Westra, 2006).

But all the available research does not 'address the fundamental structure and function common to all corporations' (Wiist, 2006). In general, public health should return to its earlier emphasis on social justice (Scutchfield, 2004). Structural factors have long been recognized as causative of 'inequities in health' (Wiist, 2006), and so are many other public health issues.

The recognition of these factors, and of the basic structure and goals of corporate activities should help to support the connection between corporate activities and public harm, either direct or indirect, that is, thorough the environment (Westra, 2004a). If 'causing serious bodily or mental harm to the members of the group' (Convention on Genocide, Article II(b)) is accepted as genocide, one does not even need to appeal, as Herz (2001) does, to other instruments. The presence of genocide in its most common physical manifestation can even be found in the public health assessment of corporate practices in general. However, it might be useful to return to the *actus reus* of genocide and revisit some of the accepted aspects of that crime, as I did above for its *mens rea* aspects.

GENOCIDE: THE *ACTUS REUS* AND CULTURAL GENOCIDE

The final draft of the Convention on Genocide, Article II, after '(a) killing members of the group', lists '(b) causing serious bodily or mental harm to members of the group', and a brief review of the case law involving indigenous peoples will support the claim that corporate harms do rise to the level of international law and that, in fact, they represent forms of genocide.

The legal aspects of indigenous rights most often referred to are 'self-determination' and 'cultural integrity', and the latter is the aspect that needs to be considered in relation to 'cultural genocide', as that is the absolute negation of 'cultural integrity'.

Cultural integrity is:

> ... *at the core of the Draft United Nations Declaration on the Rights of Indigenous Peoples and previous drafts that were produced by the chair of the U.N. working group on Indigenous Populations pursuant to that body's standard setting mandate.* (Anaya, 2000)

The language of an early draft is explicit in this regard:

> *3. The [collective] rights to exist as distinct peoples and to be protected against genocide... 4. The [collective] right to maintain and develop their ethnic and cultural characteristic and to distinct identity including the right of people and individuals to call themselves by their proper names.*[23]

The draft's language provides protection for the efforts to assimilate rather than respect indigenous cultures found in North America (including Canada) and elsewhere. But given the close identification of indigenous groups with their ancestral lands (see Chapter 1), the protection should be explicitly extended to their territorial integrity as the indispensable component of cultural integrity for all land-based minorities. The nexus between land and peoples is also recognized by the Convention on Biological Diversity, which states that each party shall:

> ... *[s]ubject to its national legislation respect, preserve and maintain knowledge, innovations and practices of indigenous and local communities embodying traditional lifestyles relevant to the conservation and sustainable use of biological diversity.*[24]

The extensive history of the debates on the inclusion (or non-inclusion) of 'cultural genocide' (Schabas, 2000) demonstrates that it is not, at this time, the equivalent of 'genocide', 'because no international instrument exists making it a punishable act' (Schabas, 2000). Yet all the arguments presented by various state parties in the ATCA cases we have discussed totally ignore the *sui generis* connection between indigenous peoples and their traditional lands, for which I have argued (see Chapters 1 and 2).

Destroying a Catholic church or a minaret may well represent an act of aggression and disrespect toward Catholic or Muslim worshippers, but whatever its intent and motivation, it does not effectively eliminate either group, as the displacement of the Chagos people in *Beanal* or the U'wa in Colombia, effectively attempted to do.

Genocide: The *actus reus* and ethnic cleansing

> *Considered in the context of the conflicts in former Yugoslavia, 'ethnic cleansing' means rendering an area ethnically homogenous by using force or intimidation to remove persons of given groups from the area.*[25]

The same Commission of Experts also stated that 'ethnic cleansing is contrary to international law', and that, in certain cases 'ethnic cleansing could be considered a breach of the Genocide Convention'.[26] Nevertheless, the judgement in *Tadić*[27] refers several times to 'ethnic cleansing' without, however, equating that crime to genocide.

The judgements under ATCA and in various tribunals discussed in Chapters 4 and 5, do not even consider the *actus reus*, the material aspects of the cases as presented in the detailed accusations of the indigenous groups, because the courts did not even get past the procedural aspects of the cases regarding the appropriate venue, or who should or should not be named as defendant. That is why, unlike the language in the cases from the former Yugoslavia, the judgements I have listed do not have much that can be used to clarify the present issue of the various aspects of genocide in the jurisprudence concerning indigenous peoples.

In contrast, it is what the judgements *do not* say that is enlightening; there is, for the most part, no dispute about the factual presentation of the cases. Hence it seems clear that the factual aspects of each of the cases tried under ATCA and, in general, involving corporate activities and their impact on indigenous peoples, are correct and can be accepted as not presenting frivolous complaints. That said, the next step is not to study only the judgements and the final dispositions of the cases but, most of all, to consider the factual components of the *actus reus* claimed, in order to evaluate the status of each of those components in international law.

The most obvious case of 'ethnic cleansing' is the *Talisman* case (see Chapter 5). The corporation involved was accused of complicity with the government of Sudan to ensure that the area where their mining operations were to be conducted was no longer home to the original indigenous and Christian inhabitants. The *Doe v. Unocal* case (see Chapter 4) does not have indigenous population physically removed or killed. Instead the population was enslaved to provide the required labour for the corporate operations. We noted also the total removal and deportation of the Chagossian population in *Bancoult* to make way for a US military establishment on Diego Garcia (see Chapter 5).

Schabas (2000) distinguishes 'ethnic cleansing' from 'genocide' on the basis of the intent of the acts committed:

> *While the material acts performed to commit the crimes may often resemble each other, they have two quite different specific intents. One is intended to displace a population, the other, to destroy it.*

Of course, even if it is not genocide, 'ethnic cleansing' is at least 'deportation or forcible transfer of population'.[28] But, while Schabas' (2000) interpretation is obviously correct in regard to the cases he analyses – from Eichman and other Nazi crimes, to crimes related to the Ad Hoc Tribunals for the former Yugoslavia – when 'deportation' and 'forcible transfer' are applied to indigenous, land-based minorities, the 'two intents' combine in the final result accomplished by the corporate activities in the ATCA cases. Both a Chagos population 'transferred' *ad absurdum* to the Canadian Rockies, and a First Nation of Canada moved to an island in the Indian Ocean or the Philippines, effectively cease to exist as peoples, at least, as the peoples they were in their original traditional lands. Hence, it may not be immediate 'killing' of the individuals comprising the group, but I suggest it may well be a form of genocide nonetheless, by 'depriving them of the necessary conditions of (their) existence (as a people),' as well as remaining a crime against humanity and a war crime.

A close kin of 'ethnic cleansing' is 'ecocide', particularly relevant from our point of view:

> *[Ecocide] Threats to the integrity of the environment can conceivably imperil the survival of a group of people. If associated with the intent to destroy the group, the definition of genocide may apply.* (Schabas, 2000)

Richard Falk (1974) also couples genocide with ecocide, as does Ken Saro-Wiwa in his description of the effects of the activities of Royal Dutch Shell Petroleum in Ogoniland, Nigeria (Westra, 2006). However, there is no history of established jurisprudence linking 'ecocide' and 'genocide', although public health research provides ample evidence for the unavoidable interface between the two.

Genocide: Causing serious bodily or mental harm

> *What is now paragraph (b) did not really emerge until the meeting of the Ad Hoc committee. It was based on a French proposal: 'Any Act directed against the* **corporal integrity** *of the members of the group'.* (Schabas, 2000, emphasis added)[29]

The original understanding of 'serious bodily harm' is far more specific than the actual phrasing of Article II(b). Bodily harm can be far more than physical attacks resulting in wounding or other harms, short of actual killing. Environmental harms due to the alteration of the physical environment, or the introduction of processes and products that are known to impair normal human function, all can be subsumed under attacks on the 'corporal integrity' of members of the group. For instance, open flares and spreading of oil and tar on the fertile farmlands in Ogoniland, as well as the effects of Texaco's operations in *Jota v. Texaco* (see Chapter 5), produce grave effects beyond wounds that are immediately observable and eventually can heal (WHO, 2002). These harms include harms to the unborn and to future generations (Westra, 2006). The significant aspects of these harms include not only their origin and their intergenerational reach, but also the fact that the activities that produce the harmful results are invariably produced by corporate activities (legal individuals), *not* by single natural individuals, who would have neither the power nor the interest to engage in such widespread and complex operations. In fact, even states themselves, the primary subjects in international law, can be and most often are complicit with corporations and conspire with them to support their activities, but seldom engage in hazardous activities on their own in peacetime.

Mental harms, according to Lester Pearson (cited in Schabas, 2000), could only mean 'physical injury to the mental faculties'.[30] Although Pearson's interpretations were not officially accepted, again, in an early proposal we find an important aspect of this crime. At a recent meeting of the Collegium Ramazzini in Bologna, Italy (22–25 September 2005), a yearly meeting of prestigious medical and epidemiological scholars and practitioners, Philip Grandjean presented a paper entitled 'Only One Chance to Develop a Brain', where he explained that certain pre-birth and early exposures permanently eliminated any chance of an embryo or a foetus developing normal brain function (see Westra, 2006; see also Grandjean and Landrigan, 2006).

Hence, exposures to certain chemical substances *only* result from corporate endeavours, and they are scientifically proven to irreversibly alter a person's mental abilities, as are pesticide exposures of the preborn, infants and young children (WHO, 2002; Licari et al, 2005). When industrial or extractive operations are conducted near to indigenous peoples' territories, and a specific group is affected, one aspect of the 'mental harm' component of genocide appears to be present.

In addition, threats, intimidation, rapes and other sexual crimes, as well as torture, may well affect peoples' mental abilities, and the judgements of the Ad Hoc Tribunals of the former Yugoslavia and Rwanda present many examples of the effects of such acts of violence, including sexual violence, on both bodily and mental aspects of a targeted group. Given the presence of the specific intent to destroy, it appears that in this sense at least, it is appropriate to claim that genocide has been committed in all these cases.

Genocide: Deliberately inflicting conditions of life calculated to destroy the group

> The 1946 Saudi Arabian draft contained '[d]estruction of the essential potentialities of life of a group, people or nation or the intentional deprivation of elementary necessities for the preservation of health or existence'. (Schabas, 2000)[31]

Once again an early, tentative definition captures very well the interface between environmental deprivation and the preservation of the 'health and existence' of indigenous peoples.

Almost each one of the cases considered in Chapter 5 describes eloquently for the corporate activities imposed just the sort of conditions that would cause a current or eventual grave threat to the existence of the group, although this particular aspect of genocide 'does not require proof of a result' (Schabas, 2000). Deportation or forcible removal of populations from their traditional lands was tantamount to committing genocide. If we consider this aspect of genocide, formally entrenched in Article II, the harm perpetrated upon indigenous populations becomes more evident.

In Chapter 1 the example of a First Nation surrounded by the industrial operations of Ontario's well-known 'Chemical Valley' showed results that can only be described as genocide. Because of a number of chemical exposures, the normal ratio of male to female births no longer exists (a result akin to that caused by the Seveso disaster in Italy) (Westra, 2006). Without enough male births in the tribe, all females could not expect to marry within the group, but needed to go beyond its borders for husbands. Therefore, the group could be said to live under conditions that, with or without the intent to eliminate that First Nation on the part of various corporate actors, are essentially such that the First Nation would ultimately be destroyed. Currently there is an inquiry by Health Canada into this issue, and the final result of the inquiry must precede any possible legal action in defence of the First Nation. However, this case clearly lacks in deliberate intent to eliminate or harm a specific population, thus neither 'ethnic cleansing' nor 'genocide' appears to be *prima facie* an appropriate description of the result of the corporate activities. Yet the question remains, whether 'wilful blindness' in the face of the well-known results of chemical exposures, coupled with the knowledge that the manufacturers and producers of those substances must have, might be sufficient as 'knowledge', if not intent.

Well-known Canadian Judge, Claire L'Hureux-Dubé, has argued from the results or effects of certain forms of discrimination (regarding gender issues, primarily gay rights), to demonstrate the injustice of certain practices (Westra, 2004a). Schabas (2000) also argues that acts of omission (such as failing to provide necessities of life, and 'withholding sufficient living accommodations') come close to committing genocide by 'omission'. He adds, 'As a general rule domestic criminal law takes the position that intentional acts of omission are criminal in nature where there is a positive duty to act.'[32]

Also, the 'positive duty to act' to prevent genocide 'is imposed upon military and civilian supervisors' in the Statute of the ICC (Schabas, 2000), and it is also present in the Canadian Criminal Code (see Chapter 5). Hence, those in charge of the various chemical industries had full knowledge of their own processes and products, and had the responsibility to halt the production in that specific harmful form; although it could be argued that it was the combination of exposures that rendered them more harmful, and that possibly, taken one by one, the chemicals might not have been equally as hazardous. Nevertheless, each corporate official knew full well that their products did not exist in isolation and were to be produced and released among other hazardous substances, rather than under sterile laboratory conditions.

The answer here lies in the 'thin skull' rule: criminals must accept their victims as they find them. By analogy, the presence of other hazardous products in the bodies of the corporate victims should not represent a way to lessen the responsibility of those who exposed the indigenous populations, rather, it should only increase the responsibility of the corporate criminals.

GENOCIDE AND *JUS COGENS* NORMS
AS APPLIED TO ECO-CRIME

The goal of reviewing corporate crimes against indigenous populations in all their aspects is to show that genocide is committed on a regular basis, as well as other crimes against humanity, and that for the most part, these crimes are perpetrated with impunity. The highest possible penalties they encounter are economic liability under

ATCA. But when the corporate activities and their results on indigenous peoples are carefully considered, the results are forms of 'eco-crimes' (Westra, 2004a) and should be proscribed by non-derogable (*jus cogens*) norms, not tried simply as torts, at best (Scott, 2001a), or simply ignored as 'not rising to the level of international law'.

The application of *jus cogens* norms to the issues I have examined will help to support the obligation to abstain from activities that impose such grave harms on indigenous groups, both directly and through their habitat/environment. According to Janis (1988):

> *Verdross, one of* jus cogens' *earliest advocates, explained that the concept of* jus cogens *was quite alien to legal positivists, but the situation was quite different in the natural law school of international law.*

Over the last few years, we have seen increasing public unrest and even violence in defence of global human rights, understood as encompassing the right to a healthy, protected environment. The chosen target was and is currently the WTO and the high-powered economic representatives of today's richest nations. The main objections to these meetings and their agendas, I believe, address what is presently lacking in the substance of their deliberations: first, the lack of explicit human rights concern; second, the lack of environmental and public health concern; and third, the lack of openness and transparency in their eventual agreements.

The main emphasis on the part of the protesters is on both 'civil and political rights', as well as 'social and economic rights', both of which ought to imply the right to life and the healthy conditions required to support this right. Article 53 of the Vienna Convention on the Law of Treaties (1969, in force 1980), however, spells out explicitly the existence of norms that cannot be 'forgotten' or simply ignored through other treaties or agreements arranged for the economic advantage of certain states:

> *A.53 Treaties conflicting with a peremptory norm of general international law (*jus cogens*). A treaty is void if, at the time of its conclusion, it conflicts with a peremptory norm of general international law. For the purposes of the present Convention, a peremptory norm of general international law is a norm accepted and recognized by the international community of states as a whole as a norm from which no derogation is permitted and which can be modified only by a subsequent norm of general international law having the same character.*

Article 53 sets the stage, giving the clarification of what is an international crime according to the description of examples of *jus cogens* norms in the former Article 19 of the International Law Commission (1996), although this article is strongly positivistic and thus not entirely helpful from our point of view.

If these articles and the corresponding obligations to which they give rise are taken seriously, then the so-called 'hooligans' who riot and protest against the environmental abuses fostered and supported by certain WTO policies, might be seen in the light of freedom fighters, not only engaging in self-defence, but even in the defence of our common humanity and our common rights (Gilbert, 1994). The character of *jus cogens* norms is precisely that of providing the strongest possible citadel in defence of humanity; their role is to rise above the economic and power interests of various states that could band together (and often do), for purposes that conflict with the respect due to all humans. Hence, *jus cogens* norms are uniquely apt to provide and defend substantive global justice beyond the purely procedural emphasis present in many other legal instruments. Bassiouni (1996) writes that 'The term *jus cogens* means "the compelling law" and as such a *jus cogens* norm holds the highest hierarchical position among all other norms and principles'.

An example may be that of massive pollution of the Mediterranean basin. Mediterranean states are directly injured, but the 'objective interests' of countries as far away as Australia or New Zealand ensures that they, too, will feel and be 'indirectly injured' (Sir Alan Sinclair, cited in Spinedi, 1989). This is a good example because the converse was true of the *Nuclear Tests* case.[33] Both of these reflect the interests of a much wider constituency than that of the immediately and directly affected states. On 28 March 2007, the Italian Association of Environmental Doctors[34] issued a 'declaration on Nuclear Energy' demanding the elimination of nuclear power.

Like aggression or genocide, both of which represent the most widely accepted, least controversial forms of these sorts of injuries affecting the international community, I argue that grave environmental pollution (in the quantitative or qualitative sense), should indeed be treated as a crime, whether or not the term 'crime' is present in the language of any international law instrument.

The existing literature on crimes under international law shows a difference in emphasis between those who see *jus cogens* norms as based on universal principles, such as those of natural law (Ragazzi, 1997), and others, such as Brownlie (1979), who appear to emphasize the procedural aspects of these breaches of international law. Speaking of the laws of war and of the Hague Convention of 1907 concerned with just war, and the 1949 Geneva Conventions IV (Civilians) and the punishment of those responsible, Brownlie (1979) says:

> *This is often expressed as an acceptance of the principle of universality, but this is not strictly correct since what is punished is the breach of international law … and the case is thus different from the punishment under national law of acts in respect of which international law gives a liberty to all states to punish, but does not itself declare criminal.*

I believe that Brownlie envisages 'crimes against humanity' in the context of war or genocide, so that it might be difficult for him to agree with the 'extension' to 'eco-crimes', for which I have argued under that same category, although these crimes can and do occur in peacetime. From the standpoint of the argument of this work, I argue that eco-violence should be viewed in the same light as the unequivocal crimes of 'genocide', 'attacks against the human person', and all forms of unprovoked and unjustified 'aggression'. The clear condemnation of all these internationally wrongful acts will then support my conclusions in regard to environmental offences, if that case can be made.

In addition, one can consider as a very positive development, the emergence of the International Criminal Court (ICC), although the court is concerned only with acts of individuals, which should include corporate individuals, not states. Williams (1998) writes:

> *An independent, just and effective international criminal court (ICC) is an imperative for the twenty-first century. The ICC will have jurisdiction over most serious international crimes. Its value is not only in prosecuting and punishing perpetrators of crimes, such as genocide, war crimes, crimes against humanity and potentially aggression, but in its deterrence capability.*

But neither in this work, nor in the Rome Statute of the International Criminal Court (1998), is there a clear reference to the environment (except in the context of 'war crimes'). In sum, not only do environmental crimes committed against indigenous peoples meet the standards of international law crimes but, I believe, they should be forbidden by non-derogable (*jus cogens*) norms, and the obligation to avoid committing these eco-crimes ought to be an obligation *erga omnes*, transcending all other conventions and agreements.

In his discussion of the application of *jus cogens* norms to land-based minorities, Pentassuglia (2002) states that the protected 'existence' of such minorities 'has been conceptualized as including a "basic right to be protected against genocide"'. In addition, he also argues that the existence of such distinctive groups, depends on the 'active awareness of their members' based on their 'language, culture or religion, a shared sense of history, a common destiny'. Hence, the destruction of the specific traits of an indigenous group is equally a form of cultural genocide, as are 'ethnocide' or forced assimilation.

In contrast, Anaya (2000) views the right to self-determination as a 'foundational principle', affirmed in the United Nations Charter[35] and other major legal instruments. Neither Pentassuglia (2002) nor Anaya (2000) envision the possibility that the indigenous groups' physical environment might be used as the source of grave attacks on their life and health, not only on each individual, but also on the group itself.

This is one of the most serious problems we have encountered. The problem has been the difficulty of holding corporate criminals accountable for their crimes, even when the crimes were clearly specific and well defined. The other problem has been the fact that 'ecocrime is not viewed as a crime at all' (Westra, 2004a). A recent case demonstrates precisely how damaging to the cause of indigenous peoples are the effects of this 'blind spot' in international law: the *Rio Tinto* case.[36]

This is yet another case tried under the ATCA, where the defendants mining operations on Bougainsville were the source of several crimes:

> *The defendants' mining operations on Bougainsville destroyed the islands' environment, harmed the health of its people, and incited a ten-year civil war, during which thousands of civilians died or were injured... the defendants are guilty of war crimes and crimes against humanity, as well as racial discrimination and environmental harm that violates international law.*[37]

The court did recognize that the war crimes had been committed, but when it came to environmental harms, they granted – in part – the defendants' motion to dismiss, on the basis that international law prohibits only activities that 'cause damage to the environment of other States or of areas beyond the limits of national jurisdiction'.[38]

The plaintiffs had both Professor Gunther Handl and Professor Steven Ratner presenting expert testimony. Gunther Handl started from the human right to life and health, and he argued that both are principles established in international law:

... in relation to environmentally injurious activities that threaten human health and well-being there is general recognition of the fact that such activities also may abridge basic human rights of the victims concerned.[39]

Handl also cited the ICCPR, the Universal Declaration of Human Rights, the African Charter of Human and Peoples' Rights, the American Convention on Human Rights, the European Convention for the Protection of Human Rights and Fundamental Freedoms, and other instruments, as well as the case concerning the *Gabcikovo-Nagymaros Project* (Westra, 2004a)[40] The court, however, found that questions of environmental harm are not addressed or defined in detail, hence that the right to health and the environment are not 'sufficiently specific', and that, therefore, it cannot be said that the law of nations can be violated by perpetrating environmental harm (Westra, 2004a).

This is the crux of the matter, as I have argued (Westra, 2004a; 2006) in different contexts, and I return to the details of this case below. At this time, and in the context of the 'recognized' *jus cogens* violation of genocide, we need to note that the fact the courts rightly do not find an explicit condemnation of environmental harms, let alone a prohibition, represents a grave lacuna in law. Until the missing link between health/ life on one side, and environmental degradation on the other, is generally accepted and the special connection between them is acknowledged and established in law, there is little hope that justice will prevail in indigenous human rights.

Jus cogens norms and *erga omnes* obligations in eco-crimes against indigenous peoples

> *In its dictum, the International Court restricted its list of examples of obligations erga omnes in the area of human rights to three examples only, namely the prohibition of genocide, and the protection from slavery and racial discrimination.* (Ragazzi, 1997)

In addition, the American Law Institute restatement lists other obligations: 'the murder or causing the disappearance of individuals', 'torture or other cruel, inhuman, or degrading treatment or punishment', 'prolonged arbitrary detention' and 'a consistent pattern of gross violations of internationally recognized human rights' (Third Restatement, Section 702).

The important question is which ones of these categories may best fit the treatment of indigenous groups we have noted in the case law discussed in Chapters 4 and 5. In his definitive treatment of *jus cogens* norms and *erga omnes* obligations, Ragazzi (1997) touches on this question as he discusses candidates in the area of Development Law, starting with the 'right to development', a position that is usually ascribed to Keba Mbaye, a former Vice-President of the International Court (Ragazzi, 1997). That right, however, is not separate from the fundamental rights of human persons, but it is firmly anchored in the traditional fundamental rights, both individual and collective (see Crawford, 1988), which include the right to self-determination, supported by a number of international instruments, as note above.

Therefore it is impossible to support 'development', while, at the same time, denying the very human rights upon which it is based, not only on moral, but also on legal grounds. The brief list of specified *erga omnes* obligations supports the approaches proposed by both Anaya (2000) and Pentassuglia (2002), the former emphasizing the right to self-determination, and the latter, racial discrimination, as both are much better defended in international law than the obligations for which I argue. However, self-determination is not covered in the list of *erga omnes* obligations, whereas racial discrimination fares somewhat better in this regard.

Prima facie, one would think that the right to life and health would certainly count as protected fundamental rights. But in the *Rio Tinto* case, for instance, when Gunther Handl advanced this argument for the plaintiffs, he based his position for both the environment and the right to life and health on various instruments, including the American Convention of Human Rights. The Report of the Inter-American Commission states that:

> ... *respect for the inherent dignity of the person is the principle which underlies the fundamental protections of the right to life and to preservation of physical well-being. Conditions of severe environmental pollution, which may cause serious physical illness, impairment and suffering on the part of the local populace, are inconsistent with the right to be respected as a human being... The realization of the right to life, and to physical security and integrity is necessarily related to and in some way dependent upon one's physical environment. Accordingly, where environmental contamination and degradation pose a persistent threat to human life and health, the foregoing rights are implicated.*[41]

But, although Handl argues that the right to life and health are established principles in international law, the court responded that, the American Convention on Human Rights, 'does *not* address issues of environmental harm', as well as conflicting with US laws regarding both abortion and capital punishment.[42] Because the US has signed but not ratified the American Convention on Human Rights, the court did not recognize it as a treaty 'that created binding obligations'.[43]

When we turn to environmental harm, the situation is even bleaker; the court maintained that only trans-border environmental harm is proscribed by international law.[44] Hence, there is a fundamental need to accept modern scientific evidence that ties inescapably human life/health issues to environmental condition before the case can be made that – despite the US claims regarding abortion and capital punishment – at least in international law, the dignity of the human person and her life/health are protected. In that case, the environmental conditions required for the achievement of that protection should impose non-derogable obligations on both states and legal entities.

Ragazzi (1998) further argues that Bedjaoui (1987) supports this position:

> ... *it would be contradictory to say on one hand that the prohibition of genocide, which aims at protecting the elementary right to life, derives from a rule of jus cogens, but on the other hand, that the right to development which aims at protecting the same right to life, does not also derive from a rule of jus cogens.*

In turn, the right to development does not imply that certain alien, Western conditions of life can be freely imposed as part of 'development' of an area, even when they are not viewed as 'development' by the indigenous inhabitants. The interface between 'development' and the rights of the human person and her dignity, should include – minimally – life, health, an acceptable 'habitat' and, necessarily, also the consent of the indigenous peoples to the proposed development. I return to this topic in Chapter 8, but for now we need to consider another important instrument with serious implications for indigenous peoples' rights: the Statute of the International Criminal Court.

Genocide, crime against humanity and the Rome Statute of the ICC

The 'situation' in Darfur has galvanized public opinion over recent years because of the gravity of the ongoing internal conflict in the area. Sudan had signed the Rome Statute of the ICC on 8 September 2000 (without, however, ratifying it) (Schabas, 2006b). Speaking of a state party, Schabas (2006b) writes, 'As a signatory of the instrument, it is bound to refrain from acts that would defeat the object and purpose of the Statute'. But the US government and the international community believed that genocide has been committed in Darfur (Schabas, 2006b; see also, Powell, 2004). Eventually, after a commission of inquiry, chaired by Anthony Cassese and mandated by Resolution 1564 of the Security Council in 2004, the acts committed in the region were declared to be crimes against humanity rather than genocide (see Article 5(1)(b) of the Rome Statute). Article 7 describes crimes against humanity in detail, and several subsections are particularly apt to describe most of the cases we have discussed. The *Talisman* case is a good example. For instance, Article 7(1)(h) states:

> *Persecution against any identifiable group or collectivity on political, racial, national, ethnic, cultural, religious, gender as defined in paragraph 3, or other grounds that are universally recognized as impermissible under international law, in connection with any act referred to in this paragraph or any crime within the jurisdiction of the Court.*

Similarly, Article 2(d) pronounces:

> *'Deportation or forcible transfer of populations' means forcible displacement of the persons concerned by expulsion or other coercive acts from the area in which they are lawfully present, without grounds permitted under international law:*

Both are accurate descriptions of the facts of the *Talisman* case. The US is not a party to the ICC, but this appears to be an egregious example of a case that ought to be considered by the prosecutor, acting *proprio motu*, although several countries, including the US, China and Israel, were opposed to the clause that permits that option. Nevertheless, the Darfur situation in western Sudan was referred to the court by the Security Council (Schabas, 2006b), and all the other three cases (Uganda, Easter Congo, and the Central African Republic) that have appeared before the court to date were referred by state parties.

It would be wrong to minimize in any way the atrocities taking place in Darfur, but there are some countervailing considerations in respect to *also* promoting the addition to the court's docket of cases like *Talisman*. First, the existence of a *proprio motu* prosecutor is a very significant aspect of this *sui generis* court and it was fought for and eventually gained precisely because of its importance to the international community. Hence it would be a significant move to use those powers in this new direction.

Second, the numbers of people killed, deported or tortured in any given situation was never explicitly listed as a condition for prosecution priority. In fact, there do not seem to be any specific conditions listed in order to establish priorities and, as Article 17 'Issues of Admissibility' states under 1(d), 'The case is not of sufficient gravity to justify further action by the Court' as a guideline. But it neither specifies numbers required to trigger prosecution, nor does it attempt to define 'gravity' in either a qualitative or quantitative sense.

For the most part, human rights issues are judged from a Kantian standpoint, that is, they are based on an understanding of the absolute value of life, any life, and the non-derogable obligation to respect it. In contrast, utilitarian considerations, such as the question of affected numbers, do not seem to be explicitly mentioned in any human rights instrument.

In fact, the Human Rights Court has heard and issued a judgement on a case involving a single woman (from the Canadian First Nations), that of Linda Lovelace (see Chapter 3) without requiring the involvement of a larger number of women. No doubt, the judgement, once pronounced, will serve large numbers who will be able to appeal to the precedent. This is equally true of corporate crime, and any and all judgements concerning the gravity of the consequences that follow upon it.

Hence, third and most important, it is possible that to include an apparently 'lesser' crime perpetrated by corporate offenders, might send ripples of awareness and spur corporate decision-makers to rethink their strategies, once these have been deemed to be unequivocally criminal.

As we noted in this and the last two chapters, corporate activities that involve Northern power and Southern resources have become routine and – for the most part – the harmful, often lethal effects of those practices, have been and are regularly viewed as the collateral effect of business as usual. The burden of proof is left entirely on the victims, a practice long condemned by defenders of minorities everywhere (Bullard, 2001).

In contrast, Articles 22 and 25 indicate clearly the major stumbling blocks facing any attempt to criminalize corporate human rights abuses. Article 22(2), *Nullum Crimen Sine Lege*, expects that the crime be 'strictly construed' and not 'extended by analogy' and, as noted, there are no clear definitions of environmental crimes in international law. Article 25(1) declares that the court has jurisdiction over 'natural persons', thus not specifically excluding legal persons from its reach.

However, this is the less serious problem because responsible parties may indeed be isolated (see discussion of 'intent' above), as in civil cases they are routinely involved in money laundering, illegal accounting practices, insider trading and the like. And if we consider the question of equity, it is hard to justify the lengthy jail sentences given in cases such as Enron, Worldcom and others, in comparison with the effective immunity of corporations that have been accused of crimes against humanity or genocide; that is, crimes of a gravity that surely exceeds that of economic misdeeds, no matter how severe. In addition, the connection between corporate offender and the crimes discussed, particularly those brought to the attention of American courts under ATCA, may well fare better at the ICC. Schabas (2006b) writes that 'Early in his mandate, the Prosecutor pointed towards the economic actors as those who might bear the greatest responsibility, and therefore merit his attention'.

In his discussion on policy issues,[45] the prosecutor points the way by speaking of future investigations, involving 'financial links with crimes', such as purchasing and providing arms used in crimes, and evidence of possible collaboration with rebels or state parties. The prosecutor adds, 'Such prosecutions will be a key deterrent to the commission of future crimes, if they can curb the source of the funding.'[46]

This is indeed the key point: insurgents, warlords in Africa and others, such as the Sudanese government in the *Talisman* case, cannot operate on their hate alone. International investors and institutions provide not only the armaments as tools, they also incite criminal activities with the incentive of their financial capabilities. In that way, they keep the criminal activities and their perpetrators alive and well, to the ongoing detriment of indigenous peoples and local inhabitants in the global South.

GENOCIDE AND CRIMES AGAINST HUMANITY

In effect, the act of genocide of 'killing' has the same underlying elements as the crime against humanity of 'murder', the grave breach of 'willful killing' and the war crime 'murder', subject of course to the various contextual elements of each category of offences. Accordingly, the analysis of the act of genocide of 'killing' draws upon relevant precedents from these other categories. (Schabas, 2006a)

As we saw above, it is not easy to fit the aspects of genocide that appear in the definition, characteristics and applications of the concept in case law to the forms of genocide that apply to aboriginal groups. It is easier to advance claims about 'intent', at least through the presence of 'knowledge' or of awareness of the results of certain activities, than it is to fit the harms inflicted upon aboriginal peoples under the heading of 'genocide', understood in its technical sense, that is, as used in the UN international courts.

But it is worthy of note that the Trial Chamber of the International Criminal Tribunal for Rwanda (ICTR), in *Kayishema et al*,[47] defines causing serious bodily and mental harm as 'harm that seriously injures the health, causes disfigurement or causes any injury to the external, internal organs or senses'. This description fits almost precisely the sort of harm that we have noted above. Equally interesting, in *Akayesu*,[48] 'According to an ICTR Trial Chamber, rape and sexual violence may constitute genocide on both a physical and mental level' (Schabas, 2006a; see also, Russel-Brown, 2003).

Hence, other forms of 'bodily and mental harm' to the individual within a group may be serious enough to merit the appellation of genocide. The crux of the problem is that courts, legislators and judges remain ignorant of the public health dimensions of environmental harms, just as Victorian judges, no doubt, would not have taken as seriously cases of sexual assaults or rapes. Rapes allow survival, despite the terrible immediate and long-term harms they cause. They are easily recognized as 'constituting genocide' when a particular group is targeted, as was the case of Tutsi women in Rwanda, for example.[49]

Analogously, it is unclear why activities that *irreversibly* affect the health, reproductive abilities and normal organ function of individuals within a group, are judged to be unworthy of fitting under the heading of genocide (see Westra, 2004a). Also, there is yet another aspect of genocide (in the legal/technical sense) that should be considered in relation to aboriginal peoples: 'deliberately inflicting conditions of life calculated to destroy the group', and several cases discussed in the preceding chapters fit this description well, especially if we accept knowledge as sufficient proof of awareness and hence intent. According to Schabas (2006a), 'This act of genocide corresponds closely to the crime against humanity of "extermination", where similar language has been used in the judgments.'

The problem of intent was discussed earlier in the chapter, hence it appears possible, in fact desirable, to apply also the category of crimes against humanity to aboriginal grievances. These crimes are not limited to specific ethnic or religious groups, but are now simply required to be directed 'against any civilian population', according to the Nuremberg Charter, and the population must be the 'object of widespread or systematic attack' (Schabas, 2006a). Hence this category remains pertinent to indigenous groups, as the reference to a civilian population is 'intended to imply crimes of a collective nature and thus exclude single or isolated acts' (Schabas, 2006a).[50] For instance, one of the punishable acts of crimes against humanity, besides the expected 'murder', 'extermination' and 'enslavement', is 'deportation' or, according to Article 7(2)(d) of the Rome Statute, 'deportation or forcible transfer'. Above we noted the case of *Chagos* (see Chapter 5), describing the full extent of this crime on the inhabitants of an island in the Indian Ocean, committed by the US government. Moving from Oceania to Alaska, we can see another version of the same plight in Shishmaref, a small village only 22 feet above sea level. This village was originally protected from storm surges by a layer of ice in the Chukchi Sea. But in 1997, a storm 'scoured away a hundred-and-twenty-five-foot wide strip from the town's northern edge' and in October 2001, the whole village was threatened by 12 foot waves (Kolbert, 2006). The US Government intends to move the whole village apparently with their consent to an even more remote and unaccessible area. Climate change is the main cause, not a single specific industrial activity, but a combination of all of them, globally. The question remains whether this choice is 'free', or whether it should be viewed as coerced, since the alternative is almost certain death. It seems as though it should be viewed as 'coerced', as it always is under the threat of a gun or other weapon. Once again, the removal of a whole population, under threat of death from cumulative effects of Western commercial activities, is nothing but another form of 'forcible transfer'. In the next chapter, I consider in detail the impact of climate change on Arctic populations in the case of the Nunavut people of Canada.

NOTES

1 *Barcelona Traction, Light and Power Company Ltd* (Second Phase); ICJ Reports 1970:32; see also Schabas (2000).
2 See the Rome Statute of the International Criminal Court (ICC), of 17 July 1998, UN Doc. A/CONF.183/9.
3 ibid.
4 UN Doc. E/447.
5 *Prosecutor v. Akayesu*, (Case No. ICTR-96-4-T) Judgement, 2 September 1998, para. 477.
6 ibid.
7 *Draft Elements of Crimes*, UN Doc. PCNICC/1999/DP.4, p.7; see discussion in Schabas (2000).
8 ibid.

9   Report by Mr Maurice Gkeke-Ahanhanzo, Special Reporter on Contemporary Forms of Racism, Racial Discrimination, Xenophobia and Related Intolerance, on his mission to the United States of America from 9 to 22 October 1994, Submitted Pursuant to Human Rights resolution 1993/20 and 1994/64, UN Doc. E/CN.4/1995/78/Add. 1, para. 21.
10 370 Dupp. 2d1. US Dist. LEXIS 27882 – 21 December 2004 decided.
11 *Bancoult v. McNamara*, 217 FRD 280, 2003 US Dist. LEXIS 17102 (DDC, 2003, #2).
12 ibid.
13 ibid.
14 ibid.; see also *Baker v. Carr*, 369 US 186, 217 2d.663, 82 S. Ct. 691 (1962).
15 ibid.
16 ibid.
17 ibid.
18 Agreement for the Prosecution and Punishment of Major War Criminals of the European Axis, Establishing the Charter of the International Military Tribunal (IMT) (1951), 82 UNITS 279. Annex.
19 *France et al v. Goering et al* (946) 22 IMT 203, p. 528.
20 Report of the International Law Commission to the General Assembly, UN Doc. A/1316 (1950), reprinted in 1950 [II] ILC Y.B. 364.
21 Case No. IT-94-1-A; Judgement, 15 July 1999.
22 *Beanal* 969 F. Supp. 362, 373 E.D.La 1997, 197 F. 3d 161 (5th Cir. 1999).
23 First Revised text of the Draft Universal Declaration on Rights of Indigenous Peoples, UN Doc. E/CN.4/Sub.21/1989/33 (1989), paras. 3 and 4.
24 Convention on Biological Diversity, 5 June 1992, UNCED, Art. 8(j), 1992, UN Doc. UNEP/ Bio.Div./N7INC.5/4 (1992).
25 Interim Report of the Commission of Experts Established Pursuant to Security Council Resolution 780 (1992), UN Coc.S/35374 (1993) para. 55.
26 ibid., para. 56; see also Schabas (2000).
27 *Prosecutor v. Tadic* (Case No. IT-94-I-T, Opinion and Judgement, 7 May 1997.
28 Statute of the International Criminal Court (ICC), Articles 8(1)(d) and 8(2)(d).
29 See UN Doc. E/AC.35/SR.13, p. 12 (five in favour, one against with one abstention).
30 Parliamentary debates, House of Commons, Canada, 21 May 1952; p. 2442.
31 UN Doc. A/C.6/86.
32 See *Prosecutor v. Delalic et al*, Case No. IT-96-21-T, Judgement, 16 November 1998.
33 *Australia v. France*, 1974, ICJ Reports 1974, 253; and *New Zealand v. France*, 1974, I.C.J. 457.
34 ISDE, 'Declaration Against Nuclear Energy,' an association of 100,000 doctors in 40 countries, 28 March 2007.
35 UN Charter, Art. 1, para. 2.
36 *Alexis Holyweek Sarei et al v. Rio Tinto plc and Rio Tinto United*, US District Court for the Central District of California, 221 F. Supp. 2d 1116; 2002 US Dist. LEXIS 16235; 156 Oil and Gas Rep. 403, 11 July 2002, Entered.
37 ibid.
38 ibid.
39 ibid.
40 *Hungary v. Slovakia*, where the ICJ declared the protection of the environment to be 'a vital part of contemporary human rights doctrine'.
41 Declaration of Gunther Handl in Opposition to Motion to Dismiss, p. 23.
42 *Rio Tinto*, p. 112; Supporting Carter Decl., p. 34.
43 ibid.
44 ibid.
45 Draft paper on some policy issues before the Office of the Prosecutor, for discussion at the public hearings in The Hague on 17 and 18 June, 2000: pp. 2–3.

46 ibid.
47 *Kayishema et al* (ICTR-95-I-T), Judgement and Sentence, 21 May 1999, para. 109.
48 *Akayesu* (ICTR-96-4-t) Judgement, 2 September 1998.
49 ibid.
50 See *Bagilishema* (ICTR-95-1at) Judgement, 7 June 2001, para. 80; see also Article 7(I) of the Rome Statute of the International Criminal Court.

CHAPTER 8

Aboriginal Rights in Domestic and International Law, and the Special Case of Arctic Peoples

FROM DOMESTIC LAW TO INTERNATIONAL LAW: THE CASE OF THE LUBICON CREE

It is very clear that the Lubicon people cannot survive the destruction of our traditional lands and the expropriation of our natural resources any more than could any other society.[1]

The cases reviewed in Chapter 6 indicate clearly the lacunae present in Canadian laws regarding its aboriginal peoples. Most often, cases and conflicts brought to the courts are based on principles and involve traditional cultural and religious beliefs, yet they are treated – for the most part – simply as land deals. The historical roots and background of the legal instruments used in the cases are treated seriously and systematically, but the principles upon which aboriginal peoples based their adherence to those documents (even when they did so) are largely ignored. Both the reasons for and the form of their agreements are consistently misunderstood (Imai, 2001). Indigenous peoples thought that allegiance, cooperation and respect were to govern their interaction with the Europeans, a hope that never truly materialized.

It is sad to find that when deliberate misunderstanding and the 'wilful blindness' appear to govern both the federal and provincial governments, as well as the courts, then the quest for justice does not fare well, even under international law. The clearest case in point is that of the Lubicon Cree from Alberta.[2] The Lubicon Cree Nation had been asking the Alberta government to demarcate their lands in the boreal forests of Alberta for many years, but to no avail, as mining, lumbering and agriculture were increasingly taking over their traditional lands (Huff, 1999). Eventually, the Lubicon Cree decided to abandon their efforts at gaining recognition in the courts, and decided instead to 'erect checkpoints on all roads entering their traditional territory' (Goddard, 1991). Chief Ominayak decided they had the right to protect their territories, declaring, 'the Lubicon Nation intends to assert and enforce its aboriginal rights and its sovereign jurisdiction as an independent nation' (cited in Goddard, 1991).

The Lubicon Cree depend on the boreal forest for hunting, fishing and trapping, their traditional pursuits, but the provincial courts did not recognize their claim. The provincial government sent in the Royal Canadian Mounted Police who arrested 27 people at the checkpoint where the Lubicon were blocking the highway (Huff, 1999), thus justifying the Lubicon's lack of trust in Canadian legal institutions and the promises of the Alberta government.

In 1984, the Lubicon took their case to the United Nations Human Rights Committee:[3]

> *In March 1990, the United Nations Human Rights Committee (UNHRC) concluded that 'historical inequalities' and 'more recent developments' have endangered the way of life and the culture of the Lubicon Cree. The Committee ruled that 'so long as they continue, these threats are a violation of the Lubicon's fundamental human rights.*

Yet the rights to the traditional territory of the Lubicon Cree had not been extinguished by any treaty that might affect them. Although they live within Treaty 8 territory, they had not signed that treaty. The Canadian government assured the UNHRC that it was working to find a way to settle with the Lubicon in a mutually satisfactory way. Since the time when this commitment was made, until 2007, no settlement has been reached. In contrast, while the Lubicon Cree live in squalor, with no running water in their homes, 'billions of dollars more in oil and gas resources have been extracted from Lubicon territory'.[4]

It is vital to keep two points in mind: the first is that as long as Canada stalls by saying it is 'negotiating' or 'trying to settle', somehow it continues to avoid taking any concrete action on this urgent matter; however, since there have been no negotiations since 2003, this is no longer a valid argument. The second point is that what is being taken away from the Lubicon is far more than revenue, although an equitable share of the profit being made by Alberta might be at least a beginning. Nevertheless, the harms they are suffering are incompensable harms, and even if they were offered a fair share of the profits of those industries, still it would not be right to continue the present rate and mode of resource extraction and 'development', given the irreversible effects of those operations, as we shall see below.

Although eventually the UN decision came down in favour of the Lubicon, their territory has yet to be demarcated. The problem originated because they lived in an isolated area, north of the land where treaties, such as Treaty 8, had been negotiated, so that the Lubicon Cree were essentially missed when other treaties were signed for other aboriginal people in Alberta and Saskatchewan (Goddard, 1991; Huff, 1999). But the main problems started after the discovery of what some believe are among the most extensive petroleum fields in America, adding to the threats to traditional Lubicon lifestyle from agriculture, settlement, mining and especially the exploitation of timber. 'The Story of the Lubicon Case shows what can happen in Canada when a native community tries to assert rights to a territory rich in oil' (Goddard, 1991). Oil companies were pressing for development and by 1979 'The Province of Alberta completed the construction of an all-weather road to the previously remote Lubicon territory' (Huff, 1999). The road was built without ever solving the question of the legal boundaries of the Lubicon territory, yet:

> *Since the all-weather road completion in 1979, more than 400 oil wells have been installed by more than one hundred oil companies, all within fifteen miles of the main Lubicon community of Little Buffalo.* (Huff, 1999; see also Goddard, 1991)

Hence the issue is even more complex than the lack of aboriginal title or the recognition of the appropriate boundaries of the Lubicon territory.

Huff (1999) lists several of the attacks on the life and health of the Lubicon. First, the proximity of operating oil wells to the Cree settlement. Second, 'Gasoline and motor oil spills have fouled many traditional gathering areas', hence traditional gathering and trapping is much reduced, as is market demand for pelts. This reality has affected the Lubicon in several ways. The elimination of the income from trapping has forced most families in the community to depend on welfare for their survival. Also, traditional kills of moose or other animals were followed by a feast and by the distribution of extra meat to people in need.

Hence the lack of favourable hunting conditions means more than a reduction in income for the Lubicon, it also implies an unravelling of their traditional social interaction. Chief Ominayak explains:

> On welfare groceries, one is embarrassed because he or she cannot share food with kin
> – who wants hot dogs and a half can of spam? As the inability to share continues,
> social relations deteriorate because one is embarrassed to visit empty-handed.[5]

The third problem reflects a combination of direct and indirect harms. The disappearance of the traditional lifestyle and the demands of subsistence resulted in a 'dramatic rise in alcoholism, domestic violence, fights, car accidents, theft and suicide' as well as a series of health problems. Some of the harms described represent a threat to their life as a people, others attack their life as human beings whose health and normal function has not been considered or protected by a government who had the fiduciary duty to do so. The extent of these harms must be fully understood before laws that reflect that reality are put in place.

INDUSTRIAL AND EXTRACTIVE OPERATIONS: THE UNRESTRAINED THREAT OF CHEMICAL EXPOSURES

It is imperative that the results of chemical and other industrial exposures be fully understood, especially when these are combined with ecological disintegrity in their lands and, increasingly, the effects of climate change. Because of the Lubicon's problems with oil wells, epidemiological studies dealing with oil exploration should be our first consideration.

Surprisingly, or perhaps as expected, it is hard to find any credible scientific literature outlining the health results of the oil wells in Alberta. Fred Lennerson, an advisor to the Lubicon, declared that:

> ... since 1978, when the first road was constructed on Lubicon territory, the moose
> population – the staple of the Lubicon diet – swiftly declined. Moreover, environmental
> pollutants caused by oil and gas companies have created numerous health problems
> including a high number of still births, birth defects, asthma, tuberculosis, and
> various cancers. (Huff, 1999)

One can find the reason for the lack of research if one considers the history of published works attempting to determine what oil explorations do to the health of those who live nearby. Chevron-Texaco's oil development in Ecuador gave rise to acrimonious critiques on the part of Chevron-Texaco's scientific consultants when credible studies appeared in the literature.[6] Those studies reported on the 'geographical differences in cancer incidence in the Amazon basin of Ecuador' (Hurting and San Sebastian, (2002), abnormal pregnancy outcomes (San Sebastian and Cordoba (1999), and acute leukemia and environmental exposure (Steffen et al, 2004).

David Hewitt, one of Chevron-Texaco's scientific consultants, criticized all these studies for methodological and data quality problems. Yet a large number of scientists, especially epidemiologists, published a strongly worded article in the popular magazine *The Scientist*, criticizing the rejection of those studies. The scientists agreed that this represented yet another example of the grievous harm perpetrated and supported by 'science for sale', while serious and well-respected scientists have gone on record to support the exposées of the epidemiological studies that showed the effects of oil extraction and other hazardous operations. These scientists made their convictions clear:

> *In response, 50 scientists from around the world have written a letter arguing that the company's statement (that is that of Chevron-Texaco) was a 'blatant attempt to influence an ongoing court case in Ecuador, in which residents were suing Chevron-Texaco for allegedly polluting the region and endangering their health. The plaintiffs argue it will cost [US]$6 billion to correct environmental damage. (McCook, 2005)*

Hence, the same health problems encountered by aboriginal people forced to live near oil extraction and production are rendered even more serious by the fact that any credible scientific analysis of their problems may be blocked from reaching the courts or any other possible source of redress. It is ominous to note that despite the length of time elapsed from the start of oil exploration, even a thorough epidemiological search of specific literature related to the situation in Alberta failed to turn up any article analysing the issue. Are the Lubicon physically different from other aboriginal people in other areas? Are they perhaps more resistant to the chemical attacks they are subjected to, whether with intent or simply through wilful blindness? (Westra, 2004a).

These questions are neither logical nor sensible, hence it must be concluded that the Lubicon's plight cannot be and apparently has not been reported in reputable scientific journals because of overt or covert political opposition to the frank discussion and publication of such data, which may affect potentially interested researchers. In addition, young untenured scholars may also find it hard to express their concern, as it might be viewed as disregard for the broad interests of their home institutions, their provincial governments, or any source of grants and other academic support. Thus we note that for the Lubicon Cree, we only find arguments presented on their behalf based on personal observation or experience, both of which are hard to admit as 'expert evidence'.

A recent article by Clapp et al (2006) summarizes the problems endemic to oil extraction. The authors list the studies published in reputable, peer-reviewed journals, addressing the results of Texaco Corporation's 28-year operation of the Napo concession in Ecuador, constructing approximately 350 wells and extracting about 1.5 billion barrels of oil:

> *As a consequence of this activity there was and remains today widespread contamination of the environment and exposure of local populations living in the former concession area to a variety of hydrocarbon compounds, metals and gasses.* (Clapp et al, 2006)

We shall return to these findings and conclusions in Chapter 9, when I assess responsibility and accountability for the harms caused to indigenous populations. For now, the closing sentence of this Clapp et al's (2006) annex supports the contentions of this chapter:

> *... it is evident that there are numerous dangerous chemicals and metals that are produced and to which peoples are exposed in the oil extraction process. Most of this information is in general scientific literature and is based on studies of workers and communities in settings outside Ecuador. Nevertheless toxic and carcinogenic properties of these compounds are as relevant to the residents of Eastern Ecuador as they are to people anywhere.*

Neurotoxic effects of chemical exposures: A life sentence

> *One in every six children has a developmental disability and in most cases these disabilities affect the nervous system. The most common neurodevelopmental disorders include learning disabilities, sensory deficits, developmental delays and cerebral palsy. Some experts have reported that the prevalence of certain neurodevelopmental disorders – autism and attention deficit disorder, in particular – might be increasing.* (Grandjean and Landrigan, 2006)

Clear evidence can be found in general reports on the far-reaching toxicity of all industrial chemicals, especially in the medical/epidemiological literature coming from Europe, as that research is somewhat less likely to be tainted by political bias than work by local scholars, dependent on local funding and institutions. The gravity of the problem is recognized by Amnesty International (2003) and other international NGOs like Women in Europe for a Common Future.[7] The prestigious medical journal, *The Lancet,* published a groundbreaking article with far-reaching implications by Grandjean and Landrigan (2006), demonstrating how common chemicals affect human beings when they are most vulnerable, that is before and right after birth, while their brain is developing:

> *The developing human brain is inherently much more susceptible to injury caused by toxic agents, than is the brain of an adult. This susceptibility stems from the fact that during the nine months of prenatal life, the human brain must develop from a strip of cells along the dorsal ectoderm of the fetus, into a complex organ consisting of billions of precisely located, highly interconnected and specialized cells.*

In theory, irreversible neurobehavioural damage is preventable (Grandjean and Landrigan, 2006). But only five major groups of chemicals have been admitted to be toxic: lead, methylmercury, arsenic, polychlorinated biphenyls (PCBs) and solvents (Granjean and Landrigan, 2006), yet at least 201 chemicals are known to be neurotoxic in man. The lists of 'metals and inorganic compounds' and 'organic solvents' include most, but not all, of the industrial substances to which aboriginal peoples are exposed, both in Canada and globally (see table opposite).

Children are not a species apart from the adults they will eventually become. They will exhibit either the diseases resulting from their earlier exposure, or other neurological outcomes of their irreversible earlier exposures. Evident in the lists in the table are arsenic and cyanide compounds used in gold and silver mining operations and the lead and benzene present in petroleum and its by-products. In addition are all the pesticide exposures resulting from too close proximity to farming or forestry operations, or even from the participation of individuals in farming operations that produce occupational health problems in the working adults and in their offspring.

These are not diseases that are susceptible to treatment or cure. Not only are the diseases mentioned in the *Lancet* article incurable, but they include equally irreversible instances of altered normal function (Boyle et al, 1994; Grandjean and White, 2002). Oil and other extractive industries, together with other environmental pollutants, ensure the presence of a variety of neurobehavioural impairments (Janssem and Slovaxk, 1991; Kimbrough et al, 1989; Landrigan, 2002). Nor are developmental abnormalities the only hazards, 'The combined evidence suggests that neurodevelopmental disorders caused by industrial chemicals have created a silent pandemic in modern society' (Grandjean and Landrigan, 2006).

This pandemic carries with it a number of consequences to the general population, and these consequences become acute and unavoidable when the recipients are unable to move away from or stop the chemical attacks. The consequences include 'increased likelihood of school failure, diminished economic productivity, and possibly increased risk of antisocial and criminal behaviour' (Grandjean and Landrigan, 2006; see also Needleman et al, 2002). Other consequences include 'increased risk of Parkinson's disease or other degenerative diseases' (Calne et al, 1986; see also Landrigan et al, 2005).

Although these scientific studies are all non-specific, it is easy to extrapolate for a far better understanding of the true nature of the environmental exposures of aboriginal peoples. In addition, there are more specific studies regarding uranium mining and pesticide exposure, and they are discussed below. For now, the lack of consideration of these facts and general ignorance of the effects of chemicals (see figure on p194) is a major part of the problem. As long as the courts and legislators do not understand fully what the cases before them imply, there is little hope that justice will be applied to the beleaguered indigenous groups that are affected not only by what the law proscribes but, unfortunately, even more by what it does not forbid.

Because these consequences are far better known to the general public, the cancer epidemic related to oil extraction has not been mentioned thus far. On that issue, it is instructive to turn to a recent article by Waters (2006):

> *Cancers related to occupational and environmental conditions, pose additional risks for disease. For example, men and women who live around oil fields in the Amazon provinces of Sucumbior, Orellana, Napo, and Pataza face elevated risks of cancer of*

Neurotoxic chemicals

Metals and Inorganic Compounds	Organic Solvents
• Aluminium compounds	• Acetone
• Arsenic and arsenic compounds	• Benzene
• Azide compounds	• Benzyl alcohol
• Barium compounds	• Carbon disulphide
• Bismuth compounds	• Chloroform
• Carbon monoxide	• Chloroprene
• Cyanide compounds	• Cumene
• Decaborane	• Cyclohexane
• Diborane	• Cyclohexanol
• Ethylmercury	• Cyclohexanone
• Fluoride compounds	• Dibromochloropropane
• Hydrogen sulphide	• Dichloroacetic acid
• Lead and lead compounds	• 1,3-Dichloropropene
• Lithium compounds	• Diethylene glycol
• Manganese and manganese compounds	• N,N-Dimethylformamide
• Mercury and mercuric compounds	• 2-Ethoxyethyl acetate
• Methylmercury	• Ethyl acetate
• Nickel carbonyl	• Ethylene dibromide
• Pentaborane	• Ethylene glycol
• Phosphine	• N-Hexane
• Phosphorus	• Isobutyronitrile
• Selenium compounds	• Isophorone
• Tellurium compounds	• Isopropyl alcohol
• Thallium compounds	• Isopropylacetone
• Tin compounds	• Methanol
	• Methyl butyl ketone
	• Methyl cellosolve
	• Methyl ethyl ketone
	• Methylcyclopentane
	• Methylene chloride
	• Nitrobenzene
	• 2-Nitropropane
	• 1-Pentanol
	• Propyl bromide
	• Pyridine
	• Styrene
	• Tetrachloroethane
	• Tetrachloroethylene
	• Toluene
	• 1,1,1-Trichloroethane
	• Trichloroethylene
	• Vinyl chloride
	• Xylene

Source: Grandjean and Landrigan, 2006

Diagram of the extent of knowledge of neurotoxic chemicals

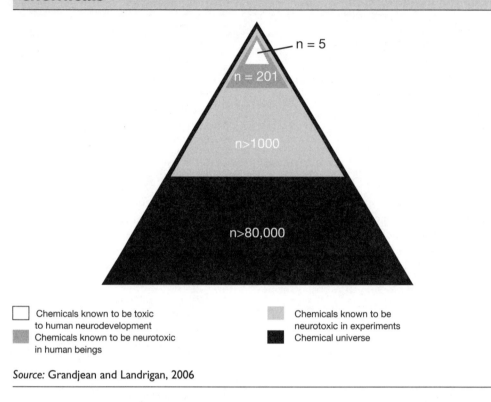

☐ Chemicals known to be toxic
to human neurodevelopment

▨ Chemicals known to be neurotoxic
in human beings

▨ Chemicals known to be
neurotoxic in experiments

■ Chemical universe

Source: Grandjean and Landrigan, 2006

> *the stomach, rectum, skin, soft tissue, and kidneys. In addition, women have increased risk of cancers of the cervix and lymph nodes; and children under the age of ten have higher risk of haematopoietic cancers.*

More non-specific evidence and the intent to suppress relevant health-related information: The results

> *Nor has the Government performed any health studies that pinpoint exactly what people and animals are breathing in heavily developed areas such as Grand Prairie, Sundre, Lloydminster or Pincher Creek. Even the oil and gas industry agrees that this scientific gap needs to be filled.* (Nikiforuk, 1999)

Although this article does not address any aboriginal issues, it gives an excellent overview of the health impacts on both animals and humans of oil development, particularly regarding Alberta's farmers (Nikiforuk, 1999). Nikiforuk also points out that, despite the fact that both oil companies and the provincial government have claimed there are no proven harms from those oil operations, many scientific studies show the contrary to be true, especially in the case of sour gas (hydrogen sulphide). As research at both US and Alberta locations shows, even low doses of sour gas exposure 'can cause persistent neurobehavioural dysfunction' (Nikiforuk, 1999), as well as higher than normal levels of bronchitis and pneumonia, and congenital heart anomalies in children, and this evidence may also be linked to the Lubicon.[8]

In Chapter 7 we addressed the thorny question of what constitutes genocide, especially the aspect of intent. We also noted that the facts that came to light regarding the effects of residential schools on indigenous children fit the bill in a very real sense, given their deliberate effort to eliminate, if not individuals, certainly the Indian children as a 'people'. The courts and the government itself stepped into the breach, and eventually the Royal Commission catalogued the painful evidence of all the wrongs done to Indian children in those institutions, and the consequence in adulthood of the crimes perpetrated.

However, in the light of the information about the consequences of harms so grave to indigenous children, before and after birth, that they shaped and altered intellectual function, economic abilities, and the ability to fully distinguish right from wrong and follow the law, it is possible that the religious and state/provincial institutions who perpetrated those crimes are by no means the only guilty parties.

Considering Grandjean and Landrigan's (2006) laundry list of results following upon 'business as usual', it is clear that indigenous peoples are totally vulnerable and unprotected *now*. Noting the eerie similarity between one set of consequences (for example, those following oil extraction and mining operations exposures), and those observed after the imposition of state institutional standards of treatment upon the children. Perhaps we need to reconsider a few main points.

The first point is the issue of viewing church institutions as fully responsible, as that may represent an oversimplification in the effort to isolate a convenient scapegoat. Hundreds of thousands of dollars were paid when the churches cooperated and assisted while admitting this public shame. Their crimes are not in question. But there may be another side to the story. What we have detailed above, the disease, despair, lack of ability to continue a traditional lifestyle, are all present in today's aboriginal peoples too, despite the elimination of the residential school system in Canada. In fact, all the effects listed occur everywhere when their territorial integrity is breached, their cultural rights are not respected and, worst of all, when hazardous industrial operations are placed close enough to their villages and settlements to harm children and adults, with results that match and also exceed the harms produced by the institutions discussed by the Royal Commission.

What is needed is a lot of research by independent and credible scientific sources because, unlike the case of the residential schools' effects that can be researched and documented almost *in vivo* by listening to affected individuals and their children, the other harms are *not* readily known, allowed to surface and explained to the public. No Royal Commission has even attempted to attack the 'sacred cow' of corporate freedom, and the over-consumption that results in the urgent need for oil and other products, no matter the cost. As we saw, only scholars far removed from the actual situation appear to have attempted that sort of research, and their courage and integrity is rewarded with immediate attacks from 'big oil' and their 'prostitute science'. The history of big tobacco is instructive in this regard: their fraudulent assertions and endless, well-funded efforts to distort reality and manipulate the public and the courts provide the right perspective from which to judge what is happening.

Perhaps that is what is needed to protect the rights of First Nations and other aboriginal groups, far more than endless debates on self-governance and sovereignty. Less abstract argument and far more independent scientific research is needed, including the publication of detailed and thorough case studies, in order to show the full impact of an economic system without conscience or respect for life, health and normal function and its impact on the 'canaries' of the world. This claim is pursued further in the next section, when I consider Nunavut, a self-governing Inuit territory north of the Arctic Circle. Does its self-governance grant the Inuit immunity from harm?

At any rate, it must be acknowledged, it will be extremely hard to convince any government, including that of Canada or of any province, to pursue a course that runs counter to the economic interests of their corporate friends and supporters. Yet justice demands that this course be followed. If reparation and restitution were accepted as necessary and appropriate, following the actions of religious and other institutions, the fact that the latter are not rich corporate allies of any government should not deter Canada's provinces and others from accepting the obvious. Similar harmful effects mean that similar condemnation and reparation should follow corporate criminals. In addition, the harmful activities should be eliminated immediately, no matter what the economic hardship in order to protect life/health and normal function as soon as possible.

IS SELF-GOVERNANCE ALONE THE ANSWER? THE CASE OF THE ARCTIC PEOPLE OF NUNAVUT

Pack ice to the white man seems like a barrier, something to fear. But to the Inuit it's their highway. It's their communication system, their freedom, their independence. Without it there is no Inuit culture. (Kendall, 2006)

For the most part, the case law we have considered thus far represents aboriginal claims requesting self-governance, or even sovereignty, border demarcation, and the right to consent to commercial intrusions on their lands (see Chapter 6). Self-governance, as noted in Chapter 1, is one of the two pillars of aboriginal rights, together with cultural integrity. The suggestion advanced at that point was to add the foundational right of biological/ecological integrity to the rights that are currently acknowledged. Perhaps the extensive general research summarized in this chapter from public health sources indicates the vital necessity of that addition.

The question, however, remains that even if my proposal is accepted, how are the three principles to be ranked? Does self-determination remain primary, while the other two are viewed as ancillary principles? Or is my claim valid that the biological/ ecological integrity of the indigenous peoples and their lands should instead be viewed as primary? The situation of the Inuit of northeast Canada is a case in point: they enjoy self-governance but their position is by no means ideal, although the pressing hazards of oil extraction found in Alberta or Ecuador are not present at this time and, to my knowledge, there is only one gold mine (although more are presently under development) and one diamond mine in the area. Nevertheless from 1960 to 2002, a zinc mine existed at Nanisivik, and the animals that form the staple of the Inuit diet have the highest DDT content in the world in their bodies (Colborn et al, 1996).

As we shall see below, these indigenous peoples suffer grave health and social problems, which arise at least in part, from the carelessness and short-sightedness of industrial operations and consumerist lifestyles, many far removed from their borders and almost totally beyond their control (Ford et al, 2006).

Global warming and vulnerability in the Canadian Arctic

The Arctic Climate Impact Assessment (ACIA) suggests that future climate change will be experienced earlier and more acutely in polar regions. These changes will occur on top of recent climate change which has been documented by instrumental records and indigenous observation in the Arctic. (Ford et al, 2006; see also ACIA, 2004; Ford, 2005)

While Western developed nations debate the existence of global warming and what to do about it, the Inuit have been plunged right into the effects of it, with no way out:

In 2004 scientists with the Arctic Climate Impact Assessment, a comprehensive study of climate change in the Arctic, reported that the region as a whole has undergone the greatest warming on Earth in recent decades with annual temperature now averaging 2–3 degrees Celsius higher than in the 50s. (Ford, 2005)

This change affects the region's ice, as the 'late Summer Arctic sea ice has been thinned by 40 percent in some parts, and shrunk in the area of roughly 8 percent over the past 30 years' (Ford, 2005; see also Kattsov and Kallen, 2005).

What are the major effects of these drastic changes? The first thing to note is that Arctic people are particularly vulnerable to these changes, as a recent study (Ford et al, 2006) of the Inuit in Arctic Bay, Nunavut, indicates. For that study, Ford and his collaborators used the 'Conceptual Model of Vulnerability', as indicated by the United Nations Framework Convention on Climate Change (UNFCCC, 1992). This convention defines vulnerability 'as a function of the climate conditions to which a system is exposed, its sensitivity, and its adaptive capacity' (McCarthy et al, 2001).

The special vulnerability of the Inuit arises principally because of their dependence on the land and sea for their subsistence, a condition they share with most indigenous peoples' communities. Their main defining activity is hunting:

Considerable time is spent by most community members 'on the land' (a term used by Inuit to refer to any traditional activity, camping, hunting, or traveling) that takes place outside the settlement. (Ford et al, 2006)

There are several main issues that manifest the basic vulnerability of the Inuit hunting and gathering activities, when either preparing to go or already out 'on the land', in relation to global warming. The first is the ability to predict weather-related dangers and to be able to adjust plans according to that knowledge. But, as Lisha Levia, a resident of Arctic Bay puts it:

> *Normally, when the wind starts coming, it comes gradually, then it gets stronger later on. But today when it starts getting windy, it comes on really strong. I cannot predict the weather through looking at the clouds when I used to.* (cited in Ford, 2005)

Eva Inukpuk reports a similar experience of her 70-year-old mother, who used to live in igloos and could predict accurately what the next day's weather would be like. She adds, 'Now, it could be anything: all her knowledge counts for nothing these days' (Kendall, 2006).

Hence, what we are witnessing in the Arctic is much more than climate change, it is, as the people in Nunavik describe it, 'climatic disruption' (Kendall, 2006). It is more than just warmer temperatures; it is the total unpredictability those changes produce, the related elimination of the Inuit's knowledge base, and the severe impact on their cultural life (Ford et al, 2006).

If the Inuit are traditionally dependent on their hunting activities and the ability to predict the weather in order to prepare ahead of each trip, this is much more than a source of inconvenience in their travel; it could be, and often is, a matter of life and death. For example, if the expectations are for spring temperatures that might be too warm to build igloos, then tents might be a better alternative. Making this decision ahead of a trip may well prove fatal if the temperature drops suddenly in the night and the hunters may then freeze to death.

Similarly, the arrival of freak blizzards and sudden snowmelts may prove equally fatal to hunters unexpectedly falling through thinner ice (Kendall, 2006). Thus, the importance of traditional knowledge is drastically diminished, as is the respect due to experienced hunters. Hunters were formerly the keepers of the 'collective social memory' (Ford et al, 2006).[9]

When this knowledge base fails and this failure is combined with climatic conditions that change the historically known accessibility of hunting grounds, this gravely undermines the very existence of their cultural integrity, as rising weather unpredictability forces changes in lifestyle on local inhabitants.

Nor does the addition of modern technology guarantee mitigation of the increasingly hostile environmental conditions I have described. Traditional travel involved dog sleds, and these animals' instincts and knowledge base ensure safety for hunters, for the most part. Modern snowmobiles, instead, often permit sudden plunges through thin ice hidden under snow (Ford et al, 2006). Perhaps the use of global positioning systems (GPS) might help preserve, at least in part, the continuity of traditional ways. Yet, when those man-made devices fail, as they often do, the stranded hunters are left with neither technology nor traditional knowledge to guide them to safety (Ford et al, 2006):

> *The results of these increasingly unmanageable hazards give rise to ... an even more pressing concern ... [which is] the social fallout from the transformation of these traditional subsistence-based societies, to 'southern' wage-based economies. Unemployment in both Arctic Bay and Igloolik stands at over 20 percent, and alcoholism is a major problem. Nunavut's suicide rate, at 77 deaths per 100,000 people, is one of the highest in the world, and six times higher than in the rest of Canada.*

The inability to continue traditional practices leads to dependence on waged positions, hence the change to a 'dual economy' or 'mixed economy', where both traditional

Harvesting activities sensitive to observed climatic conditions

Activity	Time of year	Conditions	Implications
General hunting/ travel on the sea ice	October– December	Thin ice	New areas of open water, areas of unusually thin ice, and a change in the location of leads[a] have increased the dangers of travelling on sea ice and lake ice. People have lost and damaged equipment.
	October–July	Weather	More unpredictable weather and sudden weather changes have forced hunters to spend extra unplanned nights on the land. Unusual weather – rain in winter, extreme cold in spring – is dangerous because hunters are not prepared.
Narwhal hunt	June–July	Ice break-up	Sudden and unanticipated wind changes causing sea ice to unexpectedly disintegrate. Incidence of hunters being stranded on drifting ice[b] and having to be rescued by helicopter.
General hunting/ travel by boat	July– September	Waves/ stormy weather	Sudden changes in wind strength and direction, combined with stronger winds, have forced hunters to spend extra nights out on the land waiting for calm weather to return to the community.

Source: Ford et al, 2006
Note: a) A crevice or channel of open water created by a break in a mass of sea ice.
    b) Drift occurs if the ice is blown away from ice that is attached to the land.

living and market-based activities coexist (Chabot, 2003; Damas, 2002). In addition, in the 1960s, the government promoted 'fixed settlements', which further complicated traditional access to hunting areas (Ford et al, 2006). Finally, the dependence on a 'mixed economy' implied the reduction of traditional foods and increased dependence on store-bought and fast food, with the expected rise in obesity and diabetes resulting from unhealthy diets (Ford, 2005).

The corollary of this change is not only a grave threat to the health of the Arctic Bay Inuit, but also, increasingly, to the cultural survival of the Inuit as a people. The 'social networks' typical of these societies are seriously eroded, as Lisha Qavavang puts it, 'that's the only way we survive, by supporting one another' (cited in Ford et al, 2006). But the existence of a 'mixed economy' does not facilitate the redistribution and transfer mechanisms of food sharing (Ford et al, 2006; see also Damas, 1972).

Further, as the difficulties encountered in the changed physical environment dissuade current and older generations from persisting in their traditional ways, the results have been even worse for the young:

> *English has replaced Inuktikut as the dominant language among younger generations, older generations think the young Inuit are not interested in learning the traditional ways, and the Euro-American social norms of youth are far removed from the traditional upbringing of older generations.* (Kral, 2003)

Many younger people have lost the traditional skills necessary for successful hunting, but without those skills their abilities are insufficient to ensure their safety, and their economic prospects are bleak, as they now depend on elusive monetary resources to acquire the technology and the gadgets they would need to survive. Private sector jobs are limited in number and high unemployment is a fact of life.

Self-governance in defence of Nunavut's people?

> *People form governments for their common defence, security and welfare. The first thing that public officials owe their constituents is protection against natural and man-made hazards.* (Gostin, 2004)

Gostin (2004) stresses the most important function of a government: the security of citizens and the protection of public health. And that is the question that needs to be answered at this point: can self-government, even one based on a separate territory like Nunavut do enough to help alleviate or even eliminate the threats against the Inuit people? [10]

We have noted the grave problems that beset them: loss of cultural integrity and identity, primarily based on the loss of an appropriate land base but also on the erosion of their traditional knowledge, so that even on the land, under conditions of changing climate and altered geographical characteristics, the Inuit are becoming strangers in their own lands, without the reassuring presence of their age-old skills to guide them.

For these problems, even established self-governance institutions can do little, although, as we shall see, by confirming the existence of Nunavut as a territory, these institutions can reinstate a First Nation's presence as a subject of international law. Thus, presumably, it can gain protection available through those instruments from trans-boundary harms,[11] although there is no present case law to support my proposal. Nevertheless, the problems the Inuit are facing are not open to internal solutions: they are both systemic and collective at the same time. Both aspects render them almost intractable within the present governance and regulatory systems, and the difficulties inherent to these categories are discussed in turn.

SYSTEMIC PROBLEMS AND SELF-GOVERNANCE

> *Her Majesty the Queen in right of Canada and the Inuit of the Nunavut Settlement Area have negotiated an agreement based on and reflecting the following objectives:*

to provide for certainty and clarity of rights to ownership and use the land and resources and of right for Inuit to participate in decision-making concerning the use, management and conservation of lands, water and resources, including the offshore,

to provide Inuit with wildlife harvesting rights and rights to participate in decision-making concerning wildlife harvesting,

to provide Inuit with financial compensation and means of participating in economic opportunities,

to encourage self-reliance and the cultural and social well-being of the Inuit.[12]

The first question that arises is whether the territorial government of Nunavut (where 85 per cent of the population is Inuit) can be held responsible for delivering fully on the list of desirable outcomes that Her Majesty the Queen commits to their care? It can indeed ensure that the citizens make decisions regarding their territory, but, as we saw in the discussion of climate change issues, it is the irresponsible decisions made *outside* their territories that affect, probably irreversibly, their basic rights. 'Self-reliance' and 'cultural and social well-being' are nothing but empty ideals when the conditions necessary for their actualization are no longer present.

'Ownership' and 'use' of 'lands and resources' are also increasingly empty promises when the land (including the sea ice) is shrinking fast and what remains is quickly losing its 'resources', so that 'wildlife harvesting rights' are becoming more and more elusive. The 'conservation of land water resources' is something that, no matter how good the governance and how sensitive it might be to the Inuit's lifestyle, is no longer within their power. Things might have been somewhat better in 1993, when the Nunavut Act became law, but at least one aspect of the environmental harms the Inuit are exposed to was well documented already in the scientific literature, and summarized in a generally accessible form in 1996 by Colborn et al, reporting on the highest concentration of DDT and other harmful chemicals in mammals and birds in the Arctic. Therefore, even then, their 'resources', when caught and consumed, were tainted and presented a grave threat to the health and normal function of the Inuit, although at that time wildlife might have been more readily available and the climate conditions less disastrous (see also Grandjean and Landrigan, 2006).

The Nunavut government, as we saw, can and does provide 'compensation' as required. But that compensation, even if it is the result of self-governance and the only humane choice in the face of deteriorating climatic conditions, remains an option in direct contrast with the 'cultural integrity' of the Inuit. Hence, in their dire situation, the best that can be done pits the only available choices to support their survival through self-determination against their survival as a 'people'.

Nor can the Nunavut government be blamed now for the results of choices initiated many years prior to their coming into force, in locations far from their territory. We are witnessing the results of globalization and the spread of the primacy of economic considerations over any other. These can be witnessed in the disposition of most cases involving aboriginal people throughout the world. What we are seeing, in addition, is our own plight, wherever we are living, but in the case of the Inuit, it is significantly magnified by the two considerations that characterize aboriginal peoples: their full dependence on the land, and their inability to move away from their homeland, even to seek safety or subsistence.

The presence of self-governance, however, adds one hopeful variable to the Inuit's plight, as noted above: their existence as a nation might enable them to better assert their rights in international law, a topic I return to below.

Collective rights and self-governance

> *The concept of collective interest potentially provides a valuable tool for promoting human rights enforcement in international law. Over the past century, there has been a growing consensus that the international community as a whole has a collective interest in the fulfillment of certain fundamental human rights obligations.* (Kaplan, 2004)

There are significant obstacles to any individual or group trying to defend their human rights because states are still primary in international law (Kaplan, 2004). The law of nations is intended to govern the dealings between states; individuals and groups cannot simply expect that their rights will be respected, let alone enforced by a system designed for interstate legal relations. Nevertheless, there are already several venues where individuals, at least, can bring their grievances, such as the European Court of Human Rights, the United Nations Human Rights Committee, the Inter-American Court of Human Rights (IACHR), and the International Criminal Court,[13] although the last of these is limited in scope to the gravest human rights breaches in times of war, such as attacks against the human person, crimes against humanity and genocide.

In addition, state consent is normally required when individuals want to complain to such a high court:

> *Four United Nations Agreements give individuals or groups of individuals the right to complain about violations of protected rights by state actors: The First Optional Protocol to the International Covenant on Civil and Political Rights (ICCPR); the Optional Protocol to the Convention on the Elimination of all Forms of Discrimination Against Women (CEDAW); the Convention Against Torture and Other Cruel, Inhuman or Degrading Treatment or Punishment (Convention Against Torture); and the International Convention on the Elimination of All Forms of Racial Discrimination (CERD).*[14]

Essentially, collective rights are, as Kaplan (2004) indicates, best viewed under the category of *erga omnes* obligations, dictated not by treaties but by *jus cogens* norms.

These issues were discussed in Chapter 7. Essentially the earlier debates between various ways of viewing crimes of states were never fully solved. The International Law Commission (2000) eliminated Article 19, intended to draw the distinction between 'crime' and 'delict', and to propose examples of the former, including grave environmental pollution. But the 2000 ILC Reports only retained some of the original distinctions, in the language of Articles 41 and 42.[15] That is why placing all these internationally wrongful acts in the same category, the one that contravenes *jus cogens* norms, makes good sense. The effects of widespread environmental pollution, climate change, nuclear threats, and food and water scarcity or contamination share the characteristics of doing injury to the most basic human rights in all states and evoking widespread global condemnation.

Alain Pellet (1997) notes that not only is there a difference of degree between what can be termed a delict and what must be termed a crime, but there may also be a difference in kind between some illicit acts and others: 'Malgré une thèse souvant soutenue, il n'y a pas une simple différence de degré entre ces deux categories de faits internationalement illicites, mais, bel et bien, une différence de nature' ('despite a thesis often held, there is not a simple difference of degree between these two categories of internationally illicit acts, but, rather, a difference in kind'). Pellet (1997) explains further: it is more than the society of states that is affected, it is a question of affecting humanity. And this is more than a theoretical argument; it is necessary to recognize the difference between an act of genocide and a 'banale' violation of a commercial treaty's clause, a dispute between two states. It is the former, not the latter, that primarily has 'humanity' as its target.

There are indeed differences between illicit acts that can be termed delicts and crimes. Only crimes run counter to non-derogable norms; hence, only illicit acts of extreme gravity will fit this understanding. Yet, even Pellet (1997) recognizes the flaws in the list of examples provided in former Article 19.3.[16] Most of them are questionable, Pellet argues, because the concepts used are 'open and indeterminate':

> *... les examples données font appel à des concepts eux-memes largement ouvert et indéterminés: violations 'grave' (quantitativement ou qualitativement?); violations 'à une large échelle'; obligations 'd'une importance essentielle'; 'aggression' (aggression armée ou également aggression economique?).*

> [*... the examples given appeal to concepts that are themselves largely open and indeterminate: violations that are 'grave' (quantitatively or qualitatively?); violations 'on a grand scale'; obligations that are 'essentially important'; 'aggression' (only armed or also economic aggression?).]*

No doubt the specifics are insufficient and do not add the clarity required in such a foundational distinction. But we must consider the spirit as well as the letter of the relationship between the concept of crime and that of *jus cogens*, keeping in mind both Article 53 and Article 64 of the Vienna Convention of the Law of Treaties.

When Pellet (1997) wholeheartedly approves of the distinction between crimes and delicts, he appears to have in mind the pre-eminent position of international crimes as breaches of human rights in relation to other wrongful acts. Lauterpacht (1968), for example, speaks of the Nuremberg Tribunal, as 'the basis of codification of international law on the subject... In an indirect but compelling manner the enactment of "crimes against humanity" constitutes the recognition of fundamental human rights, superior to the law of the Sovereign State.' Lauterpacht also considers the role of the Security Council (Chapter VI and Chapter VII of the UN Charter), in order to understand the relationship between human rights and peace:

> *The correlation between peace and observance of fundamental human rights is not a generally recognized fact. The circumstances that the legal duty to respect fundamental human rights has become part and parcel of the new international system upon which peace depends, adds emphasis to that ultimate connection.* (Lauterpacht, 1968)

Speaking of the 'General Principles of Humanitarian Law', Brownlie (1998) remarks upon the repeated appearance of this concept, for instance, in the *Nicaragua v. United States of America* case (1986 ICJ 14) (six passages in the judgement). It is worth citing the court's interpretation of the collective right to self-defence (Article 51 of the charter):

> ... *[with] regard to the existence of the right of self-defense and in particular collective self-defense, the Court ... notes that in the language of Article 51 of the United Nations Charter, the inherent right (or 'droit naturel') which any State possesses in the event of an armed attack covers both collective and individual self-defense.* (at para. 102)

Particularly significance from the point of view of our argument, is the dubious translation of 'droit naturel', easily understood as 'natural right' or 'inherent right' instead. The right to self-defence is one of the cornerstones of natural law, and perhaps the translation used is intended to disguise the presence of natural law in humanitarian law theory. This switch raises the question: if the right to defend myself inheres to me (or to a state), why is this the case, unless the argument of natural law supports self-defence by providing the principle upon which it is based? Brownlie (1998) also notes that 'there is an incremental progression toward an *actio popularis*', although even the presence or an obligation *erga omnes* may not be sufficient for the court to take action. In the *East Timor* case:[17]

> *In the court's view, Portugal's assertion that the rights of peoples to self-determination as it evolved from the Charter, and from United Nations practice, has an* erga omnes *character, is irreproachable. However, the court considers that the* erga omnes *character of a norm and the rule of consent to jurisdiction are two different things.* (Brownlie, 1998)

In conclusion, it is clear that neither internal domestic reforms nor treaties will succeed in addressing and correcting the human rights breaches suffered by Arctic peoples. The only possible approach is to place their harms in a category that transcends the limited capabilities of even the best-intentioned instruments of self-governance.

THE *TRAIL SMELTER ARBITRATION* AND CLIMATE CHANGE

> *The Trail Smelter principles persist in international instruments, casebooks and scholarly footnotes, as the locus classicus of international environmental law. So it is not at all surprising that one need only scratch the surface to find trace elements of these Trail Smelter principles in global climate change regimes.* (Miller, 2006)

The question is whether Nunavut is indeed a 'nation', with its own boundaries, and hence with rights within those boundaries. Also, is it a 'nation' in the sense that it could participate in international law meetings as a separate entity aside from Canada? But it might be worth considering, from the standpoint of *lex ferenda*, whether their separate 'self-governance' might entitle the Inuit to more legal protection than they enjoy as a separate minority within Canada. In fact, the thrust of Miller's (2006) chapter, is precisely the important role played by non-state actors both in the *Trail Smelter Arbitration* and climate change, a precedent that might help their case:

> *The rise of these non-state actors suggests a new world order in which the nation state's Westphalian prerogative is increasingly suspect. The literature is right to remind us that non-state actor involvement in international affairs is nothing new. But the nature and degree of the contemporary involvement of non-state actors is a genuine phenomenon.* (Miller, 2006; see also Paust, 2004)

NGOs and major corporate individuals play a determinant role today in climate change negotiations, and this 'novel' pressure has a tradition based on *Trail Smelter* itself, where the Citizens Protection Association, a Washington residents' group that would not allow the issue of Canadian pollution to rest, took a forceful stance. They forced the reopening of the case in 1933, they refused the $350,000 judgement proposed by the International Joint Commission as compensation and insisted on additional investigations (Miller, 2006).[18]

In contrast, corporate mining and smelting interests (on the American side), tried unsuccessfully to side with the Canadians, hence, the *Trail Smelter Arbitration*:

> *... transcended its formal framework, as a dispute between the United States and Canada, to encompass the clash of interests between non-state actors in an environmental NGO, facing off against global industrial interests on the international plane. This clash of non-state actors is paradigmatic of contemporary international environmental law.* (Miller, 2006; see also Brown-Weiss, 1997)

This reality is endemic to globalization, as we noted especially in Chapter 4 where the review of the international case law led inexorably to a discussion of the part the IMF and the World Bank Group (powerful non-state actors) play in those cases, through their support of corporate criminal activities. Their main focus is on economic outcomes, without any regard to the serious human rights violations that result from those corporate activities.

For Arctic people, the effects of the extended ecological footprint of a globalized economy are so severe and so diffuse, that it would be extremely hard to bring home the responsibility for these results to either corporate individuals or complicit governments. This is especially true since the connections between environmental harms and public health/medical harms has been consistently ignored by courts and legislators from *Trail Smelter* onwards. This ignorance might have been justified in 1933, even in 1941, but it is a total anachronism today when, as we saw, the connection between environmental exposures to industrial products and processes and human health are backed by solid research from the WHO, epidemiology and other scientists. Yet even today, that connection, together with the damage accelerant provided by climate change, appears to be invisible, a clear case of 'wilful blindness', as I have argued (Westra, 2004a).

In contrast, the strong presence of NGOs in current environmental debates may be profitably used by Nunavut. NGOs, now as then, 'advised and even participated as members of government delegations' (Miller, 2006). Today, NGOs are even more vocal and powerful, and they are much in evidence at climate change meetings:

... the tiny nation of Vanuatu turned its delegation over to an NGO, with expertise in international law ... thereby making itself and the other sea-level islands states major players in the fight to control global warming. (Mathews, 1997)

In fact, by the year 2000, when COP 6 was convened in The Hague, The Netherlands, 'representatives of NGOs outnumbered representatives of states' (Betsill, 2002). Hence, even if the self-governing territory of Nunavut may not have the full credentials of a state, the present operation of international law permits the participation of a much greater constituency, at least as capable of being heard, in the area of climate change:

Any Body or Agency, whether national or international, governmental or non-governmental, which is qualified in matters covered by the Convention, and which has informed the secretariat of its wish to be represented at a session of the Conference of the Parties as an observer, may be so admitted.[19]

Less obvious, but no less important, is the connection between Arctic indigenous peoples and the requirements of the Convention on Biological Diversity (CBD), the topic of the next section.

INDIGENOUS PEOPLES OF THE ARCTIC AND THE REQUIREMENTS OF THE CONVENTION ON BIOLOGICAL DIVERSITY: THE INTERFACE

Article 8 – In Situ Conservation

Each contracting Party shall, as far as possible and as appropriate:

(a) *Establish a system of protected areas or areas where special measures need to be taken to conserve biological diversity;...*
(d) *Promote the protection of ecosystems, natural habitats and the maintenance of viable populations in natural surroundings;...*
(i) *Endeavour to provide the conditions for compatibility between present uses and the conservation of biological diversity and the sustainable use of its components;*
(j) *Subject to its national legislation, respect, practices of indigenous and local communities embodying traditional lifestyles relevant for the conservation and sustainable use of biological diversity.* (CBD, 1992)

Other items on the list under Article 8 show clearly that, at least originally, the main concern was with the biodiversity of small islands and developing countries in the South. This is indicated by the many references to 'alien species', to genetically modified organisms, to the management and conservation of biological diversity, the restoration of 'degraded ecosystems', and to 'viable populations', although this last item may also be applied to the Arctic. Later, with the addition of high-altitude regions and montane areas as well as the Arctic, the development of the principles of the CBD in response to the real issue of climate change and industrial pollution is clearly in evidence.

The points emphasized above are particularly relevant to the main argument of this work. Note the first point (a) on the establishment of protected areas, as well as the presence of special measures to conserve diversity, which, as I argued above, must include a buffer zone and general restraint of industrial activities (Noss and Cooperrider, 1994). When this point is considered together with the promotion of the ecosystem protection (d), the centrality of biological ecological integrity, proposed in Chapter 1 and throughout this book, is clearly in evidence.

Whatever the country, the climate and the specifics of biological diversity, conservation *in situ* starts with the absolute requirement for protected areas; in addition, those areas must be protected from inappropriate activities even beyond the borders of the area itself. Note that in 'Island Specific Priority Actions for the Parties'[20] the issue of 'pollution' and its impact on island biodiversity, with 'special attention to hazardous waste', is especially relevant, given the fact that most Arctic communities are also 'coastal communities'. The 'Rationale' provided is instructive:

> *Rationale: Islands are largely coastal communities, where it is particularly difficult to dispose of wastes without impacting biodiversity. The siting of landfills, the disposal of liquid wastes and the uptake of solid wastes and plastics by marine organisms are all of considerable significance to islands.*[21]

Essentially, the conservation of biodiversity starts necessarily with the protection of ecosystems, hence, not only biodiversity itself, but its precondition; the protections of ecological integrity and the biological integrity of the species living therein, also require the protection of the ecosystemic function to which they all contribute. Recognizing that the key to this protection is conservation *in situ* represents the basis of any conservation ethic, including the proposed 'Code of Ethics' the IUCN is supporting (Bosselmann, 2006).

But it is in Article 8(j), that the intimate connection of ecological integrity and aboriginal cultural rights can be best seen, particularly with reference to the Arctic peoples' situation, such as those of the Nunavut people. Perhaps originally Arctic people were not front and centre in the mind of the drafters of this article. But, as we saw, it is impossible to 'preserve and maintain knowledge, innovations and practices of indigenous and local communities embodying traditional lifestyles', unless the biological/ecological integrity of the area is preserved minimally in 'special areas' (Article 8(e)), as both traditional Arctic knowledge and the Inuit's traditional lifestyle and culture are utterly dependent on the conditions of the land and climate.

In fact, the COP 8 Decisions (VIII/5. Article 8(j) and related provisions) in its Composite Report (*B. Composite Report on Status and Trends Regarding the Knowledge Innovations and Practices Relevant to the Conservation and Sustainable Use of Biological Diversity*), The Conference of the Parties, at point 6:

> *6. Notes with concern the specific vulnerability of indigenous and local communities, inter alia of the Arctic, small island states and high altitudes, concerning the impacts of climate change and accelerated threats, such as pollution, drought, and desertification, to traditional knowledge innovations and practices.*

Thus, whatever the original intent behind the formulation of Article 8(j), in the 2006 Conference of the Parties, Eighth Meeting in Curitiba, Brazil, the catastrophic impact of climate change influenced the drafters to move to a more inclusive understanding of that article.

The argument of this work, first, the primacy of biological/ecological integrity as a right of aboriginal communities, and second, the genocidal impact of the present primacy of trade over ecological and health protection in national and international law, are clearly in evidence in the case of the Nunavut people in the Arctic. Their cultural integrity and their existence as a people is threatened as clearly as their individual physical existence, despite the presence of borders and self-government, unless the recommendations of the COP 8 as well as the *jus cogens* norms against the destruction of ethnic groups are observed.

THE ARCTIC PEOPLES FIGHT BACK: THE PETITION TO THE INTER-AMERICAN COMMISSION ON HUMAN RIGHTS

In a frozen land, where even small changes in the climate can be significant, the rapid changes being wrought by global warming are nothing short of catastrophic. Global warming is forcing the Inuit to shoulder the burden of the rest of the world's development with no corresponding benefit...

Inuit Qaujimajatuqangit [knowledge] tells the Inuit that the weather is not just warmer in the Arctic, but the entire familiar landscape is metamorphosing into an unknown land.[22]

Contrast these passages with the terse response of the Inter-American Commission on Human Rights (Organization of American States), which declined to rule on the complaint of the Arctic Peoples 'that global warming caused by the United States violates their right to sustain traditional ways,' as 'there was insufficient evidence of harm' (Revkin, 2006).

The petition had been filed a year earlier, in December 2005, by Sheila Watt-Cloutier, Chair of the Inuit Circumpolar Conference, on behalf of the 155,000 Inuit of Canada, Greenland, Russia and the US. When discussing the petition, it is useful to return once again to the evidence, as listed by the Inuit and their representatives in the petition. This evidence comes not only from those who are witnessing and living with the effects of what I have termed 'eco-crime' in regard to climate change, but also many exceptional legal scholars, such as James Anaya (2000; 2001; 2004), one of the leading experts on indigenous peoples' human rights.

The petition indicates the extensive number of international legal instruments that support the claims of the Inuit:

The impacts of climate change, caused by acts and omissions by the United States, violate the Inuit's fundamental human rights protected by the American Declaration of the Rights and Duties of Man and other international instruments. These include their right to the benefit of culture, to property, to the preservation of health, life, physical integrity, security, and the means of subsistence, and to residence and the inviolability of the home.[23]

The petition painstakingly takes us through some familiar territory, problems I have addressed on these pages, such as the harm to their traditional hunting and gathering culture, to their economy, to their social and cultural practices, and to Inuit traditional knowledge regarding climate conditions.[24] The petition also reviews the now well-known facts about global warming and the particular vulnerability of the Arctic, as accepted by the most creditable scientists and researchers today. Hence, to ignore the melting of polar ice sheets and glaciers, the rising of sea levels, a hazard Arctic peoples share with island and coastal states, the 'alteration of species and habitats', and the changed conditions that amount to a physical and intellectual attack on their life, individually and collectively, is to exhibit not only unacceptable ignorance, but also wilful blindness, that is, a criminal approach to the reality of the Inuit's conditions (Westra, 2004a).

In a recent speech[25] to the American Geographical Union, Al Gore acknowledges 'the end of the age of print' and with it, much of the desire for real information and the ability to think and weigh issues, supplanted instead by television's emphasis on 'entertainment.' Gore added: 'There is now willful blindness among both the public and the politicians'.

The petition also cited the conditions of Shishmaref, Alaska, and the ongoing erosion of that settlement. It also refers to the Lubicon case, and the importance of the UN Human Rights Committee decision in that case based on the right to enjoy culture as a violation of Article 27 of the ICCPR, despite the fact that not much has changed for the Lubicon since then.[26]

I have argued, albeit with far less support from legal precedent in either international or domestic law, that the right to life, health and normal function should be considered first, as the most basic human right (Westra, 2006). The petition states:

> *International health and environmental law also lend support to the American Declaration's right to health. The preamble of the Constitution of the World Health Organization recognized that, '[t]he enjoyment of the highest attainable standard of health is one of the fundamental rights of every human being'.*[27]

Given the main focus of this work, the references of the petition to health are particularly important; it indicates what the law should proscribe as a general obligation, and what is perhaps the most important aspect of the Arctic peoples' plight: their survival, both individual and collective. It is clear that Anaya (2000; 2001; 2004) and other scholars involved emphasized the threats to cultural survival because the right to 'cultural integrity' can be found in several international instruments, whereas the right to health, although clearly widespread, is seldom, if ever, clearly coupled with environmental degradation or pollution of any kind.

Nevertheless Sheila Watt-Cloutier was nominated with Al Gore for a Nobel Prize and, on 20 June 2007, she won the 2007 Mahbub ul Haq Award for Outstanding Contributions to Human Development at the UN, in New York. Niamh Collier-Smith, a spokeswoman for the United Nations Development Programme, told CBC News that 'Sheila Watt-Cloutier's dedication and her tireless work with the Inuit people, especially in the face of devastating climate change, is a real inspiration to us all.'

The petition and the right to health

> *The right to health as conceptualized under Article 12.1 of the ICESCR can be viewed as extending not only to timely and appropriate health care, but also to the underlying determinants of health.* (Musungu, 2005)

The previous discussion on Nunavut emphasized the difference between the healthier lifestyle of 'living on the land' and pursuing the traditional hunting and gathering practices of the Arctic, and the unhealthy food choices available when hunting is no longer safe or possible, leading to obesity, diabetes and other diseases. In addition to these problems, the petition cites the distress, confusion and alienation of the Arctic peoples, leading to mental health difficulties. Even in the cases cited by the petition, the main problem emerges: environmental health effects of the pollution tend to be characterized as 'environmental nuisances' or impediments to the rights to one's home life, rather than what they are, attacks against the human person, a far more accurate description of the consequences of environmental/industrial exposures.

In the case of *Fadereyeva v. Russia*,[28] Article 8 of the European Charter of Human Rights is invoked. The European Court of Human Rights (ECHR) held:

> *Article 8 had been involved in various cases, yet it was not violated every time environmental deterioration occurred: no right to nature preservation was as such included among the rights and freedoms guaranteed by the Convention. In order to raise an issue under Article 8, the interference should directly affect the applicant's home and family life. Further, the adverse effects of environmental pollution should attain a certain minimum level if they were to fall within the scope of Article 8.*

The text of Article 8 requires a breach of the 'effective enjoyment of the applicant's home and private life', as well as striking a 'fair balance between the interests of the community' and those of the affected party. The ECHR is almost the only court whose jurisprudence can be cited in such cases, as violation of Article 8.[29] In all ECHR cases, the emphasis is on the violation of home life of the complainant, not on the real consequences of environmental hazards. In addition, in 1991 in *Fredin v. Sweden*,[30] the court 'recognized that in today's society the protection of the environment is an increasingly important consideration', as the applicant was not allowed to 'extract gravel from his property on the ground of nature conservation'.[31]

Hence, the court accepts the very personal and the most general environmental policy issue in *Fredin*, but nowhere is there a true appreciation of the criminal aspects of environmental attacks on individuals and groups exposed to toxins or other pollutants. At best, at times, some 'mitigation' is recommended to diminish the harm, and perhaps some monetary compensation, while the industrial practices that generate the exposure are taken for granted as being 'in the interest of the community'.

But one could envision a poor neighbourhood, say, in Naples where many young men can only find work by being part of an illegal organization such as the Camorra. In that case, as in cases of other groups being involved in drug trafficking or prostitution elsewhere, the fact that the persistence of these activities is in the community's economic interest does not render them legal or acceptable, let alone such that a 'fair balance' must be struck between their interests and those of others in the community.

The problem remains the lacunae in the law, the distorted view of environmental assaults, and the wilful blindness of legislators, courts and governments in this regard. If we consider 'the conditions necessary for health' (Musungu, 2005), or, as I have argued, 'the preconditions of agency' (Westra, 2004a) (that is, the environmental/health conditions that are needed to make human beings what they should be), developing normally into normal thinking people, it is clear that these issues are a significant, even primary aspect of the meaning of the 'right to health':

> *The right to health can therefore be said to embrace two main parts, namely, elements related to health care and elements concerning the underlying preconditions of health, with the first being the core content of the right.* (Musungu, 2005)

I have argued elsewhere that not the first, but the second element should be considered 'the core content of the right', because the preconditions of health are required to ensure normal development, long before any need for corrective health care might be required. In general, the right to health is a fundamental human right, but it is often in conflict with the obligations 'imposed by international trade' (Ranjan, 2005).

It is unusual to see such a clear case of conflicting values as those espoused by the Nunavut Inuit and other Arctic peoples, and the values and interests of international trade, and in general, economic interests. In addition, the fact that neither domestic nor international law is capable or willing to link environmental harms to the ecological degradation that ensues and to the biological/physical harms suffered by all those exposed is also clearly in evidence in the case of the Arctic peoples.

A parallel and a goal: The Framework Convention on Tobacco Control (FCTC)

> *Although health has traditionally been a limited area of international legal cooperation, there is a growing awareness that contemporary globalization has led to the proliferation of cross-border determinants of health status and is undermining the capacity of states to protect public health through domestic action alone.* (Taylor, 2005)

After reviewing the numerous health issues that have had such a grave impact on Arctic peoples, and in particular on the Inuit of Nunavut, it is easy to see the parallels between their exposures and those of smokers, as well as the similarity between the great profits of 'big tobacco' and those of 'big oil' and chemicals. There is, however, a vast difference in favour of the rights of Arctic peoples. While one must acknowledge that, at least initially, there is an element of choice about smoking (discounting the deliberate addictive components that largely eliminate choice later and the well-funded marketing campaigns, both of which limit substantially such 'choice'), that is totally lacking from industrial and chemical exposures, let alone climate change. According to the WHO (cited in Taylor, 2005):

> *... cigarette smoking and other forms of tobacco use currently kill 4.9 million people per year, with the majority of deaths occurring in industrialized countries...*

It is expected that by 2020 tobacco will kill up to 10 million people per year with 70 per cent of deaths occurring in developing states, if the epidemic is left unchecked.

The number of affected peoples' morbidity and death from climate change is also great and increasing: as many as 150,000 deaths are occurring every year, and 5 million 'disease incidents each year, from malaria and diarrhea, mostly in the poorest nations' (Patz, 2005; see also Epstein, 2005). Climate change, as noted, is particularly grave for Arctic peoples who are absolutely dependent on their territories' normal seasons and temperatures for survival, and have the highest exposure of any individuals or collectives, in addition, to several of the worst chemicals in existence, as their traditional diet consists primarily of animals high on the food chain.

At any rate, the FCTC was adopted in 2003 by the 192 member states of the World Health Organization, and it entered into force on 27 February 2005. Taylor (2005) describes and analyses the lengthy negotiations that finally reconciled the demands of trade law with those of public health, as most industrialized states, including Australia, New Zealand, Canada, China, Cuba, Argentina, the US, Japan and even the European Union, took a strong position against advancing the demands of public health over those of international trade:

- *States are committed to the protection of public health. However both health and trade are of national interest and should not be subject to prioritization. Rather health and trade should be 'mutually supportive'.*
- *Measures taken to protect public health should not discriminate against international trade: states should treat domestic and foreign tobacco products on the same footing.* (Taylor, 2005)

Given the presence of such self-contradictory statements, one can appreciate the difficulties dogging the negotiations, especially since the only explicit references to international law excluded almost all references to human rights (the final document included some references to Article 12 of the ICESCR, the Convention on the Rights of the Child, and the Convention on the Elimination of Discrimination Against Women (CEDAW). But Taylor (2005) states that, essentially, all attempts to prioritize 'public health over international trade were based upon the sovereign right to protect public health, not the human right to health'. Of course, this is the crux of the problem. As Taylor notes, most of the those participating in the negotiations were public health experts, not human rights experts on international law instruments, as would be required if the interface between 'trade law and human rights law' were to be truly understood. 'In the year before the end of the negotiations, the draft still contained two provisions that would have confirmed the priority of the WTO law over the convention' (Werner, 2005).

Although the final version of the convention eliminated the disputed provisions, replaced by a statement that 'the contracting parties are determined to give priority to the right to protect public health', this statement remains far short of what would be just and appropriate.[32] The lack of emphasis on individuals' and peoples' right to health, except in the evolving and pressing field of protection from the HIV/Aids epidemic (Taylor, 2005), is the main problem. Unless that obstacle is cleared, and the unavoidable connection between environmental/industrial exposures and the defence of that right is emphasized and codified, substantive justice will elude international jurisprudence.

It seems that, once again, as in the fight against nuclear weapons and against big tobacco, the WHO ought to take the lead with another convention against the attacks to the human person described in this chapter. In this instance, though, the WHO will need to broaden the range of experts it employs. Given the fact that most people at this time view the environment as their main concern, it seems that the time for action is now.

CONCLUSIONS

Part Three bears the brunt of the argument of this work: what is the meaning of 'genocide' in law? How far can the concept reach? Environmental law, as such, has been repeatedly treated as though it does *not* rise to the level of international law, hence, *ipso facto*, it is not viewed as open to claims that its obligations should be viewed as *erga omnes*, rather than simply prescribed by treaty law.

This is the essential goal of yet another volume on a topic that has been extremely well analysed already by some of the greatest publicists of today (such as Anaya, 2000; 2001; 2004; Pentassuglia, 2002; Schabas, 2000; 2001; 2006a; 2006b). The aim of this work is to raise the bar by showing why the highest and most serious human rights breaches are the ones that apply to the aboriginal peoples and other ethnic and religious groups.

The reader will judge whether that aim has been achieved, both at the conceptual level in Chapter 7, and in the real case that exemplifies the application of all aspects of genocide to a specific indigenous nation. The people of Nunavut are a particularly apt example, as when we consider their situation, we are not distracted by the issue of self-determination or by the lack of decided borders. In addition, they are in a position that is especially timely, as they are gravely affected by global warming, far more so than most of the other groups we have discussed.

Armed with these conclusions, the fourth and final part of the book discusses the question of responsibility and accountability for the harms I have noted. The last chapter finishes with some proposals for better, saner forms of governance, based on laws that recognize and incorporate the scientific advances I have documented.

NOTES

1 Affidavit of Bernard Ominayak, *Dashowa Inc. v. Friends of the Lubicon*, (1998) 158 DLR (4th) 699 (Ont. Gen. Div.).

2 ibid.

3 *Bernard Ominayak, Chief of the Lubicon Cree Band v. Canada*, Communication No. 167 /1984, Report of the Human Rights Committee, UN GAOR, 45th Sess., Supp. No. 40, Vol. 2, at 10, UN Doc. A/45/40, Annex IX (A) (1990), view adopted on 26 March 1990 at the 38th Sess.

4 17 October 2005, 'Support Lubicon Presentation to the United Nations'; see also Goodard (1991).

5 Affidavit of Bernard Ominayak, *Dashowa Inc. v. Friends of the Lubicon,* (1998) 158 DLR (4th) 699 (Ont. Gen. Div.).

6 See www.texaco.com/sitelets/ecuador/docs/report_hewitt_en.pdf

7 WECF, a leading network of women's organizations in 31 European countries, issued a press release on 23 November 2006, on 'health and environmental issues – ordinary chemicals in low doses are undermining the health and intellectual capacities of children'.

8 I am indebted for the research related to epidemiological publications on this topic to Dr Colin L. Soskolne and Mr Brian Ladd at the University of Alberta, Edmonton, Canada. They have pointed to the dearth of epidemiological research on the links between oil and other natural resource development and the health of First Nations communities in Alberta. They also pointed to the challenging, but not prohibitive, methodological constraints to meaningful epidemiological research in the area, stressing the need for considerations, other than those informed by the very limited body of retrospective scientific research, to protect the health and well-being of traditionally marginalized small communities.

9   The 'memory' is based on the knowledge and skills passed on by elders, and it is known as Inuit *Qaujimajatuqangit,* pronounced cow-yee-ma-ya-tu-kant-eet.

10 Nunavut Act, 1993, c.28 (assented to 10 June 1993); Nunavut Land Claims Agreement Act, 1993, c.29 (Assented to 10 June 1993).

11 *Trail Smelter Arbitration,* 35 *American Journal of International Law,* 1941 684.

12 Nunavut Land Claims Agreement Act, 1993, c.29.

13 Rome Statute of the International Criminal Court, 17 July 1998, Art. 1, 37 ILM 1002, 1003.

14 Optional Protocol to the International Covenant on Civil and Political Rights, Art. 1, 1999 UNTS 302; Optional Protocol on the Elimination of All Forms of Discrimination Against Women, Art. 2, 39 ILM 281, 282; Convention Against Torture and other Inhuman, Cruel or Degrading Treatment or Punishment, Art. 13, 1465 UNTS 85, 116, 23 ILM 1027, 1030; International Convention on the Elimination of All Forms of Racial Discrimination, Art. 14(1), 660 UNTS 195, 230 5 ILM 350 361.

15 In fact, Chapter III (ILC, 2000), 'Serious breaches of essential obligations to the international community', reintroduces the difference in kind between certain sorts of breaches of international obligations and others (described in Article 19), by the 'back door', so to speak, as we see in the language of Articles 41 and 42:

> *Article 41 Applications of this Chapter*
> 1. *This chapter applies to the international responsibility arising from an internationally wrongful act that constitutes a serious breach by a state of obligation owed to the international community as a whole and essential for the protection of its fundamental interests.*
> 2. *A breach of such an obligation is serious if it involves a gross or systematc failure by the responsible State to fulfill the obligation risking substantial harm to the fundamental interests protected thereby.*
>
> *Article 42 [51, 53] Consequences of serious breaches of obligations to the international community as a whole*
> 1. *A serious breach within the meaning of Article 41 may involve, for the responsible State, damages reflecting the gravity of the breach*
> 2. *It entails, for all other States, the following obligations:*
>   (a) *Not to recognize as lawful the situation created by the breach;*
>   (b) *Not to render aid or assistance to the responsible State in maintaining the situation so created;*
>   (c) *To cooperate as far as possible to bring the breach to an end.*
> 3. *This article is without prejudice to the consequences referred to in Chapter II and to such further consequences that a breach to which this Chapter applies may entail under international law.*

The language of either article can be interpreted to say, more vaguely and imprecisely perhaps, and in the context of consequences rather than through the description of examples, what the former Article 19 said, more explicitly and clearly.

16 Article 19:

> 1. *An act of a State which constitutes a breach of an international obligation is an internationally wrongful act, regardless of the subject matter of the obligation breached.*
>
> 2. *An internationally wrongful act which results from the breach by a State of an international obligation so essential for the protection of fundamental interests of the international community that its breach is recognized as a crime by that community as a whole, constitutes an international crime.*
>
> 3. *Subject to paragraph 2, and on the basis of the rules of international law in force, an international crime may result, inter alia, from:*
>
>   (a) *a serious breach of an international obligation of essential importance for maintenance of international peace and security, such as that prohibiting aggression;*
>
>   (b) *a serious breach of international obligation of essential importance for safeguarding the right of self-determination of peoples, such as those prohibiting massive pollution of the atmosphere or of the seas;*
>
>   (c) *a serious breach on a widespread scale of an international obligation of essential importance for safeguarding the human being, such as those prohibiting slavery, genocide, apartheid;*
>
>   (d) *a serious breach of international obligation of essential importance for the safeguarding and preservation of the human environment, such as those prohibiting massive pollution of the atmosphere or of the seas.*
>
> 4. *Any internationally wrongful act which is not an international crime in accordance with paragraph 2, constitutes an international delict.*

17 1995 ICJ 90.

18 See also the Arctic Contaminants Action Program at www.arctic-council.org/news/main.htm.

19 Article 7, para. 6, UNFCCC; Article 13, para. 8, Kyoto Protocol; the Inuit of Nunavut as well as other Inuit also have a voice in the ICC.

20 UNEP/CBD/.COP 8/L.20; Decision VIII/30; Target 7.2.

21 ibid.

22 *Petition on Human Rights – Violations Resulting from Global Warming Caused by the United States,* Sheila Watt-Cloutier and others, 7 December 2005.

23 ibid.

24 ibid.

25 Op.Ed.News.com, 26 January 2007, Sarah Hoffman, 'Gore Speaks to 6,000 Earth Scientists in San Francisco'.

26 *Petition on Human Rights – Violations Resulting from Global Warming Caused by the United States,* Sheila Watt-Cloutier and others, 7 December 2005.

27 ibid.

28 [2005] ECHR 55723/00, decided 19 May 2005, p.1.

29 See *Lopex-Ostra v. Spain* [1994] ECHR 16798/90; *Hatton and Other v. UK* [2003] ECHR 360 22/97; *Guerra v. Italy* [1998] ECHR 14967/89.

30 *Fredin v. Sweden* [1991] ECHR 12033/86.

31 *Fadeyeva v. Russia.*

32 See final text of the Convention, www.who.int/tobacco/fctc/text/en/fctc_en.pdf

PART FOUR

Some Modest Proposals
for Global Governance

CHAPTER 9

Indigenous Human Rights and the Obligations of State and Non-State Actors

INTRODUCTION: TRANSNATIONAL CORPORATIONS AND THE LAW

TNCs are key players in terms of development activity, and the perception that they operate in a vacuum between ineffective national laws and non-existent or unenforceable international laws has heightened concerns about the correct reach and effectiveness of environmental regulations, especially where TNCs are operating in developing countries. (Fowler, 1995)[1]

If anything, this quote underestimates the lawlessness, and hence the criminality of transnational corporations (TNCs), particularly in regard to indigenous peoples. This reality has emerged throughout this book and it is helpful to review the various points made so far in order to reinforce this claim.

Essentially, the claim is not that *either* present instruments, whether domestic or international, *or* current or past jurisprudence support an obvious argument for the criminality of corporate activities, despite the presence of some encouraging recent additions, for instance, to the Canadian Criminal Code (Westra, 2004a). The claim instead proposed the conclusion that, failing *lex lata* at this time, *lex ferenda* of a stronger, different character is clearly indicated. Equally needed are fully prepared and informed judges, and vigorous and uncompromising intervention by UN agencies, such as the World Health Organization (WHO), United Nations Environment Programme (UNEP), United Nations Children's Fund (UNICEF) and others, and powerful NGOs such as the World Conservation Union (IUCN) and Amnesty International.

Some possible avenues to change the status quo are examined in Chapter 10. The present task is to pull together the strands woven in the previous pages in order to prepare a summary, of sorts, of all the elements that result, at the very least, in crimes against humanity.

In Chapters 5 and 6, and throughout the discussion of cases involving aboriginal peoples, the language of 'genocide' or 'ethnocide' was often used, although, it is acknowledged, following Schabas (2006a), the technical sense of the concept as used in current and recent jurisprudence may not be either inclusive enough or wide-reaching enough to permit that usage. However, that is the terminology favoured by many publicists, especially by specialists in aboriginal rights. For the most part, the latter accept that the 'intent' required by the technically correct use of the concept of genocide is lacking.

Nevertheless, the Supreme Court of Canada in a 1995 decision has clearly separated 'intent' from 'motive', thus allowing that 'knowledge' is sufficient for *mens rea*. In essence, in *R. v. Hibbert* the court affirmed that 'desire' for the consequences of an act to occur is not a necessary component of a crime, as long as 'knowledge' that the consequences *will* occur is present. Hence, in those cases, *mens rea* is present and motive may, perhaps, be reintroduced at the sentencing stage.[2]

I have argued that 'knowledge' is always present, as is the deliberate planning and preparation leading any TNC to activities that have an impact on the territories of aboriginal peoples. Martin Geer (1998) explains:

> *A basic outline of the TNC's 'order of business' can be delineated as (1) site identi-fication; (2) cost-benefit and scientific analyses; (3) obtaining government approval; (4) infrastructure construction, including roads for the initial exploration; (5) exploration and drilling, with accompanying introduction of substantial changes in local economies and social structures, including labor relations and cash economics; and (6) production-extracting, primary source processing, storage and transportation of crude oils.*

It is important to point out that this accurate (though somewhat dated) analysis, as well as the whole article by Martin Geer (1998), fails to include the full range of harms to health and normal function we have noted in the previous chapters, including the impact of climate change, all of which render indigenous peoples 'strangers in their own land' today (see especially Chapter 8). It should also be noted that the brief discussion of genocide in his article does not include the possibility of 'wilful blindness', an important category I proposed in Chapter 7 and elsewhere (Westra, 2004a).

Even the US, in its 'Restatement (Third) of the Foreign Relations Law of the United States' says:

> *A State violated international law, as a matter of state policy, when it practices, encourages or condones*

> - *genocide,*
> - *slavery or slave trade,*
> - *the murder or causing the disappearance of individuals,*
> - *torture or other cruel, inhumane or degrading treatment or punishment,*
> - *prolonged arbitrary detention,*
> - *systematic racial discrimination, or*
> - *a consistent pattern of gross violations of internationally recognized human rights.*[3]

The United Nations Draft Declaration on the Rights of Indigenous Peoples,[4] lists the activities against indigenous peoples already noted in this work, including the actions which have 'the aim or effect of depriving them of their integrity as distinct peoples or of their cultural or ethnic identities'; a particularly important statement, as the intent or motive is not required, just the 'effect' produced. Perhaps then, the 'intent to destroy', an element of genocide, may be understood in a similar way. Unfortunately, the draft convention remains a 'draft' to date, despite the evidence and despite the fact that with the UN Draft:

> ... *a compelling argument was presented to the world that the Ache and other indigenous groups in Paraguay were the victims of genocidal acts by the government seeking to promote TNC oil exploration on Ancestral Lands. The Ache are now considered an extinct cultural group.* (Geer, 1998)

The Draft Declaration on the Rights of Indigenous Peoples has 'aim or effect' language for acts of cultural genocide, instead of the classic 'intent to destroy', and perhaps this change might be part of what makes it so difficult for the wealthy nations of the North to adopt this document.

There is a further element that is almost always left unchallenged, namely, the legality (and morality) of the corporate activity itself, even before considering how and where it should or could be done. We can consider the concept of ecological footprint analysis (EFA). William Rees (2006) explains that EFA quantifies:

> ... *the total ecosystem area that the population effectively 'appropriates' to meet its final demand for economic goods and services, including the area it needs to provide its share of certain (normally free) land and water-based services of nature such as the carbon sinks function.*

This clarification provides the 'bridge' between EFA and the law: the language of 'appropriation', especially when it addresses 'nature's services' (Daily, 1997); that is, the services provided to humans by water and land (and I would add air, which could be affected by effluents that render it unhealthy, as in Azerbaijan, for example).

There are, at the outset, two separate issues that must be considered: first, the question of rightful ownership/possession; and second, the problem of the commons (Westra, 2004b). The first issue considers whether the 'appropriation' involved a legal contract of purchase, taking into consideration the conditions prevailing in such contracts, such as full disclosure of all information relative to the goods to be appropriated, and free consent on the part of the 'seller' whose property has been 'appropriated'. Unless such conditions are met, any purchase contract is null and void.

The problem of the appropriation from the global commons is even more complex and many questions arise about the legitimacy of such appropriation when harm may be perpetrated not only to humans, immediately, but also to the environment and hence to their habitat, the future of human health and normal function, and the territorial integrity of neighbouring countries, especially in North–South dealings (Westra, 2004a).[5]

On this second issue, the North–South interaction in respect of both resources and wastes is highly problematic and most often involves gross breaches of human rights (Westra, 2006).[6] When people are unconsenting targets of such forms of 'appropriation', then crimes are being committed and we need to review the instruments in existence intended to redress or, even better, to prevent these wrongs.

In Chapter 4, the difference between 'consultation' and 'consent' was discussed against the background of major sources of funding of TNCs' harmful large projects, that is, the World Bank Group and the IMF. Lacking either fair procedures in any meaningful sense of the term, or just outcomes, the resulting corporate activities appear to be conducted in the commission of another crime, that of 'illegal appropriation' of others' property, and hence, to put it bluntly, theft.

As the basis for the activity's legality itself appears to be shaky at best, the subsequent effects of the activity ought to be viewed far more severely than they presently are. Of course, this is simply a general statement, and each case would require a thorough assessment of the antecedents of each specific activity, although Geer's (1998) description of the 'order of business' listed above indicates the normal framework of steps that must be taken prior to the commencement of any activity. Neither a legal study of the ownership of the territory in question, nor a medical/epidemiological study of the effect to be anticipated, are included.

Still on the question of corporate activities, in Chapter 3 the 'wrong turn' promoted by the 18th century work of de Vattel (1758) was discussed. The idea of permitting 'states' to be 'subjects' of natural law principles, like human individuals, not only represented a complete misunderstanding of the strength and reach of natural law (Westra, 2004a), but it also set a 'precedent' of sorts, possibly paving the way for the eventual 'personhood' of corporations.[7]

Recent Canadian case law is not fully taking one side or the other on the question of whether the Canada Charter of Rights and Freedoms (S.15(1)) entitles corporations, as well as natural persons, to enjoy 'equality' and 'protection' in similar ways (Gertner, 1986). Some of the 'prohibited grounds of discrimination listed in s.15(1) obviously have no applications to corporations (for example, race, colour, religion)' (Gertner, 1986).

Prior to the existence of the charter, the Canadian Bill of Rights[8] was cited in similar cases. For instance, in *R. v. Colgate-Palmolive Ltd,*[9] the court observed:

> *It seems clear from the context of s. 1 of the* Canadian Bill of Rights, *with its reference to 'discrimination by reason of race, national origin, colour, religion or sex' and its reference to the 'right of the individual to life, liberty, security of the person and enjoyment of property', 'the right of the individual to equality before the law and the protection of the law'; to 'freedom of religion'; 'freedom of speech', 'of assembly and association' and the 'freedom of the press' that reference is made to natural person and not to corporations.*

With the advent of the Canadian Charter, the courts have moved towards more, rather than less, protectionism for corporations. In general, the courts have leaned towards interpreting the charter in 'the way most favourable to the subject' (Gertner, 1986) with some notable exceptions.[10]

We have also seen the clear support of corporate and institutional 'rights' in US law, at least in the ATCA jurisprudence discussed in Chapter 5. Later in the chapter, I pull together the arguments advanced in each of the previous chapters in order to build a case not only for corporate responsibility, but for corporate criminality as well, after reviewing the reasons why the protection of indigenous peoples represents an obligation of *erga omnes* character, and hence an obligation of states that is both domestic and international.

INTERNATIONAL OBLIGATIONS *ERGA OMNES* AS APPLIED TO INDIGENOUS PEOPLES' RIGHTS

> ... *according to Judge Weeramantry, the test of the performance of an international obligation (and specifically the obligation* erga omnes *to respect self-determination) would be compliance not only with the particular directions or prohibitions that it may contain, but also with its 'underlying norms or principles'.* (Ragazzi, 1997)[11]

Whether the non-derogable obligation is that of a corporation, institution or national state, they are all clearly implicated in the activities that harm the physical and cultural existence of indigenous peoples. The classic *locus* of *erga omnes* obligations, is found in the *dictum* of the *Barcelona Traction Light and Power* case, where the phrase 'basic human rights' appears.[12] Both principles and rules are coming into play here, so that 'the propositions that obligations *erga omnes* may derive in general not only from rules, but also from principles introduces an element of analogy with *jus cogens*' (Ragazzi, 1997).[13]

The Barcelona *dictum* lists several examples of obligations *erga omnes*. The first is 'outlawing of acts of aggression',[14] intended to eliminate interstate 'threat or use of force against the territorial integrity or political independence of any State', now existing as a rule of *jus cogens*, although it is clear that the form of aggression that is meant was the example of one state invading another with its armed forces. This understanding does not preclude all other kinds of uses of force, as self-defence is permitted and viewed as justified, although I do not believe that pre-emptive strikes are equally justified (Ragazzi, 1997).[15]

The second example is the 'outlawing of genocide', and we have discussed the question of genocide in relation to indigenous rights several times in the earlier chapters (especially Chapter 7). The third example, 'the protection from slavery' is relevant to several of the cases tried under ATCA (see Chapter 5). But perhaps the strongest example is the fourth one: 'protection from racial discrimination', a particularly obvious *erga omnes* obligation, together with 'genocide' and non-warlike 'acts of aggression' in regard to aboriginal peoples.

The *erga omnes* obligation to protect against racial discrimination

All modern democracies, as well as the conventions, treaties and declarations of international law, explicitly protect human rights 'for all without distinction as to race, sex, language or religion'.[16] The crux of the problem for aboriginal peoples is that absolute equality with all others is not sufficient, as 'equality' in their case needs to be qualified. The relation between aboriginal peoples and their lands is a *sui generis* one, quite different from that of citizens who may simply purchase the land where their home is built, but without therefore having that as their 'cultural land' (Geer, 1998) because their possession does not support their culture, religion or a separate identity.

Ragazzi (1997) argues that the court had distinguished between 'equality in law' and 'equality in fact', as 'equality may require different treatment to achieve an equilibrium between different situations'. Hence an objective justification is required in order to admit differentiated treatment between racial groups, and such justification must demonstrate the necessity of the differences. It is important also to keep in mind that, as Richard Goldstein, chief prosecutor at the International Criminal Tribunal for Yugoslavia indicated, 'discrimination of any kind, anywhere, contains the seed of genocide' (Ragazzi, 1997).

· It is therefore particularly important that when discrimination occurs it should be viewed as a grave breach of international law, of an *erga omnes* obligation, not just as a trade disagreement and at best a compensable one. At any rate, the prohibition of racial discrimination is a non-derogable obligation, as Judge Tanaka clearly states: 'States which do not recognize this principle [i.e. the protection of human rights] or even deny its existence are nevertheless subject to its rule'.[17]

Can the four proposed candidates of obligations *erga omnes* be extended?

> *... all four examples are those of obligations instrumental to the main political objections of the present time, namely the preservation of peace and the promotion of fundamental human rights, which in turn reflect basic goods (or moral values), first and foremost life and human dignity.* (Ragazzi, 1997)[18]

The fundamental human rights to life and respect for human dignity are basic to the understanding of *erga omnes* obligations, so that not all human rights have the particular character that might make them 'fundamental'. But the right to have one's normal functions protected, to healthy development and to the respect for one's life, all appear to be basic and fundamental in the sense that no other right is as important as these (Westra, 2004a). Our natural person, our biological integrity is inviolable, even more obviously than the integrity of another nation's territory.

Prohibition against all forms of genocide, attacks against the human person, enslavement, racially motivated maltreatment, are *all* based upon that principle. Hence this is the main principle to keep in mind when we follow Ragazzi's (1997) observation that both 'development law', and 'environmental law' are 'good candidates' for further developments in the concept of obligations *erga omnes*. As far as 'development law' is concerned, most conventions and court decisions regarding self-determination are increasingly considered serious enough to transcend reciprocal obligation based on agreement only.

The case law I have considered and discussed indicates that new approaches are urgently needed, given the grave problems affecting indigenous peoples, and I address this question in the next chapter. But it is clear that for both development and environment, the traditional approaches, at least as they are practised today, are insufficient and justice is not served.

> *Brownlie remarked that pollution of the atmosphere and the high seas is such a dispersed and gradual process that a traditional approach based on liability can hardly lead to positive results because of the difficulties, for example, of identifying the tortfeasor and establishing the evidences of causation.* (Ragazzi, 1997)

Ragazzi appeals to intergenerational rights, citing Edith Brown-Weiss (1984) (Westra, 2006). Brownlie's work, however, is more oriented to 'customary rules' than it is to non-derogable ones. Nevertheless the same problem is equally present for the multiple actors and multiple cases apparent in the case law regarding indigenous peoples and their so-called 'development'.

Valencia-Ospina (1944), over 40 years before Brownlie's remarks, pointed out 'that the current problems of international environmental law clearly show the need for a departure from traditional rules of standing'. In addition, as we have seen, environmental and indigenous developmental law are too clearly interwoven to separate fully, although there are some cases that deal with torture, forcible removal and the like, where their environment or territory is perhaps secondary in some sense (see Chapter 5).

Nevertheless, even in 1998, the full complement of harms due to pollution, climate change and the forced acceptance of 'development', fostered by mining and other extractive industries, was present, though perhaps less obviously so than it is now. Today we need to move forcefully in the direction of establishing full responsibility for these harms through *erga omnes* obligations, so that the imperative to avoid and to cease does not have to be fought laboriously and endlessly by corporations, while the victims' plight is not eased. I proposed that neither 'liability' nor 'tort' regimes, but criminal ones would and should be most appropriate to deal with eco-crime (Westra, 2004a).

If it is not always possible to isolate one corporate criminal for each case, or one complicit government, but if the criminal effects follow upon the actions and inactions of many, then the first step must be to revise the way these crimes are understood, codified and tried. Adding non-derogable obligations to desist from hazardous activities to the present short arsenal of obligations *erga omnes* before these activities kill or inflict disease and abnormal development, appears to be the only solution, and some of the literature already points in that direction (Dupuy, 1991a; Ragazzi, 1997). Christopher Cline applies this approach directly to indigenous peoples. He argues that 'global unity ... requires global law', and that, despite the presence of a large body of international human rights law, 'many nations have refused to either recognize or obey such law' (Cline, 1991). Further he argues that the disregard for these laws is particularly obvious when states deal with indigenous tribes and communities. Commercial enterprises often violate these groups' rights to their 'religion and culture' through unwanted intrusion and activities in their territories.

These rights ought to be recognized under international law *jus cogens*, 'and the actions that affect their rights to maintain their religion and culture [could be characterized as] a denial of self-determination, an act of apartheid, and ultimately cultural genocide' (Cline, 1991; see also *Lyng v. NW Indian Cemetery Protective Association*, 485 US 439 (1988), and discussion in Rievman, 1989).

Further considerations on international obligations of states

> *... si l'on se tourne a présent non plus vers les propositions normative mais vers la pratique, on constate tout au contraire que non seulement l'avenment de la responsabilité objective de l'État pour dommage catastrophique est loin d'être advenu mais encore que l'État se tient le plus souvent a l'écart de toute intervention directe dans l'allocation des réparations.* (Dupuy, 1991b)

Even today, this remains the gravest problem: despite the presence of *erga omnes* obligations in law, and despite the ease with which these may also be understood to fit the crimes against indigenous peoples, for the most part states work to distance themselves from any responsibility for the consequences of activities presently not forbidden by international law (Handl, 1985; Magraw, 1986).

Before turning away from state responsibility to corporate/institutional responsibility, I should stress one major point: in this work 'responsibility' is used in two senses, each of which will be clarified by the context in which it is used:

1 The public international law term to indicate the legal state of affairs, following a breach of state obligation;
2 As a moral term to indicate the general duty or obligations owed to those who are or might have been harmed by an activity on the part of those who initiated that activity or sanctioned it.

In addition, however, the emphasis of the previous pages on the importance of *erga omnes* obligations, which are entirely principled, shows that the moral aspect of 'responsibility' may not be fully separated from its sense in international law. In fact, *erga omnes* obligations *must* be retained, especially for the injurious consequences arising from activities not prohibited by international law:

> *In a shrinking world, where any activity that modifies fragile ecological patterns tends to have repercussions beyond national borderlines, it becomes even more necessary to establish standards suited to save those natural cycles and thereby to ensure the foundations of human survival.* (Tomuschat, 1991)

State responsibility arises both when an unlawful act has been committed and when there are harmful consequences from legal activities. In both cases *jus cogens* norms can be invoked to deal with environmental damage (Ago, 1990; Tanzi, 1987). Two points must be clarified before proceeding. First, on the question of fault v. consequences, the hostages case in *United States v. Iran* (1980 ICJ 3, at 69, 70) shows that the duty of the Iranian government was to take 'every appropriate step' to bring 'the flagrant infringements' of international law to a speedy resolution. In fact, 'No such step was taken', although states have the duty to regulate private actors in their territory. In this case it appears that the fault element makes an even stronger case that 'Iran had violated ... its obligation toward the United States' (Kindred et al, 2000). Another point of clarification is that of moral implications of *jus cogens* norms beyond their legal status.

In *Wiwa v. Royal Shell Petroleum* (ATCA, March 2002), for instance, it is clear that because no state was involved, one could not bring a case against Shell for the breach of a treaty obligation. Shell had to be charged with the breach of *erga omnes* obligations, supported by *jus cogens* norms, because of the moral and legal principles they violated in flagrant conflict with international law, especially 'crimes against humanity'. The second problem is the possibility that although the harm is visible and present, the act that generated the harmful consequences was itself legal. The classic example is once again the *Trail Smelter Arbitration*. As various forms of technology become more widespread and complex, the environmental harm that ensues, whether it is immediate or (as is most often the case) delayed, it becomes precisely what this work suggests: a legal, institutionalized form of violence, producing harms that are often irreversible.

The problem of trans-boundary harm was first considered in a study by a sub-committee of the International Law Commission in 1963 to deal with the 'conspicuous gap' left in international law by the exclusion of 'liability that derives from … legal grounds' (Tomuschat, 1991). Several rapporteurs and many iterations of that particular aspect of state responsibility uncovered some major points. First, states are in a position to control specific activities. Hence, they should bear responsibility for the consequences arising from such activities. This appears unobjectionable. The second point, however, is more debatable, as it raises the question of trans-boundary liability for the 'global commons', as introduced by Rapporteur Barboza (1989 ILC Rep. 242, para. 348). The third point follows upon the other two: often negative effects are produced that reach well beyond the intended effects, thus producing a 'normative gap' that ought to be addressed by international law (Tomuschat, 1991). Fourth, modern scientific developments have indicated the immense scope of environmental problems such as climate change, global warming or biogenetic engineering, all of which are 'dangerous activities' and 'for whose consequences states must bear full responsibility' (Tomuschat, 1991). Last, whether the dangerous activities are undertaken by public or private sources, states must ensure that they assume full responsibility for all activities that place human rights in jeopardy. In addition, no private person or institution can ensure prevention, a responsibilty that lies with the state:

> *Experience has taught that more often than not damage to the environment cannot be made good after it has occurred. When a species of animals has disappeared it cannot be revived again. Soil that has been contaminated may have to rest for decades before it can be recultivated. Radioactive particles that have escaped a nuclear installation pose a threat to their environment as long as their radiation continues. The ozone layer, once destroyed may never build up again. Thus the primary goal must be to prevent harm from occurring. Second, pollution caused by a major disaster, but also pollution caused by accumulation, may easily take on such huge dimensions that both in financial and in technological terms, reparation is simply impossible.* (Tomuschat, 1991)

Against this background, we can consider now some specifics. The elements of the International Law Commission (ILC) Convention's work on legal trans-boundary environmental harm were 'prevention, co-operation, and strict liability for harm', but they were considered 'too controversial' (Birnie and Boyle, 2002). The 2001 amended draft of this convention[19] divided the topic into two parts, 'prevention and liability', and the main concern remained with the former (Birnie and Boyle, 2002). Although the latest draft prescribes 'all appropriate measures that must be taken to prevent or minimize the risk', it does nothing to prohibit the activities that give rise to trans-boundary harm (Birnie and Boyle, 2002).

Risk itself 'is defined to encompass both "a low probability of causing disastrous harm" and "a high probability of causing significant harm"' (Birnie and Boyle, 2002). However, neither 'disastrous' or 'significant' are defined, and neither international lawyers, nor judges nor even scientists can hope to express with any certainty what might constitute the desired 'clear and convincing' scientific proof of possible harm.

But there remains a radical conflict between the sonorous proclamations and the normatively powerful preambles of international instruments noted in the previous chapters, and the 'persistent silence' of state practices, intent on 'seizing all occasions and all pretexts to disappear behind private persons instead' (Dupuy, 1991a, author's translation). In order to foster any hope that state practice might change, it will be vital to ensure that *erga omnes* obligations are clearly entrenched in international law regarding environmental and developmental issues.

THE OBLIGATIONS OF NON-STATE ACTORS: SOME GENERAL REMARKS

> Recognizing *that even though States have the primary responsibility to promote, secure the fulfillment of respect, ensure respect and protect human rights, transnational corporations and other business enterprises, as organs of society, are also responsible for promoting and securing human rights set forth in the Universal Declaration of Human Rights.*[20]

The third paragraph of the 'Preamble' here cited makes several important points. First, it is part of a document stating 'norms', not suggestions, or trying to achieve an agreement. Second, it bases its statement of 'norms' (normally thought of as non-derogable and not as optional choices, at least in moral discourse), on the fact that corporations and other business enterprises are 'organs of society', that is, they are not arising spontaneously, like mushrooms after the rain. They must fulfil certain bureaucratic requirements in order to register their name and the purpose of their association, and they must declare whether they intend to request incorporated status to be able to assume their 'right' to operate. Hence, it would seem obvious that, at least in principle, the permission granted by society ought not to include the 'rights' to harm the society that gave it birth. Moreover, if the proposed activities also involve criminal or quasi-criminal actions, there should be clear mechanisms available to withdraw their licence to operate, as a drunk driver may have his licence revoked if he does serious harm.

International legal regimes ensure that criminals may not operate with impunity when moving from one country to another, although such movement may well shield them, at least for a time. But TNCs, unlike individual criminals, do not hide. They advertise, they market, they openly promote themselves and their products, although they are not so open about the harmful implications of their products and operations. Hence the pivotal importance of clearly stating and declaring their obligations, and the *erga omnes* character of the protection of human rights that are unavoidably their responsibility.

First considerations: Negligence and conspiracy

> *Negligence ... essentially consists in the mental attitude of undue indifference with respect to one's conduct and its consequences... Negligence, as so defined is rightly*

> *treated as a form of* mens rea, *standing side-by-side with wrongful intention as a formal ground of responsibility.* (Salmond, 1924; see also Edgerton, 1927).

If negligence is indeed a form of *mens rea*, then the connection between the result of corporate activities, the consequences that are not desired as a deliberate goal of those actions, but result from those actions nevertheless, are the responsibility of the corporation. The corporations involved are 'nevertheless indifferent or careless' whether or not the consequences ensue, as they do not 'refrain from the act notwithstanding the risk' (Edgerton, 1927). This understanding of negligence reinforces the proposed requirement to consider full criminality for these corporate activities, based on the presence of this form of *mens rea*.

In addition, one may consider that, just as the classic locus for trans-border harm is *Trail Smelter* for international law, the classic locus for domestic responsibility for harm in common law is *Rylands v. Fletcher*.[21] Without a detailed analysis of that case, the main point is that the impact of TNCs on indigenous peoples is almost always based on activities that reflect what that British court termed 'non-natural use' (Newark, 1961), that is, an activity that involves a treatment of land that may result in harms of any kinds, when it is not a 'natural use', ensures that the actor(s) is responsible for the harm:

> *If the owner of the land used it for any purpose which from its character may be called non-natural use, such as for example the introduction onto the land of something which in the natural condition of the land is not upon it, he does so at his peril.* (Newark, 1961)

It is worthy of note that it is the owner's land and action that are at stake in this classic case, not, as in present cases, the impact of TNCs' activities on the ancestral lands of indigenous peoples. It is that question of 'ownership' that is also problematic, while the responsibility remains.

Nevertheless the simplicity of the case where there is *one* person directing and ordering the activity is not available in corporate land use cases, as many different people, institutions and organizations may be involved. An old case from the British Columbia Court of Appeal makes the case for complicity very well. In *Rex v. Dunbar*,[22] Mr Dunbar was the one chosen to drive the 'getaway' car, while three confederates entered a branch of the Canadian Bank of Commerce and executed a planned robbery, during which one of the tellers was shot. Dunbar claimed he had been coerced into driving the car, and while he had been told simply to circle the block twice before returning, he was not sure about the robbery and certainly knew nothing about the killing, as he had not been there when it happened. A report on the original 'directions' given by the court regarding the understanding of the case state:

> *There is an aspect of law which is outstanding in this case, and it is this, that if two or more join to commit a felony, to rob a bank which involves violence, and the violence be shown as such that any reasonable person must have thought it likely that injury would befall the person towards whom the violence was to be exercised, injury of such a character as might cause death, then all person participating in or inciting the crime are guilty of murder if death ensues.*[23]

This passage brings up the question of 'common intention', as well as that of 'concerted action'.[24] The question may well remain open on whether a charge of manslaughter or one of murder may be more appropriate, but in general, collective plans, even participation in a common plan or conspiracy, are sufficient to establish criminal guilt.

This approach to common criminality can also be found in humanitarian law. Speaking of the Charter of the International Military Tribunal at Nuremberg (1947), Richard Wasserstrom (1974) writes, 'Conspiracy to do certain things is itself a crime. But even more than this, responsibility is derived from membership in a group.' The language of culpable conspiracy, such as 'encouraging', 'enticing', but most of all, 'enabling', fits well with being part of a group or of a collectivity like a multinational corporation. In 2003, the Canadian Criminal Code had an important addition made to it, which is worth considering. On 7 November 2003, the final draft of An Act to Amend the Criminal Code S.C. 2003, C.21 (formerly Bill C-45) was completed and received Royal Assent (and thus became law). This bill addressed some of the lacunae and limitations of the Canadian Criminal Code, amending the language of several sections with that aim in mind (see also Chapter 5). Corporations were originally formed and given a juridical personality separate from that of the aggregate of their officers, shareholders, employees and agents for one reason only: to ensure their economic protection, thus to encourage investment in their activities. It was never the intention of the legislators and the courts to declare that corporations would be granted a new form of immunity from criminal prosecution, similar to the immunity enjoyed by the representatives of states and those involved in activities on behalf of various nations. Thus criminal prosecution should equally be available when the accused is an organization, that is, a group joined in a common purpose as well as a corporation. The example given in Bill C-45 is that of a municipality. The substitution of 'organization' for 'corporation' in several sections of the Criminal Code is one of the objectives of Bill C-45.

Another main objective of Bill C-45 is to address the question of *mens rea*, which posed a serious difficulty for any court attempting to impose criminal liability on an organization, as was discussed in Chapters 4 and 5. The inability to ascribe the requisite form of criminal intent on the part of corporations and associations, ensured that a wide array of regulatory breaches of workplace safety and public health or environmental offences would be viewed as 'quasi-crimes', rather than 'true crimes'.

This work has argued for other forms of *mens rea*, and it is gratifying to realize that, although there is no case law at this time based on Bill C-45, many of the changes proposed earlier as possible *lex ferenda* have now acquired the status of *lex lata* instead.

The main changes effected to the Criminal Code are as follows:

> *S 1. (1) extends the definition of 'every one,' 'person,' and 'owner' to include 'an organization.' In turn, 'organization' means'*
> *(2) (a) a public body, body corporate, society, company, firm, partnership, trade union or municipality, or*
> *(b) an association of persons that*
> *(i) is created for a common purpose,*
> *(ii) has an operational structure, and*
> *(iii) holds itself out to the public as an association of persons.*

Here, and in the amendments to section 22.1, Bill C-45 ensures that a wide array of actors within an organization may be viewed as responsible for an offence, 'whether by act or omission' (section 22.1 (ii)); it also ensures that if the prosecution is required 'to prove fault other than negligence' (section 22.2), then senior officers or representatives may manifest the requisite 'mental state' also by '(c) knowing that a representative of the organization is or is about to be a party to the offence, or does not take all reasonable measures to stop them from being a party to the offence'. The bill also adds section 217.1 to define 'the legal duty to take reasonable steps to prevent bodily harm' on the part of anyone who is in the position to direct and order how work is to be done (see also discussion in Chapter 5). Thus far neither international humanitarian law, nor Canadian criminal law has been applied to corporate crime against indigenous peoples.

Most often, obscuring language is used to describe the factual component of cases involving indigenous groups, not only in the courts, but also in the literature, by those attempting to address these issues. For instance, Mark Stallworthy's (2006) recent work is instructive in this regard:

> ...*environmental protection measures can often conflict with other important priorities. Unsurprisingly, problems are encountered when we seek to value the costs of environmental harm against other economic and social interest.*

The question of course is, whose harm and whose economic and social interests? Stallworthy (2006) acknowledges that 'There are political dimensions to public risk' and that the present 'burden of proof' regulations 'tend to favour risk creators' (see also Savant and Aranda, 1994).

A recent example of treatment of 'risk creators' at the hand of the law, is the March 2007 dumping of hazardous waste in Abidijan, Ivory Coast.[25] The ship *Probo/Koala*, registered in Panama, was chartered by Trafigura Trading Company. Trafigura's aim was to produce petrol on the high sea, resulting in hazardous waste as a by-product. The petrol was to be shipped to Nigeria and sold there. But the ship docked at Amsterdam, and there was an attempt to unload the hazardous waste on shore (at least in part), contrary to EU laws. Equally illegal was the fact that the waste was eventually brought back on board, without the required special licence, when it transpired that dumping fees would have been too high. Hence the 'poison drama' continued to unfold when Dutch harbour officials were charged, as well as those who approved the eventual dumping in Abidijan. So far, there have been 15 casualties resulting from the dumping, and the numbers of injuries are uncertain. At least 4000 to 5000 victims are now preparing a multi-million collective claim for compensation for their damages. The Dutch Ministry of the Environment is currently investigating the case and an international order for the arrest of the captain of the vessel has been issued. However, Trafigura Trading Company has settled with the Ivory Coast authorities for about €150 million, and the employees that had been arrested, have been released as part of that deal.

This case does not involve harm to a specific indigenous population, but the difficulties of preventing such a disaster, as well as the obstacles to the achievement of a just resolution of the case, are extremely instructive. Mr Ruessink of the Dutch Ministry of the Environment terms this event, 'the tip of the iceberg', and states that dumping laws must be changed. The report of the Hulsof Commission, charged with investigating these events, concurs. The law regarding the discharge of toxic material is extremely complicated, with over 15 separate laws, regulations and licensing procedures, and most are inconsistent.

In addition, the definition of waste is equally unclear, and the various departments and ministries involved are often at odds with one another on those issues. Toxic waste is hard to control, especially because so many borders have been eliminated, and because organized crime is now involved in that trade. Hence it is necessary to establish clear definitions and easy-to-follow regulatory regimes to ensure the protection of human rights everywhere.

The main problem, as noted already, is that the consequences of impacts on indigenous peoples, which are both spatially and temporally removed, as well as arising from multiple and diffuse sources (Stallworthy, 2006), are still viewed as though the sustainability objectives sought are still part of yet another economic activity. But to recognize that the impacts are breaches of fundamental human rights, rather than economic issues, is to concede the justice of the arguments reviewed in this work. It is also to accept that for indigenous peoples, any impact on their territory is *not* a more or less favourable real estate or other business deal, and it is never simply a question of economics. In each and every case, it is a question of survival, of respect for their culture and identity, of the protection of their history, but also of their health, their normal function and their future.

It is the original classification (or misclassification) that directs the impeccably argued follow-up, in the cases cited: if a duck is defined as a mammal, none of the observations that follow will apply. Hence the efforts in this work to recognize the true import of the harms perpetrated on indigenous peoples, so that only after those harms are fully understood there might be a hope of enacting just regulatory regimes to correct the present situation. Stallworthy (2006) also recognizes this need: 'In the end, though incremental adjustments are possible, we look to regulations for real shifts in direction.'

INDIGENOUS PEOPLES IN NATURE AND CORPORATE RESPONSIBILITY

Humankind is engulfed by the planetary environment, even while people tend to behave as if they were outside of nature. In antiquity, all was sacred, except humankind. Mountains, springs, water, the winds and the sea were deified; the people did not enjoy any particular rights. With the advent of Judaeo-Christian civilization and humanism, this relationship has been reversed and Man alone is sacred. (Dupuy, 1991b)

The gravity of the impact of corporate activities on indigenous communities can only be understood when we acknowledge the reality of the human condition regarding the natural world, and we then combine that understanding with the specific circumstances of those communities. In principle at least, the rest of us can move away when environmental degradation threatens us. That, however, is not entirely true, or not equally true for rich and poor. Those of us who can influence to some degree the political and environmental decisions of the powerful home countries where TNCs originate, are also, marginally, better off.

Indigenous peoples are entirely vulnerable instead: they cannot move, they cannot make decisions about the activities that affect them, they cannot even say 'no' (as noted in Chapter 4) to the consultation process, and cannot say 'no' to the outcome of the process. So, if it seems that appealing to criminal laws, and to *jus cogens* norms is too radical an approach, their extreme vulnerability should explain the extreme tone of some of the conclusions reached here. If, *per absurdum*, we could substitute large communities of women for the same numbers of indigenous peoples, male and female, the present circumstances and treatment would not be tolerated, either in domestic or in international law.

Much has been written about self-determination and cultural integrity in the literature about aboriginal peoples. In the first chapter, a more basic right was proposed, the right to biological/ecological integrity, and the full implications of the double aspects of that right should be our main focus now, as all other rights are practically meaningless without it. The double aspect referred to is that both biological or individual integrity is at stake (though the attacks on health and normal function as well as life itself we have noted), and ecological integrity or the integrity of their lands, that is, their habitat is equally under attack.

In the last chapter, the plight of the Nunavut people was discussed. Like the Nunavut people, other indigenous groups of North America – the Mohawk, Six Nations and others – may have self-determination, but even with it, they still have no protection against the force of corporate 'collateralism' (Leader, 2004). 'Collateralism' describes the lack of focus of corporations on human rights, against the background of laws that protect corporate freedom rather than victims. Leader (2004) discusses the example of the 'Baku-Ceyhan pipeline' between the Caspian and the Mediterranean:

> *The company has thereby given ultimate priority to a right to a safe environment, but it has given priority in adjustment to the property rights of its investors. It has sought this adjustment not because it simply has a preference for building and operating the pipeline at a profit, but because it feels this is its primary mandate. Health, safety, and environmental protection thereby take their place as collateral concerns.*

Collateralism is the public policy counterpart to the lack of legal responsibility. Like wilful blindness or negligence, it is a state of mind. Given the ultimate results of that attitude, I would consider it yet another component of *mens rea*. The corporation does not deny the importance of human rights considerations, such as health or environment, but does not give these rights priority. As Leader (2004) points out, the roots of collateralism are to be found in a 'functional outlook', which essentially fixes the boundaries and the scope of corporate responsibility. 'For example the WTO is in this functionalist view, primarily responsible to the producers of goods and services, who will benefit from the exercise of its particular mandate' (Leader, 2004). This 'mandate', the main 'necessity' within corporate operations and the institutions and legal regimes that support them, is related to 'the central objective of a trading treaty: the integration of markets' (Leader, 2004). Whether or not it is a single corporate entity pursuing 'the integration of markets', functionalism marginalizes all other human concerns, which are viewed as 'collateral' to its main enterprise and goals.

Hence, the 'attacks' that ensue, are not 'meant' in the sense that the elimination of an indigenous group is not the prime target of corporate operations. In some sense, perhaps, the functionalist approach is even worse, as it renders indigenous peoples invisible, nonentities, mere obstructions to be removed or manipulated with the least possible fuss, in the service of corporate aims. In humanitarian law, when an offensive is undertaken that may (and most often does) result in 'collateral damage', at least in principle, any justification rests on the just war theory. In principle, there might be some wars that could be justified in this manner, and the Second World War is often cited as a possibility.

But it is hard to see under what conditions corporate activities could claim a justification that might be strong enough for the 'collateral effects of their operations'. Neither the 'integration of trade' nor the resulting profits, nor even the production of oil or gold, no matter how high the demand for these products, could possibly be cited as justifying the grievous harms perpetrated.

The 'third model' for the protection of biological and ecological integrity and eco-footprint appropriations

The lack of normative justification is the root cause of most of the problems encountered by indigenous peoples as the industrialized world moves onto their territories, or even just close to their lands. In Chapter 1 the role of buffer zones was discussed (Noss and Cooperrider, 1994). Their importance cannot be overstated, although for some environmental harms, even buffer zones are not enough for protection. Also in the first chapter, the plight of the Aamjiwaang First Nation located in Ontario's 'Chemical Valley' near Sarnia was described. The pattern of abnormal births of that people did not require a disaster or catastrophic event as explanation; the regular business operations surrounding their lands were more than sufficient to result in the effects described (Helstaedt, 2007).

The question is why are industrial operations with such dangerous effects legally placed that close to human habitations occupied by First Nations? Consider instead what happened in the UK. In January 2007 there was an outbreak of avian flu at a turkey farm in England, later confirmed to be caused by the H5N1 virus that can be transmitted to humans, potentially fatally. One of the several measures adopted almost immediately, and well publicized by both Euronews and BBC television channels, was the decision to establish a ten-kilometre buffer zone around the affected farm, to minimize the likelihood of spreading the virus.

One wonders how many proven diseases, from cancers, to asthma, to reproductive anomalies, even to DNA alterations, are necessary before provincial and federal governments of Canada might decide to protect its aboriginal people with a buffer zone surrounding their territory. Even better, why are these operations permitted in their present hazardous form? And why are both the biological integrity of citizens and the ecological integrity of their land and water not considered worthy of respect? The same is true for other mining/extraction operations.

Of course, such rhetorical questions are not going to solve the problem, but they might help us situate the reality of circumstances of indigenous peoples in context, so that perhaps better regulatory regimes can be designed:

> *Notably, individuals living in Texaco's former concession area in Ecuador were (and are) not simply exposed to one toxin, but to a cocktail of various toxins. Thus the effects of synergistic interactions of various toxins on human health must also be considered. The simplest interaction is an additive effect... However a more complex synergistic effect may also occur whereby the effects of two toxins acting together is substantially greater and more harmful than the sum of their effects when being alone.* (Clapp et al, 2006)

Synergistic effects of multiple exposures are seldom, if ever, studied or taken in consideration in feasibility studies, and neither are exposures of children and other subpopulations with increased vulnerabilities.

Another example of industrial harms can be found in uranium mining (Eichstaedt, 1994). The history of uranium mining in the four-corner area (Utah, Colorado, Arizona and New Mexico, and the Navajo Reservation between the Grand Canyon and the Petrified Forest National Park) appears to have been written in blood.

The evidence of the narrative is unequivocal. It is consistently one group and one group alone that is targeted. I have termed this approach 'institutionalized ecological violence'. This form of violence does more than destroy the unfortunate miners working in hazardous unventilated 'dog holes', accumulating in one week multiple doses of the yearly maximum 'safe' radiation exposure in their bodies, and eventually succumbing to untreatable cancer and other diseases. Some mill workers also had up to 60 micrograms of uranium in their urine samples. The yellowcake dust they inhaled and swallowed was making them radioactive from the inside out (Eichstaedt, 1994).

This intolerable violence also destroys families who attempt to survive on the pitiful sums allotted to them, or with no compensation at all for surviving wives and children. Finally, this same violence, discriminating against Native Americans, also attacks their survival as a people, hence the appeal to genocide in this case. Although we all depend on a healthy, non-toxic environment, native people have a particular right and claim to the lands they inhabit and from which they assert their identity as a nation. Hence, when the Navajo miners, their families and supporters took on the 'fight for justice', requesting child support and simple compensation to survive, they were asking far less than what should have been theirs by right:

> *at the age of forty, Peter Yazzie knew the end was near and was driven to a hospital in Albuquerque. He died eight days later, on June 6, 1970. He left a home that was a simple adobe Hogan heated with wood, a wife Dolores, age thirty-six, and ten children ranging in age from two to eighteen. His wife began to collect $250.00 a month on which to raise a family.* (Eichstaedt, 1994)

The final injustices were disclosed in February 1993, when even the evident physical damages to the miners were shown to have been calculated improperly. '(Dr Louise) Abel demonstrated to the assembled doctors, lawyers and government officials that the medical tests are inadequate' (Eichstaedt, 1994).

This resulted in hundreds of miners being excluded from 'compassion payments' ordered by the Radiation Exposure Compensation Act of 1990. When a group is singled out for special treatment that effectively eliminates most of their basic rights to life, health and free information and consent, then all those involved are guilty of complicity in the crimes perpetrated against them. Through each sad interview describing the story of individual miners and their families (Eichstaedt, 1994), and through the appendices detailing the hearing on radiation exposure and the Radiation Exposure Compensation Act of 1990 (Eichstaedt, 1994), the story that unfolds is one that should fill everyone with shame. Nor is the US the only country with that problem. A report by Minchin and Murdoch (2006) relates a similar story in Australia:

> *Cancer rates among Aborigines near Australia's biggest uranium mine, according to a study by the Federal Government's leading indigenous research body, appear to be almost double the normal rate. The study also found there had been no monitoring in the past 20 years of the Ranger mine's impact on the health of local indigenous peoples. Yet since 1981 there have been more than 120 spillages and leaks of contaminated water at the mine located in the World Heritage listed Kakadu National Park.*

Energy Resources of Australia (majority owned by Rio Tinto), which operates the mine, denied that the Aboriginal peoples in the area were exposed to radiation, and in fact announced that the mine would continue to operate until 2020, despite the fact that:

> *... [a] study compared Aboringines diagnosed with cancer in the Kakadu region with the cancer rate among all Aboriginal peoples in the Northern Territory from 1994 to 2003. It found the diagnosis rate was 90 percent higher than expected in the Kakadu region.* (Minchin and Murdoch, 2006)

In this case too, neither the corporation(s) responsible for the extractive activities, nor the Australian government that allowed and, in fact, defended this operation, accepted responsibility for the harms they had perpetrated or attempted to close the mine and redress the injustice for which they shared responsibility.

Examples can be multiplied, and the factual recitations of aboriginal groups in the ATCA cases reviewed earlier bear witness to a number of similar exposures. Thus, it is neither the facts nor the science that are lacking, but the functionalist approach of industry and institutions that needs to accept the scientific reality and enact the required corrections.

The cultural integrity protection that is already present in international law, though insufficient in itself, opens the door to the ecological integrity aspect of the model of protection proposed here. The land's integrity is necessary to ensure the continuation of cultural and religious practices, traditional lifestyles, and even traditional knowledge, as noted in the discussion of Arctic peoples in Chapter 8.

Thus, if cultural integrity requires ecological integrity, the latter has a twofold function. It serves to support the ongoing identity of aboriginal communities, but also to ensure the protection of the health and normal development of those communities, and hence their biological integrity too. Biological and ecological integrity cannot be separated but must be viewed as an integrated whole. There may be other ways of protecting people's health and normal development/function, but, given the circumstances of indigenous communities, there is no other way for them.

There is yet another aspect of cultural and ecological integrity that we have not discussed, and that is its factual and symbolic aspects, representing a 'critique' of the present overwhelming pressures of capitalism and globalization.

Indigenous peoples' challenges to global domination by Western states as fundamental challenges to the logic of capitalism

> *So the question remains how and why have indigenous peoples survived the onslaught against them? In particular, why have they survived into the late twentieth century and early twenty-first century when there are no regions remaining outside global capitalism, and no regions that have not been claimed by one or more states?* (Hall and Fenelon, 2004)

This work by Hall and Fenelon (2004) includes a comprehensive critique of corporate incursions on aboriginal rights, and of the non-accountability of states regarding this ongoing phenomenon. Perhaps we need to look at the problem again not from the standpoint of aboriginal peoples as victims, but from that of their own stand against the forces that attempt to eliminate them. If we consider the 'puzzle of continual indigenous survival' (Hall and Fenelon, 2004), we note that indigenous peoples have survived a violent takeover, especially in North and South America, which included both genocide and systematic exploitation as industrialization and globalization forced themselves upon those communities.

At best, the violence was muted and indirect, as in the establishment of Indian schools for their children, intent upon eliminating any form of 'Indianness' (Westra, 2006). Yet today everywhere and in each continent, there are still strong surviving indigenous groups, from the Sami in Northern Europe to the Maori in New Zealand, the Inuit in the north of Canada and the Kurds in west Asia and Turkey. They all insist, with varying degrees of success, upon maintaining their identities and their cultural and religious practices. But, as Hall and Fenelon (2004) argue, 'Many of these practices contradict, challenge, or threaten deeply held values in state-based systems.'

The greatest challenge to the globalizing capitalism that engulfs these indigenous 'islands' in the midst of modern states, is the fact that aboriginal peoples believe in the communal ownership of resources, and hence they deny 'the legitimacy of private property rights' (Hall and Fenelon, 2004). The main form of resistance to capitalism has been the central importance of their 'traditional culture'. This includes their customs, crafts, religious ceremonies and their language.

More than formal 'sovereignty' or self-governance, important though these are, the perpetuation of the traditional cultural integrity of each group represents a clear and living ongoing rejection of capitalist values, starting with the inviolability of private property, despite state efforts to alter or repress this 'difference'.

'Ethnocide and culturicide involve attempts to destroy a group's identity, and/or culture, without necessarily killing human beings' (Hall and Fenelon, 2004). Yet the aboriginal groups have resisted by refusing economic takeover, by remaining small (for the most part), and by remaining isolated from globalizing pressures, unless the encroachment upon them becomes too violent to resist. Hence, in addition to the biological/physical integrity of individuals, and the multifaceted ecological integrity I have discussed, their cultural integrity not only depends on both other aspects to survive, but it also represents a symbol and a powerful tool of resistance to both capitalism and globalization. Clearly, their example is not enough to change the rest of the world. In the next chapter, I consider some other possible tools of change to establish regimes that are truly capable of protecting indigenous communities.

NOTES

1   *R. v. Hibbert* ([1995] 2 SCR 973, 99 CCC (3rd) 193.
2   *R. v. Paquette* ([1977] 2 SCR 189 30 CCC 22417, rejected by the court, whereas it reaffirmed *Dunbar v. the King* (1936).
3   Restatement (Third) of the Foreign Relations Law of the United States 702 (1987).
4   UN Rights Committee, Sub-Commission on Prevention of Discrimination and Protection of Minorities, Res. 1994/44, 16 August 1994, UN Doc. E/CN, 4/1995/2, E/CN.4/Sub.2/1994/56 (1994) Article 7.
5   *Trail Smelter Arbitration.*
6   *Talisman* case; *Wiwa v. Royal Dutch Petroleum.*
7   *Santa Clara County v. Southern R.R. Corp* (1886).
8   RSC 1970, App. III.
9   (1972), 8 CCC, (2d) 40, SCPR (2d) 179 (CA).
10 *Surrey Credit Union v. Mendonca* (1985), 67 BCLR 310 SC; *Smith, Kline and French Laboratories Ltd. T. et al v. A.-G. Canada* (1985), 7 CPR (2d) 145 (FCTD), where Strayer states: 'It is clear that the term individual does not include bodies corporate.'
11 *East Timor (Portugal v. Australia)*; IJC Reports 1995, p. 211.
12 *Barcelona Traction, Light and Power Co. Ltd.* Second Phase, Judgement, ICJ Reports 1970, p. 3, para. 34; see also UN Charter, A.1, para. 3.
13 See also International Law Commission, Draft Articles on the Law of Treaties, pp. 67–8, para. 3. This paragraph lists the principles of self-determination as one of the suggested examples of peremptory rules.
14 UN Charter, in force 24 October 1945, A.2, para. 4 cites the prohibition of the illegal use of force.
15 *Corfu Channel* case, Merits, Judgement, ICJ Reports 1949, where the court found that Albania was responsible for the explosions in the channel and the deaths that occurred; the court also found that the UK passing through the channel did not 'violate' Albanian sovereignty, but the setting of minesweeping operations did.
16 Charter of the United Nations, Article 1(3), 13(1)(b), 55(c), 56, 59 and 76(c).
17 ICJ Reports 1966, p.298.
18 See UN Charter's opening paragraphs: 'Peoples of the United Nations are determined to save succeeding generations from the scourge of war and to reaffirm faith in fundamental human rights.'
19 Report of the ILC (2001) GAOR A/56/10.
20 *Norms on the Responsibility of Transnational Corporations and Other Business Enterprises with Regard to Human Rights*, UN Doc. E/CN.4/Sub.2/2003/12/Rev.2 (2003).
21 *Rylands v. Fletcher* (1865-68), 3H. and C. 744 (Exch.); L.R. 1 Ex.265 (Exch. Ch.); L.R.3 H.L. 330 (H.L.).

22 *Rex v. Dunbar* [1935] BCJ No. 6, [1936] 3 WWR 99, 51 BCR 20.
23 ibid.
24 ibid.
25 I am grateful to Henk Ruessink of the Environmental Ministry of the Netherlands for the information on this ongoing case.

CHAPTER 10

Governance for Global Integrity:
Present Instruments, Trends and Future Goals

REVIEW OF SOME PRESENT INSTRUMENTS FOR THE PROTECTION OF INDIGENOUS PEOPLES

The evolution of environmental law and the development of human rights represent the gradual erosion of the so-called exclusive national jurisdiction. Both international environmental rights and international indigenous rights were developed as a response from the international legal community to the nations' inefficiencies in dealing with those issues. (Kastrup, 1997)

Throughout this work, the multiple conflicts between indigenous peoples' rights and the environmental degradation to which they are exposed have emerged as a major source of global disagreement. In 1993, the United Nations World Conference on Human Rights issued a declaration[1] in partial response to the ongoing discrimination against aboriginal peoples. The main aspect of such discrimination is the lack of environmental protection of their territories (Kastrup, 1997). Governments from the Americas to Australia and New Zealand have not been doing enough, hence the need for an international focus to bring about change.

In Chapter 8 we noted that the Lubicon Cree attempted to follow the road to the UN, with theoretical success but not much change on the ground. On 19 February 2007, in Geneva, a UN committee started hearings that will include the case of the Lubicon Cree. This new UN committee will focus on a different angle this time, that is, on the elimination of racial discrimination, and hence on a violation on the part of Canada (and of the oil corporation involved) of a *jus cogens* norm, not to be lightly dismissed if the committee, whose work ends on 9 March, is to actually pronounce on this issue. This is a very important development because normally environmental racism is not taken seriously enough, even in developed democratic countries (see Westra and Lawson, 2001).

Although environmental racism or, more generally, eco-crime (Westra, 2004a) has not been codified either as a crime or even as a breach of *erga omnes* obligations, international indigenous rights appear to be developing apace with international environmental law (Kastrup, 1997). The most important early documents in this regard are the Universal Declaration of Human Rights and the Stockholm Conference on the Human Environment.[2] In 1958, the Tehran Conference on Human Rights and, in

1977, the UN General Assembly Resolution[3] both defended the interdependence of human rights and their indivisibility.

An even clearer assessment of the global environmental problems and those of human beings everywhere was provided by the 1992 Rio Declaration on Environment and Development.[4] The development of human rights instruments and that of environmental international law, however, are parallel and, to some extent, complementary. But there is no single instrument that emphasizes the unavoidable interconnection between the two. At any rate, the UN Charter 'represents the official adoption of the concept of *jus naturale* by the international community', as it sets forth the general human rights of all mankind (Kastrup, 1997). In that manner, although not specifically named, indigenous peoples were covered by the document, although 'whether indigenous tribes should be considered a "person" under international law' remains an open question (Kastrup, 1997). Given the immense difficulties brought to jurisprudence by the acceptance of that status for corporations and business institutions, it seems as though the acceptance of communities and tribes as 'persons' would be a step forward when a conflict in the courts involves both an indigenous community and one or more corporations.

After the Covenant on Civil and Political Rights and the Covenant on Economic, Social and Political Rights, [5] the provisions of the Vienna Convention on the Law of Treaties[6] under Article 60(5) states that the principle of reciprocity and treaty obligations may not be cited 'for not complying with *erga omnes* obligations' (Kastrup, 1997). Hence, fundamental rights, like the right to life, are accorded a status different from that of other rights. The right to a safe/healthy environment, as was argued in the previous chapters, should be understood simply as an extension of that right.

The 1972 Convention for the Protection of the World Cultural and Natural Heritage[7] is particularly relevant and discussed separately below. Important are also the International Labour Organization Convention Concerning Indigenous and Tribal Peoples in Independent Countries,[8] discussed earlier, and the 1992 UN Framework Convention on Biological Diversity,[9] discussed in Chapter 8. However, despite the numerous conventions and declarations, the UN designation of 1993 as 'The International Year of Indigenous Peoples', the Decade of Indigenous Peoples (1994–2004), and a second Decade (2005–2015) adopted by the General Assembly in December 2004, the situation of indigenous peoples and their environment have continued to decline. Even the Rio Conference (1992) declaring its 'twin aims' of eradicating poverty and protecting the integrity of the Earth's ecosystems (Kastrup, 1997) did not make any appreciable difference.

It seems that there are at least two major reasons for this decline. The first is the ongoing juxtaposition of poverty eradication and development, without any under-standing of the connection between these issues and environmental protection. The way these 'goals' are presently understood and codified in law are in direct conflict with one another: the result is that the former issues (the eradication of poverty and development) are almost always incompatible with the latter. So-called 'development' in aboriginal territories and in nearby areas is harmful and unwanted, for the most part, nor does it lead to economic betterment of the aboriginal communities' circumstances. The expected enrichment is not theirs, but remains with the 'developing' corporate actors and, at best, in some small measure with the complicit governments where the indigenous peoples reside.

The second reason is the refusal to accept the scientific evidence on the connection between 'development' processes and products and their health effects, as noted above, and I return to this topic below. For now, it might be best to continue our overview of some existing instruments, before turning to more radical proposals in conclusion.

THE CONVENTION FOR THE PROTECTION OF THE WORLD CULTURAL AND NATURAL HERITAGE AND ABORIGINAL RIGHTS

Toutes les manifestations des droits culturels de l'homme ont une y dimension individuelle (droit de l'individu) et une dimension collective (droit des groupes sociaux, comme les peoples, les minorités, les populations autochtones).

[All examples of human cultural rights have an individual dimension (right of the individual) and a collective dimension (right of social groups, such as peoples, minorities, and indigenous populations).] (Scovazzi, 2007)

Article 1 of the Convention for the Protection of the World Cultural and Natural Heritage defines 'sites' as 'works of man or the combined works of nature and man, and areas including archaeological sites which are of outstanding universal value from the historical, aesthetic, ethnological or anthropological point of view'. Article 2 defines the 'natural heritage' as:

- *natural features consisting of physical and biological formations or groups of such formations, which are of outstanding universal value from the aesthetic or scientific point of view;*
- *geological and physiographical formations and precisely delineated areas which constitute the habitat of threatened species of animals and plants of outstanding universal value from the point of view of science or conservation;*
- *natural sites or precisely delineated natural areas of outstanding universal value from the point of view of science, conservation or natural beauty.*

The duty to identify and protect cultural and natural sites that are part of the world's global heritage accrues to states, but the international community has increasingly recognized its obligation to protect endangered species, as many areas that are the habitats of these species, or the location of these natural sites, exceed the boundaries of one state, and often, the state's economic capacity.

Although, thus far, the convention has not been interpreted as providing special protection for indigenous peoples, the fact that the latter are the best existing source of protection for both natural sites and threatened and endangered species should ensure that this connection be noted, and that the convention's use be extended this way in the future. In addition to the protection of physical elements of sites and the sites themselves, there is also a further component that adds to the appropriateness of this convention to indigenous rights. Speaking of the protection of non-commercial goods, Tulio Scovazzi writes:

> *Les Etats peuvent aussi établir un régime spécial visant certain biens-dont les biens culturel-afin d'assurer la jouissance de leurs bénéfices non vénaux (émotionnels ou conceptuels) par les générations présentes et futures, et de partager les sacrifices liés a leur protection.*
>
> *[States may also establish a special regime regarding certain goods, such as cultural goods, in order to ensure the enjoyment of the benefits of non-commercial goods (emotional or conceptual) by present and future generations, and to participate in the sacrifices required for their protection.]* (Scovazzi, 2007)

The cultural/emotional/conceptual special goods here proposed, fit well with the cultural/religious aspects of aboriginal rights in international law for the protection of cultural integrity of those communities. Without special reference to indigenous peoples, Scovazzi adds:

> *Un aspect important de la protection transfrontière est constitué par la préoccupation de l'intégrité des biens culturels, avec la conséquente obligation de restitution des biens, à l'Etat qui en aurait été dépouillé (principe du non appauvrissement du patrimoine culturel des autres Etats).*
>
> *[An important aspect of trans-border protection is the concern for the integrity of cultural goods, with the consequent obligation of restitution of these goods to the state that has been deprived of them (the principle of non-impoverishment of the cultural patrimony of other states).]* (Scovazzi, 2007)

The deprivations suffered by aboriginal peoples are not as simple as the theft of a statue, a fresco or some other art treasure; no 'restitution' is possible for the devastation of the Arctic lands and the ongoing extermination of the wildlife and the ecosystem services upon which Arctic peoples depend. The health of the Lubicon peoples and their lands is also not easily compensable (see Chapter 8).

Further, it is not only that the exclusive possession of an artefact has been violated, but the violation of Arctic people's rights to their heritage is, *ipso facto*, a violation of our heritage, globally. Hence the previous arguments insisting that the derogation from the norms of environmental and human rights protection ought to be considered breaches of *erga omnes* obligations:

> *Human right interests ... have worked a revolutionary change upon many of the classic rules of international law as a result of the realization by states in their international practice, that we have a deep interest in the way other states treat their own interest.* (D'Amato, 1987)

The lack of ecological integrity in the territories of aboriginal peoples *may* be corrected with a lot of restoration work, but it may never be returned to its original condition. That, once again, is not only a problem for the people directly involved in the area, but also an ongoing disaster for humankind, as indicated by the interface between the melting of the polar ice and glaciers, the increase in the number and severity of hurricanes, sea surges and tsunamis, and the hazardous rising of sea levels near island states and sea-level cities. Other cases of eco-crimes on aboriginal territories always include the disintegrity of those lands and surrounding areas, often also involving water scarcity, desertification and alteration of ecosystem function, and hence the loss of 'nature's services' (Daily, 1997).

In all such cases, the problems of 'restitution' are immense, as the appropriated territorial integrity is not an object that can simply be put back. The same is true of the industrial operations that result in the loss of biological integrity, and hence, in the loss of health and normal function of the indigenous peoples affected. It might be possible to provide some decent compensation for the surviving families of those killed in uranium mines (see Chapter 9), or by the processes and the products of other extractive and mining operations (see Chapters 8 and 5), but the prematurely dead or disabled represent incompensable harms, as do the children with various neurodevelopmental dysfunctions, so that for the most part in these cases restitution is not possible.

Responsibility for incompensable appropriations and international humanitarian law

> *Il est intéressant de voir jusqu'a quel point l'individu pourrait être assujetti a des poursuites et condamnations pénales pour avoir violé des obligations existant dans les domaines des biens culturels (crimes de guerre ou crimes contre l'humanité).*
>
> *[It is interesting to consider how far an individual can go before facing an indictment in the law for having violated the obligations existing within the domain of cultural goods (as in war crimes or crimes against humanity).]* (Scovazzi, 2007)

Emmerich de Vattel (1714–1767) wrote about the necessity to safeguard the 'beautiful buildings that do honour to mankind', the temples, tombs and other public buildings, in time of war, as there is nothing to be gained by destroying them when a city is attacked (de Vattel, 1758). 'Beautiful buildings' are the expression of cultures and, as such, were recognized as part of the heritage of mankind even in the 18th century. Hence, even in the event of a genuine 'necessity of war', considerations for the heritage of mankind ought to have priority, and principles ought to be respected by all nations, even in the absence of a specific treaty among them. The primacy of respect for all human beings and their life and culture is one such culture. Not to allow this primacy to stand is to become an enemy of humankind, a pirate, to use the language found in the well-known *Le Louis* case,[10] where the British court condemned a vessel carrying on the slave trade on *moral* grounds, that is, on strong principles alone, in terms that clearly viewed the obligations of all states in this matter as *erga omnes*, despite the fact that no treaty existed at that time regarding slavery.

Later conventions regarding the treatment of monuments and cultural sites in wartimes were adopted, and they codified the same beliefs. Similar beliefs were expressed by General Dwight D. Eisenhower (29 December 1943), during the Second World War:

Today we are fighting in a country which has contributed a great deal to our cultural inheritance, a country rich in monuments which by their creation helped and now in their old age illustrate the growth of the civilization which is ours. We are bound to respect those monuments as far as war allows. (cited in Merryman, 1986)

General Eisenhower even emphasized the fact that, although the principle of 'military necessity' should have primacy, sometimes it becomes a misnomer for 'military convenience or even personal convenience' (cited in Merryman, 1986).[11] Hence, if even a general committed to a war was prepared to give a lot of weight to cultural artefacts and, even more important, to consider excuses based on 'convenience' to be unacceptable, then on what grounds can we possibly justify the relentless elimination of our natural heritage without any comparable 'necessity'? We need to keep in mind that there is no treaty or charter that lists 'profit making' as the right of natural or legal persons, let alone that ensures that goal should be defensible, even with the sacrifice of human life.

In May 1954, the Convention of The Hague for the Protection of Cultural Goods in Armed Conflict was adopted under the aegis of UNESCO. By April 2006, 114 states had become signatories. Thus, not only armies but individuals (such as for instance Goering, for his stealing of art works for his own collection or for that of Hitler) may be convicted of these crimes of unlawful appropriation.[12] Both the cultural and natural patrimony of mankind are included, and protection is based upon granting a collective assistance to ensure efficient protection without, however, any substitution of the actions and responsibility of the state involved.

Cultural heritage and natural patrimony of mankind

Article 1.
Sites: works of man or the combined works of nature and man, and areas including archaeological sites which are of outstanding universal value from the historical, aesthetic, ethnological or anthropological point of view.

It is equally possible to consider that the patrimony of mankind should have a 'mixed' character, that includes both nature and culture (Scovazzi, 2007), although the rights to environment and to culture are normally kept separate. However, the two, as argued in Chapter 1, coincide neatly in the rights of indigenous peoples, where the two represent different emphases perhaps, but essentially a single, inseparable whole. The presence of aboriginal 'guardians' of cultures intimately connected with nature represents this mixed character of the heritage of mankind very well.

In 2005 a special reunion of experts on the concept of 'exceptional universal value'[13] lists six conditions that must be met, in order for a site to warrant this status. Numbers v and vi are worth listing verbatim for their close relation to our topic:

(v) be an outstanding example of a traditional human settlement, land-use, or sea-use which is representative of a culture (or cultures), or human interaction with the environment, especially when it has become vulnerable under the impact of irreversible change;

(vi) be directly or tangibly associated with events or living traditions, with ideas or with beliefs, with artistic or literary works of outstanding universal significance. (The Committee considers that this criterion should preferably be used in conjunction with other criteria);

The presence of natural sites possessing these characteristics, impose on the state which they are located, the non-derogable obligation to ensure the sites' protection. The exceptional value, however, is not only a value to each state, but is universally valid:

Cette valeur est entendue en général comme dépassant a la fois les frontières de l'espace et les frontières du temps. Elle intéresse en effet, tous les Etats, mais aussi les générations présentes et futures.

[This value in general is understood as transcending both spatial borders and temporal limits. In effect, it concerns all states and present and future generations as well.] (Scovazzi, 2007)

Nevertheless the UNESCO Convention for the Protection of the World Cultural and Natural Heritage clearly speaks of the cooperation of the international community, rather than any intent to replace the sovereign state, which holds the primary responsibility (Article 6.1; see also Article 4), as in fact no site may be added to the list of the heritage of mankind without the consent of the state in question.

It is particularly important to extend explicitly the definitions of this convention, and the requirements of 'exceptional sites', to the territories of indigenous peoples, because once a site has deteriorated to the point that it no longer possesses the characteristics that constituted its 'exceptional value', then the site's name is withdrawn from the list.[14]

The exceptional combination of, for example, Arctic landscapes and wildlife, together with the particular traditional lifestyles of the Arctic peoples in each area, are thus highly vulnerable, once the specific properties of that territory and of the peoples that inhabit it have been 'profoundly altered'[15] by climate change and by the consequences of industrial pollutants and toxins.

Notwithstanding the apparent strong connection here outlined between the obligation to protect the cultural and natural heritage of mankind, and the right of aboriginal peoples to their own protection and that of their lands, not only has this approach not been used in either international or domestic jurisprudence, to my knowledge, but even recent scholarship attempting to describe the 'conceptual structures' of indigenous claims does not even contemplate this possibility.

We need to understand why any entrenched support or protection measure regarding indigenous peoples is viewed as troubling and controversial from the outset by the international community. In 1977, the Sub-Commission of the ICCPR, appointed Francesco Capotorti (Italy) to study the implications of Article 27 of the covenant. Capotorti (1977) indicates why states in general are 'reluctant' to accept that indigenous peoples are entitled to special protection:

any international mechanism set up for that purpose may be viewed as a pretext for interference in a state's internal affairs; the usefulness of a uniform approach in such profoundly different contexts is questionable; preservation of the ideal of minorities was seen by some as a threat to unity and stability; and the need for special protection could be used to justify reverse discrimination.

The combined weight of these issues has ensured that the Draft Declaration on the Rights of Indigenous Peoples has been studied at length, but only the Human Rights Council stopped the debate (still ongoing in 2006) by adopting the declaration in June 2006, referring it to the UN General Assembly for adoption.[16] Hence, the draft remains soft law for now.

In order to complete even an overview of existing instruments and approaches to the protection of aboriginal peoples, it is useful to summarize once again what is presently available, before venturing towards what might be desirable, and perhaps even possible, in the future.

BENEDICT KINGSBURY (2001) ON 'FIVE COMPETING CONCEPTUAL STRUCTURES OF INDIGENOUS PEOPLES' CLAIMS'

Somebody else has it and tells you you may have it, and so you try to find it; but every time you try to find it, it is not there... If something serves the purpose of the state, it is sovereign;... and it serves the government's purpose to recognize Indian sovereignty, because it then does not have to abide by the rules and regulations that govern nuclear waste elsewhere in the United States. (Lyons, 1993)

Kingsbury (2001) cites the Haudenosaunee Leader, Oren Lyons, to demonstrate what he terms the 'chimerical element of the modern quest for "sovereignty" among Indian Nations in the United States'. The quest for sovereignty represents one of the 'five fundamentally different conceptual structures employed in claims brought by indigenous peoples' (Kingsbury, 2001):

1   *human rights and non-discrimination claims;*
2   *minority claims;*
3   *self-determination claims;*
4   *historical self-determination claims;*
5   *claims as indigenous peoples, including claims based on treaties or other agreements between indigenous peoples and states.*

The first thing to note about this list is that neither claims about environmental rights, nor about the natural heritage of mankind are present; nor are any claims regarding the right to life, to health, or to be spared exposures to harmful and toxic substances. Hence, we are firmly within the realm of what has been tried in law thus far. We are also within the realm of claims that have been far from successful to protect indigenous peoples, as the successes of these claims have been limited and few, as we saw in the previous chapters. Nevertheless, before attempting to reach beyond existing approaches, it is useful to briefly review the conceptual structures summarized by Kingsbury (2001).

The first two claim structures:
Human rights and non-discrimination and minority claims

The first 'conceptual structure', that is, the appeal to human rights to non-discrimination, is, on one hand, a timely and desirable approach. For example, the Committee on Human Rights is hearing the case of the Lubicon Cree on these grounds. On the other hand, the human rights approach may be insufficient on various grounds. For example, too many government institutions in North America and elsewhere pay lip service to human rights but, in practice, allow the rights of non-state, non-natural 'persons', such as mining corporations, to assert their own rights to the detriment of indigenous peoples.

In addition, freedom from racial discrimination is a powerful right, as it grounds both genocide and ethnocide, although neither has been successfully argued in the courts thus far regarding indigenous peoples. In addition, the question of individual v. collective rights may be the source of problems. The second aspect of this approach then is supported by all the instruments against discrimination, so that the universality required by human rights is modified in favour of indigenous peoples by appealing to the historical harms to which they have been subjected, a position similar to that of African Americans regarding affirmative action programmes or quotas. This approach has been debated in that context in the business ethics literature (see, for example, Velasquez, 1998).

For applications of the concept of minorities we can appeal to several older UN instruments[17] and especially to the ICCPR, Article 27,[18] which provides:

> *In those states in which ethnic, religious or linguistic minorities exist, persons belonging to such minorities shall not be denied the right in community with other members of their group, to enjoy their own culture, to profess and practice their own religion, or to use their own language.*

Article 27, by citing culture, ties self-determination to their territory, which is the most appropriate way to think of indigenous communities. The Human Rights Committee in *Ominayak v. Canada*, decided that the oil and timber concessions in the area 'threaten the way of life and culture of the Lubicon Lake Band, and constitute a violation of Article 27, as long as they continue'.[19]

Nevertheless, even that decision did nothing to stop the ongoing industrial operations, and the committee is reviewing the case in March 2007 from the perspective of racial discrimination instead. However Kingsbury (2001) notes that the use of Article 27 does little to address 'the assimilationist provisions' of the Canadian Indian Act of 1985. If aboriginal communities are to be treated as 'minorities', their *sui generis* status is not really considered.

But it is often false to term indigenous peoples 'minorities', as in the second structural approach, at least in certain regions where they may be in the majority instead. It is also an incorrect understanding of the true position of aboriginal peoples, as this approach does not incorporate the *sui generis* relation between them and their territories, a relation that separates them sharply from other minorities, for example the Roma in Eastern Europe and elsewhere.

Two more conceptual structures:
Self-determination and historical self-determination

The third approach is closer to the *sui-generis* claims of indigenous peoples, based on their traditional sovereignty and their distinctive histories. In New Zealand, the case of *Maori Council v. Attorney General*,[20] based on the principles of the Treaty of Waitangi, envisions Maori people and the Crown itself as two nations participating in a treaty, describing the relations between indigenous peoples' environment and their history. Not just human rights in general, but the specific aboriginal traditions and history, in relation to their territories make the difference.

The European Commission on Human Rights depends for the most part on Article 8.1 of the European Convention, as a person is entitled 'to claim the right to respect for the particular lifestyle it may lead', as 'private life, family life or home' are protected under that article.[21] However, this article is not used in the jurisprudence we have discussed, whether in Canada or elsewhere, in claims by indigenous groups asking for the protection of their home and lifestyle. The right to self-determination is often appealed to, but the results of those appeals are often less than optimal. The UN Working Group on Indigenous Populations defends that right (Pritchard, 1998). The UN Draft Declaration, Article 3, states that 'Indigenous peoples have the right to self-determination. By virtue of that right, they freely determine their political status and freely pursue their economic, social and cultural development.'

There are several categories of 'self-determination' that are applied to different socio-political units. At any rate, although complete independence could, at least theoretically, be an available choice for indigenous peoples, it is not often chosen or even desired. Rather, some improved relation with the state where the group is located is what is wanted, and perhaps more equality in the relations with that state (Kingsbury, 2001). At any rate, self-determination is not a panacea: 'It can be state-threatening or state-reinforcing, liberating or chauvinistic, democratic or demagogic. In its legal operation since 1920, it generally has buttressed the states system' (Kingsbury, 2001).

The UN Draft Declaration of the Working Group on Indigenous Peoples (1993), Article 31, emphasizes the freedom of organizing their own institutions, but does not include the powers related to 'foreign affairs and military security', as well as 'policing, taxation and judicial proceedings (Kingsbury, 2001). Worst yet, it does not specifically tie any group to a specific land base.[22]

Kingsbury (2001) analyses several of the imprecisions and problematic aspects of the draft declaration, as even a desirable environmental/health component in the draft is not treated in the best possible manner:

> States are required for instance to 'take effective measures to ensure that no storage or disposal of hazardous materials shall take place in the lands and territories of indigenous peoples', a formulation that deliberately did not provide for indigenous consent to the receipt of such materials.

Nevertheless some internal form of self-determination is accepted by several countries, including Canada, New Zealand, Denmark and Australia (Kingsbury, 2001), and the 1995 Mexico City Agreement on Identity and Rights of Indigenous Peoples[23] also supports self-determination, as does the Philippines Indigenous Peoples Rights Act of 1997.[24]

However, according to Kingsbury (2001), some view the right to self-determination as foundational to all other rights, or, like James Anaya (2000), connect it with a human rights approach. In contrast, I have argued (Westra, 2004b; see also Chapter 1) that the basis of all human rights, including the capacity to decide, hence including self-determination itself, is to be found in the preconditions of agency – that is, in the right to health and normal intellectual and physical development – and I return to this topic below in the discussion of health and the role of the WHO.

The fourth approach, 'historical sovereignty', is close to one of the aspects of the final approach, the 'claims as indigenous peoples', and hence I discuss them together. The final classic basis for claims, that is, the arguments about treaties, is not so much a conceptual approach as a political one. Historical sovereignty, together with the related condition of being a *sui generis* community, is the conceptual structure that I believe should be emphasized in both cases and instruments. The main reason for this is twofold: first, it is focused on sovereignty, something that is inextricably related to land and territories, and hence something that clearly distinguishes indigenous peoples from other 'minorities'; and second, this approach recognizes both the historical and the essential 'Indianness' of these communities, with all its traditional/cultural components.

In this sense, sovereignty also supports the extensive series of treaties between aboriginal communities and the governments of New Zealand, Canada and the US.[25] It seems that, given the geopolitical situation and the heavy hand of globalization today, sovereignty is at times something of a 'red herring'. Aboriginal groups do argue for it forcefully, and it does have a component of dignity and power attached to it. But the other side of the coin is its powerlessness regarding the harmful conditions surrounding or even infiltrating the 'sovereign' nations, as we saw in the clear indictment of US practices regarding radioactive waste by Oren Lyons, and generally in the conditions of the Nunavut people.

It is only when sovereignty is coupled with the special existence of indigenous peoples as a distinct category that the concept starts to fit, and perhaps even provides a useful tool in conflict situations. In Chapter 6 we saw the case of the Mohawk at Oka, where the joint claim was precisely that of sovereignty and the special respect for the traditional burial grounds at Oka. Another similar case, albeit in a different region, is that of 'native Tahitians against a French government decision to allow construction of a hotel complex in an area impinging on an ancient Polynesian grave site' (Kingsbury, 2001).[26]

Nevertheless, this approach, which shows 'special respect' for indigenous communities, whose 'traditions, culture, lands and beliefs had been ignored and impaired' (Kingsbury, 2001), is not enough. It remains a conceptual approach that focuses exclusively on the past of indigenous peoples, viewed as 'victims'. This may well be the best approach available against the ongoing harms affecting these groups, and law, at least common law, is primarily focused on precedent. But it remains focused on 'history and culture' (Kingsbury, 2001), rather than on the indigenous peoples themselves, as a unique, distinct society, whose *sui generis* relation to their territories makes them a beacon of hope for the future of humankind and not only a relic of the past, even if the latter is well worth saving.

Simply, it is not those groups who join with corporate enterprises as 'partners' who want to be free of their 'frozen rights' (Borrows, 1997–1998), whether it is in conjunction with Shell Oil in the Canadian oil sands of Alberta, or with the fishery corporations of New Zealand (see Chapter 4). Instead, those who stand up to and against the corporate second conquest, who are and must continue to be, the inspiration and model to the rest of the world to recapture the oneness with the natural world that we have lost, represent that beacon of hope.

This brief summary cannot possibly do justice to the richness and thoroughness of Kingsbury's (2001) treatment of this important topic, but it serves for our purpose to conclude the survey of what instruments and conceptual tools are 'out there' at this time and are, at least in principle, capable of being extended to keep pace with today's science, and with the reality of the present circumstances of climate change and the unchecked proliferation of chemical and toxic substances. Below, I turn to concepts and instruments that have not yet been used in defence of aboriginal peoples, but which show some evidence of possible renewal and re-evaluation in that direction, or that represent, as they stand, obstacles that must be acknowledged in our quest for justice for aboriginal peoples.

CORPORATIONS AND THEIR HUMAN RIGHTS?

The fundamental rights regime of the European Union is a potent example at the level of supranational law, of fundamental rights and freedoms to corporate actors: corporate claims make up a large part of the fundamental rights litigation brought before the European Court of Justice. (Emberland, 2006)

In the last chapter we discussed the responsibility of non-state actors, including corporations, for the protection of aboriginal rights. But we need to attempt a deeper understanding of the origins of the present cavalier disregard for those rights by corporate actors. That disregard, I submit, started with the *Santa Clara* case,[27] as discussed in conjunction with de Vattel's 'wrong turn', which proposed viewing states as subjects of natural law like human persons (see Chapter 3).

The thrust of this work, thus far, has argued for viewing corporate actors as open to criminal prosecution for breaches of human rights, rather than attempting to view them as beneficiaries of human rights law (see, for example, Jagers, 2002; Joseph, 2004). In fact, corporations are powerful entities, and human rights law, for the most part, is intended to defend the vulnerable and the poor against abuses of power. Hence, even the use of human rights language in relation to corporations does not fit well. 'Experience shows, besides, that uninhibited free enterprise often is at odds with respect for individual integrity, a central tenet of international human rights' (Emberland, 2006).

Emberland's (2006) focus is on Europe, viewing the European Convention on Human Rights[28] as the most effective human rights regime in the realm of civil and political rights. Like other courts, the European Court is primarily seeking to implement the right to equality and, in general, the European Court of Human Rights:

In accordance with the Vienna Convention on the Law of Treaties Article 31(1), the Court places 'considerable emphasis ... in the interpretation of the Convention, upon a teleological approach,' that is, the method by which the object and purpose of the ECHR had not been exhaustively identified, but that it encompasses subjective as well as objective elements. (Emberland, 2006)

The convention is intended to protect human rights, but also it is designed to promote the ideals of a democratic society and the rule of law and other values. Emberland (2006) shows that:

... the scope of Arts. 8, 10 and 41 has been widened to include private activity that was formerly believed to lack the characteristics required for protection under the relevant rights and entitlements: the ambit now covers corporate and for-profit activities to an extent that at least was not discussed at the time of the Convention's adoption.

Perhaps the most important article that should be 'protected' from such 'extension', is Article 8(1), because this article is the only one appealed to in defence of the right to life and health, not only in European courts, but in international law as well.[29] In Europe, several cases were successful applications of Article 8(1); however, in cases involving indigenous peoples, Article 8(1) has been appealed to but with no success so far.

Article 8(1) states that 'Everyone has the right to respect for his private and family life, his home and correspondence'. In some sense, corporate offices do represent the 'home' of a company, despite the fact that no 'family life' takes place on those premises, except by a very convoluted extension. Emberland (2006) adds:

Here, as elsewhere in Article 8, a distinction is drawn between matters concerning a person's 'private sphere' and matters more broadly connected with private activity. When a company asserts 'home protection', it seeks safeguards for its for-profit activity, but for-profit activity as such is not an issue with which 'privacy' and 'home protection' are concerned.

In fact, even the private sphere of individual persons, their 'home life', represents, at best, an effort to treat as simply formal a right that ought to be substantive and principle-based instead. Hence, it seems right to conclude that Article 8 primarily 'protects the natural person', the individual human being, rather than the offices of a corporation (Emberland, 2006).[30] The article is intended to protect the individual against arbitrary interference by public authorities or others. Emberland (2006) argues that the 'philosophical justification' of the article depends on the fact that 'the individual cannot make free moral and rational choices, establish an identity, and develop his or her personhood' unless there is an area free from 'outside intrusion' that permits this development. Not only is this an indisputable point, but its counterpart is the fact that without an area free from outside 'physical' intrusion, no normal intellectual, moral and physical development is possible. This is precisely what I have argued for here, and I return to this point below.

By denying, for the most part, this area of similarity between natural individuals and legal entities, perhaps the present emphasis on equality in corporate rights might be stemmed, although the present problems are not solved. Objective international law does have 'gaps' that need urgent attention:

> *The idea of 'gaps' in law is premised on the idea that normally the law is there to be found as a tangible object of professional scrutiny, external to the way lawyers argue about it, or the perspectives from which they do this.* (Koskenniemi, 2000; see also Lauterpacht, 1933)

A very serious gap in international law is the lack of explicit protection of life and health in the non-preambulary portions of international instruments (Westra, 2006). The severity of this gap emerges from the very possibility of 'joint' rights between natural individuals and corporations, even if, in the final analysis, the analogy does break down in practice.

At any rate, as long as the 'sources of international law' still include natural law, and as long as normative principles can be appealed to beyond treaties, there ought to be some study devoted to the gap between human rights in general and the basic or fundamental human rights for which this work argues. Not applying Article 8 to corporate persons is a first step towards the recognition of fundamental human rights against corporate attacks. A fuller appreciation of the necessity to recognize the normativity that derives from natural law, beyond treaties and beyond the exclusive reliance on state practice, is a necessary condition to achieve the protection of aboriginal peoples. Before turning to some possible newer roads to reach that goal, it might be best to start by acknowledging the foundation of that tentative enterprise. Sir Hersch Lauterpacht (1946) says it well:

> *The fact is that while within the State it is not essential to give to the idea of a higher law – of natural law – a function superior to that of providing the inarticulate ethical premises underlying judicial decisions... in the international society the position is radically different. There – in a society deprived of normal legislative and judicial organs – the function of natural law, whatever may be its form, must approximate more closely to that of a direct source of law. In the absence of the overriding authority of the judicial and legislative organs of the State there must assert itself – unless anarchy or stagnation are to ensue – the persuasive but potent authority of reason and principle derived from the fact of the necessary co-existence of a plurality of States. This explains the pertinacity, in the international sphere, of the idea of natural law as a legal source.*

FUTURE TRENDS: THE INFLUENCE OF SOFT LAW AND NGOS

it is a principle of international law, and even a general conception of law that any breach of an engagement involves the obligation to make reparation.[31]

This principle is recognized in the jurisprudence, for the most part. But the form of recognition it achieves is usually economic. The question then remains: how can 'reparation' take place when a culture, hence a people, has been attacked, or when the ecological basis for their traditional lifestyle has been altered beyond the conditions required to support that lifestyle? Thus, the need to review available legal instruments that might be used to deal with these problems. There are a number of instruments available for the protection of indigenous peoples that are not fully utilized. Some could have a stronger impact if political and economic constraints did not conspire to minimize their potential reach. A clear example of these constraints in another field can be found in the conflict between the WTO and the European Community regarding SPS Agreements (WTO Agreements on the Application of Sanitary and Phytosanitary Measures) in the *EC-Biotech* case.[32] Under '2. Risk Assessment and Precaution', the Panel Report states:

> 21. *The SPS agreement strives for balance between the right of WTO members to adopt and enforce measures necessary to protect human, animal or plant life or health, and the need to restrict the use of sanitary and phytosanitary measures for protectionist purposes.*[33]

And this is not a 'special plot' or aberration, it is a routine 'business' assessment of a situation where a bizarre 'balance' is attempted between incommensurables: human, animal and environmental health, all of which are obviously connected, and the protection of trade. The point of the previous discussion of Article 8 is that the human right to life and health cannot be 'balanced' with commercial interests, and in the cases cited, health and 'home' did indeed gain primacy. Norms for the protection of human beings and their habitat cannot even be compared to agreements for the protection of profit, a non-existing category in itself.

Although this issue is not directly related to indigenous peoples, this normative conflict represents the main issue in the case law involving indigenous communities discussed so far. Hence, it is necessary to correctly assess this basic problem and state that it is so important to retain a principled approach in international law, particularly regarding indigenous peoples rights. The appeal to natural law, above, indicates the only way that such problems should be approached and, ultimately, solved. No agreement or treaty is sufficient by itself, primarily because all decisions that arise from the negotiations of multiple state actors are disproportionately governed by the interests of the richest and most powerful nations so that, for the most part, their economic interests prevail over the legitimate human rights claims of the poor and vulnerable, including indigenous groups.

Hence positivism alone – that is, the practice of basing policy and even court decisions on state practice and jurisprudence – is necessary but not sufficient if justice is to be achieved. There are no countervailing benefits that may account for the imposition of grave costs against human rights in indigenous peoples communities. Even a state's self-defence ultimately requires a just war to be legitimate (Westra, 2004a), and there are principles governing just wars too, such as *jus ad bellum* to define the just war and the actions leading to it, and *jus in bello* to circumscribe what is and is not permissible within it.

A just war presumably defends a people from grave human rights violations, but that is not the case for the industrial and trade activities whose results are the imposition of morbidity and fatalities on peoples, with no countervailing benefits. In addition, for the most part, those communities are excluded from the decision-making process that precedes most extractive and mining industrial operations, and hence they are, for all intents, unconsenting to the harms that befall them. If they are included in the discussions preceding those operations, it is only in the most cursory manner (see Chapter 4).

Although direct appeals to natural law are not easily found in either public policy or jurisprudence, except perhaps by reference to the 'principles of civilized nations' or such similar euphemisms, appeals to moral principles and to justice are routinely incorporated in declarations, proclamations and charters, known as 'soft law'. Principal among these is the Earth Charter, as we shall see below.

The reasons why we do not see explicit appeals to natural law have been discussed elsewhere in my work (Westra, 2004a). Essentially, natural law has been mistakenly viewed as based on religious principles, ignoring the ancient basis for its formulations in the work of Aristotle. Hence, it has been viewed as inappropriate for governance instruments intended to direct non-religious policies. In addition, some (see Baxi, 1998) view the principles of natural law as unavoidably based on Western ideals, out of step with modern global realities and aspirations, especially those of the global South (see, however, the response of Higgins, 1994, who argues for the unity of all humans whatever their region of origin).

Finally, the tenets of natural law are viewed as expressing an unacceptable essentialism, thus denying the ideals of freedom that are implicit in modernity. This objection does not consider the fact that natural law implies adaptation to modern situations – provided the basic principles are not abandoned – and most important, denies the appellation of 'law' to any instrument that favours one group (or elite) over another, and that is not intended to bring about just ends. For instance Thomas Aquinas defines this sort of 'law' as 'somebody's violence', and thus not to be obeyed but to be disregarded as a legitimate obligation and actively fought against by citizens (Aquinas, 1988 [c. 1260]).

These critiques are easily rebutted, but it is to the advantage of most today to view them as fatal to natural law instead, and to rely on state voluntarism and the positivist approach that allows them a stronger voice than the one they might have if strong normativity prevailed. Hence it is left to 'soft law' instruments and to NGOs to take principled positions without apology, and without the need to appeal explicitly to any specific source of international law (see Koskenniemi, 2000). Koskenniemi (2000) explains the role of norms in international law:

> By the 'binding force' of norms, is usually meant that norms govern the solution of normative problems. This may be further elaborated into two propositions:
>
> 1 Norms control *decisions in the sense that if they are applicable, they must be applied and the solution they provide excludes recourse to other solutions;*
>
> 2 Norms explain *the decision by making the sequence leading from the identification of the normative problem to its solution seem rational. Normative problems appear as problems of content and problems of subsumption. The former relate to the*

establishment of the meaning of an individual norm-formulation. The latter are concerned with the legal qualification of facts.

In addition to this conceptual analysis of the role of norms, there are several principles established, for instance, by the Declaration on the Principles of International Law of 1970.[34] Whatever its legal force today, this contains several principles that require no further defence when applied, and hence they are foundational. The document includes at least seven principles that carry normative force in international law, and three of these are very relevant to indigenous peoples:

1 the principle of peoples' self-determination;
2 the principle of political independence of states; and
3 the principle of non-use of force.[35]

These principles could play a determinant role in litigation involving indigenous peoples, and they should influence the formulation of regulatory instruments and treaties that concern them. Particularly relevant is the principle forbidding the use of force, as the concept of 'aggression' has not been exhaustively defined yet by the Statute of the International Criminal Court of Rome, or in general in international law. As noted above, especially in Chapter 5 in the factual descriptions of the cases appearing in the US courts under ATCA, the use of force in various forms is commonplace against indigenous communities on the part of TNCs and the governments involved.

It is also clear that, from the scientific information regarding the Arctic peoples discussed in Chapter 8, even forms of environmental or non-military aggression that originate from places far removed from the 'home' locations of aboriginal nations may result in serious harms. At any rate, the explicit reliance on principles and clear appeal to normativity are not commonplace in international law. Hence it is better to examine what soft law might have to offer to counterbalance the emphasis on trade and other commercial rights, which remains evident in the interaction between the courts, policymakers and aboriginal peoples.

The Earth Charter and indigenous peoples

12. Uphold the right of all without discrimination, to a natural and social environment supportive of human dignity, bodily health, and spiritual well-being, with special attention to the rights of indigenous peoples and minorities...
b. Affirm the right of indigenous peoples to their spirituality, knowledge, lands and resources and to their related practice of sustainable livelihoods.

The Earth Charter is the product of a process initiated by Steven Rockefeller, Ron Engel and others, with the representatives of people everywhere, to provide an environmental 'moral charter' to guide public policy. It has remained 'soft law' so far, despite its adoption by the IUCN in 1998, and many other adoptions elsewhere. Principle 12 of the Earth Charter (see Appendix 1; see also Westra, 2004b) represents part of a grouping defining 'social justice' and it recognizes and acknowledges the determinant role played by the environment in the support of 'human dignity, bodily health and spiritual well-being'. In addition, it affirms the special rights of indigenous peoples to their own spirituality and knowledge and, most important, the connection between this and their lands.

The Earth Charter[36] is unique for several reasons; it is also especially relevant as it represents both soft law and the NGO influence, as it has been adopted by the IUCN and other organizations, as well as a number of cities throughout the world. I believe it is the most important soft law document regarding indigenous people for several reasons:

1   It embodies a sense of the sacred without, however, representing exclusively a specific 'holy book' or tradition.
2   It promotes and supports the primacy of all life, as 'the community of life' (Principle I, 1.a).
3   It supports the obligation to future generations (Principle I, 4.a and 4.b).
4   It gives primacy to ecological integrity, the basis and foundation of cultural integrity for indigenous peoples (Principle I, 5, 5.a, 5.b, 5.c, 5.d, 5.e).
5   It demands prevention from pollution and embraces the precautionary principle (Principle II, 6.a, 6.b, 6.c and 6.d).
6   It demands strict observance of 'social and environmental standards' for all production (Principle II, 7.d, 7.f).
7   It requires that science should inform the knowledge of ecological sustainability, with particular attention to developing nations (Principles II, 8.a).
8   It emphasizes the importance of 'traditional knowledge and spiritual wisdom' to 'environmental protection,' as well as to 'human well-being' (Principle II, 8.b).
9   It requires the eradication of poverty and emphasizes the right of all people 'to potable water, clean air, food security, uncontaminated soil'; it demands that the international community should shoulder that obligation (Principle III, 9.a).
10 It demands accountability on the part of 'multinational organizations' and 'international financial organizations'; they must be responsible for all the consequences of their activities (Principle III, 10.d).
11 It is committed to uphold the 'right of all ... to a natural and social environment supportive of human dignity, bodily health, and spiritual well-being', with particular reference to indigenous peoples (Principle III, 12 see also 12.b).

It is easy to recognize in the principles listed here, the answer to most, if not all, the problems and conflicts I have noted between aboriginal communities and state and non-state actors. If the Earth Charter were to be adopted not only by NGOs and organizations and cities, as it has been so far, but by the governments of the powerful Western countries that are home to most TNCs, the needed legal principles and framework for the protection of aboriginal peoples would be in place.

We have now moved so far from the respect for nature and for life, that even a cursory review of these 11 points, focusing on those most relevant to indigenous peoples, indicates the vast gulf that separates our present practices and legal instruments from what should be done to ensure the survival of indigenous groups (and, incidentally, our own). As with the changes in current practices required by global warming, this analysis indeed represents an 'inconvenient truth' (Gore, 2006).

Ron Engel (2000) terms the Earth Charter a 'transcendent' democratic covenant':

> *The experience of transcendence has been thematized in a wide diversity of religious and secular traditions throughout human history. The Earth Charter takes the radical democratic posture that underneath all these different interpretations there is natural religious piety we can all share and a common covenant we can all make with the ultimately reliable powers of life.*

Here, moral principles, natural law and a strong respect for the sacred in general are combined in a way that does not permit rebuttal on positivist or agnostic grounds, either based on theoretical or practical objections. Steven Rockefeller, who promoted and guided the development of the Earth Charter from its inception after the 1992 Rio Declaration until its completion in 2000, ensured that people all over the world were involved in the preparation and writing of the charter, so that critiques based on North/South or rich/poor distinctions are not applicable to this document. It is not the product of Northern ideals and it does not embody rich nations' preferences. Theoretically, it reflects the 'reconstruction of old ways of thinking' (Rockefeller, 2002), in the same way as was advocated by Christian Weeramantry (1997) in his masterful 'dissenting opinion' on the *Gabcikovo-Nagymaros* case,[37] where he lists the beliefs of all past civilizations regarding the environment and respect for the Earth. Nor is the Earth Charter a purely environmental treatise because it 'recognizes that caring for Earth and caring for people are closely interconnected' (Rockefeller, 2002).

I cannot propose any way of making the Earth Charter an immediate instrument of change. But I can and do recognize that the ideal relationship between the community of life on Earth presented by the Earth Charter finds its closest embodiment in the traditional lifestyle of aboriginal peoples the world over. If the Earth Charter represents the newest and most radical call to sanity and to a new way of interacting with each other and with the Earth, then the *current* importance of respecting and protecting the remaining indigenous groups living in a traditional lifestyle cannot be overestimated.

This brief evaluation does not do justice to the Earth Charter's additional emphasis on science and on the use of the precautionary principle to ensure that ecological sustainability is well grounded. That is the focus of the next section devoted to the issue that might be the most important among the possible new categories under which to search for better protective regimes for indigenous communities: science, or more specifically, epidemiology and public health.

PUBLIC HEALTH, EPIDEMIOLOGY AND THE RESEARCH OF THE WHO: SCIENCE IN DEFENCE OF ABORIGINAL PEOPLES

> *Health disparities are, first and foremost those indicators of a relative disproportionate burden of disease on a particular population. Health inequities point to the underlying causes of the disparities, many if not most of which sit largely outside the typically constituted domain of 'health'.* (Adelson, 2005)

After the influence of 'soft law' and the efforts of NGOs, best combined in the example of the Earth Charter, the health aspects of the human rights of indigenous peoples represent the second of the partially untried ways to achieve environmental justice for these communities. 'Partially untried' because only one aspect of the 'health question' regarding indigenous peoples has already been considered in litigation and regulatory regimes, at least in Canada. The health question has two separate though interwoven strands: first, the 'social, economic, political inequities' that emerge clearly from the expanding research and literature, including Canadian documents and reports; and second, the breaches of human rights originating in part from government policies, but primarily from the current primacy of trade and commercial enterprise over human life and health, which clearly emerges from the case law discussed from Canada, the US, Australia and elsewhere.

For the second aspect of health, the literature focuses mainly on the law itself and the limits of accountability and responsibility of TNCs, as well as state and non-state actors. But there is very little to be found on the health implications of harmful activities and the true reach of the results of these activities and of the harms produced.

Health disparities in aboriginal Canada:
Social, economic and political aspects

> *Suicide, injuries, drug and alcohol abuse, sexual violence and even some chronic diseases – all occurring in disproportionate numbers across aboriginal Canada – are not just problems of individuals.* (Adelson, 2005)

Some of these issues were discussed in relation to the Lubicon Cree and the Nunavut in Chapter 8.[38] The legacy of the residential schools, which not only removed children from their family and cultural milieu, but also indoctrinated them on the need to abandon both and even punished them for non-compliance, figures largely in the genesis of the emotional and physical ills described above and acknowledged by Canadian government sources (Millroy, 1999; Napoleon, 2001; Neu, 2003).

The inequities that persist affect all aboriginal peoples, including First Nations, Métis and Inuit. They also affect equally all aboriginal peoples, whether they are still traditional hunters in remote locations, or whether they are simply yet another impoverished and largely overlooked group in urban or rural non-traditional settings (Adelson, 2005). For all, there are far greater numbers of young aboriginals than the comparable numbers of non-aboriginal Canadians, 'due to both the high birth rate and lower overall life expectancy' (Adelson, 2005).

In addition, the Royal Commission on Aboriginal Peoples reports other differences that have a grave impact on health[39]. For the most part, aboriginal people live in housing that is in need of major repairs, often with no piped water supply (aboriginals are more than 90 times as likely to suffer this as other Canadians), with no flush toilets (aboriginals are more than ten times as likely to suffer this as other Canadians), and about 34 per cent fewer aboriginals own their own dwelling in comparison with other Canadians (overcrowding is the key to the spread of infectious diseases).[40]

Some of these hazardous conditions arise from poverty, from bureaucratic failures and socio-political blunders. But other harms, not necessarily specific only to Canada, originate from ecological and biological causes. Hence, in the next section I consider those who represent the main focus of this work: traditional aboriginal peoples living in non-urban settings, on reserves or other historically assigned territories, not only in Canada but in various regions and continents.

Aboriginal health disparities: Ecological and biological aspects

Once fashionable during the Industrial and Progressive eras, the ideals of population health began to wither with the rise of liberalism in the late 20th century. In its place came a sharpened focus on personal and economic freedom. (Gostin, 2004)

Concerns with population health surely apply to the anomalous groupings of aboriginal peoples, regardless of their locations and living arrangements, as the common thread joining all is their aboriginal background and ancestry. It is not my intent to dispute this point, which is an obvious one, but the social and economic disadvantages that affect aboriginal peoples *now* owe a lot to the residential school systems in Canada, and to the general inaction and bureaucratic failures in Canada and elsewhere (Johnston, 1983).

However, there are other components to public health that do not appear in those analyses reflecting the Canadian situation. Perhaps they are not considered seriously because they are viewed as part of the common burden of ill-health affecting all people in developed and developing countries, originating from industrial operations and their products and processes, rather than being a specific burden on indigenous peoples. In addition, the well-established approach to environmental harms present in the discipline of ecological epidemiology, understood as research into the relationship between ecosystem health and human health at various scales, has not been used, to my knowledge, either by the courts or legislators to properly assess the exposures of indigenous peoples (see Soskolne, 2002).

In contrast, I have argued that because traditional aboriginal communities have a *sui generis* relationship to their lands, there are several differences between the rest of the developed world and aboriginal peoples in all continents:

1 Traditional aboriginal communities may be viewed as the proverbial 'canaries in the mine', as their exposures are involuntary and unavoidable, and therefore far more extreme than those affecting the rest of the populations of all countries.
2 Traditional aboriginal communities, therefore, are entitled to particular respect and protection, over and above the protection that is rightfully due to all other human beings.
3 The health impacts on traditional aboriginal communities are – in a sense – like the result of 'case studies', albeit involuntary on the part of researchers who simply record what has happened (see the case of the Nanavut nation discussed in Chapter 8). These 'cases' demonstrate why *in general* the present trade/corporate attacks perpetrated by 'business as usual' should not be tolerated.
4 Therefore, traditional communities *alone* deserve immediate special consideration, changed circumstances and comprehensive redress (as much as possible for *restitutio ad integrum* of all they have been deprived of, as indicated in the law governing the cultural heritage of mankind). Those who have abandoned traditional ways,

require the same support and assistance as all impoverished groups, plus additional consideration and redress for the discrimination they have suffered, as do, for instance, other groups that have suffered discrimination, such as women in the workforce.[41]

Other groups that were discriminated against in Canada included those of Japanese descent during the Second World War and African Canadians in Nova Scotia (see McCurdy, 2001). This is a radical position because it divides aboriginal peoples, including First Nations, Métis and Inuit along traditional and non-traditional lines. It seems to glorify what John Borrows (1997–1998) terms 'frozen rights', over parity with other Canadians and freedom of choice, and, in a sense, it does. However, even accepting this distinction must not blind us to the reality of the situation faced by many indigenous groups, even in Canada. Often, the decision to leave the land and to abandon traditional lifestyles is not the result of a free choice. When the land is depleted, the animals that used to be plentiful are no longer available – in short, when industrial or military activities, or the impact of climate change, or both, conspire to render traditional activities insufficient to ensure survival on their lands, indigenous peoples are forced to leave.

Their status then should be considered that of environmental refugees or exiles, not that of people who freely decided to abandon their land: they should receive special treatment to assist them in their plight (I am indebted to Bradford Morse for his insightful discussion of this issue). Nevertheless, in Canada, a country that embraces and promotes multiculturalism, rather than the US-style 'melting pot' approach, various groups can maintain respectful allegiance to their ethnic and racial background, without abandoning the mainstream Canadian choices most of us have consciously embraced. Readily available for most ethnic groups are language classes, clubs and meeting places with organized events and sponsored classes and tours. Some of these groups have, no doubt, been happier and more successful than others, but essentially, the conceptual division I propose is not a 'step back' but a step forward for both of the groupings I suggest.

In fact there is a precedent of sorts for this approach to aboriginal rights in the treatment of Sami peoples in Sweden. The 1886 Reindeer Grazing Act forms the basis for the current Reindeer Husbandry Act, 1971 (Thampapillai, 2007) and states:

> *The right to use land and water according to this law to support oneself and one's reindeer (the reindeer herding right) belongs to the person of Sami ancestry if his father or mother or one of his grandparents had reindeer herding as a steady occupation. Under special circumstances, the county administration can grant a person with Sami ancestry the reindeer herding right even in cases not covered by the above paragraph.*
> (cited in Korsmo, 1993)

This 'graded' approach grants special resource rights solely to Sami who pursue a traditional lifestyle and it has met with some approbation because it demonstrates 'Sweden's efforts to ensure the distinct cultural heritage of the Sami linked to reindeer herding' (Thampapillai, 2007). It also met with disapproval in some quarters, as the Sami Rights Commission was criticized for failing to protect the resource rights of all Sami, 'while [it] merely protected the entrenched rights of the minority reindeer herders' (Korsmo, 1993).

As far as health issues are concerned, Adelson (2005) recognizes that it is not possible to treat as one all aboriginals in Canada precisely because of their different locations and lifestyles, so that unitary assessment is precluded. For the traditional indigenous communities, the grave health problems, from the genetic mutations affecting the Aamjiwaang First Nation in Sarnia's 'Chemical Valley' in Ontario, to the generally documented effects of oil and other mining extractive industries on the Lubicon in Alberta, as well as those affecting most of the aboriginal groups who are litigating for their rights, from Colombia, Ecuador, Guatemala, Ghana, Sudan and Cambodia, cannot be denied.

In addition, there is an aspect of these problems I have not considered yet, as it encompasses both social and physical/mental harms: 'the social amplification of risk' (Sunstein, 2007). Sunstein cites an example:

> *Consider this in regard to the 'Buffalo Creek Syndrome', documented several times in the aftermath of major disasters. Nearly two years after the collapse of a dam that left one hundred twenty people dead and four thousand homeless, psychiatric researchers continued to find significant psychological and sociological changes; survivors were characterized by a loss of direction and energy, other disturbing character changes, and a loss of communality. One evaluation attributed this loss of direction specifically to 'the loss of traditional bonds of kinship and neighbourliness'.* (Sunstein, 2007)

This loss reflects much of what was observed in Nunavut as well as the narratives of many other affected groups, although in the Arctic we face a slow, ongoing disaster, rather than a sudden, natural one. Sunstein's argument seriously supports the modified version of the precautionary principle that he proposes, particularly with reference to climate change and related disasters. He argues that most people find it difficult to accept present losses in order to ensure favourable outcomes that are not immediately observable, and this is clearly the case with climate change's 'worst-case scenarios'. Sunstein proposes adopting a special version of the precautionary principle, modified as 'the catastrophic harm precautionary principle':

> *In deciding whether to eliminate the worst-case scenario under circumstances of uncertainty, regulators shall consider the losses imposed by eliminating that scenario and the magnitude of the difference between the worst-case scenario and alternative scenarios.* (Sunstein, 2007)

But two grave problems remain: one is that alternative scenarios *today* are based on current knowledge, but the knowledge of the possibilities involved in other scenarios would increase regularly as time goes on. As our knowledge expands, we might discover that both the decision to wait to acquire better understanding was a mistake, and that alternative scenarios we believed might present a better, less costly choice, may have been entirely mistaken. Sunstein (2007) writes:

> *... the failure to take precautionary action may be irreversible, or reversible only at very high cost. For example greenhouse gasses stay in the atmosphere for a very long time,*

and inaction may saddle posterity with a catastrophic risk that future generations are effectively powerless to eliminate.

Hence, if we accept Sunstein's analysis, the situation of aboriginal communities is something about which uncertainty remains, so that we can hesitate among various scenarios for the far future. In contrast, the catastrophic aspects of their situation are, for the most part, present and evident, although the long-term implications of their precarious situation – that is, the 'social amplification' of the harms they have suffered, as well as of the risks to which they are exposed – have not been fully researched or understood, let alone factored into regulatory instruments or judicial analysis, whether domestic or international.

These health effects are environmentally related and globally distributed, and they point to the responsibility not only of the trade regimes that govern TNCs and their interaction with indigenous groups, but also to the accountability of governments that are complicit with those who inflict harm. We should return briefly then to the possibility of intervention by the WHO, as a UN organ and, in a sense, as the global 'policeman' of health issues, as noted in the discussion of the Tobacco Convention above.

The WHO and the scientific component of aboriginal protection

WHO's advancement of national and international public health and supervisory institutions is critical to furthering the realization of the right to health. Encouraging countries to develop specific binding legal obligations with respect to the right to health, and publicizing their compliance and non-compliance with those obligations, can powerfully influence states to rethink priorities and redirect national resources to national health care. (Taylor, 1992)

WHO's mandate of 'Health for All' was declared in 1977 and was to be achieved for all the world's citizens by 2000.[42] Nevertheless, it is hard to find any appeals to science or health in the jurisprudence concerning indigenous peoples' rights. There appears to be a disjoint between the WHO health mandate, despite its position in the UN, and other documents which, even if they address the question of health, do so in general terms and with no reference to the WHO, let alone to the possibility of binding regulations. For instance, Article 7 of the Human Rights Council[43] states:

1 *Indigenous individuals have the right to life, physical and mental integrity, liberty and security of persons.*
2 *Indigenous peoples have the collective right to live in freedom, peace and security as distinct peoples and shall not be subjected to any act of genocide or any other act of violence including forcibly removing children of the group to another group.*[44]

The problem is that at this time these articles and the whole draft do not represent binding legal obligations. Hence, the desirability of involving the WHO or, better yet, the World Health Assembly (WHA), to add their authoritative voice to the requirements proposed by this report. The WHA has power that should be exercised in addition to the technical recommendations it normally issues:

WHA also enjoys authority to adopt regulations regarding sanitary and quarantine requirements to deter the international spread of disease, and standards for safety, purity and potency of biological and pharmaceutical products that move in international commerce, among other things. (Taylor, 1992)

Thus, a precedent exists whereby an arm of the WHO – that is, the WHA, its legislative organ – is empowered to limit trade and also to limit freedom of action of individuals in the usual public health fashion, through sanitary regulations and quarantines. Those who attempt to defend the rights of indigenous peoples in the courts, might consider the possibility of using this precedent for the protection of aboriginal communities as it remains one of the few approaches that has not been tried to limit, legitimately, the power and freedom of TNCs.

Public health is the mandate and the duty of the WHO, internationally, and they do have a history of speaking for the most vulnerable, for instance for children's exposures and diseases. All the signatories of the Convention on the Rights of the Child (CRC) are obliged to report periodically to Geneva on how their countries are integrating the mandates of that document into their own domestic laws (see Westra, 2006). This obligation to report applies to all states that are signatories to the CRC (all nations except the US and Somalia), but to my knowledge, it does not oblige each state to report any particulars about its indigenous communities (although I have found in my research that some do) and indigenous peoples can press to make their own submissions. In developed countries, the dissonance between the conditions of aboriginal and non-aboriginal communities is obvious if you examine the statistical information:

Developing countries in general have a much lower life expectancy.
High infant and child (below the age of five) mortality rates are the main factors contributing to low life expectancy rates in developing nations… Infant mortality in developing countries is still more than five times that in industrialized countries. (Taylor, 1992; see also El-Badry, 1989)

But, in addition to the malnutrition, infectious and parasitic diseases, measles, whooping cough, diphtheria, pneumonia and malaria – the main diseases that affect children under five years of age in developing countries (Taylor, 1992; see also Chapter 8 of Westra, 2006) – there is also a plethora of chemical and toxic exposures in developed countries, especially as a particular burden imposed on aboriginal communities. Unlike the latter, the former diseases prevalent in developing countries tend to arise for the most part from poverty and from inactions of governments.

The WHO has been very active organizing ministerial conferences on health in Europe, where the 'silent epidemic' of chemical/toxic exposures is described and presented based on the exhaustive research the WHO has accumulated (WHO 2002; Licari et al, 2005). They have also organized a meeting addressing questions of aboriginal peoples' health recently in Vancouver, Canada. As an organ of the UN, its presence ought to make a stronger impact, as it indicts specific threats as grave global challenges persist, from the return of drug-resistant tuberculosis, to cholera epidemics and the persistence of malaria, as well as the presence of an ever-growing body of research on exposures (Grandjean and Landrigan (2006). Taylor (1992; see also Gelert, 1989) adds:

These global health challenges have not only exposed the inadequacy of national public health systems, but also evidenced the increasing interdependence of world health. Indigenous public health issues can no longer be regarded as purely a matter of domestic concern. Increasingly public health challenges are recognized as transcending national boundaries.

Essentially then, the right to health, guaranteed by the International Covenant on Economic, Social and Cultural Rights,[45] Article 12(1) provides for 'the right of everyone to the enjoyment of the highest attainable standard of physical and mental health', hence it recognizes that the right to health 'is an essential element of human dignity' (Taylor, 1992). The 'guarantee' intended, of course, is not for the absence of disease for all, a patently impossible requirement. The right is instead intended to ensure certain preconditions for health and normal function, not to health care (see Westra, 2004a). I have argued elsewhere that the preconditions to physical and mental health, as well as that to normal development, are specifically based on the requirement to ensure ecological health for all human beings.[46]

This requirement is particularly relevant and necessary for aboriginal individuals and groups, as ecological concerns are basic to their traditional lifestyle. The United Nations Declaration on the Rights of Indigenous Peoples was adopted by the Human Rights Council on 29 June 2006, although consensus could not be reached among all (it was adopted by a recorded vote of 30 to 2 with 12 abstentions). It adds its voice (although it is still a draft, not a binding document), to the covenant and the UN Declaration of Human Rights, so that the protection of health should include aboriginal peoples, and should emphasize their protection from *all* attacks to their health, not only the traditional infectious diseases and other health problems arising from poverty and unsanitary conditions. One of the main concerns of the nations and lands participating in the discussion of the declaration, was the question of 'their lands and territories', according to Article 27. Nevertheless, that article does not specify whether their 'right' to specific territories is only quantitative or whether the question of the quality of the lands has been considered. The problem is that even establishing aboriginal 'rights' to a certain area or region is insufficient unless that area or region is protected from pollutants of various kinds and is actually available for traditional pursuits. This is a critical point that could be used to defend indigenous peoples' rights and that should inform the legal instruments designed to protect those rights.

The land is needed to exercise their rights to hunt, fish and gather wild foods, but if the chemicals affecting the land have made it unsafe for animals and plants, then their right cannot be exercised, and, in fact, their own health must be equally affected. It is instructive to listen to yet another aboriginal voice, attempting to frame the subject of their individual and collective right to life, in terms neither their country nor the international community seem willing to accept. The case involves the Buffalo River Dene Nation (BRDN) of Saskatchewan, Canada; the speaker is Adelard Blackman (2006):

Unabated resource development is killing the land, our water, and our people. We've asked for a moratorium and discussion to address the issues. Silence and inaction have been the response. We have nowhere to turn, but to the international arena and

*pleas for help and support from other nations and nation states. This is our last move
as the tide of genocide turns against our people. When our land is no more, then we
are no more.*

In the case of BRDN, it is not only TNCs who are attacking the community, but the
Canadian federal government itself has ignored the provisions of Treaty 10 (signed by
the British Crown and BRDN in 1906) that established that their nomadic, traditional way
of life would be respected. From 1986, when the first road was build, the community was
forced into the 21st century, through the destruction of their lifestyle and their territory
and resources (Blackman, 2006). Canada authorized the Department of National
Defense to lease a large tract of land for air weapons training (Blackman, 2006), and
is also actively involved in the exploitation of BRDN's natural resources, including oil,
timber, diamonds and uranium within BRDN traditional territory (Blackman, 2006).

Neither the Saskatchewan court nor the Supreme Court of Canada (the latter, on
18 April 2002, dismissed the application of Mr Catarat and Mr Sylvestre to appeal to the
Court of Appeal of Saskatchewan) defended the rights of this community, and a petition
is presently before the Inter-American Court of Human Rights. The community also
would like to present its case before the International Court of Justice (but so far the
court has not given it standing to do so), as well as the International Criminal Court, as
a human rights violation under CERD.

This is just one of the many examples of such cases of human rights abuses we
have discussed in this work. That is the main reason that intervention by the WHA is
advocated:

> *The destruction of the land to which the people of BRDN is connected leads to the
> destruction of the Dene as a people and Nation. As this kind of destruction carried out
> by multinational societies and governments is now global, this process of genocide of
> indigenous communities is also global.* (Blackman, 2006)

This statement by the representative of the indigenous community puts the reality of
the situation in simple terms, and much better than many of the court decisions I have
examined. But it remains mostly rhetoric, unless the clear connection between industrial
and other activities and the land and its inhabitants is made clear in scientific, rather
than purely emotional terms. The truth is plainly there, in the words of this Dene, but
the scientific proof to lay bare the connection of which he speaks must be provided by
the appropriate scientific organs of the UN, if the protection of human rights is to be
more than a collection of high-sounding words.

ENVIRONMENTAL JUSTICE: GLOBAL
GOVERNANCE FOR ECOLOGICAL INTEGRITY

The promotion of the right to health is explicitly present in the 'Preamble' of the
WHO Constitution.[47] In addition, the WHO 'has the legal capacity to initiate discussion
among member nations and to serve as a platform for international law-making efforts

in relation to the right to health' (Taylor, 1992). It can also develop regulations under its constitution (Article 21), and under Article 19 it can work on conventions; under Article 23, it can make recommendations to states on any matter on which it is competent to speak.[48] In contrast, it is important to note that, according to Susan Connor (1990), a legal consultant to the WHO, 'We have the ability under WHO Constitution to issue regulations and conventions that can be legally binding in form. We generally do not do that.'

Hence, even a right proclaiming the intent to foster 'Health for All' with a target year of 2000, indicating an evolution of the WHO towards human rights, does not demonstrate a clear change in priorities, 'from its traditional functional role to a more assertive posture addressing health crises' (Taylor, 1992).

A major stumbling block remains the passive stance of the WHO, except when it addresses clearly defined technical issues (for example, SARS, avian flu, and the like), rather than taking an aggressive, prescriptive stance on issues affecting global health. Nevertheless the Tobacco Convention was one such leadership role that the WHO did not shirk.

The Eighth General 'Programme of Work', in response to emerging global issues,[49] includes the need to address 'toxic chemicals,' after listing tobacco but before HIV/ Aids. Hence, perhaps there is hope that, like other UN organs, the WHO will move forward indicting present human rights abuses and bringing to task all nations that do not prioritize the right to health for all, starting with their most vulnerable populations, the aboriginal communities.

The difficulties involved in such a plan are vast. First, the change from a traditional, low-key, technically advisory role, to one of law/policymaking cannot be an easy one. Second, the economic question is usually brought in as an insurmountable obstacle, but the WHO could respond by underlining the fact that 'it is more a question of priorities than of resources', and that the health sector is, presently, 'one of the most underfunded areas of national financing' (Taylor, 1992). On this topic, especially for countries with social health care, the expenditures funded by taxes to mitigate the surge of disease following the continuation of the status quo, would more than outweigh the expenses required to ameliorate/restrain current practices, whose 'benefits' (for example, profits) are limited to the shareholders/CEOs of the corporations involved, and do not 'trickle down' in any meaningful way to the affected people, especially indigenous groups (in the European Ministers Conference convened by the WHO in 2002, several national representatives remarked on the question of the health costs of the status quo).

In addition, the pressure exerted on the state parties by TNCs at most WHO conferences – especially those involved in the most dangerous operations, such as the chemical industry – is undeniable. They participate in ministerial meetings and they bring their power to bear to ensure that any motion to eliminate their present hazardous activities and products is defeated, if possible, or at least modified or postponed indefinitely.

In conclusion, any effort to establish ecological integrity in global governance should start with the WHO taking its rightful place on the world stage in defence of all peoples, starting with the people of aboriginal communities. The aim of this work has been to examine the existing situation of indigenous peoples regarding the protection of their human rights.

It is obvious, and largely undisputed in international and domestic law, that justice for aboriginal communities *starts* with environmental justice: not only their right to the historical territories and lands they have occupied, but, equally, if not more important, with the ecological health of those lands. If indigenous peoples have the right to occupy certain territories and to pursue their traditional lifestyle activities there, then the *preconditions* upon which these rights are based are in fact their *first right*.

In Chapter 1, I proposed to term that right the right to biological/ecological integrity. The ecological component refers to the condition of the lands and territories; the biological aspect applies to the protection of health and normal function for individuals and populations. Neither is an easy position to adopt in a world saturated with the economic values of globalization and the post-modern, neoliberal thrust of individualism.

Lawrence Gostin (2004) noted the problem in regard to public health, which he described as an ideal that has been superseded by the quest for individual freedoms, largely incompatible with communitarian obligations. Of course, this is a universal problem and not limited to indigenous peoples. But given their communitarian belief system and their particular relations to the lands they occupy, and hence their vulnerability, consideration for their position should be primary in a generally desirable effort to correct and modify present regulatory regimes and legal instruments.

The full extent of the harms perpetrated by the status quo cannot be exposed unless the interface between environment and health is laid bare, hence this work's emphasis on public health and on the specific UN organ, the WHO, whose mandate it is to ensure and protect it. When representatives of the WHO appear at various official meetings and are reported in the media worldwide to declare on the hazards of this or that turkey or poultry operation, the fact that several industrial operations are going to suffer economic losses is not an issue that is weighed in the balance. The same was true when the origins of 'mad cow disease' were discovered (McCalman and Cook, 1998). The representatives of the WHO spoke clearly, forcefully and authoritatively, as they also do when various epidemics emerge, undeterred by the economic implications of their pronouncements.

I am simply proposing that they might follow the same path, as it is *their* research that has revealed the connection between chemical exposures and disease and abnormalities, together with work of many scientists who collaborate with them. It is also *their* research and that of their collaborators that has led to the formulation of the directive known as REACH (Registration, Evaluation and Authorization of Chemicals).[50] The powerful chemical industry cannot be compared to poultry farming, although the beef industry is also large and powerful. But the realities are similar, no matter how wealthy and powerful are those who might face an economic loss because the effects of their operations and products are made public. The WHO *was* indeed successful in the case of 'big tobacco', so that perhaps 'big chemistry' might be next in their sights.

Unless the WHO articulates clearly the results of its own research to the public, starting with legislators, judges and advocates, the descriptive, anecdotal recitations of the representative of indigenous communities remain the observations of social science, at best, rather than the hard fact of medical science that they are, and the connection to human rights and humanitarian law is lost.

Women's groups and advocates have fought long and hard to ensure the inclusion of rape among the acts of genocide. That inclusion now permits raising the level of those attacks to other crimes listed as attacks against the human person or genocide, and codified in international law. I propose that the same effort on the part of those who are already committed to the cause of aboriginal peoples might also serve to raise the level of their harms in international law. This would require, initially, a courageous stance on the part of the WHO to ensure the legitimacy of the health claims I propose. As an organ of the UN, it should be their clear obligation to work together with other UN committees to fulfil the aims of other conventions sponsored by the UN, such as CERD and others, to do their share to bring about the protection of aboriginal communities globally.

NOTES

1   UN World Conference on Human Rights, Vienna Declaration and Programme of Action, UN Doc. A/CONF.157/24 (Part I) (1993), 32 ILM 1661 (1993).
2   Universal Declaration of Human Rights, GA Res. 217A, UNGA OR, 3d Sess., pt. 1, UN Doc. A/810(198); UN Conference on the Human Environment, UN Doc. A/CONF.48/14 Rev. and Corr.1(1972), 11 ILM 1416(1972).
3   Proclamation of Tehran, International Conference on Human Rights, 1968 YB on HR 458; UN General Assembly Resolution 32/130 (1977); see also Van Boven (1979).
4   UN Doc. A/CONF.151/5/P v.1 (1992), 31 ILM 874(1992).
5   International Covenant on Civil and Political Rights, 999 UNTS 171, in force 23 March 1976, 6 ILM 368 (1967); (ICPR); and the International Covenant on Economic, Social and Cultural Rights, (1966) UNTS 3 (ICESCR).
6   Vienna Convention on the Law of Treaties, 115 UNTS 331, 8 ILM 679 (1969).
7   UNESCO Convention Concerning the Protection of the World Cultural and Natural Heritage, 11 ILM (1972) 1358.
8   Convention Concerning Indigenous and Tribal Peoples, ILO No. 169, 27 July 1989, 28 ILM 1382 (1989), into force 5 September 1991.
9   UN Framework Convention on Biological Diversity, 5 Treaty Doc. No. 103-20, ILM 818 (1992).
10   *Le Louis*, 2 Dodson, Rep. 238.
11   See also The Convention of the Hague, A.4 and A.6 regarding the imperative of military necessity.
12   See The Trials of German Major War Criminals Proceedings of the International Military Tribunal Sitting at Nuremberg, Germany, Vol. 22, 1950, London.
13   Doc. UNESCO WHC 05/29.COM/9, 15 June 2005.
14   Orientations Para.9; see also Convention, A.11, para.4.
15   ibid.
16   This had not happened by May 2007; the Draft's text is at the Sub-Commission resolution 1994/45, UN Sub-Commission on Prevention of Discrimination and Protection of Minorities, Report of the Sub-Commission on Prevention of Discrimination and Protection of Minorities on its 46th Section, UN Doc. E/CN.4/Sub.2/1994/56(1994).
17   See for instance the Declaration on the Rights of Persons Belonging to National or Ethnic, Religious and Linguistic Minorities, UNGAOR, 47th Sess., Supp., No.49, at 210, UN Doc. A/47/49 (1992); also the Framework Convention for the Protection of National Minorities, 1 February 1995, Europ.T.S. 157.
18   International Covenant on Civil and Political Rights, G.A. Res.2200 GAOR, 21st Sess., Supp. No.16, at 49, UNDoc.A/6316.

19 *Ominyak v. Canada*, UN GAOR, 45th Sess., Supp. No. 40, Annex 9 at 27, UN Doc. A/45/40 (1990).
20 See *N.Z. Maori Council v. Attorney General* [1987] 1 NZLR 1641); in Canada, *Delgamuukw v. British Columbia* [1997] 3.S.C.R. 1010, 1067-68.
21 See for instance *G. and E. v. Norway Apps.*, No. 9278/81 and 9415/81, 35 Eur. Comm'n H.R. Doc. And Rep. 30, 35 (1984).
22 Draft Declaration on the Rights of Indigenous Peoples, Working Group on Indigenous Populations (11th Sess.) Commission on Human Rights, Sub-Commission on Prevention of Discrimination and Protection of Minorities, 44th Sess. Agenda Item 14, at 50, Annex I, UN Doc. E/CN.4/Sub.2/1993/29(1993).
23 Agreement on Identity and Rights of Indigenous Peoples, UN GAOR, 49th Sess., Agenda Item 42, Annex, UN Doc. A./49/882, S/1995/256 (1995).
24 The Indigenous Peoples Rights Act, Republic Act No. 8371 (1997) (Phil.); see www.bwf.org.
25 See for instance the Treaty of Waitangi, Treaty of Cession, 5–6 February 1840, Gr. Britain-N.Z., 89 C sol.T.S. 473; also the treaties listed in Chapter 6, regarding Canadian First Nations.
26 See *Hopu and Besent v. France*, UN GAOR, 52nd Sess., Supp., No. 4, UN Doc. A/52/40 (1997); see also *Lyng v. N.W. Indian Cemetery Protective Association*, 485 US 439 (1988).
27 *Santa Clara County v. South Pacific Railroads Corp.*, 1886.
28 Convention for the Protection of Human Rights and Fundamental Freedoms, Rome, 4 November 1950 T.S. 71 (1953).
29 See *Guerra v. Italy*, 116/1996/735/932, 19 February 1998; *Lopez-Ostra v. Spain*, (1995) EHRR 277, (1994) ECHR 16798/90.
30 The Oxford University Press English Dictionary Online (Oxford University Press, 2003, at www.oed.com) defines 'home' as a 'dwelling place, house, abode; the fixed residence of a family or household; the seat of domestic life and interest; one's own house; the dwelling in which one habitually lives, or which one regards as one's proper abode'.
31 *Chorozow Factory* case, PCIJ, Ser. A, No. 17, p. 29.
32 Trade and Development Board, 11th Sess., Geneva 19–23 March 2007, TD/B/COM.1/CRP.4; WTO Report.
33 ibid.
34 Declaration on the Principles of International Law Concerning Friendly Relations and Cooperation among States in Accordance with the Charter of the United Nations, 24 October 1970 (2625) XXV.
35 ibid.
36 A summary of the Earth Charter endorsements follows:

Approved Endorsers

Endorse Category	*Number of Endorsers*
(With no category)	158
Business	270
Faith group	278
Government agencies	25
Individual	13,240
Local government	457
NGO	1,474
School	363
University	150
Total	16,415

Not approved Endorsers

Endorse Category	Number of Endorsers
(With no category)	6
Individual	819
NGO	1
Total	826

See also www.earthcharter.org

37   *Gabcikovo-Nagymaros* case, ICJ (1997) Rep.

38   See also First Nations and Inuit Regional Health Survey Steering Committee, 2003, *First Nations and Inuit Regional Health Survey*, Ottawa.

39   Report of the Royal Commission on Aboriginal Peoples, Vol. 3, table 4.1, according to the 1991 Aboriginal Peoples Survey.

40   ibid.

41   Anecdotally, in Canada at least, several other groups were discriminated against, although it was mostly a case of discrimination and being viewed 'not quite like' other Canadians. As an Italo-Canadian I recall vividly the slurs and demeaning remarks I received, including the suggestion that, as I was blond and had light eyes, I could 'pass' for a regular Canadian at my place of employment, in the late 1950s and early 1960s in Toronto, Canada.

42   The World Health Authority (WHA) the legislative organ of WHO, issued the WHA Res. 30.43, 30th World Health Assembly, 14th plenary meeting (19 May 1977), in *2 World Health Organization, Handbook of Resolutions and Decisions of the World Health Assembly and the Executive Board,* 197301984 1 (1985).

43   Resolution 2006/2 – Working group of the Commission on Human Rights to elaborate a draft declaration in accordance with paragraph 5 of the General Assembly resolution 49/214 of 23 December 1994.

44   Report of the Working Group on its 11th Sess., Geneva, 5–16 December 2005, and 30 January–3 February (2006 (E/CN.4/2006/79).

45   UN GAOR, 21st Sess., Supp. No. 16, 49, UN Doc. A/6315 (1966).

46   International Bill of Human Rights, UN Doc. A/565 (1948).

47   WHO, *Basic Documents* 4-8 (38th edn, 1990).

48   The full texts of the articles cited are as follows:

> *ARTICLE 19:*
> *The Health Assembly shall have authority to adopt conventions or agreements with respect to any matter within the competence of the Organization. A two-thirds vote of the Health Assembly shall be required for the adoption of such conventions or agreements which shall come into force for each Member when accepted by it in accordance with its constitutional processes.*
>
> *ARTICLE 21:*
> *The Health Assembly shall have authority to adopt regulations concerning:*
> *(a) sanitary and quarantine requirements and other procedures designed to prevent the international spread of disease;*
> *(b) nomenclatures with respect to diseases, causes of death and public health practices;*
> *(c) standards with respect to diagnostic procedures for international use;*
> *(d) standards with respect to the safety, purity and potency of biological, pharmaceutical and similar products moving in international commerce;*
> *(e) advertising and labelling of biological, pharmaceutical and similar products moving in international commerce.*
>
> *ARTICLE 23*
> *The Health Assembly shall have authority to make recommendations to Members with respect to any matter within the competence of the Organization.*

49 WHO, Eighth General Programme of Work Covering the Period 1990–1995, 37–38 (1987).
50 Registration, Evaluation and Authorization of Chemicals (REACH); COM(03) 644(01) on
    REACH, COM (03) 644(02) amending Directive 67/548/EEC, REACH entered into force
    on 1 June 2007.

The Earth Charter
March 2000

PREAMBLE

We stand at a critical moment in Earth's history, a time when humanity must choose its future. As the world becomes increasingly interdependent and fragile, the future at once holds great peril and great promise. To move forward we must recognize that in the midst of a magnificent diversity of cultures and life forms we are one human family and one Earth community with a common destiny. We must join together to bring forth a sustainable global society founded on respect for nature, universal human rights, economic justice, and a culture of peace. Towards this end, it is imperative that we, the peoples of Earth, declare our responsibility to one another, to the greater community of life, and to future generations.

Earth, Our Home

Humanity is part of a vast evolving universe. Earth, our home, is alive with a unique community of life. The forces of nature make existence a demanding and uncertain adventure, but Earth has provided the conditions essential to life's evolution. The resilience of the community of life and the well-being of humanity depend upon preserving a healthy biosphere with all its ecological systems, a rich variety of plants and animals, fertile soils, pure waters, and clean air. The global environment with its finite resources is a common concern of all peoples. The protection of Earth's vitality, diversity, and beauty is a sacred trust.

The Global Situation

The dominant patterns of production and consumption are causing environmental devastation, the depletion of resources, and a massive extinction of species. Communities are being undermined. The benefits of development are not shared equitably and the gap between rich and poor is widening. Injustice, poverty, ignorance, and violent conflict are widespread and the cause of great suffering. An unprecedented rise in human population has overburdened ecological and social systems. The foundations of global security are threatened. These trends are perilous – but not inevitable.

The Challenges Ahead

The choice is ours: form a global partnership to care for Earth and one another or risk the destruction of ourselves and the diversity of life. Fundamental changes are needed in our values, institutions, and ways of living. We must realize that when basic needs have been met, human development is primarily about being more, not having more. We have the knowledge and technology to provide for all and to reduce our impacts on the environment. The emergence of a global civil society is creating new opportunities to build a democratic and humane world. Our environmental, economic, political, social, and spiritual challenges are interconnected, and together we can forge inclusive solutions.

Universal Responsibility

To realize these aspirations, we must decide to live with a sense of universal responsibility, identifying ourselves with the whole Earth community as well as our local communities. We are at once citizens of different nations and of one world in which the local and global are linked. Everyone shares responsibility for the present and future well-being of the human family and the larger living world. The spirit of human solidarity and kinship with all life is strengthened when we live with reverence for the mystery of being, gratitude for the gift of life, and humility regarding the human place in nature.

We urgently need a shared vision of basic values to provide an ethical foundation for the emerging world community. Therefore, together in hope we affirm the following interdependent principles for a sustainable way of life as a common standard by which the conduct of all individuals, organizations, businesses, governments, and transnational institutions is to be guided and assessed.

PRINCIPLES

I. RESPECT AND CARE FOR THE COMMUNITY OF LIFE

1. Respect Earth and life in all its diversity

a. Recognize that all beings are interdependent and every form of life has value regardless of its worth to human beings.

b. Affirm faith in the inherent dignity of all human beings and in the intellectual, artistic, ethical, and spiritual potential of humanity.

2. Care for the community of life with understanding, compassion, and love

a. Accept that with the right to own, manage, and use natural resources comes the duty to prevent environmental harm and to protect the rights of people.

b. Affirm that with increased freedom, knowledge, and power comes increased responsibility to promote the common good.

3. Build democratic societies that are just, participatory, sustainable, and peaceful

a. Ensure that communities at all levels guarantee human rights and fundamental freedoms and provide everyone an opportunity to realize his or her full potential.

b. Promote social and economic justice, enabling all to achieve a secure and meaningful livelihood that is ecologically responsible.

4. Secure Earth's bounty and beauty for present and future generations

a. Recognize that the freedom of action of each generation is qualified by the needs of future generations.

b. Transmit to future generations values, traditions, and institutions that support the long-term flourishing of Earth's human and ecological communities.

In order to fulfill these four broad commitments, it is necessary to:

II. ECOLOGICAL INTEGRITY

5. Protect and restore the integrity of Earth's ecological systems, with special concern for biological diversity and the natural processes that sustain life

a. Adopt at all levels sustainable development plans and regulations that make environmental conservation and rehabilitation integral to all development initiatives.

b. Establish and safeguard viable nature and biosphere reserves, including wild lands and marine areas, to protect Earth's life support systems, maintain biodiversity, and preserve our natural heritage.

c. Promote the recovery of endangered species and ecosystems.

d. Control and eradicate non-native or genetically modified organisms harmful to native species and the environment, and prevent introduction of such harmful organisms.

e. Manage the use of renewable resources such as water, soil, forest products, and marine life in ways that do not exceed rates of regeneration and that protect the health of ecosystems.

f. Manage the extraction and use of non-renewable resources such as minerals and fossil fuels in ways that minimize depletion and cause no serious environmental damage.

6. Prevent harm as the best method of environmental protection and, when knowledge is limited, apply a precautionary approach

a. Take action to avoid the possibility of serious or irreversible environmental harm even when scientific knowledge is incomplete or inconclusive.

b. Place the burden of proof on those who argue that a proposed activity will not cause significant harm, and make the responsible parties liable for environmental harm.

c. Ensure that decision making addresses the cumulative, long-term, indirect, long distance, and global consequences of human activities.

d. Prevent pollution of any part of the environment and allow no build-up of radioactive, toxic, or other hazardous substances.

e. Avoid military activities damaging to the environment.

7. Adopt patterns of production, consumption, and reproduction that safeguard Earth's regenerative capacities, human rights, and community well-being

a. Reduce, reuse, and recycle the materials used in production and consumption systems, and ensure that residual waste can be assimilated by ecological systems.

b. Act with restraint and efficiency when using energy, and rely increasingly on renewable energy sources such as solar and wind.

c. Promote the development, adoption, and equitable transfer of environmentally sound technologies.

d. Internalize the full environmental and social costs of goods and services in the selling price, and enable consumers to identify products that meet the highest social and environmental standards.

e. Ensure universal access to health care that fosters reproductive health and responsible reproduction.

f. Adopt lifestyles that emphasize the quality of life and material sufficiency in a finite world.

8. Advance the study of ecological sustainability and promote the open exchange and wide application of the knowledge acquired

a. Support international scientific and technical cooperation on sustainability, with special attention to the needs of developing nations.

b. Recognize and preserve the traditional knowledge and spiritual wisdom in all cultures that contribute to environmental protection and human well-being.

c. Ensure that information of vital importance to human health and environmental protection, including genetic information, remains available in the public domain.

III. SOCIAL AND ECONOMIC JUSTICE

9. Eradicate poverty as an ethical, social, and environmental imperative

a. Guarantee the right to potable water, clean air, food security, uncontaminated soil, shelter, and safe sanitation, allocating the national and international resources required.

b. Empower every human being with the education and resources to secure a sustainable livelihood, and provide social security and safety nets for those who are unable to support themselves.

c. Recognize the ignored, protect the vulnerable, serve those who suffer, and enable them to develop their capacities and to pursue their aspirations.

10. Ensure that economic activities and institutions at all levels promote human development in an equitable and sustainable manner

a. Promote the equitable distribution of wealth within nations and among nations.

b. Enhance the intellectual, financial, technical, and social resources of developing nations, and relieve them of onerous international debt.

c. Ensure that all trade supports sustainable resource use, environmental protection, and progressive labor standards.

d. Require multinational corporations and international financial organizations to act transparently in the public good, and hold them accountable for the consequences of their activities.

11. Affirm gender equality and equity as prerequisites to sustainable development and ensure universal access to education, health care, and economic opportunity

a. Secure the human rights of women and girls and end all violence against them.

b. Promote the active participation of women in all aspects of economic, political, civil, social, and cultural life as full and equal partners, decision makers, leaders, and beneficiaries.

c. Strengthen families and ensure the safety and loving nurture of all family members.

12. Uphold the right of all, without discrimination, to a natural and social environment supportive of human dignity, bodily health, and spiritual well-being, with special attention to the rights of indigenous peoples and minorities

a. Eliminate discrimination in all its forms, such as that based on race, color, sex, sexual orientation, religion, language, and national, ethnic or social origin.

b. Affirm the right of indigenous peoples to their spirituality, knowledge, lands and resources and to their related practice of sustainable livelihoods.

c. Honor and support the young people of our communities, enabling them to fulfill their essential role in creating sustainable societies.

d. Protect and restore outstanding places of cultural and spiritual significance.

IV. DEMOCRACY, NONVIOLENCE, AND PEACE

13. Strengthen democratic institutions at all levels, and provide transparency and accountability in governance, inclusive participation in decision making, and access to justice

a. Uphold the right of everyone to receive clear and timely information on environmental matters and all development plans and activities which are likely to affect them or in which they have an interest.

b. Support local, regional and global civil society, and promote the meaningful participation of all interested individuals and organizations in decision making.

c. Protect the rights to freedom of opinion, expression, peaceful assembly, association, and dissent.

d. Institute effective and efficient access to administrative and independent judicial procedures, including remedies and redress for environmental harm and the threat of such harm.

e. Eliminate corruption in all public and private institutions.

f. Strengthen local communities, enabling them to care for their environments, and assign environmental responsibilities to the levels of government where they can be carried out most effectively.

14. Integrate into formal education and life-long learning the knowledge, values, and skills needed for a sustainable way of life

a. Provide all, especially children and youth, with educational opportunities that empower them to contribute actively to sustainable development.

b. Promote the contribution of the arts and humanities as well as the sciences in sustainability education.

c. Enhance the role of the mass media in raising awareness of ecological and social challenges.

d. Recognize the importance of moral and spiritual education for sustainable living.

15. Treat all living beings with respect and consideration

a. Prevent cruelty to animals kept in human societies and protect them from suffering.

b. Protect wild animals from methods of hunting, trapping, and fishing that cause extreme, prolonged, or avoidable suffering.

c. Avoid or eliminate to the full extent possible the taking or destruction of non-targeted species.

16. Promote a culture of tolerance, nonviolence, and peace

a. Encourage and support mutual understanding, solidarity, and cooperation among all peoples and within and among nations.

b. Implement comprehensive strategies to prevent violent conflict and use collaborative problem solving to manage and resolve environmental conflicts and other disputes.

c. Demilitarize national security systems to the level of a non-provocative defense posture, and convert military resources to peaceful purposes, including ecological restoration.

d. Eliminate nuclear, biological, and toxic weapons and other weapons of mass destruction.

e. Ensure that the use of orbital and outer space supports environmental protection and peace.

f. Recognize that peace is the wholeness created by right relationships with oneself, other persons, other cultures, other life, Earth, and the larger whole of which all are a part.

THE WAY FORWARD

As never before in history, common destiny beckons us to seek a new beginning. Such renewal is the promise of these Earth Charter principles. To fulfill this promise, we must commit ourselves to adopt and promote the values and objectives of the Charter.

This requires a change of mind and heart. It requires a new sense of global interdependence and universal responsibility. We must imaginatively develop and apply the vision of a sustainable way of life locally, nationally, regionally, and globally. Our cultural diversity is a precious heritage and different cultures will find their own distinctive ways to realize the vision. We must deepen and expand the global dialogue that generated the Earth Charter, for we have much to learn from the ongoing collaborative search for truth and wisdom.

Life often involves tensions between important values. This can mean difficult choices. However, we must find ways to harmonize diversity with unity, the exercise of freedom with the common good, short-term objectives with long-term goals. Every individual, family, organization, and community has a vital role to play. The arts, sciences, religions, educational institutions, media, businesses, nongovernmental organizations, and governments are all called to offer creative leadership. The partnership of government, civil society, and business is essential for effective governance.

In order to build a sustainable global community, the nations of the world must renew their commitment to the United Nations, fulfill their obligations under existing international agreements, and support the implementation of Earth Charter principles with an international legally binding instrument on environment and development.

Let ours be a time remembered for the awakening of a new reverence for life, the firm resolve to achieve sustainability, the quickening of the struggle for justice and peace, and the joyful celebration of life.

The Earth Charter Initiative,
International Secretariat
The Earth Council
P.O. Box 319-6100
San Jose, Costa Rica
Tel: +506-205-1600
Fax: +506-249-3500
Email: info@earthcharter.org

'Development' and Environmental Racism: The Case of Ken Saro-Wiwa and the Ogoni

The environment is man's first right
We should not allow it to suffer blight
The air we breathe we must not poison
They who do should be sent to prison
Our streams must remain clean all season
Polluting them is clearly treason
The land is life for man and flora,
Fauna and all, should wear that aura
Protected from the greed and folly
Of man and companies unholy.

> Ken Saro-Wiwa, A Walk in the
> Prison Yard, 1994

Last Monday I got news of the five attempts
it took before they finally hanged him. In the
Wild West they would let you walk at the
failure of the first attempt. I will remember
the words, 'Why are you doing this?'. I
also heard that he said, before they were
all martyred: 'Lord take my soul, but the
struggle continues'. (Seremba, 1995)

Seremba (1995) is referring to the murder of Ken Saro-Wiwa on 10 November 1995, an unspeakable crime committed by General Abacha and his military tribunal, with the complicity of Nigeria's powerful elites, but also with the tacit support of Royal Dutch Shell Oil, and of all of us who over-consume and overuse in the affluent North–West countries. For the most part, our silent complicity and our responsibility goes unnoticed and unacknowledged. Therefore, after briefly detailing a chronology of Nigeria's history from June 1993 to February 1995 and presenting Ken Saro-Wiwa's case, I argue for the need for a new approach to personal morality and public policy that includes an *environmental* assessment of all technological projects. I also argue that a holistic assessment of all developmental issues

is the only approach capable of imposing respect for all life-support systems, and hence for all human and non-human life.

NIGERIA UNDER THE DICTATORSHIP OF SANI ABACHA: KEN SARO-WIWA AND THE OGONI PEOPLE

The events of 1995 and the killing of Ken Saro-Wiwa may be traced as the culmination of two separate but intertwined historical lines, one tracing the political developments in Nigeria, the other, that country's economic interaction with oil companies, primarily Royal Dutch Shell Oil and Exxon.

Political developments

In June 1993, General Babangida sanctioned presidential elections in Nigeria. Chief M. K. O. Abiola was the clear winner, but Babangida cancelled the elections after the fact, claiming that fraud had been committed. The international community reacted by cancelling all but humanitarian aid, suspending military cooperation and restricting visas to Nigeria. Wole Soyinka (1994) describes what happened:

> On June 23, 1993, the day of the annul-
> ment of the presidential election, the mili-
> tary committed the most treasonable act of
> larceny of all time: it violently robbed the
> Nigerian people of their nationhood.

Through the summer months of July and August, the country was plagued by demonstrations and several hundred were killed in clashes. The government in power detained human rights workers and charged them with 'sedition', 'unlawful assembly' and other 'crimes'. At this time, both Babangida and Shonekan, his intended successor, were ousted by General Sani Abacha.

In November 1993, Abacha disbanded all elected bodies, such as the state legislature, 30 houses of state assemblies, all local councils, and banned all political activity. He also suspended the 1979 Constitution, including all provisions for human rights carried by that document. In April 1994, a civil disturbance tribunal was established with the power to impose the death penalty: capital offences now included 'unrest crimes' and 'attempted murder'. By May 1994, four Ogoni leaders were murdered and several hundred people, supporters of the Movement for Survival of the Ogoni People (MOSOP) were arrested, including Ken Saro-Wiwa.

The documents of Amnesty International (1995) relate that 'he was severely beaten, his legs chained'. Former senators, governors and members of the House of Representatives were also detained without charge. From June to September, a major Gas and Oil Union went on strike, causing riots and protests, and President Clinton sent Jesse Jackson as a special envoy to attempt mediation. This effort was unsuccessful and the whole Nigerian Labour Congress, representing 40 unions and 3.5 million workers joined the strike. This prompted the authorities to dissolve all unions and to replace their leaders with government-appointed officials. In September, the strike collapsed, and General Abacha issued a series of decrees, retroactive to mid-August, allowing 'administrative detention laws, for up to three months, renewable', and specifying further that this particular law could not be challenged in court.

Abacha also fired Attorney General Olu Onagoruwa, and arrested union officials and leaders. In 1995, a ban on all political activities was executed and still, no time was set for the regime's departure. In Ogoniland, hundreds of villages were destroyed and hundreds killed, while Saro-Wiwa was still detained, suffering ongoing inhuman treatment and often tortured. He was expected to be tried by the Civil Disturbances Tribunal for the murder of four officials in Ogoniland.

Economic and technological developments

In 1958, Shell discovered oil in Ogoniland, 404 square miles of largely wild, fertile land, home to a variety of flowers, plants and animals, both terrestrial and marine, beyond its coast, and to 500,000 Ogoni people (Saro-Wiwa, 1994b). Chevron moved its oil exploration to Ogoniland in 1977, and both companies, jointly, have extracted an estimated US$30 billion worth of oil from Ogoniland. Saro-Wiwa (1994b) adds:

> *In return for this we have received nothing but a highly polluted land where associated gas burns twenty-four hours a day, belching carbon monoxide, carbon dioxide, methane and soot into the air; and oil spillage and blow-outs devastate much needed farmland, threatening human existence.*

Flora and fauna are all but dead, marine life is destroyed, the ecosystem is fast changing. Ogoni is a wasteland.

However Nigeria's military dictatorship was geographically removed from this devastation and enjoyed a mutually supportive relationship with the oil companies, as they depended on the wealth the oil companies provided. In turn, the oil companies depended on the dictatorship to ignore the environmental disasters they continued to create, without imposing restraints or demanding remediation or compensation for the land and people affected. Throughout this increasingly distressing state of affairs, Saro-Wiwa maintained that 'the environment is man's first right. Without a safe environment, man cannot live to claim other rights' (1994a). He also steadfastly opposed the devastation of Ogoniland, demanding remediation of environmental problems and royalties to assist his people. The Ogoni desperately needed help, as the families could no longer depend on the land and the sea, but had to have financial help and medical aid to mitigate the many ills besetting them and destroying not only their livelihoods, but also their health, as they were now living in 'absolute poverty' (Shiva, 1988). They had no access to safe water, to electricity, telephones, or any educational or health facilities (Saro-Wiwa, 1994a; 1994b).

Examples of the harms inflicted on the Ogoni people from Shell's economic exploitation abound. In one case, Grace Zorbidon was walking near her mud hut one night in January 1994, 'carrying a kerosene lantern to light her way'. She did not see 'the oil slick oozing from a rupture in a pipeline that runs hard up against her tiny village' (Brooks, 1994). When she put down her lantern, she was engulfed by flames and, in May 1994, was still lying on the floor of a healer's hut in terrible pain, and treated only with traditional potions made from leaves. Shell neither inquired after her, nor saw to her treatment or to the fate of the eight children of this subsistence farmer. Their excuse? Shell said they were 'hazy' on the accident, and could not substantiate Zorbidon's report because of the 'tensions in the area' (Brooks, 1994). Shell was much quicker to react to protests and demonstrations that had forced it to close its operations in early 1994. Shell's reaction was to 'ask for assistance' from the military authorities, who responded with swift and brutal retribution against the protesters.

The Nigerian government was not prepared to tolerate any interference with its business relations with Shell; neither human rights nor environmental concerns could be allowed to interfere. According to Brooks (1994), 'Nigeria's government depends on oil for 80 per cent of its income, and sees any threat to the industry as imperiling its shaky hold on power. Oil produced by Shell accounts for about half of these revenues.' Nigeria's military dictatorship and Shell operate as a 'joint venture', in which Shell holds a 30 per cent interest, the Nigerian government holds 55 per cent, Elf Aquitaine of France has 10 per cent, and Agip Francaise the remaining 5 per cent. Further, the US was also benefiting from the arrangement as they imported 36 per cent of Nigeria's oil production in 1993, which accounted for about 11 per cent of all US oil imports.

In all these large business transactions, what, if any, are the benefits the Ogoni have reaped from their land's exploitation? When large multinationals interact with impoverished developing countries, the benefits accrue primarily to their constituents in the affluent North. The usual 'trade-offs' offered in those cases are employment, 'improvements' such as roads, hospitals and schools, and remediation of environmental impacts. Shell's record appears to be dismal on all counts. 'Of Shell's 5000 employees in Nigeria, only 85 are Ogoni' (Brooks, 1994); there are 96 oil wells, two refineries, a petrochemical complex and a fertilizer plant in Ogoniland, but the only available hospital is described as an 'unfinished husk', and the promised schools are seldom open because there is no money available for teachers' salaries (Brooks, 1994).

In addition, Shell's spokesman, Mr. Nickson, claimed that Shell 'deplored' the military 'heavy-handed clampdowns and the pain and loss suffered by local communities' (Brooks, 1994). However, there is no record of Shell initiating any policy to ameliorate the Ogoni's lot or to mitigate the damage they had perpetrated. Given the strength of their economic interests in Shell's operations, the military continued to organize raids to 'punish' the Ogoni for obstructing Shell, and responded to protests by shooting into the crowd, killing and maiming civilians, using any pretext to lay entire villages to waste. The raids were often conducted by a mobile police unit, nicknamed 'Kill and Go'. On Easter Sunday, 1994, villagers who had fled the raids were felled by random shooting. 'One ten-year old girl says she was gang-raped. Three days later, the whites of her eyes were bloodshot, the flesh around them purple and swollen'; she explained that the soldiers attempted to gouge her eyes out, so that she would not be able to identify them (Brooks, 1994). Health facilities, says a European nurse, are minimal, and Shell refused to even pave the roads to prevent patients having to walk through the mud to reach the clinic.

What of the economic benefits? In response to increasing protests from the Ogoni, the government ostensibly offered 3 per cent of its oil revenues to them. In practice, these percentages never reached the Ogoni, as the money was spent in the tribal lands of the ruling majority instead, or vanished in corrupt deals (Brooks, 1994). As far as remediation is concerned, one example will suffice. More than 20 years ago, a spill near the village of Ebubu has not been cleaned to date; today, in 'an area the size of four football fields, cauliflower shaped extrusions of moist black tar cover the ground to a depth of about three feet' (Brooks, 1994). Shell claims that while unrest continues, they are not prepared to do any clean-up work, though it is worth noting that the spill occurred in the late 1960s.

As an additional corollary to the government's role in the economic development by the oil companies, foreign observers are denied access, and even a fact-finding mission from The Netherlands was denied permission to visit. Also, checkpoints were set up instead in order to monitor Western travellers. The *Wall Street Journal* reporter (Brooks, 1994) who compiled most of the data summarized in this section, concludes by relating her own experience:

> *When I approached an army officer to ask for the military's account of a violent incident, I was handed over to the secret police, held and interrogated for two days, and then deported 'for security reasons'.*

Although the US government commissioned a 'human rights report' on the Ogoni in 1993, the report only admitted 'some merit' to the Ogoni's claims, but refused to accept the definition of 'genocide' urged by Saro-Wiwa, as appropriate to describe the Ogoni's plight. Saro-Wiwa remarked that 'one thousand dead Ogonis out of five hundred thousand', is comparable to half a million dead US citizens, and had that situation occurred, it would surely have been termed a case of 'genocide'.

In essence, the perversion of human rights and the clear presence of racism (or even of attempts at 'ethnic cleansing') that was manifested by the oil companies with the support of the military dictatorship of Nigeria, was more than a particularly lethal case of environmental racism (Westra and Wenz, 1995). It was and is no less than an 'ecological war' that was being waged (and still persists); it is 'omnicide', according to Saro-Wiwa (1994b). He adds 'men, women and children die unnoticed, flora and fauna are threatened, the air is poisoned, waters are polluted, and, finally, the land itself dies' (Saro-Wiwa, 1994b).

AGAIN, A QUESTION OF RESPONSIBILITY

So far we have pointed to joint activities of the military regime under Sani Abacha and Shell Oil as the primary source of the crimes committed against the Ogoni and against their land. But are they the sole culprits? We can learn a lot from Shell's public relations response to Saro-Wiwa's murder, and the international revulsion and anger that followed. After all, Saro-Wiwa was well known as the recipient of several prizes and grants (the Goldman Environmental Prize (1995); the Right Livelihood Award (1994); and the Bruno Kreisky Human Rights Award (1995); the Goldman Environmental Prize was deliberately given to him in advance in the hope of drawing international attention to him, as he had already been declared a 'prisoner of conscience' by Amnesty International). A well-known poet, writer and activist, his death made an impact that Shell attempted to offset by buying prime space in international newspapers in an effort to shift blame for their actions and omissions; as they disclaimed any responsibility for either the environmental devastation or the murder.

In a carefully worded newspaper advertisement entitled 'Clear Thinking in Troubled Times' (Shell, 1995), Shell explicitly allied itself with 'clear thinking', and patronizingly dismissed a 'great wave of understandable emotion over the death of Ken Saro-Wiwa', together with the anger and disapprobation it faced from all nations. 'The public have been manipulated and misled', was one of its statements, as they attempted to whitewash themselves because they had spent millions on 'environmentally related projects'. The environmental problems were due, they claimed, to 'over-farming'(!), soil erosion, deforestation and population growth, in areas where only the most meagre subsistence farming existed (Shell, 1995). Geraldine Brooks (1994) describes it as 'pulling tubers from the earth with sticks'. Shell further appealed to a World Bank survey to support their position, but the World Bank was one of the few major powers who, together with the Royal Geographical Society, withdrew all their support from Nigeria in protest, and categorically denied Shell's allegations.

Shell also remarked that, after all, they were not the only ones at fault, as all humanitarian protests and even international sanctions could not (and in fact did not) succeed. One can speculate that no other 'sanctions' could prevail, as they would not carry the same clout for a money-hungry military clique as would the continued cash-producing presence of Shell and other oil companies.

Finally Shell raised a question and veiled threat common to all industries that are the target of environmental protests throughout the world. The ad continues, 'What if we were to withdraw from the project' and with it, withdraw all employment the project entails? 'The oil extraction would continue', they say, 'and it might not be done any better' (Shell, 1995). One could respond that other companies elsewhere *have* in fact done much better. For instance, Conoco DuPont drilled a well in Gabon between 1989 and 1992:

> ...*it flew in much of its equipment to avoid pushing a major road through the rain forest. When trees had to be felled, the company hired scientists to cultivate cuttings so that sites could be replanted with exactly the same species that had been removed.* (Westra and Wenz, 1995)

Hence a technology assessment based on a holistic management perspective would have made a large difference *at the outset*, rather than demand remediation after the fact, a largely useless procedure from the environmental standpoint, and – as we saw – based on total disrespect for human rights as well.

Even more appalling from the moral standpoint, was the final paragraph of Shell's page-long ad:

Some campaigning groups say we should intervene in the political process in Nigeria. But even if we could, we must never do so. Politics is the business of governments and politicians. The world where companies use their economic influence to prop up or bring down governments would be a frightening and bleak one indeed. (Shell, 1995)

It is both frightening and bleak to read such vicious travesty of the facts. Shell is a partner in the joint venture with Nigeria's ruthless and inhumane military regime, and knew full well the impact its financial support had on the latter's existence. Further, when negotiations and consent are *both* conducted and originate from unelected, unrepresentative authorities, one is clearly already meddling in the politics of the country with which one deals.

ENVIRONMENTAL ETHICS AND RESPONSIBILITY

Nevertheless, even ascribing responsibility for the gross miscarriage of justice and the environmental devastation of Ogoniland to Shell and the military regime of Nigeria is necessary, but not sufficient, for a serious ethical evaluation of the situation. Shell and others like them could quickly point out that they only have a profitable market for their operations because we, the affluent consumers, are hungry for abundant, low-cost oil and gasoline products. Hence, it is not enough to point the finger at Shell and other corporate exploiters. It is also necessary to confront the morality of our lifestyle and of our policy choices.

This is the raw, evil side of technological progress. It is eco-violence perpetrated against the most vulnerable people; it shows the worst face of environmental racism in a most deadly form. Retaliation against pro-environmental protest ended in a murder, orchestrated by a kangaroo court. Ken Saro-Wiwa was murdered by hanging in Nigeria on the morning of 10 November 1995. The dictatorial regime that plotted and executed his murder on a trumped-up charge was heavily dependent on the oil revenues generated by Shell's operations. The question now is, how should that technology have been evaluated before its impact on Nigeria was felt?

Traditional moral theories could and should indict the gross abuse of human rights that took place when Saro-Wiwa was murdered; they could decry the lack of justice and due process in his trial and sentencing and appeal to Rawlsian principles in defence of all the Ogoni people; finally, they could appeal to Bullard's (2001) 'five principles of environmental justice' to combat environmental racism (Shrader-Frechette, 1991). But all these arguments are end-of-pipe attempts at mitigation, after the fact. The fundamental question remains: how should the introduction of a large technological system of oil extraction have been evaluated in that particular part of the world and in that geographical area? From the ecocentric point of view, the environmental impact should have been anticipated, if not precisely, at least with enough accuracy to discourage Shell, unless an impartial international commission with veto powers, including both appropriate scientists and environmental ethicists, could have been put in place to oversee all Shell's plans and activities. In contrast, if we took a purely anthropocentric position for our starting point, we might still be able to put in place some restraints, based on risk assessments of the situation. But, without knowing the actual results of Shell's operations, it would have been extremely difficult to stop them or establish tight limits to their activities *before the fact*.

Hence, if we simply appealed to traditional moral principles, we might not have been able to stop the violence that followed. It also would have rendered us guilty of 'complicity', as would have our isolating ourselves from the information and simply turning our eyes while availing ourselves of these products' easy availability (Jonas, 1984). The question is one of moral responsibility, one that Hans Jonas (1984), for example, viewed as the most important question to be asked in regard to technology: for him responsibility was the 'keyword' for the ethics of human conduct in dealing with technology. Jonas (1984) argued that 'the new kinds and dimensions of action require a commensurate ethics of foresight and responsibility, which is as novel as the eventualities which it must meet'. Also, when 'foresight' is difficult because of science's lack of predictive capacities, since 'care for the future' is the 'overruling duty', we must face the fact that the only possible moral choices might be the careful application of the precautionary principle, or even abstention from certain non-basic lifestyle and technological choices (Jonas, 1984).

One wonders whether an appeal to traditional, anthropocentric moral doctrines is sufficient not only to address such problems, but also to prevent them from developing, in the face of increasing environmental disintegration and degradation, and mounting scarcity of resources as populations increase. Many have addressed the need to ensure that cost–benefit analyses and economic evaluations of technology are made to focus prominently on ethical considerations beyond aggregate utilities and majority preferences (Sagoff, 1988). I believe that the anthropocentric/non-anthropocentric distinction presents a false dichotomy in several senses, and that it is no more than a red herring, advanced by those concerned with defending the present status quo. Accordingly, they are led to propose a somewhat modified, 'greened' revamping of the same hazardous, uncritically accepted practices to which all life on Earth has been subjected.

Utilities and preferences are normally understood (in philosophical and political theory) as reflecting the wishes, and maybe the (descriptively) perceived 'good' of a society, as do appeals to rights, justice, fairness and due process. The question, however, is whether ethical considerations based on moral doctrines designed primarily for intraspecific interaction – that is, designed to guide our interpersonal behaviour – are in fact sufficient, as well as being clearly necessary to ensure that our activities conform to an inclusive and enlightened morality. Recent global change affecting our resource base everywhere *proves* the inadequacy of calculations that depend solely on economics, so that evaluations founded on moral doctrines and upholding both 'natural' and 'civil' rights appear indeed mandatory.

Would this approach have been sufficient to redress the terrible ills done to the Ogoni people and their land? In other words, had a democracy been in place, and had the citizens of Ogoniland been polled about their wishes in regard to the projects of Shell and other corporations, would that have been enough to save the environment on which they depend? One problem is that even if a technology impact assessment had been required and openly publicized, it is unlikely that a community of subsistence farmers would have been well informed enough to foresee the irreversible ecological damage that would have been their lot eventually, even if they would have received a fair percentage of the oil royalties, and roads, schools and clinics might have been built for their use. Saro-Wiwa would have known, but it is at least an open question whether he would have been listened to, before the fact.

This remains a routine problem whenever hazardous operations move into minority or economically depressed areas in their home countries, although perhaps both education and standards of living might be higher, comparatively, than those of the Ogoni (Westra and Wenz, 1995). Hence, I suggest that even in an ideal situation, where legal restraints on environmental hazards are in place and where democratic institutions prevail, the environmental and health protection of all are by no means guaranteed.

The basic problem for us, anywhere, is sustainability. Rees and Wackernagel (1996), for example, propose adopting an 'ecological world view', in contrast with the prevailing established 'expansionist world view', which represents 'the dominant social paradigm'. As Leopold (1949) did before them, Rees and Wackernagel (1996) recognize that we are not independent of, and separate from, an 'environment', but ecological sustainability is foundational, so that it makes perfectly good sense to abandon our present unsustainable and indefensible world view. They write, 'By contrast, an ecological economic perspective would see the human economy as an inextricably integrated, completely contained, and wholly dependent sub-system of the ecosphere.'

This position is supported by Rees and Wackernagels's research (1996) in the Vancouver–Lower Fraser Valley region of British Columbia, Canada, but can be easily generalized for all urban, affluent Northern centres. Their findings show that, assuming an average Canadian diet and current management practices, the local 'regional population support(s) its consumers' lifestyles [by importing] the productive capacity of at least 22 times as much land as it occupies'. To put this in a more general way, 'the ecological footprints of individual regions are much larger than the land areas they physically occupy' (Westra and Wenz, 1995).

When we continue to import others' carrying capacity, we are 'running an unaccounted ecological deficit, and our populations are appropriating carrying capacity from elsewhere or from future generations' (Rees and Wackernagel, 1996). The same can be said about 'sinks' for our wastes. For both resource appropriation and waste disposal, our Northern approach has been one of neo-colonialism in regard to less developed countries, and one of ruthless exploitation (through environmental racism) toward minorities and the disempowered in our own countries (Kamm and Greenberger, 1995).

Thus, it is both easy and even necessary to indict the military rule and the despotism that was instrumental in the killing of Ken Saro-Wiwa and the devastation of his land, plus the large corporations that wreaked havoc on the environment, leading to the Ogoni's protests and resistance, and these enterprises' callous and unjust exploitation of a vulnerable people for purely financial reasons. However, this is not enough.

On 13 November 1995, the *Wall Street Journal* reported that, although they issued 'sanction threats' and they cut (US) military aid, and although the UK banned arms sales and the EU recalled its ambassadors and suspended all aid, *no nation* had 'halted purchases of Nigerian oil or sales of drilling equipment, as a result of the hangings' (Kamm and Greenberger, 1995; see also French, 1995). Halting the oil trade would bring Nigeria to its knees, as oil represents 90 per cent of its exports and 80 per cent of its revenue; but the US would *also* be hard hit, as it imports 40 per cent of Nigeria's oil. Hence, the US recalled its ambassador, but did not make the principled stand made by the World Bank. The International Finance Corporation (private sector lending for the World Bank) withdrew its support in the form of a US$100,000 loan to Nigeria for a liquefied natural gas project (Kamm and Greenberger, 1995).

The problem is that, as long as we elect leaders and governments on the basis of promises of low taxes and low prices, as well as the 'right' to development, without any consideration of the *size* of our ecological footprint, let alone its *location* (that is to say, without considering who is to pay for our choices), we cannot claim to be free from responsibility. Each one of us is, to some extent, an accomplice and a contributor to the evil deeds perpetrated in Nigeria.

It is both what we *do* and what we *fail to do* that is at stake. In essence, we cannot continue to consume and to waste as though we had the *right* to take from the poor and the vulnerable, just because we can afford it. We must reconsider our political choices when these are explicitly insular, isolationist and segregationist in intent, and when they are both supported by and supportive of big business, such as oil companies, tobacco producers, manufacturers of chemicals or transgenics, all of which (in their present forms) often spell death for our environment, and ensure severe threats to our health and to the persistence of our species on Earth. Thus the problem is a question of personal as well as ecological integrity: it is a moral problem to which no facile solutions exist at this time. In some sense, Ken Saro-Wiwa died because of our moral failures, our negligence and our lack of commitment to justice and a moral ideal.

This, however, is one case where the law is moving slowly to attempt to redress *some* of the unspeakable harms that occurred. In New York, the son of Ken Saro-Wiwa, has initiated an action under the Alien Torts Claims Act.

DRAFT DECLARATION OF PRINCIPLES FOR THE DEFENCE OF THE INDIGENOUS NATIONS AND PEOPLES OF THE WESTERN HEMISPHERE

Developed and circulated by indigenous participants at the Non-Governmental Organization Conference on Discrimination Against Indigenous Populations, Geneva, 1977, reprinted in UN Doc. E/CN.4/Sub.2/476/Add.5, Annex 4 (1981).

Preamble

Having considered the problems relating to the activities of the United Nations for the promotion and encouragement of respect for human rights and fundamental freedoms,

Noting that the Universal Declaration of Human Rights and related international covenants have the individual as their primary concern, and

Recognizing that individuals are the foundation of cultures, societies, and nations, and

Whereas, it is a fundamental right of any individual to practice and perpetuate the cultures, societies and nations into which they are born, and

Recognizing that conditions are imposed upon peoples that suppress, deny, or destroy the cultures, societies, or nations in which they believe or of which they are members,

Be it affirmed, that,

(1) *Recognition of Indigenous Nations*: Indigenous people shall be accorded recognition as nations, and proper subjects of international law, provided the people concerned desire to be recognized as a nation and meet the fundament requirement of nationhood, namely: (a) having a permanent population; (b) having a defined territory; (c) having a government; (d) having the ability to enter into relations with other states.

(2) *Subjects of International Law*: Indigenous groups not meeting the requirements of nationhood are hereby declared to be subjects of international law and are entitled to the protection of this Declaration, provided they are identifiable groups having bonds of language, heritage, tradition, or other common identity.

(3) *Guarantee of Rights*: No indigenous nation or group shall be deemed to have fewer rights or lesser status for the sole reason that the nation or group has not entered into recorded treaties or agreements with any state.

(4) *Accordance of Independence*: Indigenous nations or groups shall be accorded such degree of independence as they may desire in accordance with international law.

(5) *Treaties and Agreements*: Treaties and other agreements entered into by indigenous nations or groups with other states, whether denominated as treaties or otherwise, shall be recognized and applied in the same manner and according to the same international laws and principles as the treaties and agreements entered into by their states.

(6) *Abrogation of Treaties and Other Rights*: Treaties and agreements made with indigenous nations or groups shall not be subject to unilateral abrogation. In no event may the municipal laws of any State serve as a defence to the failure to adhere to and perform the terms of treaties and agreements made with indigenous nations or groups. Nor shall any State refuse to recognize and adhere to treaties or other agreements due to changed circumstances where the change in circumstances has been substantially caused by the State asserting that such change has occurred.

(7) *Jurisdiction*: No State shall assert or claim to exercise any right of jurisdiction over any indigenous nation or group unless pursuant to a valid treaty or other agreement freely made with the lawful representatives of the indigenous nation or group concerned. All actions on the part of any State which derogate from the indigenous nations' or groups' right to exercise self-determination shall be the proper concern of existing international bodies.

(8) *Claims to Territory*: No State shall claim or retain, by right of discovery or otherwise, the territories of an indigenous nation or group, except such lands as may have been lawfully acquired by valid treaty or other cessation freely made.

(9) *Settlement of Disputes*: All States in the Western hemisphere shall establish through negotiations or other appropriate means a procedure for the binding settlement of disputes, claims, or other matters relating to indigenous nations or groups. Such procedures shall be mutually acceptable to the parties, fundamentally fair, and consistent with international law. All procedures presently in existence which do not have the endorsement of the indigenous nations or groups concerned, shall be ended, and new procedures shall be instituted consistent with this Declaration.

(10) *National and Cultural Integrity*: It shall be unlawful for any State to take or permit any action or course of conduct with respect to an indigenous nation or group which will directly or indirectly result in the destruction or disintegration of such indigenous nation or group or otherwise threaten the national or cultural integrity of such nation or group, including, but not limited to, the imposition and support of illegitimate governments and the introduction of non-indigenous religions to indigenous peoples by non-indigenous missionaries.

(11) *Environmental Protection*: It shall be unlawful for any State to make or permit any action or course of conduct with respect to the territories of an indigenous nation or group which will directly or indirectly result in the destruction or deterioration of an indigenous nation or group through the effects of pollution of earth, air, water, or which in any way depletes, displaces or destroys any natural resources or other resources under the dominion of, or vital to the livelihood of an indigenous nation or group.

(12) *Indigenous Membership*: No State, through legislation, regulation, or other means, shall take actions that interfere with the sovereign power of an indigenous nation or group to determine its own membership.

(13) *Conclusion*: All of the rights and obligations declared herein shall be in addition to all rights and obligations existing under international law.

DECLARATION OF PRINCIPLES OF INDIGENOUS RIGHTS

Adopted by the Fourth General Assembly of the World Council of Indigenous Peoples, Panama, September 1984, reprinted in UN Doc. F/Cn.4/1985/22, Annex 2 (1985).

Principle 1

All indigenous peoples have the right of self-determination. By virtue of this right they may freely determine their political status and freely pursue their economic, social, religious and cultural development.

Principle 2

All states within which an indigenous people lives shall recognise the population, territory and instructions of the indigenous people.

Principle 3

The cultures of the indigenous peoples are part of the cultural heritage of mankind.

Principle 4

The traditions and customs of indigenous people must be respected by the states and recognised as a fundamental source of law.

Principle 5

All indigenous people have the right to determine the person or groups of persons who are included within its population.

Principle 6

Each indigenous people has the right to determine the form, structure and authority of its institutions.

Principle 7

The institutions of indigenous people and their decisions, like those of states, must be in conformity with internationally accepted human rights both collective and individual.

Principle 8

Indigenous peoples and their members are entitled to participate in the political life of the state.

Principle 9

Indigenous people shall have exclusive rights to their traditional lands and resources; where the lands and resources of the indigenous people have been taken away without their free and informed consent, such lands and resources shall be returned.

Principle 10

The land rights of an indigenous people include surface and subsurface rights, full rights to interior and costal waters and rights to adequate and exclusive coastal economic zones within the limits of international law.

Principle 11

All indigenous peoples may, for their own needs, freely use their natural wealth and resources in accordance with Principles 9 and 10.

Principle 12

No action or course of conduct may be undertaken which directly or indirectly may result in the destruction of land, air, water, sea ice, wildlife, habitat or natural resources without the free and informed consent of the indigenous peoples affected.

Principle 13

The original rights to their material culture, including archaeological sites, artefacts, designs, technology and works of art lie with the indigenous people.

Principle 14

The indigenous peoples have the rights to receive education in their own language or to establish their own educational institutions. The languages of indigenous peoples are to be respected by the states in all dealings between the indigenous people and the state on the basis of equality and non-discrimination.

Principle 15

The indigenous peoples and their authorities have the rights to be previously consulted and to authorise the realisation of all technological and scientific investigations to be conducted within their territories and to be informed and have full access to the results of the investigation.

Principle 16

Indigenous peoples have the right, in accordance with their traditions, to move freely and conduct traditional activities and maintain kinship relationships across international boundaries.

Principle 17

Treaties between indigenous nations or peoples and representatives of states freely entered into, shall be given full effect under national and international law.

These principles constitute minimum standards which States shall respect and implement.

DECLARATION OF PRINCIPLES ON THE RIGHTS OF INDIGENOUS PEOPLES

Adopted by representatives of indigenous peoples and organizations meeting in Geneva, July 1985, in preparation for the fourth session of the United Nations Working Group on Indigenous Populations: as reaffirmed and amended by representatives of indigenous peoples and organizations meeting in Geneva, July 1987, in preparation for the working group's fifth session. Reprinted in UN Doc. E/CN.4/Sub.2/1987/22.Annex 5 (1987).

1. Indigenous Nations and peoples have, in common with all humanity, the right to life, and to freedom from oppression, discrimination, and aggression.

2. All Indigenous Nations and peoples have the right to self-determination, by virtue of which they have the right to whatever degree of autonomy or self government they choose. This includes the right to freely determine their political status, freely pursue their own economic, social, religious and cultural development, and determine their own membership and/or citizenship, without external interference.

3. No State shall assert any jurisdiction over an Indigenous nation and people, or its territory, except in accordance with the freely expressed wishes of the nation and people concerned.

4. Indigenous nations and peoples are entitled to the permanent control and enjoyment of their aboriginal ancestral-historical territories. This includes air space, surface and subsurface rights, inland and coastal waters, sea ice, renewable and non-renewable resources, and the economies based on these resources.

5. Rights to share and use land, subject to the underlying and inalienable title of the indigenous nation or people, may be granted by their free and informed consent, as evidenced in a valid treaty or agreement.

6. Discovery, conquest, settlement on a theory of *terra nullius* and unilateral legislation are never legitimate basis for States to claim or retain the territories of indigenous nations or peoples.

7. In cases where lands taken in violation of these principles have already been settled, the indigenous nation or people concerned is entitled to immediate restitution, including compensation for the loss of use, without extinction of original title. Indigenous peoples' right to regain possession and control of sacred sites must always be respected.

8. No State shall participate financially or militarily in the involuntary displacement of indigenous populations, or in the subsequent economic exploitation or military use of their territory.

9. The laws and customs of indigenous nations and peoples must be recognized by States' legislative, administrative and judicial institutions and, in case of conflicts with State laws, shall take precedence.

10. No State shall deny an indigenous nation, community, or people residing within its borders the right to participate in the life of the State in whatever manner and to whatever degree they may choose. This includes the right to participate in other forms of collective action and expression.

11. Indigenous nations and peoples continue to own and control their material culture including archaeological, historical and sacred sites, artefacts, designs, knowledge, and works of art. They have the right to regain items of major cultural significance and, in all cases, to the return of the human remains of their ancestors for burial according with their traditions.

12. Indigenous nations and peoples have the right to education, and the control of education, and to conduct business with States in their own languages, and to establish their own educational institutions.

13. No technical, scientific or social investigations, including archaeological excavations, shall take place in relation to indigenous nations or peoples, or their lands, without their prior authorization, and their continuing ownership and control.

14. The religious practices of indigenous nations and peoples shall be fully respected and protected by the laws of States and by international law. Indigenous nations and peoples shall always enjoy unrestricted access to, and enjoyment of sacred sites in accordance with their own laws and customs, including the right of privacy.

15. Indigenous nations and peoples are subjects of international law.

16. Treaties and other agreements freely made with indigenous nations or peoples shall be recognized and applied in the same manner and according to the same international laws and principles as treaties and agreements entered into with other States.

17. Disputes regarding the jurisdiction, territories and institutions of an indigenous nation or peoples are a proper concern of international law, and must be resolved by mutual agreement or valid treaty.

18. Indigenous nations and peoples may engage in self-defence against State actions in conflict with their right to self-determination.

19. Indigenous nations and peoples have the right freely to travel, and to maintain economic, social, cultural and religious relations with each other across State borders.

20. In addition to these rights, indigenous nations and peoples are entitled to the enjoyment of all the human rights and fundamental freedoms enumerated in the International Bill of Human Rights and other United Nations instruments. In no circumstances shall they be subjected to adverse discrimination.

21. All indigenous nations and peoples have the right to their own traditional medicine, including the right to the protection of vital medicinal plants, animals and minerals. Indigenous nations and peoples also have the right to benefit from modern medical techniques and services on a basis equal to that of the general population of the States within which they are located. Furthermore, all indigenous nations and peoples have the right to determine, plan, implement, and control the resources respecting health, housing, and other social services affecting them.

22. According to the right of self-determination, all indigenous nations and peoples shall not be obligated to participate in State military services, including armies, paramilitary or 'civil' organizations

with military structure, within the country or in international conflicts.

DECLARATION OF SAN JOSÉ

Adopted by the UNESCO Meeting of Experts on Ethno-Development and Ethnocide in Latin America, San José, 11 December 1981, UNESCO Doc. Fs.82/WF.32, 1982

For the past few years, increasing concern has been expressed at various international forums over the problem of the loss of cultural identity among the Indian populations of Latin America. This complex process, which has historical, social, political and economic roots, has been termed *ethnocide*.

Ethnocide means that an ethnic group is denied the right to enjoy, develop and transmit its own culture and its own language, whether collectively or individually. This involves an extreme form of massive violation of human rights and, in particular, the right of ethnic groups to respect for their cultural identity, as established by numerous declarations, covenants and agreements of the United Nations and its Specialized Agencies, as well as various regional intergovernmental bodies and numerous non-governmental organizations.

In response to this demand, UNESCO organized an international meeting on ethnocide and ethno-development in Latin America, in collaboration with FLACSO, which was held in December 1981 in San José, Costa Rica.

The participants in the meeting, Indian and other experts, made the following in a Declaration:

1. We declare that ethnocide, that is, cultural genocide, is a violation of international law equivalent to genocide, which was condemned by the United Nations Convention on the Prevention and Punishment of the Crime of Genocide of 1948.

2. We affirm that ethno-development is an inalienable right of Indian groups.

3. By ethno-development we mean the extension and consolidation of the elements of its own culture, through strengthening the independent decision-making capacity of a culturally distinct society to direct its own development and exercise self-determination, at whatever level, which implies an equitable and independent share of power. This means that the ethnic group is a political and administrative unit, with authority over its own territory and decision-making powers within the confines of its development project, in a process of increasing autonomy and self-management.

4. Since the European invasion, the Indian peoples of America have seen their history denied or distorted, despite their great contributions to the progress of mankind, which has led to the negation of their very existence. We reject this unacceptable misrepresentation.

5. As creators, bearers and propagators of a civilizing dimension of their own, as unique and specific facets of the heritage of mankind, the Indian peoples, nations and ethnic groups of America are entitled, collectively and individually, to all civil, political, economic, social and cultural rights now threatened. We, the participants in this meeting, demand universal recognition of all these rights.

6. For the Indian peoples, the land is not only an object of possession and production. It forms the basis of their existence, both physical and spiritual, as an independent entity. Territorial space is the foundation and source of their relationship with the universe and the mainstay of their view of the world.

7. The Indian peoples have a natural and inalienable right to the territories they possess as well as the right to recover the land taken away from them. This implies the right to the natural and cultural heritage that this territory contains and the right to determine freely how it will be used and exploited.

8. An essential part of the cultural heritage of these peoples is their philosophy of life and their experience, knowledge and achievements accumulated throughout history in the cultural, social, political, legal, scientific and technological sphere. They therefore have a right to access to and use, dissemination and transmission of this entire heritage.

9. Respect for the forms of autonomy required by the Indian peoples is an essential condition for guaranteeing and implementing these rights.

10. Furthermore, the Indian peoples' own forms of internal organization are part of their cultural and legal heritage which has contributed to their cohesion and to maintaining their socio-cultural traditions.

11. Disregard for these principles constitutes a gross violation of the right of all individuals and peoples to be different, to consider themselves as different and to be regarded as such, a right recognized in the Declaration on Race and Racial Prejudice adopted by the UNESCO General Conference in 1978, and should therefore be condemned, especially when it creates a risk of ethnocide.

12. In addition, disregard for these principles creates disequilibrium and lack of harmony within society and may incite the Indian peoples to the ultimate resort of rebellion against tyranny and oppression, thereby endangering world peace and therefore contravenes the United Nations Charter and Constitution of UNESCO.

As a result of their reflections, the participants appeal to the United Nations, UNESCO, the ILO, WHO, and FAO, as well as to the Organizations of American States and the Inter-American Indian Institute, to take the necessary steps to apply these principles in full.

The participants address their appeal to Member States of the United Nations and the above-mentioned Specialized Agencies, requesting them to give special attention to the application of these principles, and also to collaborate with international intergovernmental and non-governmental organizations both universal and regional including in particular, Indian organizations, in order to ensure observance of the fundamental rights of the Indian peoples of America.

This appeal is also addressed to officials in the legislative, executive, administrative and legal branches, and to all public servants concerned in the countries of America, with the request that in the course of their daily duties they will always act in conformity with the above principles.

The participants appeal to the conscience of the scientific community and the individuals comprising it, who have the moral responsibility for ensuring that their research studies and practices, as well as the conclusions they draw, cannot be used as a pretext for misrepresentation or interpretations which could harm Indian nations, people, and ethnic groups.

Finally, the participants draw attention to the need to provide for due participation by genuine representatives of Indian nations, peoples and ethnic groups in any activity that might affect their future.

CONVENTION (NO. 169) CONCERNING INDIGENOUS AND TRIBAL PEOPLES IN INDEPENDENT COUNTRIES

Adopted by the General Conference of the International Labour Organization, Geneva, 27 June 1989. Entered into force 5 September 1991.

The General Conference of the International Labour Organization, *Having* been convened at Geneva by the Governing Body of the International Labour Office, and having met in its seventy-sixth session on 7 June 1989, and

Noting the international standards contained in the Indigenous and Tribal Populations Convention and Recommendation, 1957, and

Recalling the terms of the Universal Declaration of Human Rights, the International Covenant on Economic, Social and Cultural Rights, the International Covenant on Civil and Political Rights, and the many international instruments on the prevention of discrimination, and

Considering that the developments which have taken place in international law since 1957, as well as developments in the situation of indigenous and tribal peoples in all regions of the world, have made it appropriate to adopt new international standards on the subject with a view to removing the assimilationist orientation of the earlier standards, and

Recognizing the aspirations of these peoples to exercise control over their own institutions, ways of life and economic development and to maintain and develop their identities, languages and religions, within the framework of the States in which they live, and

Noting that in many parts of the world these peoples are unable to enjoy their fundamental human rights to the same degree as the rest of the population of the States within which they live, and that their laws, values, customs and perspectives have often been eroded, and

Calling attention to the distinctive contributions of indigenous and tribal peoples to the cultural diversity and social and ecological harmony of humankind and to international co-operation and understanding, and

Noting that the following provisions have been framed with the co-operation of the United Nations, the Food and Agriculture Organization of the United Nations, the United Nations Educational, Scientific and Cultural Organization and the World Health Organization, as well as of the Inter-American Indian Institute, at appropriate levels and in their respective fields, and that it is proposed to continue this co-operation in promoting and securing the application of these provisions, and

Having decided upon the adoption of certain proposals with regard to the partial revision of the Indigenous and Tribal Populations Convention, 1957 (No. 107), which is the fourth item on the agenda of the session, and

Having determined that these proposals shall take the form of an international Convention revising the Indigenous and Tribal Populations Convention, 1957,

Adopts this twenty-seventh day of June of the year one thousand nine hundred and eighty-nine the following Convention, which may be cited as the Indigenous and Tribal Peoples Convention, 1989:

PART I. GENERAL POLICY

Article 1

1. This Convention applies to:

(a) Tribal peoples in independent countries whose social, cultural and economic conditions distinguish them from other sections of the national community, and whose status is regulated wholly or partially by their own customs or traditions or by special laws or regulations;

(b) Peoples in independent countries who are re-garded as indigenous on account of their descent from the populations which inhabited the country, or a geographical region to which the country be-longs, at the time of conquest or colonisation or the establishment of present State boundaries and who, irrespective of their legal status, retain some or all of their own social, economic, cultural and political institutions.

2. Self-identification as indigenous or tribal shall be regarded as a fundamental criterion for determining the groups to which the provisions of this Convention apply.

3. The use of the term 'peoples' in this Convention shall not be construed as having any implications as regards the rights which may attach to the term under international law.

Article 2

1. Governments shall have the responsibility for developing, with the participation of the peoples concerned, co-ordinated and systematic action to protect the rights of these peoples and to guarantee respect for their integrity.

2. Such action shall include measures for:

(a) Ensuring that members of these peoples benefit on an equal footing from the rights and opportunities which national laws and regulations grant to other members of the population;

(b) Promoting the full realisation of the social, economic and cultural rights of these peoples with respect for their social and cultural identity, their customs and traditions and their institutions;

(c) Assisting the members of the peoples concerned to eliminate socio-economic gaps that may exist between indigenous and other members of the national community, in a manner compatible with their aspirations and ways of life.

Article 3

1. Indigenous and tribal peoples shall enjoy the full measure of human rights and fundamental freedoms without hindrance or discrimination. The provisions of the Convention shall be applied without discrimination to male and female members of these peoples.

2. No form of force or coercion shall be used in violation of the human rights and fundamental freedoms of the peoples concerned, including the rights contained in this Convention.

Article 4

1. Special measures shall be adopted as appropriate for safeguarding the persons, institutions, property, labour, cultures and environment of the peoples concerned.

2. Such special measures shall not be contrary to the freely-expressed wishes of the peoples concerned.

3. Enjoyment of the general rights of citizenship, without discrimination, shall not be prejudiced in any way by such special measures.

Article 5

In applying the provisions of this Convention:

(a) The social, cultural, religious and spiritual values and practices of these peoples shall be recognised and protected, and due account shall be taken of the nature of the problems which face them both as groups and as individuals;

(b) The integrity of the values, practices and institu-tions of these peoples shall be respected;

(c) Policies aimed at mitigating the difficulties experi-enced by these peoples in facing new conditions of life and work shall be adopted, with the participation and co-operation of the peoples affected.

Article 6

1. In applying the provisions of this Convention, Governments shall:

(a) Consult the peoples concerned, through appropriate procedures and in particular through their representative institutions, whenever consideration is being given to legislative or administrative measures which may affect them directly;

(b) Establish means by which these peoples can freely participate, to at least the same extent as other sectors of the population, at all levels of decision-making in elective institutions and administrative and other bodies responsible for policies and programmes which concern them;

(c) Establish means for the full development of these peoples' own institutions and initiatives, and in appropriate cases provide the resources necessary for this purpose.

2. The consultations carried out in application of this Convention shall be undertaken, in good faith and in a form appropriate to the circumstances, with the objective of achieving agreement or consent to the proposed measures.

Article 7

1. The peoples concerned shall have the right to decide their own priorities for the process of development as it affects their lives, beliefs, institutions and spiritual well-being and the lands they occupy or otherwise use, and to exercise control, to the extent possible, over their own economic, social and cultural development. In addition, they shall participate in the formulation, implementation and evaluation of plans and programmes for national and regional development which may affect them directly.

2. The improvement of the conditions of life and work and levels of health and education of the peoples concerned, with their participation and co-operation, shall be a matter of priority in plans for the overall economic development of areas they inhabit. Special projects for development of the areas in question shall also be so designed as to promote such improvement.

3. Governments shall ensure that, whenever appropriate, studies are carried out, in co-operation with the peoples concerned, to assess the social, spiritual, cultural and environmental impact on them of planned development activities. The results of these studies shall be considered as fundamental criteria for the implementation of these activities.

4. Governments shall take measures, in co-operation with the peoples concerned, to protect and preserve the environment of the territories they inhabit.

Article 8

1. In applying national laws and regulations to the peoples concerned, due regard shall be had to their customs or customary laws.

2. These peoples shall have the right to retain their own customs and institutions, where these are not incompatible with fundamental rights defined by the national legal system and with internationally recognized human rights. Procedures shall be established, whenever necessary, to resolve conflicts which may arise in the application of this principle.

3. The application of paragraphs 1 and 2 of this Article shall not prevent members of these peoples from exercising the rights granted to all citizens and from assuming the corresponding duties.

Article 9

1. To the extent compatible with the national legal system and internationally recognised human rights. the methods customarily practised by the peoples concerned for dealing with offences committed by their members shall be respected.

2. The customs of these peoples in regard to penal matters shall be taken into consideration by the authorities and courts dealing with such cases.

Article 10

1. In imposing penalties laid down by general law on members of these peoples account shall be taken of their economic, social and cultural characteristics.

2. Preference shall be given to methods of punishment other than confinement in prison.

Article 11

The exaction from members of the peoples concerned of compulsory personal services in any form, whether paid or unpaid, shall be prohibited and punishable by law, except in cases prescribed by law for all citizens.

Article 12

The peoples concerned shall be safeguarded against the abuse of their rights and shall be able to take legal proceedings, either individually or through their representative bodies, for the effective protection of these rights. Measures shall be taken to ensure that members of these peoples can understand and be understood in legal proceedings, where necessary through the provision of interpretation or by other effective means.

PART II. LAND

Article 13

1. In applying the provisions of this Part of the Convention governments shall respect the special importance for the cultures and spiritual values of the peoples concerned of their relationship with the lands or territories, or both as applicable, which they occupy or otherwise use, and in particular the collective aspects of this relationship.

2. The use of the term 'lands' in Articles 15 and 16 shall include the concept of territories, which covers the total environment of the areas which the peoples concerned occupy or otherwise use.

Article 14

1. The rights of ownership and possession of the peoples concerned over the lands which they traditionally occupy shall be recognised. In addition, measures shall be taken in appropriate cases to safeguard the right of the peoples concerned to use lands not exclusively occupied by them, but to which they have traditionally had access for their subsistence and traditional activities. Particular attention shall be paid to the situation of nomadic peoples and shifting cultivators in this respect.

2. Governments shall take steps as necessary to identify the lands which the peoples concerned traditionally occupy, and to guarantee effective protection of their rights of ownership and possession.

3. Adequate procedures shall be established within the national legal system to resolve land claims by the peoples concerned.

Article 15

1. The rights of the peoples concerned to the natural resources pertaining to their lands shall be specially safeguarded. These rights include the right of these peoples to participate in the use, management and conservation of these resources.

2. In cases in which the State retains the ownership of mineral or sub-surface resources or rights to other resources pertaining to lands, governments shall establish or maintain procedures through which they shall consult these peoples, with a view to ascertaining whether and to what degree their interests would be prejudiced, before undertaking or permitting any programmes for the exploration or exploitation of such resources pertaining to their lands. The peoples concerned shall wherever possible participate in the benefits of such activities, and shall receive fair compensation for any damages which they may sustain as a result of such activities.

Article 16

1. Subject to the following paragraphs of this Article, the peoples concerned shall not be removed from the lands which they occupy.

2. Where the relocation of these peoples is considered necessary as an exceptional measure, such relocation shall take place only with their free and informed consent. Where their consent cannot be obtained, such relocation shall take place only following appropriate procedures established by national laws and regulations, including public inquiries where appropriate, which provide the opportunity for effective representation of the peoples concerned.

3. Whenever possible, these peoples shall have the right to return to their traditional lands, as soon as the grounds for relocation cease to exist.

4. When such return is not possible, as determined by agreement or, in the absence of such agreement, through appropriate procedures, these peoples shall be provided in all possible cases with lands of quality and legal status at least equal to that of the lands previously occupied by them, suitable to provide for their present needs and future development. Where the peoples concerned express a preference for compensation in money or in kind, they shall be so compensated under appropriate guarantees.

5. Persons thus relocated shall be fully compensated for any resulting loss or injury.

Article 17

1. Procedures established by the peoples concerned for the transmission of land rights among members of these peoples shall be respected.

2. The peoples concerned shall be consulted whenever consideration is being given to their capacity to alienate their lands or otherwise transmit their rights outside their own community.

3. Persons not belonging to these peoples shall be prevented from taking advantage of their customs or of lack of understanding of the laws on the part of their members to secure the ownership, possession or use of land belonging to them.

Article 18

Adequate penalties shall be established by law for unauthorised intrusion upon, or use of, the lands of the peoples concerned, and governments shall take measures to prevent such offences.

Article 19

National agrarian programmes shall secure to the peoples concerned treatment equivalent to that accorded to other sectors of the population with regard to:

(a) The provision of more land for these peoples when they have not the area necessary for providing the essentials of a normal existence, or for any possible increase in their numbers;

(b) The provision of the means required to promote the development of the lands which these peoples already possess.

ARTICLE 21

RECOGNIZING AND STRENGTHENING THE ROLE OF INDIGENOUS PEOPLE AND THEIR COMMUNITIES

Basis for action

26.1. Indigenous people and their communities have an historical relationship with their lands and are generally descendants of the original inhabitants of such lands. In the context of this chapter the term 'lands' is understood to include the environment of the areas which the people concerned traditionally occupy. Indigenous people and their communities represent a significant percentage of the global population. They have developed over many generations a holistic traditional scientific knowledge of their lands, natural resources and environment. Indigenous people and their communities shall enjoy the full measure of human rights and fundamental freedoms without hindrance or discrimination. Their ability to participate fully in sustainable development practices on their lands has tended to be limited as a result of factors of an economic, social and historical nature. In view of the interrelationship between the natural environment and its sustainable development and the cultural, social, economic and physical well-being of indigenous people, national and international efforts to implement environmentally sound and sustainable development should recognize, accommodate, promote and strengthen the role of indigenous people and their communities.

26.2. Some of the goals inherent in the objectives and activities of this programme area are already contained in such international legal instruments as the ILO Indigenous and Tribal Peoples Convention (No. 169) and are being incorporated into the draft universal declaration on indigenous rights, being prepared by the United Nations working group on indigenous populations. The International Year for the World's Indigenous People (1993), proclaimed by the General Assembly in its resolution 45/164 of 18 December 1990, presents a timely opportunity to mobilize further international technical and financial cooperation.

Objectives

26.3. In full partnership with indigenous people and their communities, Governments and, where appropriate, intergovernmental organizations should aim at fulfilling the following objectives:

(a) Establishment of a process to empower indigenous people and their communities through measures that include:

i. Adoption or strengthening of appropriate policies and/or legal instruments at the national level;

ii. Recognition that the lands of indigenous people and their communities should be protected from activities that are environmentally unsound or that the indigenous people concerned consider to be socially and culturally inappropriate;

iii. Recognition of their values, traditional knowledge and resource management practices with a view to promoting environmentally sound and sustainable development;

iv. Recognition that traditional and direct dependence on renewable resources and ecosystems, including sustainable harvesting, continues to be essential to the cultural, economic and physical well-being of indigenous people and their communities;

v. Development and strengthening of national dispute-resolution arrangements in relation to settlement of land and resource-management concerns;

vi. Support for alternative environmentally sound means of production to ensure a range of choices on how to improve their quality of life so that they effectively participate in sustainable development;

vii. Enhancement of capacity-building for indigenous communities, based on the adaptation and exchange of traditional experience, knowledge and resource-management practices, to ensure their sustainable development;

(b) Establishment, where appropriate, of arrangements to strengthen the active participation of indigenous people and their communities in the national formulation of policies, laws and programmes relating to resource management and other development processes that may affect them, and their initiation of proposals for such policies and programmes;

(c) Involvement of indigenous people and their communities at the national and local levels in resource management and conservation strategies and other relevant programmes established to support and review sustainable development strategies, such as those suggested in other programme areas of Agenda 21.

Activities

26.4. Some indigenous people and their communities may require, in accordance with national legislation, greater control over their lands, self-management of their resources, participation in development decisions affecting them, including, where appropriate, participation in the establishment or management of protected areas. The following are some of the specific measures which Governments could take:

(a) Consider the ratification and application of existing international conventions relevant to indigenous people and their communities (where not yet done) and provide support for the adoption by the General Assembly of a declaration on indigenous rights;

(b) Adopt or strengthen appropriate policies and/ or legal instruments that will protect indigenous intellectual and cultural property and the right to preserve customary and administrative systems and practices.

26.5. United Nations organizations and other international development and finance organizations and Governments should, drawing on the active participation of indigenous people and their communities, as appropriate, take the following measures, inter alia, to incorporate their values, views and knowledge, including the unique contribution of indigenous women, in resource management and other policies and programmes that may affect them:

(a) Appoint a special focal point within each international organization, and organize annual interorganizational coordination meetings in consultation with Governments and indigenous organizations, as appropriate, and develop a procedure within and between operational agencies for assisting Governments in ensuring the coherent and coordinated incorporation of the views of indigenous people in the design and implementation of policies and programmes. Under this procedure, indigenous people and their communities should be informed and consulted and allowed to participate in national decision-making, in particular regarding regional and international cooperative efforts. In addition, these policies and programmes should take fully into account strategies based on local indigenous initiatives;

(b) Provide technical and financial assistance for capacity-building programmes to support the sustainable self-development of indigenous people and their communities;

(c) Strengthen research and education programmes aimed at:

i. Achieving a better understanding of indigenous people's knowledge and management experience related to the environment, and applying this to contemporary development challenges;

ii. Increasing the efficiency of indigenous people's resource management systems, for example, by promoting the adaptation and dissemination of suitable technological innovations;

(d) Contribute to the endeavours of indigenous people and their communities in resource management and conservation strategies (such as those that may be developed under appropriate projects funded through the Global Environment Facility and the Tropical Forestry Action Plan) and other programme areas of Agenda 21, including programmes to collect, analyze and use data and other information in support of sustainable development projects.

26.6. Governments, in full partnership with indigenous people and their communities should, where appropriate:

(a) Develop or strengthen national arrangements to consult with indigenous people and their communities with a view to reflecting their needs and incorporating their values and traditional and other knowledge and practices in national policies and programmes in the field of natural resource management and conservation and other development programmes affecting them;

(b) Cooperate at the regional level, where appropriate, to address common indigenous issues with a view to recognizing and strengthening their participation in sustainable development.

Means of implementation

A) Financing and cost evaluation

26.7. The Conference secretariat has estimated the average total annual cost (1993–2000) of implementing the activities of this programme to be about $3 million on grant or concessional terms. These are indicative and order-of-magnitude estimates only and have not been reviewed by Governments. Actual costs and financial terms, including any that are non-concessional, will depend upon, inter alia, the specific strategies and programmes Governments decide upon for implementation.

B) Legal and administrative frameworks

26.8. Governments should incorporate, in collaboration with the indigenous people affected, the rights and responsibilities of indigenous people and their communities in the legislation of each country, suitable to the country's specific situation. Developing countries may require technical assistance to implement these activities.

C) Human resource development

26.9. International development agencies and Governments should commit financial and other resources to education and training for indigenous people and their communities to develop their capacities to achieve their sustainable self-development, and to contribute to and participate in sustainable and equitable development at the national level. Particular attention should be given to strengthening the role of indigenous women.

DRAFT UNITED NATIONS DECLARATION ON THE RIGHTS OF INDIGENOUS PEOPLES

As agreed upon by the members of the UN Working Group on Indigenous Populations at its eleventh session, Geneva, July 1998, adopted by the UN Sub-Commission on Prevention of Discrimination and Protection of Minorities by its resolution 1994/45, 26 August 1994, UN Doc. E/CN.4/1995/2, E/CN.4/Sub2/1994/56 at 105, 194.

Affirming that indigenous peoples are equal in dignity and rights to all other peoples, while recognizing the right of all peoples to be different, to consider themselves different, and to be respected as such,

Affirming also that all peoples contribute to the diversity and richness of civilizations and cultures, which constitute the common heritage of humankind,

Affirming further that all doctrines, policies and practices based on or advocating superiority of peoples or individuals on the basis of national origin, racial, religious, ethnic or cultural differences are racist, scientifically false, legally invalid, morally condemnable and socially unjust,

Reaffirming also that indigenous peoples, in the exercise of their rights, should be free from discrimination of any kind,

Concerned that indigenous peoples have been deprived of their human rights and fundamental freedoms, resulting, inter alia, in their colonization and dispossession of their lands, territories and resources, thus preventing them from exercising, in particular, their right to development in accordance with their own needs and interests,

Recognizing the urgent need to respect and promote the inherent rights and characteristics of indigenous peoples, especially their rights to their lands, territories and resources, which derive from their political, economic and social structures and from their cultures, spiritual traditions, histories and philosophies,

Welcoming the fact that indigenous peoples are organizing themselves for political, economic, social and cultural enhancement and in order to bring an end to all forms of discrimination and oppression wherever they occur,

Convinced that control by indigenous peoples over developments affecting them and their lands, territories and resources will enable them to maintain and strengthen their institutions, cultures and traditions, and to promote their development in accordance with their aspirations and needs,

Recognizing also that respect for indigenous knowledge, cultures and traditional practices contributes to sustainable and equitable development and proper management of the environment,

Emphasizing the need for demilitarization of the lands and territories of indigenous peoples, which will contribute to peace, economic and social progress and development, understanding and friendly relations among nations and peoples of the world,

Recognizing in particular the right of indigenous families and communities to retain shared responsibility for the upbringing, training, education and well-being of their children,

Recognizing also that indigenous peoples have the right freely to determine their relationships with States in a spirit of coexistence, mutual benefit and full respect,

Considering that treaties, agreements and other arrangements between States and indigenous peoples are properly matters of international concern and responsibility,

Acknowledging that the Charter of the United Nations, the International Covenant on Economic, Social and Cultural Rights and the International Covenant on Civil and Political Rights affirm the fundamental importance of the right of self-determination of all peoples, by virtue of which they freely determine their political status and freely pursue their economic, social and cultural development,

Bearing in mind that nothing in this Declaration may be used to deny any peoples their right of self-determination,

Encouraging States to comply with and effectively implement all international instruments, in particular those related to human rights, as they apply to indigenous peoples, in consultation and cooperation with the peoples concerned,

Emphasizing that the United Nations has an important and continuing role to play in promoting and protecting the rights of indigenous peoples,

Believing that this Declaration is a further important step forward for the recognition, promotion and protection of the rights and freedoms of indigenous peoples and in the development of relevant activities of the United Nations system in this field,

Solemnly proclaims the following United Nations Declaration on the Rights of Indigenous Peoples:

PART I

Article 1

Indigenous peoples have the right to the full and effective enjoyment of all human rights and fundamental freedoms recognized in the Charter of the United Nations, the Universal Declaration of Human Rights and international human rights law.

Article 2

Indigenous individuals and peoples are free and equal to all other individuals and peoples in dignity and rights, and have the right to be free from any kind of adverse discrimination, in particular that based on their indigenous origin or identity.

Article 3

Indigenous peoples have the right of self-determination. By virtue of that right they freely determine their political status and freely pursue their economic, social and cultural development.

Article 4

Indigenous peoples have the right to maintain and strengthen their distinct political, economic, social and cultural characteristics, as well as their legal systems, while retaining their rights to participate fully, if they so choose, in the political, economic, social and cultural life of the State.

Article 5

Every indigenous individual has the right to a nationality.

PART II

Article 6

Indigenous peoples have the collective right to live in freedom, peace and security as distinct peoples and to full guarantees against genocide or any other act of violence, including the removal of indigenous children from their families and communities under any pretext.

In addition, they have the individual rights to life, physical and mental integrity, liberty and security of person.

Article 7

Indigenous peoples have the collective and individual right not to be subjected to ethnocide and cultural genocide, including prevention of and redress for:

(a) Any action which has the aim or effect of depriving them of their integrity as distinct peoples, or of their cultural values or ethnic identities;

(b) Any action which has the aim or effect of dispossessing them of their lands, territories or resources;

(c) Any form of population transfer which has the aim or effect of violating or undermining any of their rights;

(d) Any form of assimilation or integration by other cultures or ways of life imposed on them by legislative, administrative or other measures;

(e) Any form of propaganda directed against them.

Article 8

Indigenous peoples have the collective and individual right to maintain and develop their distinct identities and characteristics, including the right to identify themselves as indigenous and to be recognized as such.

Article 9

Indigenous peoples and individuals have the right to belong to an indigenous community or nation, in accordance with the traditions and customs of the community or nation concerned. No disadvantage of any kind may arise from the exercise of such a right.

Article 10

Indigenous peoples shall not be forcibly removed from their lands or territories. No relocation shall take place without the free and informed consent of the indigenous peoples concerned and after agreement on just and fair compensation and, where possible, with the option of return.

Article 11

Indigenous peoples have the right to special protection and security in periods of armed conflict.

States shall observe international standards, in particular the Fourth Geneva Convention of 1949, for the protection of civilian populations in circumstances of emergency and armed conflict, and shall not:

(a) Recruit indigenous individuals against their will into the armed forces and, in particular, for use against other indigenous peoples;

(b) Recruit indigenous children into the armed forces under any circumstances;

(c) Force indigenous individuals to abandon their lands, territories or means of subsistence, or relocate them in special centres for military purposes;

(d) Force indigenous individuals to work for military purposes under any discriminatory conditions.

PART III

Article 12

Indigenous peoples have the right to practise and revitalize their cultural traditions and customs. This includes the right to maintain, protect and develop the past, present and future manifestations of their cultures, such as archaeological and historical sites, artifacts, designs, ceremonies, technologies and visual and performing arts and literature, as well as the right to the restitution of cultural, intellectual, religious and spiritual property taken without their free and informed consent or in violation of their laws, traditions and customs.

Article 13

Indigenous peoples have the right to manifest, practise, develop and teach their spiritual and religious traditions, customs and ceremonies; the right to maintain, protect, and have access in privacy to their religious and cultural sites; the right to the use and control of ceremonial objects; and the right to the repatriation of human remains.

States shall take effective measures, in conjunction with the indigenous peoples concerned, to ensure that indigenous sacred places, including burial sites, be preserved, respected and protected.

Article 14

Indigenous peoples have the right to revitalize, use, develop and transmit to future generations their histories, languages, oral traditions, philosophies, writing systems and literatures, and to designate and retain their own names for communities, places and persons.

States shall take effective measures, whenever any right of indigenous peoples may be threatened, to ensure this right is protected and also to ensure that they can understand and be understood in political, legal and administrative proceedings, where necessary through the provision of interpretation or by other appropriate means.

PART IV

Article 15

Indigenous children have the right to all levels and forms of education of the State. All indigenous peoples also have this right and the right to establish and control their educational systems and institutions providing education in their own languages, in a manner appropriate to their cultural methods of teaching and learning.

Indigenous children living outside their communities have the right to be provided access to education in their own culture and language.

States shall take effective measures to provide appropriate resources for these purposes.

Article 16

Indigenous peoples have the right to have the dignity and diversity of their cultures, traditions, histories and aspirations appropriately reflected in all forms of education and public information.

States shall take effective measures, in consultation with the indigenous peoples concerned, to eliminate prejudice and discrimination and to promote tolerance, understanding and good relations among indigenous peoples and all segments of society.

Article 17

Indigenous peoples have the right to establish their own media in their own languages. They also have the right to equal access to all forms of non-indigenous media.

States shall take effective measures to ensure that State-owned media duly reflect indigenous cultural diversity.

Article 18

Indigenous peoples have the right to enjoy fully all rights established under international labour law and national labour legislation.

Indigenous individuals have the right not to be subjected to any discriminatory conditions of labour, employment or salary.

PART V

Article 19

Indigenous peoples have the right to participate fully, if they so choose, at all levels of decision-making in matters which may affect their rights, lives and destinies through representatives chosen by themselves in accordance with their own procedures, as well as to maintain and develop their own indigenous decision-making institutions.

Article 20

Indigenous peoples have the right to participate fully, if they so choose, through procedures determined by them, in devising legislative or administrative measures that may affect them.

States shall obtain the free and informed consent of the peoples concerned before adopting and implementing such measures.

Article 21

Indigenous peoples have the right to maintain and develop their political, economic and social systems, to be secure in the enjoyment of their own means of subsistence and development, and to engage freely in all their traditional and other economic activities. Indigenous peoples who have been deprived of their means of subsistence and development are entitled to just and fair compensation.

Article 22

Indigenous peoples have the right to special measures for the immediate, effective and continuing improvement of their economic and social conditions, including in the areas of employment, vocational training and retraining, housing, sanitation, health and social security.

Particular attention shall be paid to the rights and special needs of indigenous elders, women, youth, children and disabled persons.

Article 23

Indigenous peoples have the right to determine and develop priorities and strategies for exercising their right to development. In particular, indigenous peoples have the right to determine and develop all health, housing and other economic and social programmes affecting them and, as far as possible, to administer such programmes through their own institutions.

Article 24

Indigenous peoples have the right to their traditional medicines and health practices, including the right to the protection of vital medicinal plants, animals and minerals.

They also have the right to access, without any discrimination, to all medical institutions, health services and medical care.

PART VI

Article 25

Indigenous peoples have the right to maintain and strengthen their distinctive spiritual and material relationship with the lands, territories, waters and coastal seas and other resources which they have traditionally owned or otherwise occupied or used, and to uphold their responsibilities to future generations in this regard.

Article 26

Indigenous peoples have the right to own, develop, control and use the lands and territories, including the total environment of the lands, air, waters, coastal seas, sea-ice, flora and fauna and other resources which they have traditionally owned or otherwise occupied or used. This includes the right to the full recognition of their laws, traditions and customs, land-tenure systems and institutions for the development and management of resources, and the right to effective measures by States to prevent any interference with, alienation of or encroachment upon these rights.

Article 27

Indigenous peoples have the right to the restitution of the lands, territories and resources which they have traditionally owned or otherwise occupied or used, and which have been confiscated, occupied, used or damaged without their free and informed consent. Where this is not possible, they have the right to just and fair compensation. Unless otherwise freely agreed upon by the peoples concerned, compensation shall take the form of lands, territories and resources equal in quality, size and legal status.

Article 28

Indigenous peoples have the right to the conservation, restoration and protection of the total environment and the productive capacity of their lands, territories

and resources, as well as to assistance for this purpose from States and through international cooperation. Military activities shall not take place in the lands and territories of indigenous peoples, unless otherwise freely agreed upon by the peoples concerned.

States shall take effective measures to ensure that no storage or disposal of hazardous materials shall take place in the lands and territories of indigenous peoples.

States shall also take effective measures to ensure, as needed, that programmes for monitoring, maintaining and restoring the health of indigenous peoples, as developed and implemented by the peoples affected by such materials, are duly implemented.

Article 29

Indigenous peoples are entitled to the recognition of the full ownership, control and protection of their cultural and intellectual property.

They have the right to special measures to control, develop and protect their sciences, technologies and cultural manifestations, including human and other genetic resources, seeds, medicines, knowledge of the properties of fauna and flora, oral traditions, literatures, designs and visual and performing arts.

Article 30

Indigenous peoples have the right to determine and develop priorities and strategies for the development or use of their lands, territories and other resources, including the right to require that States obtain their free and informed consent prior to the approval of any project affecting their lands, territories and other resources, particularly in connection with the development, utilization or exploitation of mineral, water or other resources. Pursuant to agreement with the indigenous peoples concerned, just and fair compensation shall be provided for any such activities and measures taken to mitigate adverse environmental, economic, social, cultural or spiritual impact.

PART VII

Article 31

Indigenous peoples, as a specific form of exercising their right to self-determination, have the right to autonomy or self-government in matters relating to their internal and local affairs, including culture, religion, education, information, media, health, housing, employment, social welfare, economic activities, land and resources management, environment and entry by non-members, as well as ways and means for financing these autonomous functions.

Article 32

Indigenous peoples have the collective right to determine their own citizenship in accordance with their customs and traditions. Indigenous citizenship does not impair the right of indigenous individuals to obtain citizenship of the States in which they live.

Indigenous peoples have the right to determine the structures and to select the membership of their institutions in accordance with their own procedures.

Article 33

Indigenous peoples have the right to promote, develop and maintain their institutional structures and their distinctive juridical customs, traditions, procedures and practices, in accordance with internationally recognized human rights standards.

Article 34

Indigenous peoples have the collective right to determine the responsibilities of individuals to their communities.

Article 35

Indigenous peoples, in particular those divided by international borders, have the right to maintain and develop contacts, relations and cooperation, including activities for spiritual, cultural, political, economic and social purposes, with other peoples across borders.

States shall take effective measures to ensure the exercise and implementation of this right.

Article 36

Indigenous peoples have the right to the recognition, observance and enforcement of treaties, agreements and other constructive arrangements concluded with States or their successors, according to their original spirit and intent, and to have States honour and respect such treaties, agreements and other constructive arrangements. Conflicts and disputes which cannot otherwise be settled should be submitted to competent international bodies agreed to by all parties concerned.

PART VIII

Article 37

States shall take effective and appropriate measures, in consultation with the indigenous peoples concerned, to give full effect to the provisions of this Declaration. The rights recognized herein shall be adopted and included in national legislation in such a manner that indigenous peoples can avail themselves of such rights in practice.

Article 38

Indigenous peoples have the right to have access to adequate financial and technical assistance, from States and through international cooperation, to pursue freely their political, economic, social, cultural and spiritual development and for the enjoyment of the rights and freedoms recognized in this Declaration.

Article 39

Indigenous peoples have the right to have access to and prompt decision through mutually acceptable and fair procedures for the resolution of conflicts and disputes with States, as well as to effective remedies for all infringements of their individual and collective rights. Such a decision shall take into consideration the customs, traditions, rules and legal systems of the indigenous peoples concerned.

Article 40

The organs and specialized agencies of the United Nations system and other intergovernmental organizations shall contribute to the full realization of the provisions of this Declaration through the mobilization, inter alia, of financial cooperation and technical assistance. Ways and means of ensuring participation of indigenous peoples on issues affecting them shall be established.

Article 41

The United Nations shall take the necessary steps to ensure the implementation of this Declaration including the creation of a body at the highest level with special competence in this field and with the direct participation of indigenous peoples. All United Nations bodies shall promote respect for and full application of the provisions of this Declaration.

PART IX

Article 42

The rights recognized herein constitute the minimum standards for the survival, dignity and well-being of the indigenous peoples of the world.

Article 43

All the rights and freedoms recognized herein are equally guaranteed to male and female indigenous individuals.

Article 44

Nothing in this Declaration may be construed as diminishing or extinguishing existing or future rights indigenous peoples may have or acquire.

Article 45

Nothing in this Declaration may be interpreted as implying for any State, group or person any right to engage in any activity or to perform any act contrary to the Charter of the United Nations.

PROPOSED AMERICAN DECLARATION ON THE RIGHTS OF INDIGENOUS PEOPLES

Approved by the Inter-American Commission on Human Rights on 26 February 1997 at its 1333rd session, 95th regular session OAS Doc. OEA/Ser.L/V/II.95.Doc.7.rev (1996).

Preamble

1. Indigenous institutions and the strengthening of nations

The member states of the OAS (hereafter the states),

Recalling that the indigenous peoples of the Americas constitute an organized, distinctive and integral segment of their population and are entitled to be part of the national identities of the countries of the Americas, and have a special role to play in strengthening the institutions of the state and in establishing national unity based on democratic principles; and,

Further recalling that some of the democratic institutions and concepts embodied in the constitutions of American states originate from institutions of the indigenous peoples, and that in many instances their present participatory systems for decision-making and for authority contribute to improving democracies in the Americas.

Recalling the need to develop their national juridical systems to consolidate the pluricultural nature of our societies.

2. Eradication of poverty and the right to development

Concerned about the frequent deprivation afflicting indigenous peoples of their human rights and fundamental freedoms; within and outside their communities, as well as the dispossession of their lands, territories and resources, thus preventing them from exercising, in particular, their right to development in accordance with their own traditions, needs and interests.

Recognizing the severe impoverishment afflicting indigenous peoples in several regions of the Hemisphere and that their living conditions are generally deplorable.

And recalling that in the Declaration of Principles issued by the Summit of the Americas in December 1994, the heads of state and governments declared that in observance of the International Decade of the World's Indigenous People, they will focus their energies on improving the exercise of democratic rights and the access to social services by indigenous peoples and their communities.

3. Indigenous culture and ecology

Recognizing the respect for the environment accorded by the cultures of indigenous peoples of the Americas, and considering the special relationship between the indigenous peoples and the environment, lands, resources and territories on which they live and their natural resources.

4. Harmonious relations, respect and the absence of discrimination

Reaffirming the responsibility of all states and peoples of the Americas to end racism and racial discrimination, with a view to establishing harmonious relations and respect among all peoples.

5. Territories and indigenous survival

Recognizing that in many indigenous cultures, traditional collective systems for control and use of land, territory and resources, including bodies of water and coastal areas, are a necessary condition for their survival, social organization, development and their individual and collective well-being; and that the form of such control and ownership is varied and distinctive and does not necessarily coincide with the systems protected by the domestic laws of the states in which they live.

6. Security and indigenous areas

Reaffirming that the armed forces in indigenous areas shall restrict themselves to the performance of their functions and shall not be the cause of abuses or violations of the rights of indigenous peoples.

7. Human rights instruments and other advances in international law

Recognizing the paramouncy and applicability to the states and peoples of the Americas of the American Declaration of the Rights and Duties of Man, the American Convention on Human Rights and other human rights instruments of inter-American and international law; and

Recognizing that indigenous peoples are a subject of international law, and mindful of the progress achieved by the states and indigenous organizations, especially in the sphere of the United Nations and the International Labor Organization, in several international instruments, particularly in the ILO Convention 169.

Affirming the principle of the universality and indivisibility of human rights, and the application of international human rights to all individuals.

8. Enjoyment of collective rights

Recalling the international recognition of rights that can only be enjoyed when exercised collectively.

9. Advances in the provisions of national instruments

Noting the constitutional, legislative and jurisprudential advances achieved in the Americas in guaranteeing the rights and institutions of indigenous peoples.

SECTION ONE. INDIGENOUS PEOPLES

Article I. Scope and definitions

1. This Declaration applies to indigenous peoples as well as peoples whose social, cultural and economic conditions distinguish them from other sections of the national community, and whose status is regulated wholly or partially by their own customs or traditions or by special laws or regulations.

2. Self identification as indigenous shall be regarded as a fundamental criterion for determining the peoples to which the provisions of this Declaration apply.

3. The use of the term 'peoples' in this Instrument shall not be construed as having any implication with respect to any other rights that might be attached to that term in international law.

SECTION TWO. HUMAN RIGHTS

Article II. Full observance of human rights

1. Indigenous peoples have the right to the full and effective enjoyment of the human rights and fundamental freedoms recognized in the Charter of the OAS, the American Declaration of the Rights and Duties of Man, the American Convention on Human Rights, and other international human rights law; and nothing in this Declaration shall be construed as in any way limiting or denying those rights or authorizing any action not in accordance with the instruments of international law including human rights law.

2. Indigenous peoples have the collective rights that are indispensable to the enjoyment of the individual human rights of their members. Accordingly the states recognize inter alia the right of the indigenous peoples to collective action, to their cultures, to profess and practice their spiritual beliefs, and to use their languages.

3. The states shall ensure for indigenous peoples the full exercise of all rights, and shall adopt in accordance with their constitutional processes such legislative or other measures as may be necessary to give effect to the rights recognized in this Declaration.

Article III. Right to belong to indigenous peoples

Indigenous peoples and communities have the right to belong to indigenous peoples, in accordance with the traditions and customs of the peoples or nation concerned.

Article IV. Legal status of communities

Indigenous peoples have the right to have their legal personality fully recognized by the states within their systems.

Article V. No forced assimilation

1. Indigenous peoples have the right to freely preserve, express and develop their cultural identity in all its aspects, free of any attempt at assimilation.

2. The states shall not undertake, support or favour any policy of artificial or enforced assimilation of indigenous peoples, destruction of a culture or the possibility of the extermination of any indigenous peoples.

Article VI. Special guarantees against discrimination

1. Indigenous peoples have the right to special guarantees against discrimination that may have to be instituted to fully enjoy internationally and nationally-recognized human rights; as well as measures necessary to enable indigenous women, men and children to exercise, without any discrimination, civil, political, economic, social, cultural and spiritual rights. The states recognize that violence exerted against persons because of their gender and age prevents and nullifies the exercise of those rights.

2. Indigenous peoples have the right to fully participate in the prescription of such guarantees.

INTERNATIONAL COVENANT ON CIVIL AND POLITICAL RIGHTS

Article 1

1. All peoples have the right of self-determination. By virtue of that right they freely determine their political status and freely pursue their economic, social and cultural development.

2. All peoples may, for their own ends, freely dispose of their natural wealth and resources without prejudice to any obligations arising out of international economic co-operation, based upon the principle of mutual benefit, and international law. In no case may a people be deprived of its own means of subsistence.

3. The States Parties to the present Covenant, including those having responsibility for the administration of Non-Self-Governing and Trust Territories, shall promote the realization of the right of self-determination, and shall respect that right, in conformity with the provisions of the Charter of the United Nations.

CONVENTION ON BIOLOGICAL DIVERSITY

Article 8. In-situ Conservation

Each Contracting Party shall, as far as possible and as appropriate:

(a) Establish a system of protected areas or areas where special measures need to be taken to conserve biological diversity;

(b) Develop, where necessary, guidelines for the selection, establishment and management of protected areas or areas where special measures need to be taken to conserve biological diversity;

(c) Regulate or manage biological resources important for the conservation of biological diversity whether within or outside protected areas, with a view to ensuring their conservation and sustainable use;

(d) Promote the protection of ecosystems, natural habitats and the maintenance of viable populations of species in natural surroundings;

(e) Promote environmentally sound and sustainable development in areas adjacent to protected areas with a view to furthering protection of these areas;

(f) Rehabilitate and restore degraded ecosystems and promote the recovery of threatened species, inter alia, through the development and implementation of plans or other management strategies;

(g) Establish or maintain means to regulate, manage or control the risks associated with the use and release of living modified organisms resulting from biotechnology which are likely to have adverse environmental impacts that could affect the conservation and sustainable use of biological diversity, taking also into account the risks to human health;

(h) Prevent the introduction of, control or eradicate those alien species which threaten ecosystems, habitats or species;

(i) Endeavour to provide the conditions needed for compatibility between present uses and the conservation of biological diversity and the sustainable use of its components;

(j) Subject to its national legislation, respect, preserve and maintain knowledge, innovations and practices of indigenous and local communities embodying traditional lifestyles relevant for the conservation and sustainable use of biological diversity and promote their wider application with the approval and involvement of the holders of such knowledge, innovations and practices and encourage the equitable sharing of the benefits arising from the utilization of such knowledge, innovations and practices;

(k) Develop or maintain necessary legislation and/or other regulatory provisions for the protection of threatened species and populations;

(l) Where a significant adverse effect on biological diversity has been determined pursuant to Article 7, regulate or manage the relevant processes and categories of activities; and

(m) Cooperate in providing financial and other support for in-situ conservation outlined in subparagraphs (a) to (l) above, particularly to developing countries.

ACIA	Arctic Climate Impact Assessment
ATCA	Alien Torts Claims Act
BIOT	British Indian Ocean Territory
BRDN	Buffalo River Dene Nation
CBD	Convention on Biological Diversity
CERD	Committee on the Elimination of Racial Discrimination
CID	corporate internal decision-making
CRC	Convention on the Rights of the Child
ECHR	European Court of Human Rights
EEA	European Environmental Agency
EFA	ecological footprint analysis
FAO	Food and Agriculture Organization of the United Nations
FCTC	Framework Convention on Tobacco Control
FPIC	free, prior, informed consent
FPICon	free, prior, informed consultation
IACHR	Inter-American Court of Human Rights
IBI	Index of Biotic Integrity
ICC	International Criminal Court
ICCPR	International Covenant on Civil and Political Rights
ICESCR	International Covenant on Economic, Social and Cultural Rights
ICJ	International Court of Justice
IJC	International Joint Commission (Canada and US)
ILO	International Labour Organization
IMF	International Monetary Fund
IUCN	World Conservation Union
MNC	multinational corporation
MOSOP	Movement for Survival of the Ogoni People
MPA	marine protected area
OAS	Organization of American States
PCB	polychlorinated biphenyl
REACH	Registration, Evaluation and Authorization of Chemicals
TAN	transnational advocacy network
TNC	transnational corporation
UNDD	United Nations Draft Declaration on the Rights of Indigenous Peoples
UNDP	United Nations Development Programme
UNEP	United Nations Environment Programme
UNESCO	United Nations Economic, Scientific and Cultural Organization
UNHRC	United Nations Human Rights Committee

WHA	World Health Assembly
WHO	World Health Organization
WTO	World Trade Organization
WWF	World Wildlife Fund

AUSTRALIA

Aboriginal Community v. Victoria (2002) 194 ALR 538
Dagi; Shackles, Ambeu; Maur and others v. the Broken Hill Proprietary Company Ltd. and Ok Tedi Mining Limited (No. 2) [1997] Victoria Reports [VR] 428
Mabo v. Queensland, 83 ALR High Court of Australia, (1992) 175 CL
Western Australia v. Ward (2002) 194 ALR 538
Wik Peoples v. Queensland (1996) 187 CLR 1
Yorta Yorta Aboriginal Community v. Victoria (1998) 1606 FLR

CANADA

Corinthe v. Seminary of St. Sulpice of Montreal 5 DLR, Judicial Committee of the Jury Council, 19 July 1992
Dashowa Inc. v. Friends of the Lubicon, (1998) 158 DLR (4) 699 (Ont. Gen. Div.)
Delgamuukw v. British Columbia [1997] 3 SCR 1010
Delgamuukw v. British Columbia [1998] 1 CNLR 14, 11 December 1997
Dunbar v. the King (1936)
Guerin v. Canada [1984] 2 SCR 335
Halfway River First Nation v. British Columbia (Minister of Forests) (1999) 178 DLR (4) 666 716
Lubicon Lake Band v. Canada, Communication No. 167/1984
Marshall v. The Queen [1993] 3 SCR 456
Monsanto (Canada) Inc. v. Schmeiser [2004] 1 SCR 902
Ominayak v. Canada, UN GAOR, 45 Sess., Supp. No. 40, Annex 9 at 27, UN Doc. A/45/40(1990)
R. v. Colgate Palmolive 8 CCC (2d) 40 1972 Ontario High Court of Justice
R. v. Hibbert ([1995] 2 SCR 973, 99 CCC (3) 193
R. v. Marshall; R. v. Bernard (2005), 2 SCR 220
R. v. Paquette [1977] 2 S.C.R. 189 30 CCC 22417
R. v. Sparrow, 70 DLR 4 (1990)385 401
R. L. et al v. Canada, Communication No. 358/1989 views of 5 November 1991, [1992] Annual Report: 358
R. v. Gladstone , 137 DLR 4 648, 9 WWR1 1996
R. v. Pamajewon, 138 DLR 4 204
R. v. Sparrow [1990] 1 SCR 1075
R. v. Van der Peet, 137 DLR 4 289, 9 WWR1 (Can. 1996)
R. v. Wholesale Travel Group Inc (1991) 3 SCR 154

Reference re Secession of Quebec, 20 August 1998, SCR 2[1998], 281
Rex v. Dunbar [1935] BCJ No. 6, [1936] 3 WWR 99, 51 BCR 20
Smith, Kline and French Laboratories Ltd T. et al v. A.-G. Canada (1985), 7 CPR (2d) 145 (FCTD)
Surrey Credit Union v. Mendonca (1985), 67 BCLR 310 SC
Van der Peet, 137 DLR 4 289

EUROPE

Fadeyeva v. Russia [2005] ECHR **55723**/00, European Court of Human Rights, 1 July 2004 and
    19 May 2005
France et al v. Goering et al (946) 22 IMT 203, p. 528
Fredin v. Sweden [1991] ECHR 12033/86
G. and E. v. Norway Apps., No. 9278/81 and 9415/81, 35 Eur. Comm'n H.R. Doc. And Rep. 30,
    35 (1984)
Guerra v. Italy [1998] ECHR 14967/89
Hatton and Other v. UK [2003] ECHR 36022/97
Ilmari Lansman et al v. Finland, Communication No.511/1992: Finland, 08/11/94
Ivan Kitok v. Sweden, Communication No. 197/1985, CCPR/C/33/D/197/1985 (1988)
Le Louis, 2 Dods. Rep. 210–212, 237–259
Le Louis, 2 Dodson Rep.238, *Judgement* – Sir William Scott at 248
Lopez-Ostra v. Spain (1995) 20 HER 277m (1994) ECHR 16798/90
Lopez-Ostra v. Spain [1994] ECHR 16798/90
Rylands v. Fletcher (1865–1868), 3H. and C. 744 (Exch.); L.R. 1 Ex.265 (Exch. Ch.); L.R.3 H.L.
    330 (H.L.)

INTERNATIONAL

Advisory Opinion (WHO) [1996] ICJ Rep. 66
Australia v. France, 1974, ICJ Reports 1974, 253
Bagilishema (ICTR-95-1at) Judgement, 7 June 2001, para. 80
Barcelona Traction, Light and Power Co. Ltd Second Phase, Judgement ICJ Reports 1970, p.3
Burkina-Faso v. Republic of Mali, ICJ Reps. 1986, 586
Case concerning *East Timor* (*Portugal v. Australia*) 1995 ICJ 90
Chorozow Factory case, PCIJ, Ser. A, No. 17, p. 29
Corfu Channel (*UK v. Albania*) 1949 ICJ 4 (April 1949)
Gabcikovo-Nagymaros case, ICJ (1997) Rep. 7, Judge C. Weeramantry, Separate
Hopu and Besent v. France, UN GAOR, 52 Sess., Supp., No. 4, UN Doc. A/52/40 (1997)
Lake Lanoux Arbitration (France v. Spain) (1957) 12 RIAA 281, Arbitral Tribunal, 16 November
Lovelace, Communication No. 24/1977. 30 July 1981
Lovelace v. Canada, No. 24/1977
The Mayagna (Sumo) Awas Tingni Community Case – Series C, No. 79 [2001] 1A CHR 9 (31 August
    2001)
Minors Oposa v. Secretary of the Dept. of Environmental and Natural Resources, (Philippines 1993), 33
    ILM 173 (1994)
New Zealand v. France, 1974, ICJ 457
Nicaragua v. United States of America (1986) ICJ 14
Nuclear Tests case (*Australia v. France*) 1974 ICJ 253

Nuclear Tests case (*New Zealand v. France*) 457
Prosecutor v. Akayesu (Case No. ICTR-96-4-T) Judgement, 2 September 1998, paras 477, 731–733
Prosecutor v. Delalic et al, Case No. IT-96-21-T, Judgement, 16 November, 1998
Prosecutor v. Tadic (Case No. IT-94-I-T, Opinion and Judgement, 7 May, 1997
South West Africa cases, 1966 ICJ 4
UK v. Albania (1949) ICJ Rep. 4,17
United States v. Iran (1980) ICJ 3
United States v. EC Biotech (2005) DS 291 17, World Trade Organization dispute panel hearing (also cases for Canada (DS 292 17) and Argentina (DS 293 17) versus EC Biotech)
US v. Canada (1931–1941), 3 RIAA 1905
Western Sahara, 1975 ICJ 12, 39 (1 October)

JAPAN

Kayishema et al (ICTR-95-I-T), Judgement and Sentence, 21 May 1999
Kumamoto Minimata Disease case, 696 Hanjil 5 Kumamoto District Court, 20 March 1973
Niigata Minamata case, 642 Hanji (Niigata District Court, 29 September 1971)
Tachiona v. Omugabe, 234 S. Supp. 2d. 401, No. 00 Civ. 6666 (VM), 2002 WL 317 9018 (SDNY 11 December 2002)
Toyama Itai-Itai case, 635 Hanji 17 (Toyama District Court, 30 June 1091)
Yokkaichi Asthma case, 672 Hanji 30 (Tsu District Court, Yokkaichi Branch, 24 July 1972)

NEW ZEALAND

Maori Council v. Attorney General (1987) 1 NZLR (1641)
Ninety Mile Beach (1963) NZLR 461

UNITED KINGDOM

Continental Tyre and Rubber Co Ltd v. Daimler Co Ltd (1915) KB, 893
R. (Bancoult) v. Secretary of State for Foreign and Commonwealth Affairs and Another (2001) QB 1067 (3 November 2000)

UNITED STATES

Aguinda v. Texaco, Inc., 1945 F. Supp. 625 (5 DNY 1996); 1 & 2 F. Supp. 2d 53 (SDNY 2001)
Alexis Holyweek Sarei et al v. Rio Tinto plc and Rio Tinto United, US District Court for the Central District of California, 221 F. Supp. 2d 1116; 2002 US Dist. LEXIS 16235; 156 Oil and Gas Rep. 403, 11 July 2002, Entered
Ashanga v. Texaco, Inc., SDNY Dist. No. 94 Civ. 9266 (13 August 1997)
Baker v. Carr, 369 US 186, 217 2d.663, 82 S. Ct. 691 (1962)
Bancoult v. McNamara 370 Supp. 2dl.U.S. Dist., LEXIS 27882 (21 December 2004, decided)

Bancoult v. McNamara, 217 FRD 280, 2003 US Dist. LEXIS 17102 (DDC, 2003, #2)

Beanal v. Freeport-McMoran, Inc. and Freeport-McMoran Copper and Gold, Inc., 969 F. Supp. 362; 1997 US Dist LEXIS 4767 (April 1997, decided)

Cherokee Nations v. Georgia, 30 US 5 Pet. 17 (1831)

Derensis v. Cooper and Lybrand Chartered Accountants, 930 F. Supp. 1003, 1007 (DNJ 1996)

Doe v. Unocal Corp., 2002 W.L. 3.D 63976 (9 Cir. 2003)

Doe/Roe v. Unocal Corp., 110 F. Supp. 2d 1294, 1306 (CD Cal. 2000)

Employment Div., Dept. of Human Resources v. Smith, 494 U.S. 872 (1990)

Federation of the Yagua People of the Lower Amazon and Lower, Napo v. Texaco, Inc., 303 F 3d 470; 2002 US App. LEXIS cl6540; 157 Oil and Gas Rep. 333, 16 August 2002, Decided

Filartiga v. Pena-Irala, 630 F.2d 876, 881 (2d Cir. 1980)

Filartiga v. Pena-Irala, US Court of Appeals, 2d ct, 1980 630 F 2d 876

Jota v. Texaco, Inc., 157 F 3d 153 (2d Cir.1998)

Kadic v. Karadi, (1996) 74 F.3d 377, decided 4 January

Lyng v. NW Indian Cemetery Protective Association, 485 US 439 (1988)

The Presbyterian Church of Sudan, Rev. John Gaduel, Nuer Community, Development Services and others v. Talisman Energy, Inc., 244 F. Supp. 2d 289:2003 US Dist. LEXIS 4085:155 Oil and Gas Rep. 409, 19 March 2003, decided

Santa Clara County v. South Pacific Railroads Corp., 1886

Sequinha v. Texaco, 847 F. Supp. 61 (SD Tex. 1994)

Sequinha v. Texaco, Inc., 945 F. Supp. 625 (SDNY 1996)

Sinaltral the Estate of Isidro Sequndo Gil, Plaintiffs v. Coca Cola Company et al, United States District Court SD Florida, 256 F. Supp. 2d 1345

Trail Smelter Arbitration, US v. Canada 1931-1941 3 RIAA 1905

United States v. FMC Corporation, 572 F. 2d 902 (2 Cir. 1978)

United States v. Smith, 18 US 153, 160–161, 5 L. Ed. 57 (1920)

Wiwa v. Royal Shell Petroleum et al, 226 F. 3d 88 (2d Cir. 2000)

Worcester v. Georgia, 31 US 515 (1832)

Aboriginal Lands Rights (Northern Territory) Act, 1976 B42(6) 77A (Austl.)

African [Banjul] Charter on Human and Peoples Rights, adopted 27 June 1981, Art. 24, 21 ILM 58(1982)

Agenda 21, document of United Nations Programme of the same name, revealed at the United Nations Conference on Environment and Development (Earth Summit), Rio de Janeiro, 14 June 1992

Agreement for the Prosecution and Punishment of Major War Criminals of the European Axis, Establishing the Charter of the International Military Tribunal (IMT) (1951), 82 UNITS 279. annex

Agreement on Identity and Rights of Indigenous Peoples, UN GAOR, 49 Sess., Agenda Item 42, Annex, UN Doc. A./49/882, S/1995/256 (1995)

Alien Torts Claims Act, 28 USC 1350 (2000)

Alien Torts Claims Act, 28 USCS 1350 (2002)

American Convention on Human Rights (1969) OAS Treaty Ser./No.36; 1144 UNTS 123

Article of Agreements of the International Bank for Reconstruction and Development, Art. IV, 10, 60 Stat. 15 1449, 2 UNTS at 158

Atlantic Charter, joint declaration issued on 14 August 1941, during World War II, by the British prime minister, Winston Churchill, and President Franklin D. Roosevelt of the US, after five days of conferences aboard warships in the North Atlantic

Badinter Commission Opinion No. 1, 29 November 1991 ILM 31, 1992: 1494–1497, 'Conference on Yugoslavia'

Biodiversity Convention 5 June 1992, 1760 UNTS 79, Can. T.S. 1993 No. 24,31 ILM 818

British Indian Ocean Territory Agreement, 1999

Canadian Bill of Rights (1960) SC, c.44

Canadian Bill of Rights, RSC 1970, App. III

Canadian Charter of Rights and Freedoms, a part of the Constitution of Canada, in force 17 April 1982

Canadian Criminal Code, RSC 1985, c C-46

CERD Report (1993): UN GAOR, 47 Sess. Supp. No. 18 Doc. A/47/18

Charter of Economic Rights and Duties of States, GA Res. 3281, UN GAOR, 29 Sess., Supp. No. 31, at 50, UN Doc. A/9631 (1974)

Charter of the International Military Tribunal (1947) IMT, Nuremberg, I and II, trials of the major war criminals

Charter of the United Nations, Article 1 (3), 13(1) (b), 55(c), 56, 59, and 76(c)

Clean Water Act (1972) PL 92-500, US legislation

Committee on the Elimination of Racial Discrimination (CERD), general recommendatins (XXITTI) concerning indigenous peoples; adopted by the UN Committee on the Elimination of Racial Discrimination at its 1235 meeting, on August 18, 1997, UN Doc. CERD/C/51/ misc.13/Rev.4 (1997)

Composite Report on Status and Trends Regarding the Knowledge, Innovations and Practices Relevant to the Conservation and Sustainable Use of Biological Diversity, The Conference of the Parties, Composite Report (B), COP8 Decisions (VIII/5. Article 8 (j) and related provisions)

Constitution Act (1982) Schedule B of the *Canada Act 1982* (UK), a part of the Constitution of Canada

Constitución Política de la Republica de Nicaragua, Managua, 9 January 1982

Contemporary Forms of Racism, Racial Discrimination, Xenophobia and Related Intolerance, Report by Mr Maurice Gkeke-Ahanhanzo, Special Reporter on his mission to the United States of America, 9–22 October 1994, Submitted Pursuant to Human Rights resolution 1993/20 and 1994/64, UN Doc E/CN.4/1995/78/Add.1, para.21

Convention Against Torture and other Inhuman, Cruel or Degrading Treatment or Punishment, Art. 13, 1465 UNTS 85, 116, 23 ILM 1027, 1030

Convention Concerning Indigenous and Tribal Peoples, ILO No. 169, 27 July 1989, 28 ILM1382 (1989), in force 5 September 1991

Convention for the Protection of Human Rights and Freedoms, Rome, 4 November 1950 T.S. 71 (1953)

Convention on Biological Diversity, 5 June 1992, UNCED, UN Doc. UNEP/Bio.Div./N7INC.5/4 (1992)

Convention on the Prevention and Suppression of the Crime of Genocide (1951), 78 UNTS 277

Declaration of Independence of New Zealand, 28 October 1835

Declaration on Principles of International Law Concerning Friendly Relations and Co-operation Among States in Accordance with the Charter of the United Nations, UN GAOR, 25 Sess., Supp. No. 28, at 121, 124, UN Doc. A/8028(1970)

Declaration on the Establishment of the Arctic Council, Canada, Denmark, Finland, Iceland, Norway, Russian Federation, Sweden, and the United States, 19 September 1996, 35 ILM 1387 (Arctic Council Declaration)

Declaration on the Principles of International Law Concerning Friendly Relations and Cooperation among States in Accordance with the Charter of the United Nations, 24 October 1970 (2625) XXV

Declaration on the Rights of Persons Belonging to National or Ethnic, Religious and Linguistic Minorities, UN GAOR, 47 Sess., Supp., No. 49, at 210, UN Doc. A/47/49 (1992)

Desertification Convention, 14 October 1994, UNTS 3, Can. TS 1996, No. 51, 33 ILM 1332

Development and International Economic Co-operation: Transnational Corporation, UN ESCOR, 2d See., UN Doc. E/1990/94 (1990)

Draft Convention on the Crime of Genocide, UN Doc. E/447 (1947)

Draft Convention on the Crime of Genocide, UN Doc. A/C.6/86 (1946)

Draft Decision UNEP/CBD/.COP 8/L.20, Decision VIII/30 at the Conference of the Parties to the Convention on Biological Diversity

Draft Declaration on the Rights of Indigenous Peoples, Working Group on Indigenous Populations (11ts Sess.) Commission on Human Rights, Sub-Commission on Prevention of Discrimination and Protection of Minorities, 44 Sess. Agenda Item 14, at 50, Annex I, UN Doc. E/CN.4/Sub.2/1993/29 (1993)

Draft Elements of Crimes, UN Doc. PCNICC/1999/DP.4, p. 7

Draft Genocide Convention (1946) UN DocA/C.6/86

Draft International Covenant on Environment and Development, Commission on Environmental Law of IUCN (World Conservation Union) in Cooperation with the International Council of Environmental Law, Paper No 31, second edition, 2000

Draft United Nations Code of Conduct on Transnational Corporations, UN ESCOR, Spe. Sess. Supp.No. 7, Annex II, UN Doc. E/1983/17/Rev.1 (1983)

ECOSOC, Commission on Human Rights, 'Human Rights and Indigenous Issues: Report of the Working Group', Annex I, UNDoc. E/CN.4/2006/79 (22 March 2006), prepared by the Charpersou-Rapporteur, Luis-Enrique Chavez

Federal Racial Discrimination Act, Australian legislation, 1975

Fifth Report of the Standing Committee on Aboriginal Affairs, House of Commons, Canada, May 1991

First Revised Text of the Draft Universal Declaration on Rights of Indigenous Peoples, UN Doc. E/CN.4/Sub.21/1989/33 (1989), paras. 3 and 4

Foreign Sovereign Immunities Act, 28 USC and 1603(b) and 1604

Foreshore and Seabed Act of 2004, no 93, Parliament of New Zealand

The Framework Convention for the Protection of National Minorities, 1 February 1995, Europ.T.S. 157

Geneva Conventions: adopted on 12 August 1949 by the Diplomatic Conference for the Establishment of International Conventions for the Protection of Victims of War, held in Geneva from 21 April to 12 August 1949, entry into force 21 October 1950, 75 UNTS 287:

> First convention: *Convention for the Amelioration of the Condition of the Wounded in Armies in the Field*, first adopted in 1864

> Second convention: *Convention for the the Amelioration of the Condition of Wounded, Sick and Shipwrecked Members of Armed Forces at Sea*, first adopted in 1949

> Third convention: *Convention relative to the Treatment of Prisoners of War*, first adopted in 1929

> Fourth convention: *Convention relative to the Protection of Civilian Persons in Time of War*, first adopted in 1949

Great Lakes Water Quality Agreement (1978) between the US and Canada, signed at Ottawa, 22 November 1978; Amended Protocol signed 18 November 1987

The Hague Convention (1907) Convention (IV) Respecting the Laws and Customs of War by Land, [1910] UKTS 9

Human Rights Commission, UN Doc. A/45/40, Vol. II, Annex IV.A.

ILC Draft Articles on Jurisdictional Immunities of States, as adopted at 43rd Session, 1991, and recommended to UN General Assembly, Article 10, 30 It.Lg.Mt. 1554 (1991)

ILC Report (2001) GAOR A/56/10

ILO Convention on Indigenous and Tribal Peoples, No. 169 of 1989, International Labour Conference, entered into force 5 September 1991

Indian Child Welfare Act of 1978, 25 USC § 1901 (1978)

The Indian Self-Determination and Education Act of 1975, 25 USC § 450 (1975)

Indian Tribal Government Tax Status Act, 26 USC § 7871 (1982)

The Indian Tribal Justice Acto of 1993, 25 USC § 2901 (1993)

The Indigenous Peoples Rights Act, Republic Act, No.8371 (1997) (Phil.), www.bknet.org/laws/RA_8371.html.

Indigenous Peoples Statement at the 19 Session of the United Nations Working Groups on Indigenous Populations, 29 July 2001, http://forestpeoples.gn.apc.org/briefings.html

Interim Report of the Commission of Experts Established Pursuant to Security Council Resolution 780 (1992), UN Doc. S/35374 (1993)

International Bill of Human Rights, UN Doc. A/565 1948

International Convention on the Elimination of All Forms of Racial Discrimination (1965) Art. 14(1), 660 UNTS 195, 230 5 ILM 350 361

International Covenant on Civil and Political Rights (ICCPR), GA Res. 2000, UN GAOR, 21st Sess., Supp. No. 16, UN Doc. A/6316 (1966)

International Covenant on Economic, Social and Cultural Rights UN Doc. A/6316 (1996) 993 UNTS 3

International Law Commission, *Report on the Work of the 48th Session, Draft Articles on State Responsibility* (1995) GAOR, 51st Session, Supp. No.10, UN Doc A/51/10

Madison Declaration on Mercury Pollution, www.unbc.ca/assets/media/2007/03_march/madison_declarationon_mercury_pollution_with_nontechnical_summary.pdf

The Maori Language Act of 1987

Migratory Bird Treaty (1918) 16 USC 703

Montevideo Convention on the Rights and Duties of States of 1934, www.yale.edu/lawweb/avalon/avalon.htm

Moscow Treaty: *Treaty Banning Nuclear Weapons Tests in the Atmosphere, in Outer Space and Underwater (Moscow)*, 480 UNTS 3 (1964)

Native Title Act, 1993, Aust. Cap. Terr. Laws §223(1)

Native Title Amended Act, 1998 (Australia)

Norms on the Responsibility of Transnational Corporations and Other Business Enterprises with Regard to Human Rights, UN Doc. E/CN.4/Sub.2/2003/12/Rev.2 (2003)

Nunavut Act, 1993, c.28 (assented to 10 June 1993)

Nunavut Land Claims Agreement Act, 1993, c.29 (assented to 10 June 1993)

Nuremberg Charter: *Charter of the International Military Tribunal*, Nuremberg, 82 UNTS 279

Operational Manual Statement, World Bank, 1982, OMS 2.34

Optional Protocol to the Elimination of All Forms of Discrimination Against Women, Art. 2, 39 ILM 281, 282

Optional Protocol to the International Covenant on Civil and Political Rights, Art. 1, 1999 UNTS 302

Optional Protocol to the International Covenant on Civil and Political Rights, Art. 5, Communication No. 197/1985

Philippines Indigenous Peoples Rights Act, 1997, B3(g), 59

Prevention of Racial Discrimination, Including Early Warning and Urgent Actions Procedures: Working Paper Adopted by the Committee on the Elimination of Racial Discrimination, UN GAOR 48 Sess., Supp, No. 18, UN Doc. A/48/18, Annex III, para. 8

Proclamation of Tehran, International Conference on Human Rights, 1968 Year Book on Human Rights, 458

Proposed American Declaration on the Rights of Indigenous Peoples (1997), OR OEA/Ser./L/V/II.95 Doc. 6 (OAS Draft Declaration)

Protocol Additional to the Geneva Conventions of 12 August 1949, and relating to the Protection of Victims of International Armed Conflicts (Protocol 1), adopted on 8 June 1977 by the Diplomatic Conference on the Reaffirmation and Development of International Humanitarian Law applicable in Armed Conflicts, entry into force 7 December 1979, in accordance with Article 95

Protocol to the Framework Convention on Climate Change (Kyoto) (1998) 37 ILM 22

Queensland Coast Island Declaratory Act 1985 ('The Queensland Act'), Australia

Radiation Exposure Compensation Act (1990) 4 STAT 920, US federal statute, passed by Congress on 5 October 1990

Reindeer Grazing Act (1886) Swedish legislation

Reindeer Husbandry Act (1971) Swedish legislation

Report of the Human Rights Committee, UN GAOR, 45 Sess., Supp. No. 40, Vol. 2, at 10, UN Doc. A/45/40, Annex IX (A) (1990), view adopted on 26 March 1990 at the 38 Sess., Bernard Ominayak, Chief of the Lubicon Cree *Band v. Canada*, Communication No. 167 /184

Report of the International Law Commission to the Genera Assembly (1950) UN Doc. A/1316, reprinted in 1950 [II] ILC YB 364

Report of the UN Conference on the Human Environment, UN Doc. A/CONF.48/14/Rev.1 at 3 (1973), adopted 16 June 1972

Report of the Working Group on its 11 Sess., Geneva, 5-16 December 2005, and 30 January–3 February 2006 (E/CN.4/2006/79)

Report on the Situation of Human Rights in Ecuador OAS Doc. OEA/Ser.L/V/II.96, Doc. 10, rev. 1 (1997), Chapter VII, on 'The human rights situation of the inhabitants of the Ecuadorian interior affected by development activities'

Resolution 1994/45, Annex 26, 1994, adopted without changes from the *Report of the Working Group on Indigenous Populations on its Eleventh Session*, UN ESCOR, Commission on Human Rights, *Sub-Commission on Prevention of Discrimination and Protection of Minorities*, 45 Sess, Agenda Item 14, UN Doc. E/CN.4/Sub/1993/29, Annexl

Resolution 2006/2 – *Working Group of the Commission on Human Rights to Elaborate a Draft Declaration in accordance with Paragraph 5 of the General Assembly Resolution 49/214 of 23 December 1994*

Restatement (Third) of the Foreign Relations Law of the United States 702 (1987)

Rio Declaration on Environment and Development, Annex 1 of the *Report of the United Nations Conference on Environmental and Development,* 1992, A;CONF.151/vol.2

Royal Proclamations, 7 October 1763 (1985 RSC Appendix II, No. 1)

Statute of the International Criminal Court, Rome, 17 July 1998, Art. 1, 37 ILM, UN Doc. A/CONF.183/9 (in force 12 July 2002)

Stockholm Declaration on the Human Environment, adopted June 16, 1972, UN Doc. A/CONF.48/141 Rev.l at 3(1973) Principle 1, 11 ILM 1416(1972)

Tobacco Convention, www.who.int/tobacco/fctc/text/en/fctc_en.pdf

Trade and Development Board, 11 Sess., Geneva, 19–23 March 2007, TD/B/COM.1/CRP.4; WTO Report

Treaty of Paris (1783) between Great Britain and the US (separate agreements also signed between Britain and France, Spain and the Netherlands) signed 3 September 1783, ratified by the Congress of the Confederation on 14 January 1784

Treaty of Waitangi, Treaty of Cession, 5–6 February 1840, Great Britain–New Zealand, 89 C sol.T.S. 473

UN Conference on the Human Environment, UN Doc. A/CONF.48/14 Rev. and Corr.1 (1972), 11 ILM 1416 (1972)

UN Convention on the Rights of the Child (UNCROC) GA Res. 44/25, 44 UNGA Supp. (No. 49), UN Doc. A/44/49, 20 November 1989

UN Declaration of Human Rights, GA Res. 217A (III), UNCA at A/810, 10 December 1948

UN Doc. A/CONF.151/5/P v.1 (1992), 31 ILM 874(1992)

UN Economic and Social Council (ECN.4/2006/78/Add.3, 13 March 2006);

UN Framework Convention on Biological Diversity, 5 Treaty Doc. No. 103-20, ILM 818 (1992)

UN Framework Convention on Climate Change (UNFCCC), 31 ILM (1992) 851

UN GAOR 6 Comm. 3d Sess. 75 mtg. at 115–116 (UN Doc. A/633) (1948)

UN GAOR, 21 Sess., Supp. No. 16, 49, UN Doc. A/6315(1966)

UN General Assembly Resolution 32/130 (1977)

UN Report of the World Summit on Sustainable Development, 26 August–4 September 2002 at 10, Article 25, UN Doc. A/CONF.199/20/Corr.1, at 10, Art. 25

UN Rights Committee, Sub-Commission on Prevention of Discrimination and Protection of Minorities, Res. 1994/44, Aug. 16, 1994, UN Doc. E/CN, 4/1995/2, E/CN.4/Sub.2/1994/56 (1994) Article 7

UN Sub-Commission on Prevention of Discrimination and Protection of Minorities, Study of the Problem of Discrimination against Indigenous Populations, UN Doc. E/CN.4/Sub.2/1986/7Add.4

UN World Conference on Human Rights, Vienna Declaration and Programme of Action, UN Doc. A/CONF.157/24 (Part I) (1993), 32 ILM 1661 (1993)

UNESCO Convention Concerning the Protection of the World Cultural and Natural Heritage, 11 ILM (1972) 1358

UNESCO WHC-05/29.COM/9, June 15, 2005

Universal Declaration of Human Rights, GA Res. 217A, UNGA OR, 3d Sess., pt. 1, UN Doc. A/810 (1948)

US National Security Council Position on Indigenous Peoples (18 January 2001), www.umn.edu/humanrts/usdocs/indigenousdocs.html

Vienna Convention on the Law of Treaties, 115 UNTS 331, 8 ILM 679 (1969)

Westfall, *Federal Employees Liability Reform and Tort Compensation Act of 1988,* Fub. L. No. 100–694, 102 Stat.4563 (1988) (codified at 28 USC && 2671-2680)

WHO (IPCS) (2002) *Global Assessment of the State-of-the-Science of Endocrine Disruptors* (WHO/IPCS/EDC/02.0)

World Bank, Emergency Economic and Social Reunification Support Project (EESRSP), Technical Annex, Report No. T7601-ZR.

World Health Organization: *Basic Documents 4–8* (1990) 38th edition, WHO, Geneva

World Health Organization: *Eighth General Programme of Work Covering the Period 1990–1995*, WHO, Geneva

World Health Organization: *Handbook of Resolutions and Decisions of the World Health Assembly and the Executive Board* (1985) volumes I to III, WHO, Geneva

Bibliography

ACIA (Arctic Climate Impact Assessment) (2004) *Impacts of a Warming Arctic*, Summary Report of the Arctic Climate Impact Assessment, Cambridge, Cambridge University Press

Adelson, N. (2005) 'The embodiment of inequity: Health disparities in aboriginal Canada', *Canadian Journal of Public Health*, March/April

Agarwal, A. (1992) 'Sociological and political constraints to biodiversity conservation: A case study from India', in Sandhend, O. T., Hindar, K. and Brown, A. H. D. (eds) *Conservation of Biodiversity for Sustainable Development*, Oslo, Scandinavian University Press

Ago, R. (1990) 'The concept of the international community as a whole', in Weiler, J., Cassese, A. and Spinedi, M. (eds) *International Crime of State: A Critical Analysis of the ILC Draft Article 19 on State Responsibility*, Berlin, Walter de Gruyter

Amnesty International (1995) *Nigeria Historical Fact Sheet: June 1993, February 1995*, Washington DC

Amnesty International (2003) *Canada Time is Wasting: Respect for the Land Rights of the Lubicon Cree Long Overdue*, www.amnesty.org/library/

Anaya, J. (1999) 'Superpower attitudes towards indigenous peoples and group rights', *American Society of International Law Proceedings*, pp251-257

Anaya, J. (2000) 'Self-determination as a collective right under contemporary international law', in Aikio, P. and Scheinin, M. (eds) *Operationalizing the Right of Indigenous Peoples to Self-Determination*

Anaya, J. (2001) 'The influence of indigenous peoples on the development of international law', in Garwawe, S., Kelly, L. and Fisher, W. (eds), *Indigenous Human Rights*, Sydney, Sydney Institute of Criminology

Anaya, J. (2004) *Indigenous Peoples in International Law*, 2nd edition, New York, Oxford University Press

Anaya, J. and Grossman, C. (2002) 'The case of the Awas Tingni v. Nicaragua: A new step in the international law of indigenous peoples', *Arizona Journal of International and Comparative Law*, vol 19, spring

Aquinas, T. *Summa Theologiae*, Book II

Aquinas, T. (1988 [c. 1260]) *On Law, Morality and Politics*, Baumgarten, W. and Regan, R. S. J. (eds) Indianapolis, IN, Hackett Publishing Company

Aristotle (1900 [c. 340 BC]) *The Politics*, New York, Colonial Press

Aristotle (1968 [c. 350 BC]) *Parts of Animals, Movement of Animals, Progression of Animals*, Loeb Library no 323, Cambridge, MA, Harvard University Press

Artuso, A. (1997) 'Capturing the chemical value of biodiversity: Economic perspectives and policy prescriptions', in Grifo, F. and Rosenthal, J. (eds) *Biodiversity and Human Health*, Washington DC, Island Press

Asch, M. and Zlotkin, N. (1997) 'Affirming aboriginal title: A new basis for comprehensive claims negotiations', in Asch, M. (ed) *Aboriginal and Treaty Rights in Canada: Essays on Law, Equality and Respect for Difference*, Vancouver, BC, UBC Press

Asiema, J. K. and Situma, F. D. P. (1994) 'Indigenous peoples and the environment: The case of the pastoral Maasai of Kenya', *Colorado Journal of Environmental Law and Policy*, vol 5, winter, pp149–171

Barker, E. (1973) *The Politics of Aristotle*, London, Oxford University Press

Bassiouni, C. M. (1979) 'Has the United States committed genocide against the American Indian?', *California Western International Law Journal*, vol 9, pp271–273

Bassiouni, C. M. (1996) *Crimes Against Humanity in International Criminal Law*, Dordrecht, The Netherlands, Martinus Nijhoff Publishers

Baxi, U. (1998) 'Voices of suffering and the future of human rights', *Transnational Law and Contemporary Problems*

Baxi, U. (2001) 'Geographies of injustice: Human rights at the altar of convenience', in Scott, C. (ed) *Torture as Tort*, Oxford, Hart Publishing

Bedjaoui, M. (1987) 'Some unorthodox reflections on the "right to development"', in Snyder, F. and Slinn, P. (eds) *International Law of Development: Comparative Perspectives*, Abingdon, UK, Abingdon Professional Books

Begin, P., Moss, W. and Niemczak, P. (1990) *The Claim Dispute at Oka*, Background Paper, Research Branch, Ottawa, Library of Parliament, BP.235E

Benvenisti, E. (1999) 'Exit and voice in the age of globalization', *Michigan Law Review*, vol 167

Betsill, M. (2002) 'Environmental NGOs meet the sovereign state: The Kyoto Protocol negotiations on global climate change, *Colorado Journal of International Environmental Law and Policy*, vol 13, pp49–64

Beyerveld, P. and Brownsword, R. (2001) *Human Dignity in Bioethics and Biolaw*, Oxford, Oxford University Press

Birch, M. L. (2003) 'Torture, identity and indigenous peoples: Individual and collective rights', *Albany Law Review*, pp537–540

Birnie, P. and Boyle, A. E. (2002) *International Law and the Environment*, 2nd edition, Oxford, Oxford University Press

Blackman, A. (2007) *One Last Move Before Genocide: Buffalo River Dene Nation Take Action Against the Canadian Government*, Press Release, 15 February, Buffalo River Dene Nation of Canada

Boggs, S. W. (1980) *International Boundaries: A Study of Boundary Functions and Problems*, New York, Columbia University Press

Boileau, G. (1991) *Oka, Terre Indienne*, Montreal, Meridien

Borrows, J. (1997–1998) 'Frozen rights in Canada: Constitutional interpretation and the trickster', *American Indian Law Review*, vol 22, pp37–64

Bosselmann, K. (2006) 'Toward a code of ethics for biodiversity conservation', in *CEL Newsletter*, end of 2006, Commission on Environmental Law, available at www.iucn.org

Bowman, M. (1996) 'The nature, development and philosophical foundations of the biodiversity concept in international law', in Bowman, M. and Redgwell, C. (eds) *International Law and the Conservation of Biological Diversity*, The Hague, Kluwer Law Pubications

Boyle, C. A., Decoufle, P. and Yeargin-Allsopp, M. (1994) 'Prevalence of health impacts of developmental disabilities in US children', *Pediatrics*, vol 93, pp399–403

Bridgeford, T. A. (2003) 'Imputing human rights violations on multinational corporations: The Ninth Circuit strikes again in judicial activism', *American University International Law Review*, vol 18, no 4, July–August, pp1009–1057

Brierly, J. L. (1963) *The Law of Nations*, 6th edition, Oxford, Oxford University Press

Brooks, G. (1994) 'Slick alliance, Shell's Nigerian fields produce few benefits for region's villagers: How troops handle protests', *The Wall Street Journal*, ppA1, A4, 6 May

Brooks, R., Jones, K. and Ross, V. (2002) *Law and Ecology*, Ashgate, Dartmouth

Brown, D. A. (2002) *American Heat*, Lanham, MD, Rowman Littlefield

Brownlie, I. (1979) *Principles of Public International Law*, Oxford, Clarendon Press

Brownlie, I. (1998) *Principles of Public International Law*, 5th edition, Oxford, Clarendon Press

Brownlie, I. (2003) 'The rights of peoples in modern international law', in Crawford, J. (ed) *The Rights of Peoples*, 6th edition, Oxford, Clarendon Press

Brownsword, R. (ed) (2004) *Global Governance and the Quest for Justice, Human Rights*, vol 4, Oxford, Hart Publishing

Brown-Weiss, E. (1984) 'The planetary trust: Conservation and intergenerational equity', *Ecology Law Quarterly*

Brown-Weiss, E. (1990) 'Our rights and obligations to future generations for the environment', *American Journal of International Law*, vol 84

Brown-Weiss, E. (1997) 'The changing structure of international law', *Georgetown Law Review – Res Ipsa Loquitur*

Brunnée, J. (1993) 'The responsibility of states for environmental harm in multinational context', *Les Cahiers de Droit*

Bryant, B. and Mohai, P. (eds) (1990) *Race and the Incidence of Environmental Hazards: A Time for Discourse*, Boulder, CO, Westview Press

Brysk, A. (2000) *From Tribal Village to Global Village: Indian Rights and International Relations in South America*, Stanford, Stanford University Press

Buchanan, A. (2004) *Justice, Legitimacy and Self-Determination: Moral Foundations for International Law*, Oxford, Oxford University Press

Bullard, R. D. (1994) *Dumping in Dixie*, Boulder, CO, Westview Press

Bullard, R. (1994–1995) 'Impact of the People of Color Summit', in *People of Color: Environmental Groups, 1994–1995 Directory*, Flint, MI, Charles Stewart Mott Foundation

Bullard, R. D. (2001) 'Decision making', in Westra, L. and Lawson, B. (eds) *Faces of Environmental Racism*, Lanham, MD, Rowman Littlefield

Burger, J. (1990) *The Gaia Atlas of First Peoples: A Future for the Indigenous World*, London, Gaia Books

Callicott, J. B. (1989) *In Defense of the Land Ethic*, Albany, NY, State University Press of New York

Calne, D. B., Eisen, A., McGeer, E. and Spencer, P. (1986) 'Alzheimer's disease, Parkinson's disease, and motoneurone disease: Abiotrophic interaction between ageing and environment?", *Lancet*, vol 2, pp1067–1070

Cancado Trindade, A. A. (1985) *Coexistence and Coordination Mechanisms of International Protection of Human Rights Course*, The Hague, Academy of International Law

Cancado Trindade, A. A. (1987) *Coexistence and Coordination Mechanisms of International Protection of Human Rights Course*, The Hague, Academy of International Law

Cancado Trindade, A. A. (1992) 'The contribution of international human rights law to environmental protection, with special relevance to environmental change', in Brown-Weiss, E. (ed) *Environmental Change and International Law*, Tokyo, United Nations University Press

Capotorti, F. (1977) *Study of the Rights of Persons Belonging to Ethnic Religious and Linguistic Minorities*, UN Doc. E/CN.4/Sub.2/8 and Add.1-6 (republished by the UN Centre for Human Rights, New York, 1991)

Carson, R. (1962) *Silent Spring*, Boston, Houghton Mifflin

Cassese, A. (1995) *Self-Determination of Peoples*, Cambridge, Cambridge University Press

Castaneda, J. (1969) *Legal Effects of the United Nations Resolutions*, New York, Columbia University Press

Castellino, J. and Walsh, N. (2005) *International Law and Indigenous Peoples*, The Raoul Wallenberg Institute Human Rights Library Series, Leiden, The Netherlands, Martinus Nijhoff Publishers

Catrilli, J. F. (1984) 'Problems of proof and credibility issues in relation to expert evidence in toxic tort litigation', *Queen's Law Journal*, vol 71, pp75–79

Cavallar, G. (1999) *Kant and the Theory and Practice of International Rights*, Cardiff, University of Wales Press

Chabot, M. (2003) 'Economic changes, household strategies, and social relations in contemporary Nunavit Inuit', *Polar Record*, vol 39, pp19–34

Charlebois, C. T. (1977) 'An overview of the Canadian mercury problem', *Scientific Forum*, vol 10, no 5, pp17–36

Chick, T. (1993) *Corporation and the Canadian Charter of Rights and Freedoms*, Master of Law Thesis, Halifax, Dalhousie University

Clapp, R. W., Howe, G. K. and Mizraki, S. A. (2006) *Oil Extraction and Its Human Health Impacts in the Former Texaco Concession in Ecuador*, expert opinion used in an ongoing case

Claude, I. L. (1955) *National Minorities: An International Problem*, Cambridge, MA, Harvard University Press

Cline, C. P. (1991) 'Pursuing Native American rights in international law venues: A *jus cogens* strategy after *Lyng v. Northwest Indian Cemetery Protective Association*', *Hastings Law Journal*, no 42, p59

Clinton, W. J. (1994) *Remarks to American Native and Alaska Native Tribal Leaders*, Weekly Complilation of Presidential Documents, no 18, pp941–942 (9 May)

Colborn, T. D., Myers, D. and Patterson, J. (1996) *Our Stolen Future*, Dutton, NY, Penguin Books

Connor, S. (1990) 'Health, human rights and international law', *American Society of International Law Proceedings*, pp122–129

Cooperrider, A. Y. (1994) 'The Wildlands Project, land conservation strategy', *Wild Earth*, Special Issue, pp10–25

Craig, D. (undated) 'Presentation of the IUCN Commission for Environmental Law', in International Marine Project Activities Centre Limited (IMPAC), *Traditional Law and the Environment for Country and States of the Melanesian Spearhead Group*, IMPAC (supported by the World Bank, The CEC Reef Research Centre, Australian Government, Christenson Fund)

Crawford, J. (1987) 'The aborigine in comparative law', *Law and Anthropology*, vol 2, pp5–28

Crawford, J. (1988) *The Rights of Peoples*, Oxford, Oxford University Press

Crowe, M. B. (1974) 'St Thomas and Ulpian's natural law', in *St Thomas Aquinas 1274–1974 Commemorative Studies*, Pontifical Institute for Medieval Studies, Toronto, University of Toronto Press

D'Amato, A. (1987) 'Trashing customary international law', *American Journal of International Law*, vol 81, p101

Daily, G. (1997) *Nature's Services: Societal Dependence on Natural Ecosystems*, Washington DC, Island Press

Damas, D. (1972) 'Central Eskimo systems of food sharing', *Ethnology*, vol 11, pp220–240

Damas, D. (2002) *Arctic Migrants/Arctic Villagers*, Toronto, McGill-Queens University Press

Date-Bah, S. K. (1998) 'Rights of indigenous peoples in relation to natural resources development: An African perspective', *Journal of Energy Natural Resources Law*, vol 16, no 4, pp389–412

De Klemm, C. and Shine, C. (1993) *Biological Diversity: Conservation and the Law*, Environmental Policy and Law Paper No. 29, Cambridge, IUCN Publications Service Unit

Dennison, M. (2006) 'Right to clean environment before justices', *The Missoulian*, www.missoulian.com/articles/2006/03/09/news/mtregional/news02.txt

Dunoff, J. L. and Trachtman, J. P. (1999) 'Economic analysis of international law', *Yale Journal of International Law*, vol 24, no 1, winter, pp1–59

De Sousa Santos, B. (2005) 'Beyond neoliberal governance: The World Social Forum', in De Sousa Santos, B. and Rodriguez-Garavito, C. (eds) *Law and Globalization from Below*, Cambridge, Cambridge University Press

De Tocqueville, A. (1945) *Democracy in America*, (translation by H. Reeve) New York, Alfred A. Knopf

de Vattel, E. (1758) *Le droit des gens ou principles de la loi naturelle appliqués a la conduite et aux affaires des nations et des souverains*, Book III, London

de Vattel, E. (1872) *The Law of Nations*, (translated by J. Chitty), Philadelphia, J. W. Johnson and Co., Law Booksellers

Downs, J. (1993) 'A healthy and ecologically balanced environment: An argument for a third generation right', *Duke Journal of Comparative and International Law*, vol 3, no 2, spring, pp351–385

Draper, E. (1991) *Risky Business*, Cambridge, Cambridge University Press

Dupuy, R.-J. (1991a) 'Humanity and the environment', *Colorado Journal of International Environmental Law and Policy*, vol 2, pp201–204

Dupuy, P.-M. (1991b) 'L'Etat et la réparation des dommages catastrophique', in Francioni, F. and Scovazzi, T. (eds) *International Responsibility for Environmental Harm*, London, Graham and Trotman

Edgerton, H. W. (1927) 'Negligence, inadvertence, and indifference: The relation of mental states to negligence', *Harvard Law Review*, vol 39, p849

EEA (European Environmental Agency) (2006) *Report no 29*, European Commission Joint Research Centre, Copenhagen, Denmark

Eichstaedt, P. H. (1994) *If You Poison Us: Uranium and Native Americans*, Santa Fe, Red Crane Books

El-Badry, M. A. (1989) *Health and Human Rights*, UN Doc. IESA/P/AC.28/9 (21 March)

Emberland, M. (2006) *The Human Rights of Companies*, Oxford, Oxford University Press

Endicott, T. (2005) 'The infant in the snow', in Endicott, T., Getzler, J. and Peel, E. (eds) *Properties of Law*, Oxford, Oxford University Press

Engel, R. (2000) 'The Earth Charter as a new covenant for democracy', in Miller, P. and Westra, L. (eds) *Just Ecological Integrity*, Lanham, MD, Rowman Littlefield

Epstein, P. R. (2005) 'Climate change and human health', *New England Journal of Medicine*, vol 353, no 14, pp1433–1436

Epstein, S. (1978) *The Politics of Cancer*, California, Sierra Club Books

Evans-Illidge, E. (undated) 'Oceans of opportunity: Seeking new commercial and sustainable uses of Australia's marine biodiversity', in International Marine Project Activities Centre Limited (IMPAC), *Traditional Law and the Environment for Countries and States of the Melanesian Spearhead Group*, IMPAC (supported by the World Bank, The CEC Reef Research Centre, Australian Government, Christenson Fund)

Fahim, H. M. (1982) *Indigenous Anthropology and Non-Western Countries*, Durham, NC, Carolina Academic Press

Falk, R. A. (1974) 'Ecocide, genocide and the Nuremberg traditions of individual responsibility', in Held, V., Morgenbesser, S. and Nagel, T. (eds) *Philosophy, Morality and International Affairs*, New York, Oxford University Press

Falk, R. A. (1988) 'The rights of peoples (in particular indigenous peoples)', in Crawford, J (ed) *The Rights of Peoples*, Oxford, Clarendon Press

Falk, R. A. (1998) *Law in an Emerging Global Village*, Ardsley, NY, Transnational Publishers

Feit, H. A. (1982) 'The future of hunters within nation-states: Anthropology and the James Bay Cree', in Leacock, E. and Lee, R. (eds) *Politics and History in Bank Societies*, Cambridge, Cambridge University Press

Feit, H. A. (1987) 'Waswanipi Cree management of land and wildlife: Cree ethno-ecology revisited', in Cox, B. (ed) *Native People, Native Lands: Canadian Indian, Inuit and Métis*, Ottawa, Carleton University Press

Fidler, D. (2000) *International Law and Public Health*, Arsley, NY, Transnational Publishers

First Nations and Inuit Regional Health Survey Steering Committee (2003) *First Nations and Inuit Regional Health Survey*, Ottawa, First Nations and Inuit Regional Health Survey Steering Committee

Fitzmaurice, G. G. (1950) 'The law and procedure of the International Court of Justice: General principles and substantive law', *The British Yearbook of International Law*, vol 27, p1

Ford, J. (2005) 'Living with change in the Arctic', *WorldWatch*, Sept/Oct., pp15–21

Ford, J., Smit, B. and Wandel, J. (2006) 'Vulnerability to climate change in the Arctic: A case study from Arctic Bay, Canada', *Global Environmental Change*, vol 16, pp145–160

Fowler, R. J. (1995) 'International environmental standards for transnational corporations', *Environmental Law*, vol 25, winter, p1

Franck, T. (1978) 'The stealing of Sahara', *American Journal of International Law*, vol 70, October, pp694–721

Fraser, T. (2000) *Cambodia Forest Concession Review Report*, Sustainable Forestry Management Project, Asian Development Bank (TA-3152 Cam), Ministry of Agriculture, Forestry and Fisheries, General Directorate of Forestry, Phnom Penh, Royal Government of Cambodia

French, H. W. (1995) 'Nigeria Executes Activist Playwright', in *New York Times*, reprinted in the *San Francisco Chronicle*, 11 November

French, P. A. (1979) 'Corporate moral agency', in Beawcha, T. L. and Bowie, N. E. (eds) *Ethical Theory and Business Practice*, Englewood Cliffs, NY, Hall

French, P. A. (1984) *Collective and Corporate Responsibility*, New York, Columbia University

Freudenberg, N. (2005) 'Public health advocacy to change corporate practices', *Health Education Behavior*, vol 32, pp289–319

Friedman, M. and. Narveson, J. (1994) *Political Correctness: For and Against*, Lanham, MD, Rowman Littlefield

Friends of the Earth (2002) 'Memorandum on Camisea Project violations of World Bank safeguard policies', press release, 17 October, www.bicusa.org/bicusa/issues/misc_resources/338.php

Gaylord, C. and Bell, E. (2001) 'Environmental justice: A national priority', in Westra, L., and Lawson, B. (eds) *Faces of Environmental Racism*, Lanham, MD, Rowman Littlefield

Geer, M. (1998) 'Foreigners in their own land: Cultural and transnational corporations – emerging international rights and wrongs', *Virginia Journal of International Law*, vol 38, pp331–354

Gelert, G. A. (1989) 'The obsolescence of distinct domestic and international health sectors', *Journal of Public Health Policy*, vol 10, p421

Gelobter, M. (1988) *The Distribution of Air Pollution by Income and Race*, paper presented at the Second Symposium on Social Science in Resource Management, Urbana, IL

Gertner, E. (1986) 'Are corporations entitled to equality? Some preliminary thoughts', *Canadian Rights Reporter*, pp288–301

Gewirth, A. (1982) *Human Rights: Essays in Justiccation and Application*, University of Chicago Press, Chicago

Gilbert, P. (1994) *Terrorism, Security and Nationality*, London, Routledge

Gilbertson, M. (2006) 'Injury to health: A forensic audit of the Great Lakes Water Quality Agreement (1972–2005) with special reference to congenital minamata disease', PhD thesis

Glasbeek, H. and Tucker, E. (1993) 'Death by consensus: The Westray Mine story', *New Society*, vol 3, no 4, pp14–41

Goddard, J. (1991) *The Last Stand of the Lubicon Cree*, Vancouver, Douglas & McMillan

Goodland, R. (1982) *Economic Development and Tribal Peoples: Human Ecologic Considerations*, Washington DC, World Bank Group

Goodland, R. (2003) *Sustainable Development Sourcebook for the WBG's Extractive Industry Review*, Washington DC, World Bank Group

Goodland, R. and Daly, H. (1995) 'Universal environmental sustainability and the principle of integrity', in Westra, L. and Lemons, J. (eds) *Perspectives on Ecological Integrity*, Dordrecht, The Netherlands, Kluwer Academic Publishers

Goodwin, R. E. (1980) 'No moral nukes', *Ethics*, vol 90, no 3, pp417–449

Gore, A. (2006) *An Inconvenient Truth*, New York, Rodale Press

Gostin, L. O. (2004) 'Law and ethics in population health', *Australian and New Zealand Journal of Public Health*, vol 28, no 1, pp7–12

Grandjean, P. and Landrigan, P. J. (2006) 'Developmental neurotoxicity of industrial chemicals', *The Lancet*, Nov 8

Grandjean, P. and White, R. F. (2002) 'Developmental effects on environmental neurotoxicants', in Taburlini, G., von Ehrenstein, O. and Bertollini, R. (eds) *Children's Health and Environment*, Environmental Issue Report No. 24, Copenhagen, EEA

Greenpeace (1995) *Not in Anyone's Backyard: The Grassroots Victory over Bowning-Ferris Industries*, Greenpeace video

Grenville, J. A. S. (1974) *The Major International Treaties: 1914–1973 – A History and Guide with Texts*, London, Methuen

Gresser, J., Fugikura, K. and Morishima, A. (1981) *Environmental Law in Japan*, Cambridge, MA, MIT Press

Griffiths, T. (2003a) '10 reasons to promote the implementation of Article 10c of the CBD', *ECO* vol 9, no 4, p2

Griffiths, T. (2003b) *A Failure of Accountability: Indigenous Peoples, Human Rights and Development Agency Standards – A Reference Tool and Comparative Review*, Briefing Paper, Moreton-in-Marsh, UK, Forest Peoples Programme, available at www.forestpeoples.org/documents/law_hr/ip_devt_stds_failure_accountability_dec03_eng.pdf

Gros Espiell, H. (1980) *The Right to Self-Determination: Implementation of United States Nations Resolutions*, UN Doc. E/CN. 4/Sub. 2/ 405/Rev. 1, New York, United Nations

Grotius, (1925) *On the Law of War and Peace*, translation by Francis W. Kelsey from the 1646 edition, Classics of International Law, Oxford, Clarendon

Guradze, H. (1971) 'Are human rights resolutions of the United Nations Assembly law-making?", *Revue des droits de l'homme/Human Rights Journal*

Halewood, M. (1999) 'Indigenous and local knowledge in international law: A preface to *sui generis* intellectual property protection, *McGill Law Review*

Hall, T. D. and Fenelon, J. V. (2004) 'The futures of indigenous peoples: 9-11 and the trajectory of indigenous survival and resistance', *Journal of World Systems Research X, F*, Winter, pp153–197

Handl, G. (1985) 'Liability as an obligation established by a primary rule of international law: Some basic reflections on the International Law Commission's work', *Netherlands Year Book of International Law*, The Hague

Handl, G. (2006) '*Trail Smelter* in contemporary international environmental law: Its relevance in the nuclear energy context', in Bratspeis, R. and Miller, R. A. (eds) *Transboundary Harm in International Law*, Cambridge, Cambridge University Press

Harrington, C. (2002) 'Doe v. Unocal Corporation', *Tulane Environmental Law Journal*, vol 16, no 1, winter, pp247–9

Harris, C. E. (1990) 'The ethics of natural law', in Timmons, M. (ed) *Conduct and Character*, Belmont, CA, Wadsworth Publishing

Havemann, P. (undated) 'Kaitiakitanga: Customary fisheries management in New Zealand', in International Marine Project Activities Centre Limited (IMPAC) *Traditional Law and the Environment, for Countries and States of the Melanesian Spearhead Group*, IMPAC (supported by the World Bank, The CEC Reef Research Centre, Australian Government, Christenson Fund)

Heath, J. (2001) *The Efficient Society*, Toronto, Penguin Books,

Hecht, S. and Cockburn, A. (1990) *The Fate of the Forest: Developers and Defenders of the Amazon*, New York, Harper Perennial

Helstaedt, M. (2007) 'The Mystery of the Mission Boys', *The Globe and Mail*, 11 April

Henao, D. and Genolagani, J. (undated) 'Biodiversity and sustainable use of marine biodiversity in PNG: Policy and legal implications', in International Marine Project Activities Centre Limited (IMPAC) *Traditional Law and the Environment, for Countries and States of the Melanesian Spearhead Group*, IMPAC (supported by the World Bank, The CEC Reef Research Centre, Australian Government, Christenson Fund)

Herz, R. L. (2001) 'Indigenous rights, environmental torts, and cultural genocide', *Hasting International and Comparative Law Review*, vol 24, no 3, spring, pp503–506

Higgins, R. (1994) *Problems and Process: International Law and How We Use It*, Oxford, Clarendon Press

Hiskes, R. P. (1998) *Democracy, Risk and Community*, New York, Oxford University Press

Hoffman, S. (2007) 'Gore Speaks to 6,000 Earth Scientists in San Francisco', 26 January, *Op.Ed. News.com*

Hogg, P. (2005) *Constitutional Law of Canada*, student edition, Carslaw, Toronto

Homer Dixon, T. (1994) 'Environmental society and violent conflict: Evidence from cases', *International Security*, vol 19, no 1, pp5–40

Hossain, K. and Chowdhury, S. R. (eds) (1984) *Permanent Sovereignty over Natural Resources in International Law: Principle and Practice*, New York, St Martin's Press

Howard, M. C. (1994) 'Mining, development and indigenous peoples in Southeast Asia', *Journal of Business Administration*, vol 22–23, p93

Huff, A. I. (1999) 'Resource development and human rights: A look at the case of the Lubicon Cree Indian Nation of Canada (Bernard Ominayak, Chief)', *Colorado Journal of International Environmental Law and Policy*, vol 10, no 1, pp161–174

Human Rights Watch (1999a) *The Price of Oil: Corporate Responsibility and Human Rights Violations in Nigeria's Oil Producing Communities*, Human Rights Watch, www.hrw.org/reports/1999/nigeria

Human Rights Watch (1999b) *The Enron Corporation Complicity in Human Rights Violations*, Human Rights Watch, www.hrw.org/reports/1999/enron

Humphrey, J. P. (1979) 'The Universal Declaration of Human Rights: Juridical Character', in Ramcharan, B. G. and Nijhoff, M. (eds) *Human Rights: History, 30 Years After the Universal Declaration*, The Hague, Kluwer Law

Hurting A. K. and San Sebastian, M. (2002) 'Geographical differences in cancer incident in the Amazon Basin of Ecuador in relation to residence near oil fields', *International Journal of Epidemiology*, vol 31, no 5, pp1021–1027

Hutchinson, A. and Peter, A. (1988) 'Private rights public wrongs: The liberal lie of the Charter', *University of Toronto Law Journal*, vol 38, summer, pp278–297

Imai, S. (2001) 'Treaty lands and crown obligation: The "tracts taken up" provision', *Queen's Law Journal*, vol 27, no 1, p49

IMPAC (International Marine Project Activities Centre Limited) (undated) *Traditional Law and the Environment, for Countries and States of the Melanesian Spearhead Group*, IMPAC (supported by the World Bank, The CEC Reef Research Centre, Australian Government, Christenson Fund)

Jagers, N. (2002) *Corporate Human Rights Obligations: In Search of Accountability*, Antwerp, Intersentia

Janis, M. W. (1988) 'The nature of *jus cogens*', *Connecticut Journal of International Law*, vol 3, p359

Janssem, A. and Slovaxk, S. (eds) (1991) *Chemical Contamination in Human Milk*, Boca Raton, CRC Press

Jennings, R. Y. (1987) 'Universal international law in a multicultural world', in Bos, M. and Brownlie, J. (eds) *Liber Americorum for the Right Hon. Lord Wilberforce*, Oxford, Oxford University Press

Johnston, P. (1983) *Native Children and the Child Welfare System*, Toronto, James Lorimer and Co

Jonas, H. (1984) *The Imperative of Responsibility*, Chicago, University of Chicago Press

Joseph, S. (2004) *Corporations and Human Rights Litigation*, Oxford, Hart Publishing

Kamm, T. and Greenberger, R. (1995) 'Nigeria executions raise sanction "threat"', *The Wall Street Journal*, 13 November

Kant, I. (1957) *Perpetual Peace*, (Beck, L. (ed)) Indianapolis, IN, Bobbs Merril

Kant, I. (1964) *Groundwork of the Metaphysics of Morals*, translation by H. J. Paton, New York, Harps Torchbooks

Kant, I. (1981) *Metaphysics of Morals*, translation by J. Ellington, Indianapolis, IN, Bobbs Merril

Kapashesit, R. and Klippenstein, M. (1991) 'Aboriginal group rights and environmental protection', *McGill Law Journal*, vol 36, October, pp925–961

Kaplan, M. (2004) 'Using collective interests in ensuring human rights: An analysis of the articles on state responsibility', *New York University Law Review*, vol 79, no 5, November

Karr, J. (1993) 'Protecting ecological integrity: An urgent societal goal', *Yale Journal of International Law*, vol 18, pp297–306

Karr, J. (2000) 'Defining and measuring river health', in Pimentel, D., Westra, L. and Noss, R. (eds) *Ecological Integrity: Integrating Environment, Conservation and Health*, Washington, DC, Island Press

Karr, J. (2006) 'Seven foundations of biological monitoring and assessment', *Biologia Ambientale*, vol 20, no 2, pp7–8

Kastrup, J. P. (1997) 'The internationalization of indigenous rights from the environmental and human rights perspective', *Texas International Law Journal*, vol 32, winter, p97

Kattsov, V. M. and Kallen, E. (2005) 'Future climate change: Modeling and scenarios for the Arctic', in Hassoll, S. J. (ed) *Arctic Climate Impact Assessment Scientific Report*, Cambridge, Cambridge University Press

Kempton, K. (2005) 'Bridge over troubled waters: Canadian law on aboriginal treaty water rights', unpublished paper

Kendall, C. (2006) 'Life at the edge of a warming world', *The Ecologist*, vol 36, no 5, July/August, p26

Kimbrough, R. D., Mahaffey, K. R., Grandjean, P., Sands, S. H. and Ruttstein, D. D. (1989) *Clinical Effects of Environmental Chemicals: A Software Approach to Etiologic Diagnosis*, New York, Hemisphere Pub. Corp.

Kindred, H. M., Michelson, K., Provost, R., McDonald, T. L., DeMistral, A. and Williams, S. A. (2000) *International Law*, 6th edition, Ottawa, Edmond Montgomery Publications

King, M. L., Jr (1990) 'Letter from a Birmingham jail', in Homes, R. (ed) *Non-Violence in Theory and Practice*, Belmont, CA, Wadsworth Publishing

Kingsbury, B. (2001) 'Reconciling five competing conceptual structures of indigenous peoples' claims in international and comparative law', *New York University Journal of International Law and Politics*, vol 34, Fall, p189

Koh, H. (1996) 'Transnational legal process', *Nebraska Law Review*, vol 75, pp181–207

Koh, H. (1997) 'Why do nations obey international law?', *Yale Law Journal*, vol 106, no 8

Kolbert, E. (2006) *Field Notes from a Catastrophe*, London, Bloomsbury Publishing

Kontos, A. P. (2005) 'Aboriginal self-government in Canada', in Castellino, J. and Walsh, N. (eds) *International Law and Indigenous Peoples*, Dordrecht, The Netherlands, Martinus Nijhoff Publishers

Korsmo, F. (1993) 'Sami policy and Sami rights', *The Northern Review*, vol 11, pp32–55

Koskenniemi, M. (ed) (2000) *Sources of International Law*, London, Ashgate Publishing

Kral, M. (2003) *Unikkaartuit: Meanings of Well-being, Sadness, Suicide, and Change in Two Inuit Communities*, final report to the National Health Research and Development Programs, Ottawa, Health Canada

Kymlicka, W. (1991) *Liberalism, Community and Culture*, Oxford, Clarendon Paperbacks and Oxford University Press

Landrigan, P. (2002) 'The worldwide problem of lead in petrol', *Bulletin of World Health Organization*, vol 80, no 10, p768

Landrigan, P., Sowawanee, B., Butler, R. N., Trasande, L., Callan, R. and Droller, D. (2005) 'Early environmental origins of neurodegenerative disease in later life', *Environmental Health Perspective*, vol 113, pp1230–1233

Laponce, J. A. (1960) *The Protection of Minorities*, Berkeley, CA, University of California Press

Large, D. W. and Mitchie, P. (1981) 'Proving that the British Navy depends on the number of old maids in England: A comparison of scientific proof with legal proof', *Environmental Law*, vol 11, no 3, pp555–638

Lauterpacht, H. (1933) *The Function of Law in the International Community*, Oxford, Clarendon Press

Lauterpacht, H. (1946) 'The Grotian tradition in international law', *British Yearbook*, vol 23, pp22–23

Lauterpacht, H. (1950) *International Law and Human Rights*, London, Stevens Publishers

Lauterpacht, H. (1968) *International Law and Human Rights*, New York, Archon Books

LaVelle, J. P. (2001) 'Strengthening tribal sovereignty through Indian participation in American politics: A reply to John Porter', *Kansas Journal of Law & Public Policy*, vol 10, no 3, spring, pp533–580

Leader, S. (2004) 'Collateralism', in Brownsword, R. (ed) *Global Governance and the Quest for Justice*, vol IV, Oxford, Hart Publishing

Lemkin, R. (1944) *Axis Rule in Occupied Europe*, Washington DC, Carnegie Endowment for International Peace

Lenin, V. I. (1969) 'Thesis on the socialist revolution and the right of nations to self-determination', in *Selected Works*, New York, International Publishers

Leopold, A. (1949) *A Sand County Almanac and Sketches Here and There*, New York, Oxford University Press

Licari, L., Nemer, L. and Tamburlini, G. (eds) (2005) *Children's Health and the Environment*, Copenhagen, Denmark, World Health Organization Regional Office for Europe

Lovelock, J. E. (2006) *The Revenge of Gaia: Why the Earth is Fighting Back – and How We Can Still Save Humanity*, New York, Perseus Press

Lyon, B. (2002) 'Postcolonial Law Theory and Law Reform Conference; discourse in development: A post-colonial "agenda" for the United Nations Committee on Economic, Social and Cultural Rights', *American University Journal of Gender and Social Policy and Law*, vol 10, no 3, pp535–579

Lyons, O. (1993) 'Indigenous peoples and the right to self-determination', *Proceedings of the American Society of International Law*, 1993 edition, pp190–204

Macdonald, T., Anaya, S. J. and Soto, Y. (1998) *The Samoré Case: Final Report of the Harvard/OAS Project in Colombia*, Washington, DC, Organization of American States, available at www.wcfia.harvard.edu/ponsacs/images/Macdonald_Samore_eng.pdf

MacKay, F. (2005) 'The Draft World Bank Operational Policy 4.10 on Indigenous Peoples: Progress or more of the same?', *Arizona Journal of International and Comparative Law*, vol 22, no 1, pp65–98

Magraw, D. B. (1986) 'Transboundary harm: The International Law Commission's study of "international liability"', *American Journal of International Law*, vol 80, no 2, pp305–330

Manus, P. (2006) 'Indigenous peoples' environmental rights: Evolving common law perspectives in Canada, Australia and the United States', *British Columbia Environmental Affairs Law Review*, vol 33, no 1

Marks, G. C. (1990–1991) 'Indigenous peoples in international law: The significance of Francisco de Vitoria and Bartolomé De Las Casas', *Australia Year Book of International Law*, vol 13, pp1–51

Marrus, M. (2006) 'In France's transport of Jews, where do you draw the line?', *The Globe and Mail*, 2 June

Mathews, J. T. (1997) 'Power shift', *Foreign Affairs*, vol 76, no 1, January–February, p50

Maybury-Lewis, D. (1984) 'Demystifying the second conquest', in Schmink, M. and Wood, C. (eds) *Frontier Expansion in Amazonia*, Gainesville, University of Florida Press

McCaffrey, S. C. (2006) 'Of paradoxes, precedents, and progeny', in Braspeis, R. M. and Miller, R. A. (eds) *Transboundary Harm in International Law*, Cambridge, Cambridge University Press

McCalman, I. P. B. and Cook, M. (1998) *Mad Cows and Modernity*, Humanities Research Centre, Canberra, Australian National University

McCarthy, J., Canziani, O. F., Leary, N. A., Dokken, D. J. and White, K. S. (2001) *Climate Change 2001: Impacts, Adaptation, Vulnerability Contribution of Working Group II to the Third Assessment Report of The Intergovernmental Panel on Climate Change*, Cambridge, Cambridge University Press

McCook, A. (2005) 'News', *The Scientist*, vol 6, 29 September, p1

McCurdy, H. (2001) 'Africville: Environmental racism', in Westra, L. and Lawson, B. (eds) *Faces of Environmental Racism*, 2nd edition, Lanham, MD, Rowan Littlefield

Merryman, J. H. (1986) 'Two ways of thinking about cultural property', *American Journal of International Law*, vol 80, pp831–853

Metcalf, C. (2004) 'Indigenous rights and the environment: Evolving international law', in *Ottawa Law Review*, vol 35, no 1, winter, pp101–140

Mickelson, K. (1993) 'Rereading Trail Smelter', *Canadian Year Book of International Law*

Miller, R. A. (2006) 'Surprising parallels between *Trail Smelter* and the global climate change regime', in Bratspies, R. M. and Miller, R. A. (eds) *Transboundary Harm in International Law*, Cambridge, Cambridge University Press

Millroy, J. S. (1999) *A National Crime: The Canadian Government and the Residential School System 1879–1986*, Winnipeg, University of Manitoba Press

Minchin, L. and Murdoch, L. (2006) 'Aboriginal cancer doubles near uranium mine', *The Age*, 23 November

Mittelstaedt, M. (2005) 'Pollution debate born of Chemical Valley's girl-baby boom', *The Globe and Mail*, 15 November

Morse, B. (2002) *Comparative Assessments of the Position of Indigenous Peoples in Quebec, Canada, and Abroad*, vol 3, book 1, Executive Council, Quebec, National Assembly of Quebec

Musungu, S. (2005) 'The right to health, intellectual property, and competition principles', in Cottier, T., Puwelyn, J. and Burgi Bonanomi, E. (eds) *Human Rights and International Trade*, Oxford, Oxford University Press

Napoleon, V. (2001) 'Extinction by numbers: Colonialism made easy', *Canadian Journal of Law and Society*, vol 16, no 1, pp113–145

Nar, R. (undated) 'Linking traditional resource management approaches and practices into formal legal systems in Vanuatu', in International Marine Project Activities Centre Limited (IMPAC) *Traditional Law and the Environment, for Countries and States of the Melanesian Spearhead Group*, IMPAC (supported by the World Bank, The CEC Reef Research Centre, Australian Government, Christenson Fund)

Nations, J. (1988) 'Deep ecology meets the developing world', in Wilson, E. (ed) *Biodiversity*, Washington, DC, National Academy Press

Needleman, H. L., McFarland, C., Ness, R. B., Feinberg, S. E. and Tobin, M. J. (2002) 'Bone lead level in adjudicated delinquents: A case control study', *Neurotoxicological Teratology*, vol 24, pp711–717

Nelson, R. K. (1982) 'A conservation ethics and environment: The Koyukon of Alaska', in Williams, N. M. and Hunn, E. S. (eds) *Resource Managers: North American and Australian Hunter-Gatherers*, Boulder, CO, Westview Press

Neu, D. E. (2003) *Accounting for Genocide: Canada's Bureaucratic Assault on Aboriginal Peoples*, Black Point, NS, Fernwood

Newark, F. H. (1961) 'Non-natural user and *Rylands v. Fletcher*', *The Modern Law Review*, vol 24, no 5, pp557–571

Newman, D. G. (2006) 'Theorizing collective indigenous rights', *American Indian Law Review*, vol 31, no 2, pp1–17

Nikiforuk, A. (1999) 'It makes them sick', *Canadian Business*, vol 82, no 2, pp47–51

Noss, R. (1992) 'The Wildlands Project, land conservation strategy', *Wild Earth*, Special Issue, pp10–25

Noss, R. (2000) 'Maintaining the ecological integrity of landscapes and ecoregions', in Pimenteal, D., Westra, L. and Noss, R. (eds) *Ecological Integrity: Integrating Environment, Conservation and Health*, Washington DC, Island Press

Noss, R. and Cooperrider, A. Y. (1994) *Saving Nature's Legacy*, Washington DC, Island Press

O'Neill, O. (1996) *Towards Justice and Virtue*, Cambridge, Cambridge University Press

Pannenborg, C. O. (1979) *A New International Health Order*, Germantown, MD, Sijthoff and Noordhoff

Parent, A. (1887) *The Life of Rev Armand Parent: Forty-seven Years Experience in Evangelical Work in Canada; Eight Years Among the Oka Indians*, Toronto, Briggs Publishing

Patz, J. (2005) 'Impact of regional climate change on human health', *Nature*, vol 384, pp310–317

Paust, J. (2004) 'The reality of private rights, duties, and participation in the international legal process', *Michigan Journal of International Law*, vol 25, no 4, pp1229–1249

Pellet, A. (1992) 'The opinion of the Badminter Arbitration Committee: A second breath for the self-determination of peoples', *European Journal of International Law*, vol 3, pp178–185

Pellet, A. (1997) 'Vive le crime! Remarques sur les degrees de l'illicite en droit international', *International Law on the Eve of the Twenty-First Century*, United Nations, p287

Pentassuglia, G. (2002) *Minorities in International Law*, Strasbourg, Council of Europe Publishing

Pentassuglia, G. (2006) 'Inside and outside the European Convention: The case of minorities compared', *Baltic Yearbook of International Law*, vol 6, pp261–289

Pidgeon, N., Kasperson, R. E. and Slovic, P. (eds) (2003) *The Social Amplification of Risk*, Cambridge, Cambridge University Press

Pimentel, D. (1991) 'Environmental and economic effects of reducing pesticide use', *BioScience*, vol 41, no 6

Pimentel, D. (1992) 'Conserving biological diversity in agricultural/forestry systems', *BioScience*, vol 42, no 5

Pimentel, D. (1993) 'The relationship between "cosmetic standards" for food and pesticide use', in Pimentel, D. and Lehman, H. (eds) *The Pesticide Question: Environment Economics and Ethics*, New York, Chapman and Hall

Pindera, G. and York, L. (1991) *People of the Pines: The Warriors and the Legacies of Ok*, Ottawa, Little Brown Co. (Canada)

Pogge, T. (ed) (2001) *Global Justice*, Oxford, Blackwell Publishers

Powell, C. (2004) 'Testimony Before the Senate Foreign Relations Committee', Washington DC, Senate Foreign Relations Committee

Pritchard, S. (ed) (1998) *Indigenous Peoples, the United Nations and Human Rights*, London, Zed Books

Pureza, J. M. (2005) 'Counter-hegemonic uses of international law', in De Sousa Santos, B. and Rodrigues-Garavito, C. (eds) *Law and Globalization from Below*, Cambridge, Cambridge University Press

Rabb, D. (1995) 'Is there an Amerindian Philosophy?', unpublished paper presented at the Ontario Philosophical Society Meting, University of Windsor, Ontario, 28 October

Racine, J, (1946) *Phedre*, Paris, Edition du Seuil

Ragazzi, M. (1997) *The Concept of International Obligations Erga Omnes*, Oxford, Clarendon Press

Ramasastry, A. (2002) 'Corporate complicity from Nuremberg to Rangoon: An examination of forced labor cases and their impact on the liability of multinational corporations', *Berkeley Journal of International Law*, vol 20, no 1, pp91–159

Ranjan, P. (2005) 'International trade and human rights: Conflicting obligations', in Cotter, T., Pauwelyn, J. and Burgi Bonanomi, E. (eds) *Human Rights and International Trade*, Oxford, Oxford University Press

Ratner, S. (2001) 'Corporations and human rights: A theory of legal responsibility', *Yale Law Journal*, vol 111, no 3, pp443–447

Ratner, S. and Abrams, J. (2001) *Accountability for Human Rights Atrocities in International Law*, 2nd edition, Oxford, Oxford University Press

Rawls, J. (1999a) *A Theory of Justice*, 2nd edition, Cambridge, MA, Harvard University Press

Rawls, J. (1999b) *The Law of Peoples*, Cambridge, MA, Harvard University Press

Read, J. E. (1963) 'The Trail Smelter Dispute', *Canadian Yearbook of International Law*, vol 1, Vancouver, University of British Columbia Press

Rees, W. (2000) 'Patch disturbance, ecofootprints and biological integrity: Revisiting the limits to growth or why industrial society is inherently unsustainable', in Pimentel, D., Westra, L. and Noss, R., *Ecological Integrity: Integrating Environment, Conservation and Health*, Washington, DC, Island Press, pp139–156

Rees, W. E. (2006) 'Ecological footprints and bio-capacity: Essential elements in sustainability assessment', Chapter 9 in J. Dewulf and H. Van Langenhove (eds) *Renewables-Based Technology: Sustainability Assessment*, Chichester, UK, John Wiley and Sons, pp143–158

Rees, W. E. and Wackernagel, M. (1996) *Our Ecological Footprint*, Gabriold Island, BC, New Society Publishers

Revkin, A. C. (2005) *The North Pole Was Here: Puzzles and Perils at the Top of the World*, Boston, MA, Kingfisher

Revkin, A. C. (2006) 'World briefing Americas: Inuit climate change petition rejected', *New York Times*, 16 December

Ridenour, A. (2001) 'Apples and oranges: Why courts should use international standards to determine liability for violations of the law of nations under the Alien Tort Claims Act', *Tulane Journal of International and Comparative Law*, vol 9, Spring, pp581–603

Ridep-Morris, A. (undated) 'Traditional management of marine Resources in Palau', in International Marine Project Activities Centre Limited (IMPAC) *Traditional Law and the Environment, for Countries and States of the Melanesian Spearhead Group*, IMPAC (supported by the World Bank, The CEC Reef Research Centre, Australian Government, Christenson Fund)

Rievman, J. D. (1989) 'Judicial scrutiny of Native American free exercise rights: *Lyng* and the decline of the *Yoder* Doctrine', *Boston College Environmental Law Review*, vol 17, pp169–200

Robinson, J. D., Higgins, M. D. and Bolyard, P. K. (1983) 'Assessing environmental impacts on health: A role for behavioural science', *Environmental Impact Assessment Review*

Rockefeller, S. (2002) 'Foreword', in Miller, P. and Westra, L. (eds) *Just Ecological Integrity*, Lanham, MD, Rowman Littlefield

Rodriguez-Garavito, C. A. and Arena, L. C. (2005) 'Indigenous rights, transnational activism and legal mobilization: The struggle of the U'wa people in Colombia', in De Sousa Santos, B. and Rodriguez-Garavito, C. (eds) *Law and Globalization from Below*, Cambridge, Cambridge University Press

Rogan, W. J. and Regan, B. N. (2003) 'Evidence of effects of environmental chemicals on the endocrine system in children', *Pediatrics*, vol 112, pp247–252

Rolston, H. (1993) 'Rights and responsibilities on the home planet', *Yale Journal of International Law*, vol 18, pp259–262

Romano, R. (1984) 'Metabolics and corporate law reform', *Stanford Law Review*, vol 36, no 4, p923

Russell-Brown, S. L. (2003) 'Rape as an act of genocide', *Berkeley Journal of International Law*, vol 21, no 2, pp350–374

Sagoff, M. (1988) *The Economy of the Earth: Philosophy, Law and the Environment*, Cambridge Cambridge University Press

Salmond, J. (1924) *Jurisprudence*, 7th edition, London, Sweet and Maxwell

San Sebastian, M. and Cordoba, J. A. (1999) *Yana Curi Report: The Impact of Oil Development on the Health of People of the Ecuadorian Amazon*, London, Departmento de Pastoral Social del Vicariato Apostolico de Aguarico and the London School of Hygiene and Tropical Medicine

Sandler, R. (2006) 'Comments on Bill Lawson's "Racist property holdings and environmental coalitions", and Laura Westra's "The rights of indigenous peoples: Ecofootprint crime and the biological/ecological integrity model', unpublished paper

Sarfaty, G. A. (2005) 'The World Bank and the internationalization of indigenous rights norms', *Yale Law Journal*, vol 114, no 7, pp1791–1818

Saro-Wiwa, K. (1994a) 'Right Livelihood Award Acceptance Speech', 9 December, Stockholm

Saro-Wiwa, K. (1994b) 'Human Rights, Democracy and an African Gulag', unpublished talk, 2 March, New York

Savant, K. P. and Aranda, V. (1994) 'The international legal framework of transnational corporations', in Fatouros, A. A. (eds) *Transnational Corporations: The International Legal Framework*, London, Routledge

Schabas, W. (1997) *The Abolition of the Death Penalty*, Cambridge, Cambridge University Press

Schabas, W. (2000) *On Genocide in International Law*, The Hague, Kluwer Publishing

Schabas, W. (2001) 'Enforcing international humanitarian law: Catching the accomplices', *International Review of the Red Cross (IRRC)*, vol 83, no 42, pp439–459

Schabas, W. (2006a) *The UN International Criminal Tribunals*, Cambridge, Cambridge University Press

Schabas, W. (2006b) 'First prosecutions at the International Criminal Court', *Human Rights Law Journal*, vol 27, no 1, p4

Schmidt-Jortzig, E. (1991) 'The Constitution of Namibia: An example of a state emerging under close supervision and world scrutiny', *German Yearbook of International Law*, vol 34, pp413–428

Scott, C. (2001a) *Torture as Tort*, Oxford, Hart Publishing

Scott, C. (2001b) 'Multinational enterprises and emergent jurisprudence on violations of economic, social and cultural rights', in Eide, A., Krause, C. and Rosas, A. (eds) *Economic, Social and Cultural Rights: A Textbook*, 2nd revised edition, The Hague, The Netherlands, Kluwer Law International

Scott, J. B. (1934) *The Spanish Origin of International Law*, Oxford, Clarendon Press

Scovazzi, T. (2007) *Le Patrimoine Culturel de l'Humanité*, Leiden, Martinus Niijhoff

Scutchfield, F. D. (2004) 'A third public health revolution', *American Journal of Preventive Medicine* vol 27, no 1, July

Sedjo, R. (1992) 'Property rights, genetic resources, and biotechnological change', *Journal of Law and Economics*, vol 35, pp199–213

Seremba, S. (1995) 'Playwright Grieves for Saro-Wiwa and Africa', *The Globe and Mail*, 18 November

Sevigny, H. (1993) *Lasagne – L'Homme derriere le masque*, St Lambert, Quebec, Editions Sedes

Sheehy, E. A. (1982) 'Regulatory crimes and the charter: *R.v. Wholesale Travel, Inc.*', *Journal of Human Justice*, vol 3, no 2, pp111–124

Shell (1995) 'Clear thinking in troubled times', newspaper advertisement placed by Shell in *The Globe and Mail*, Toronto, Canada, 21 November, pA17

Shelton, D. (1994) 'Fair play, fair pay: Preserving traditional knowledge and biological resources', *Year Book of International Environmental Law*, Oxford, Oxford University Press

Shiva, V. (1988) *Staying Alive*, London, Zed Books Ltd

Shrader-Frechette, K. (1982) *Nuclear Power and Public Policy*, Dordrecht, The Netherlands, Kluwer Academic

Shrader-Frechette, K. (1991) *Risk and Rationality*, Berkeley, CA, University of California Press

Shrader-Frechette, K. (1993) *Burying Uncertainty*, Berkeley, CA, University of California Press

Shrader-Frechette, K. (1995) 'Hard ecology, soft ecology, and ecosystem integrity', in *Perspectives on Ecological Integrity*, Dordrecht, The Netherlands, Kluwer Academic

Shrader-Frechette, K. and McCoy, E. D. (1993) *Method in Ecology*, New York, Cambridge University Press

Shue, H. (1996) *Basic Rights: Subsistence, Affluence and American Foreign Politics*, Princeton, NJ, Princeton University Press

Sidgwick, H. D. (1878) *A Selection of American and English Cases in the Measure of Damages (Arranged by Subject with Notes)*, New York, Baker, Voorhuis

Slattery, B. (1987) 'Understanding aboriginal rights', *The Canadian Bar Review*, vol 66, pp727–783

Sopinka, J. (1989) 'The Charter of Rights and the corporations', *The Cambridge Lectures*, Cambridge, Cambridge University Press

Soskolne, C. (2002) 'Eco-epidemiology: On the need to measure the health effects from global change', *Global Change and Human Health*, vol 3, no 11, pp58–66

Soskolne, C. and Bertollini, R. (1999) *Global Ecological Integrity and 'Sustainable Development': Cornerstones of Public Health*, discussion document based on an international workshop at the World Health Organization European Centre for Environment and Health, Rome Division, Rome, Italy, 3–4 December 1998, www.euro.who.int/document/gch/ecorep5.pdf

Soyinka, W. (1994) 'Nigeria's long, steep, bloody slide', *New York Times*, 22 August

Spinedi, M. (1989) 'Convergences and divergences on the legal consequences of international crimes of states', in Weiler, J. H., Cassese, A. and Sinedi, M. (eds) *International Crimes of State: A Critical Analysis of the ILC Draft Article 19 on State Responsibility*, Berlin, Walter de Gruyter

Stallworthy, M. (2006) 'Sustainability, the environment, and the rule of UK corporations', *International Company and Commercial Law Review*, vol 17, no 6, pp155–165

Stavenhagen, R. (2002) *Report of Special Rapporteur on the Situation of Human Rights and Fundamental Freedoms of Indigenous Peoples*, submitted pursuant to Commission res.2001/57, UN Doc. E/CN.4/2002/97

Steffen, C., Auclerc, M. F., Auvrignon, A., Baruchel, A. (2004) 'Acute childhood leukemia and environmental exposure to potential sources of benzene and other hydrocarbons: Case control study', *Occupational and Environmental Medicine*, vol 61, no 9, pp773–778

Steiner, H. J. and Alston, P. (2000) *International Human Rights in Context*, 2nd edition, Oxford, Oxford University Press

Stephenson, M. (2004) 'Native title: An overview', *Australian Commercial Law*, 25th edition, Pyrmont, Australia, Lawbook Co.

Stone, C. (2000) 'Should trees have standing? Towards legal Rights for Natural Objects', in Dojan, L. (ed) *Environments Ethics*, Belmont, CA, Wadsworth Publishers

Stone, J. (1965) *Human Law and Human Justice*, Stanford, CA, Stanford University Press

Strange, S. (1996) *The Retreat of the State: The Diffusion of Power in the World Economy*, Cambridge, Cambridge University Press

Strickland, R. (1986) 'Genocide-at-law: An historic view of the native American experience', *University of Kansas Law Review*, vol 34, summer, pp713–755

Sunstein, C. (2007) *The Catastrophic Harm Precautionary Principle*, The Berkeley Electronic Press

Tamburlini, G. (2002) 'Children's special vulnerability to environmental health hazards: An overview', in Tamburlini, G., Von Ehrenstein, O. and Bertollini, R. (eds) *Children's Health and Environment: A Review of Evidence*, EEA Report No 29

Tanzi, A. (1987) 'Di ritto, di veto ed esecuzione della sentenza della Corte Internazionale di Giustizia fra Nicaragua e Stati Unit', *Rivista di Diritto Internazionale*, pp293–308

Taylor, A. L. (1992) 'Making the World Health Organization work: A legal framework for universal access to the conditions for health', *American Journal of Law and Medicine*, vol 18, pp301–346

Taylor, A. L. (2005) 'Trade, human rights and the WHO Framework Convention on Tobacco Control: Just what the doctor ordered?', in Cottier, T., Puwelyn, J. and Burgi Bonanomi, E. (eds) *Human Rights and International Trade*, New York, Oxford University Press, pp322–333

Taylor, C. (1992) 'Can Canada survive the Charter?', *Alberta Law Review*, vol 30, pp440–441

Taylor, P. E. (1998) 'From environmental to ecological human rights: A new dynamic in international law?', *Georgetown International Environmental Law Review*, vol 10, p309

Terry, J. (2001) 'Taking Filartiga on the road', in Scott, C. (ed) *Torture as Tort*, Oxford, Hart Publishing

Thampapillai, V. (2007) *Water Governance in Sweden*, Working Paper Series, Uppsala, Swedish University of Agricultural Sciences

Thornberry, P. (1991) *International Law and the Rights of the Minorities*, Oxford, Clarendon Press

Tomei, M. and Swepston, L. (1996) *Indigenous and Tribal Peoples: A Guide to ILO Convention No.169*, Geneva, ILO

Tomuschat, C. (1991) 'International liability for injurious consequences arising out of acts not prohibited by international law: The work of the International Law Commission', in Francioni, F. and Scovazzi, T. (eds) *International Responsibility for Environmental Harm*, London, Graham and Trotman

Tripp, L. and Thorleifson, M. (1998) *The Canadian Mercury Cell Chlor-Alkali Industry: Mercury Emissions and Status of Facilities 1935–1996; Report to Transboundary Air Issues Branch*, Hull, Quebec, Environment Canada

Troyer, W. (1977) *No Safe Place*, Toronto, Clarke Irwin

Tuivanuavou, S. (undated) 'Community involvement in the implementation of ocean policies: The Fiji Locally Managed Marine Area (FLMM) network experience', in International Marine Project Activities Centre Limited (IMPAC) *Traditional Law and the Environment, for Countries and States of the Melanesian Spearhead Group*, IMPAC (supported by the World Bank, The CEC Reef Research Centre, Australian Government, Christenson Fund)

Ulgen, O. (2000) 'Aboriginal title in Canada: Recognition and reconciliation', *Netherlands International Law Review*, vol 47, no 2, pp147–150

United Church of Christ Commission for Racial Justice (1987) *Toxic Wastes and Race in the United States: A National Study of Racial and Socioeconomic Characteristics of Communities with Hazardous Waste Sites*, New York, United Church of Christ

Valencia-Ospina, E. (1944) 'The International Court of Justice and international environmental law', *Asian Yearbook of International Law*, vol 2, pp1–10

Van Boven, T. C. (1979) 'United Nations policies and strategies: Global perspectives?', in Ramcharan, B. G. (ed) *Human Rights: Thirty Years After the Universal Declaration*, The Hague, The Netherlands, Kluwer

Velasquez, M. (1998) *Business Ethics, Concepts and Cases*, Belmont, CA Prentice-Hall Publishing

Wallace, P. (1994) *The Iroquois Book of Life: White Roots of Peace*, Santa Fe, Clear Light Publishers

Wasserstrom, R. (1974) 'The relevance of Nuremberg', in Cohen, M., Nagel, T. and Scanlon, T. (eds) *War and Moral Responsibility*, Princeton, NJ, Princeton University Press

Waters, W. F. (2006) 'Globalization and local responses to epidemiological overlap in 21st century Ecuador', *Globalization and Health*, vol 2, pp1–13

Weeramantry, C. (1997) '*Dissenting Opinion*', Gabcikovo-Nagymaros case, ICJ Rep-4, 14

Wellington, A., Greenbaum, A. and Cragg, W. (eds) (1997) *Canadian Issues in Environmental Ethics*, Peterborough, Ontario, Broadview Press

Werner, M. (2005), 'Conflicting rules in the WHO FCTC and their impact', in Cottier, T., Puwelyn, J. and Burgi Bonanomi, E. (eds) *Human Rights and International Trade*, New York, Oxford University Press

West, L. (1987) 'Mediated settlement of environmental disputes: Grassy Narrows and White Dog revisited', *Environmental Law*, vol 18, pp131–150

Westra, L. (1990) 'Terrorism, self-defence and whistleblowing', *Journal of Social Philosophy*, vol 20, no 3, pp46–58

Westra, L. (1994a) *An Environmental Proposal for Ethics: The Principle of Integrity*, Lanham, MD, Rowman Littlefield

Westra, L. (1994b) 'On risky business: Corporate responsibility for hazardous products', *Business Ethics Quarterly*, vol 4, no 1, January, pp97–110

Westra, L. (1995) 'The foundational value of wilderness', in *Perspectives on Ecosystem Integrity*, Dordrecht, the Netherlands, Kluwer

Westra, L. (1997) 'Terrorism in Oka', in Wellington, A., Greenbaum, A. and Cragg, W. (eds) *Canadian Issues in Environmental Ethics*, Peterborough, ON, Broadview Press

Westra, L. (1998) *Living in Integrity*, Lanham, MD, Roman Littlefield

Westra, L. (2000a) 'Institutionalized violence and human rights', in Pimentel, D. Westra, L. and

Noss, R. (eds) *Ecological Integrity: Integrating Environment, Conservation and Health*, Washington, DC, Island Press, pp279–294

Westra, L. (2000b) 'The global integrity project and the ethics of integrity', in Crabbe, P., Holland, A., Ryszkowski, L. and Westra, L. (eds) *Implementing Ecological Integrity: Restoring Regional and Global Environmental and Human Health*, NATO Science Series, Dordrecht, The Netherlands, Kluwer Academic Publishers

Westra, L. (2004a) 'The Earth Charter: From global ethics to international law instrument', in Pojman, L. (ed) *Environmental Ethics*, Belmont, CA, Prentice Hall

Westra, L. (2004b) 'Environmental rights and the human rights: The final enclosure movement', in Brownsword, R. (ed) *Global Governance and Human Rights*, vol 4, Oxford, Hart Publishing

Westra, L. (2004c) *Ecoviolence and the Law: Supranational Normative Foundations of Ecocrime*, Ardsley, NY, Transnational Publishers, Inc.

Westra, L. (2006) *Environmental Justice and the Rights of Unborn and Future Generations: Law, Environmental Harm and the Right to Health*, London, Earthscan

Westra, L. and Lawson, B. (2001) *Faces of Environmental Racism*, 2nd Edition, Lanham, MD, Rowman Littlefield

Westra, L. and Wenz, P. (1995) *The Faces of Environmental Racism: The Global Equity Issues*, Lanham, MD, Rowman Littlefield

WHO (World Health Organization) (2002) *Health and Environment: A Review of the Evidence*, EEA Report No 29m, Geneva, WHO

Wiessner, S. (1999) 'Rights and status of indigenous peoples: A global comparative and international legal analysis', *Harvard Human Rights Journal*, vol 12, spring, pp57–93

Wigley, D. C. and Shrader-Frechette, K. (2001) 'Consent, equity, and environmental justice: A Louisiana case study', in Westra, L. and Lawson, B. (eds) *Faces of Environmental Racism*, Lanham, MD, Rowman Littlefield

Wiist, W. H. (2006) 'Public health and the anticorporate movement: Rationale and recommendations', *American Journal of Public Health*, vol 96, no 8, pp1370–1375

Williams, G. (1961) *Criminal Law: The General Part*, 2nd edition, London, Stevens and Sons Ltd

Williams, S. A. (1986) 'Public international law and water quantity management in a common drainage basin: The Great Lakes', *Case Western Reserve International Law*, vol 18, no 1, pp155–201

Williams, S. A. (1998) 'Light out of darkness: The new international criminal court', *Proceedings of the Annual Conference of the Canadian Council on International Law*, vol 23

Wilson, E. O. (1992) *The Diversity of Life*, Cambridge, MA, Harvard University Press

Woodliffe, J. (1996) 'Biodiversity and indigenous peoples', in Bowman, M. and Redgwell, C. (eds) *International Law and the Conservation of Biological Diversity*, Boston, MA, Kluwer Law International

World Bank (1991) *OD 4.20: Indigenous Peoples*, Washington DC, World Bank

World Bank (1992) *Wapenhaus Report, Effective Implementation: Key to Development Impact*, discussion draft, Portfolio Management Task Force, Washington DC, World Bank

World Bank (2004) *Global Witness, Taking a Cut, Institutionalizing Corruption and Illegal Logging in Cambodia's Aural Wildlife Sanctuary*, Washington DC, World Bank

World Bank Group (2004) *The World Bank Operational Manual, Operational Policy 4.10: Indigenous Peoples*, 1 December, Washington DC, World Bank